Talk About Good II

A Toast To Cajun Food

published by

**The Junior League of Lafayette, Inc.
Lafayette, Louisiana**

The purpose of the league is exclusively educational and charitable and is to promote voluntarism: to develop the potential of its members for voluntary participation in community affairs: to demonstrate the effectiveness of trained volunteers.

Copies of *Talk About Good* II may be obtained from:
The Junior League of Lafayette
504 Richland Avenue
Lafayette, Louisiana 70508
(337) 988-2739 • (800) 757-3651
Fax (337) 988-1079
www.juniorleagueoflafayette.com

ISBN: 0-935032-50-9
Library of Congress Catalog Card Number 80-81675
Copyright ©1979
by
Junior League of Lafayette, Louisiana

First Printing 30,000
Second Printing 50,000
Third Printing 20,000
Fourth Printing 15,000
Fifth Printing 20,000
Sixth Printing 20,000
Seventh Printing 40,000
Eighth Printing (Hardback) 10,000

All recipes herein have been tested and represent favorite recipes of League members, their relatives and friends.

Manufactured by
Favorite Recipes® Press
an imprint of

FRP™

P.O. Box 305142
Nashville, Tennessee 37230
800-358-0560

Proceeds from the purchase of this cookbook help the Junior League of Lafayette provide children's programs in the areas of substance abuse, child abuse prevention and educational enrichment, social service support to the homeless and family counseling programs.

TABLE OF CONTENTS

ACKNOWLEDGEMENTS

Introduction

Vaughan Burdin Baker is an Acadian descendant and holds a Ph.D. in History. She has published books and articles on European history and on Louisiana and Acadian history and culture. She currently is Director of the Women in Louisiana Collection at the University of Southwestern Louisiana.

Color Reproductions

George Rodrigue is internationally known for his printings and books depicting Cajun culture. His first book *The Cajuns of George Rodrigue* was selected Best Southern Book Listing 1976 and picked by the First Lady Rosalyn Carter as an official State Department gift. Mr. Rodrigue's second book *Le Petit Cajun* was published in 1978.

A native of New Iberia, Louisiana, his permanent residence is in Lafayette. Mr. Rodrigue has received many awards, among them: Gold Medal, Italian Government; Le Salon Exhibition Award Paris, France; and Malno, Sweden. He is listed in Who's Who in American Art, International Directory of Art, French Artist's Society and the Official Guide to Collectors Prints. His works are in the Public Collection of: President of France, Louisiana Governor's Mansion, Brockton Museum, Everson Museum, Fine Arts Museum of the South, Art Center for Southwestern Louisiana, Slater Museum and Butler Institute of American Art.

Pen and Inks

Mary Lenny Perrin is a direct descendant of the famous "Beausoleil" brothers, Alexandre and Joseph Broussard, who made their way down with their band of Acadian followers from Nova Scotia, by way of the island of Martinique and finally settling in south Louisiana.

She received a B.A. in Art Education form U.S.L. and taught art in the public school system for a number of years, including three years teaching art at the Louisiana School for the Deaf in Baton Rouge. Presently, she is teaching private art classes to adults and children through her own art studio and is also involved in "Bright New Worlds," a community project which brings local artists and craftsmen into the classroom to demonstrate and teach their art to the children.

TALK ABOUT GOOD II has been "in the making" for four full years. Many hours and many minds have been expended on this project. It is impossible to thank individually each person's valuable contribution to the publication of our new cookbook, however, some special acknowledgements and thank yous must go to a few:

To Robert and Jolie Shelton for their gracious donation of the copyrights to the cover "A Toast to Cajun Food" and "Winning Cakes."

To Dr. Amos E. Simpson, professor of History at the University of Southwestern Louisiana, for the valuable time he gave in editing, proofing and even typing the historical background for the Menu section, and also for his persistent support when Murphy's Law came to visit.

To Terry Veron, Ann Stewart, Dick Dowty and Dr. Bernard Bienvenu for their assistance in preparing the Wine Sampler.

To the local restaurants for their cooperation in submitting recipes that have added flavor and fame to the book.

To the sustainers especially Sarah Beacham and Yvonne Bienvenu for their advice and guidance.

To all who submitted recipes, even those we could not use for lack of space.

To my committee and the entire membership for their devotion to the concept of this book.

To each and every one who ever had a "finger in the pie" my deep appreciation and gratitude for they have helped to preserve forever that "piquant" Cajun Heritage which is ours alone.

Editor

Committee

Elaine Abell	Marcie Lecky
Bootsie Arceneaux	Kathy Leonard
Carola Bacqué	Ann Martin
Barbara Black	Nancy McDonald
Alonda Duos	Judith Pelletier
Ibby Eggart	Barbara Pooler
Maureen Goldware	Kathleen Short
Mary Jeansonne	

ACADIANA'S CULINARY HERITAGE

By VAUGHAN BURDIN BAKER

Halfway between New Orleans and Houston in the southwestern section of Louisiana lies Acadiana, widely known as Cajun Country. Named for the French-speaking exiles who settled there in the mid-eighteenth century and whose descendants still dominate the population, the region is justly famous for its distinctive culture and renowned cuisine.

The Cajuns—a corruption of "Acadian"—are descendants of the French colonists expelled from Nova Scotia in 1753. After years of dispersal, wandering, and searching for a land where they could reconstruct the pastoral lifestyle they had enjoyed in Acadie, as their homeland was then known, they came to Louisiana. Their story and the story of the *grand dérangement,* as history calls their sad odyssey, have been immortalized in song and story.

The most famous of the legends is familiar to most Americans through Henry Wadsworth Longfellow's poem *Evangeline.* Longfellow told of a beautiful young Acadian girl torn from her lover, Gabriel. The two were finally reunited under a spreading oak tree on the banks of Bayou Teche, but Gabriel had married someone else and Evangeline died, heartbroken and still faithful to her youthful love. While the legend has captured the fancy of all who visit Acadiana, it has perpetuated a romantic conception of both the land and its people.

A resurgent interest in ancestral roots and regional ethnic cultures has awakened a widespread fascination with Evangeline's people, the French-speaking Cajuns of lower Louisiana. Popular conceptions are, however, usually distorted. One stereotype follows Longfellow's idealization and pictures a simple, religious folk living close to the land, preserving the old virtues of religion and family and a *bon vieux temps* that existed only in imagination. Another, less attractive, depiction is of the "coonass"—a term connoting an ignorant and superstitious individual speaking ungrammatical and thickly-accented English, eating boudin and two-stepping to a cacaphonous accordian.

The Cajun actuality is far more interesting and appealing than either fantasy. Like most stereotypes both popular misconceptions are caricatures, but, as do all caricatures, exaggerate aspects of reality. It is true that many Cajuns prefer French to English and like to eat boudin, that spicy-hot stuffed sausage redolent of peppers and onions. It is also true that the Cajun has kept a unique sense of values characterized by a fun-filled outlook on life and strong family ties. The Cajun lifestyle has never been static, but has changed in response to new challenges and changing times. Today's Cajuns are proud of their heritage and aware that life is good because of it. They have not, however, failed to adapt to the modern world. A twentieth-century Cajun may choose to spend Saturday night at a cock fight or dancing at a *fais-do-do,* but an oil rig may rise from the corner of his rice field, and his wife is likely to prepare the jambalaya in a microwave oven.

Flexibility and ingenuity are among the traits which encouraged the survival of Cajun culture and led to the creation of an exceptional cuisine. Cajun cooking, one of the culture's distinguishing marks, reflects Cajun adaptability, concern with sensory pleasure and let's-take-life-as-it-comes attitude.

The land that welcomed the Acadians is bayou country, rimmed by the Gulf of Mexico on the south and on the east by the once-forbidding recesses of the Atchafalaya Swamp. Gulf, swamp and bayou have played important roles in shaping the Louisiana Cajun's unique identity and a culinary tradition. Through bountiful gifts of seafood and wildlife, the land encouraged the creation of a cuisine unlike any other in the world and matched in gustatory satisfaction by few.

Cajun cooking reflects both the affluence of the geographic locale and its French-flavored legacy. It is a lush land, easy to paint in romantic colors. Moss-draped oaks form surrealistic patterns against a sky more often blue than gray, despite the frequent Louisiana rains. Bayou and gulf waters teem with shrimp, crabs, oysters and a rich variety of fish. In winter the marshes attract thousands of ducks and geese flying south from Canada to Mexico. Even the swamp, once dark and mysterious, produces crawfish, catfish, and frog legs in abundance. The land along the banks of the bayous and on the perimeter of the swamp is rich in its yield of okra, eggplant, peppers, yams and sugar cane. The great prairies to the west not only produce rice for much of the world, but graze cattle and hogs which provide the meat for the popular Cajun gathering, the *boucherie*. These were the ingredients which served as raw materials for a peerless cuisine created by a people who braved the hardships of life in an environment as remote, arduous and capricious as it was idyllic.

The Cajun tradition still characterizes the cultural outlook in the area, but it has been enriched by successive waves of new immigrants to these swamps and prairies. Spanish, Germans, Irish, Negro and Anglo-American planters, slaves and entrepreneurs came, stayed and left their mark. In recent decades the oilmen entered, bringing a new zest as well as wealth. The Cajuns tended to absorb all these strains, but not without at the same time absorbing influences from their traditions as well. New customs and practices entered into and modified Cajun ways like spices into a gumbo, subtly altering the flavor without changing the basic stock. Gumbo, in fact, is an appropriate symbol of Cajun culture as well as Cajun cuisine. Pungent, nourishing, spicy and soul-satisfying, it is a rich blend of flavors and ingredients which evolved from the simmering together of a locale and its complex cultural legacy.

Like gumbo, Cajun cooking is unpretentious yet exotic in flavor. It takes and adapts whatever is at hand and blends it into taste-tempting dishes. It is rich in its variety. The culinary inheritance of Acadiana ranges from a simple *coush-coush* of cornbread and milk to an elegant *Terrine de Poisson aux Écrivisses* boasting a crawfish filling and fit for the most aristocratic table. Cajun cooking is an unending delight which conquers the most skeptical of newcomers, seduces them into the local lifestyle, and converts them into self-proclaimed Cajuns.

Cajun *joie-de-vivre* is not a sometime thing. Gala festivities follow a yearly cycle of celebration, from Mardi Gras in the spring to the harvest festivals of autumn. Each occasion demands feasting with traditional custom. This cookbook salutes the enduring vitality of the Cajun cultural heritage and the culinary artistry of Acadiana. The recipes reflect the mixed legacy and the versatility of the region, and are as diverse as the population which lives there.

CAJUN BELLE

Here I have painted a girl who is a descendant of those people exiled from Canada (Acadie) who are now called "Cajuns".

For me as an artist, it was very difficult to portray the Cajun, for there are so many aspects of his culture that are truly unique in America. The first quality that I wanted to convey was the timelessness of this culture. Whether I paint a contemporary scene, or one out of the past, I use the same style or technique, trying to show that the culture has not changed significantly in 200 years. This painting, Cajun Belle, to me, represents the past as well as the present.

MENU SECTION

TWELFTH NIGHT

Traditionally King's Cake or Twelfth Night parties have been celebrated throughout Acadiana. January 6, the twelfth night after Christmas, opens the Mardi Gras season. The parties follow a simple pattern. Groups of friends gather and decide who shall host the first of the series of parties which continue until Mardi Gras.

For the first party the hostess makes a large circular or oval cake—usually a brioche—decorated with candied fruit and a sugar glaze. The most significant ingredient is a tiny china doll, or a bean, or a silver coin. At the appropriate time the cake is sliced into as many pieces as there are guests, and everyone is served. The person who receives the piece containing the hidden "prize" is then designated King or Queen. The reign lasts only a week, however, as the ritual must be repeated weekly, with each new monarch required to host the next party in a similar manner for the same guests. This ritual, rooted in a custom centuries old, is still popular among Acadians. Although each family or group of friends has its own variation, each adds to the festivity of the pre-Lenten season in Acadiana.

Twelfth Night

Cochon de Lait
Mushroom Tenderloin
Marinated Barbecued Chicken Wings
Caponata
Fritto Misto
Tequeños
Crabmeat Kate
Shrimp Toast
King's Cake

COCHON DE LAIT

1 (30 pound) pig with feet,
  ears and tail intact
  (when dressed approximately
  20 pounds) will fit in
  conventional oven

Paste: ½ cup salt
  ½ cup red pepper
  1 tablespoon garlic salt
  ¼ cup vinegar
  ¼ cup oil

Place pig in large pan. Rub pig well inside and out with paste. Marinate over-night. When you are ready to roast pig, curl rear feet and extend fore legs. Place tent of foil over pig, loosely. Bake for 3 hours at 275°. Remove foil, raise heat to 300° and bake for 4 hours or until done. While pig is still hot, glaze with pan drippings. Insert apple in mouth. Use dark grapes for the eyes. Decorate around pig with fresh fruit and flowers. Cover feet with parsley. Place a gold paper crown on pig's head and tie Mardi Gras colored ribbon (purple, green, gold) around tail. Miss Fanny Cornay is a well-known caterer in Lafayette. She tradi-tionally prepares the roasted pig for the Krewe of the Troubadors cocktail party, and caters for many other festivities.   Fanny Cornay

MUSHROOM TENDERLOIN

1 whole beef tenderloin, 3-5 pounds
soy sauce

Worcestershire

Mushroom Sauce:
1 stick margarine
3 tablespoons worcestershire
1 tablespoon vinegar
1 tablespoon lemon juice

1 teaspoon garlic salt
2 tablespoons sweet basil, can use fresh
1 (8 ounce) can sliced mushrooms, or ½
  pound fresh sliced mushrooms

Marinate tenderloin by covering with soy sauce first then Worcestershire, 2-3 hours. Barbecue to desired doneness, 30-40 minutes for medium. Cut into serv-ings about 1½ inches thick. Spoon on 1 serving of mushroom sauce for each serving.
Sauce: Melt margarine. Add all other ingredients and simmer 5-10 minutes. Serve hot. Serves 6-8.   Mary Buie Skelton

MARINATED, BARBECUED CHICKEN WINGS

Disjoint and discard tips of 35-50 chicken wings. Place into a flat pan and pour the following marinade over the wings. Let stand for 1 hour.

Heat:
1 stick margarine
1 cup brown sugar
½ cup soy sauce
½ cup red wine

2 teaspoons dry mustard
garlic salt and pepper to taste
¼ cup fresh lemon juice

Be sure wings are thoroughly marinated, then put in oven that is 350°. Reduce heat to 250°. Bake 4-5 hours, turning wings carefully at least 2-3 times. If all the sauce has not been absorbed, pour off and dry out the wings a bit in oven, not too much, before serving. UMMMMM, Finger Licking Good!!! Serves 8-10 as a main course.   Frances Wallace

CAPONATA

2 large eggplants
1 tablespoon salt
¾ cup olive oil
2 cloves garlic, crushed
2 onions, chopped
1 (Number 2) can Italian Plum
  tomatoes
3 celery stalks, diced

1 (1 pound) can pitted black olives
1 (12 ounce) jar Italian olive salad mix
¼ cup capers
½ cup pine nuts
¼ cup wine vinegar
2 tablespoons sugar
salt and pepper to taste

Wash and cube unpeeled eggplant. Sprinkle with salt and let stand in colander for 2 hours. Squeeze dry. Sauté in heated olive oil until soft. Remove from pan and sauté chopped onions and garlic in same oil. Add strained tomatoes, olives and celery and cook until celery is tender, about 15 minutes. Return eggplant to pan. Add capers and pine nuts. In another pan heat vinegar and sugar until dissolved and pour over eggplant. Season to taste and cook an additional 20 minutes. Serve hot or cold on melba rounds or sliced French bread. This is an Italian appetizer. Serves 50.

Stephanie Bacque

FRITTO MISTO

1 pound zucchini, washed and sliced
1 bunch broccoli, washed and cut into
  flowerets
1 (9 ounce) package frozen artichoke
  hearts, thawed and dried well
1 head cauliflower, washed and cut
  into flowerets

1 quart oil
coarse salt
2 lemons, quartered
1 tablespoon finely chopped
  parsley

Batter:
1 cup flour
½ cup cornstarch
1 teaspoon baking powder
1 teaspoon salt

2 eggs
3 tablespoons olive oil
1 cup water

Combine flour, cornstarch, baking powder and salt. Beat eggs with whisk, add oil and water. Combine with flour mixture and beat with whisk. Heat oil to 360° or sizzling. Dip vegetables into batter and carefully lower into oil. Fry until golden brown. Drain well on paper towels. May keep warm in oven for 30-45 minutes. Sprinkle liberally with salt, parsley and garnish with lemon wedges. Serves 8.

Carola L. Bacqué

TEQUENOS

4 cups flour	1 egg, beaten
1¼ teaspoons salt	½ cup butter, melted
¼ teaspoon thyme	1 cup warm milk
¼ teaspoon marjoram	1 pound sharp cheese
⅛ teaspoon pepper	oil for deep fat frying
1 cup bite size shredded wheat, crushed	

Heat fat to 400°. Sift flour and seasonings together. Stir in cereal crumbs. Add egg, butter and milk, mix until smooth. Knead several times on floured board, divide dough into thirds. Roll and stretch until thin. Cut into ½ inch wide strips. Wrap dough strips tightly around cheese strips which have been cut into 1 inch x ⅛ inch strips. Dough should be wrapped in spiral form, overlapping slightly to cover and seal cheese. Fry one minute or until brown. These can be frozen before frying. If so, thaw one hour at room temperature before frying. This recipe was given to us by friends in Venezuela as this is a favorite hors d'oeuvre there. Yield 6-7 dozen.   Don Burts

CRABMEAT KATE

1 stick butter	6-7 drops Tabasco
8-10 shallots and tops, chopped	½ teaspoon salt
1 tablespoon corn starch	1 cup sour cream
½ cup sherry	3½ cups crabmeat
2 cans mushrooms, drained	

Sauté the shallots in butter. Add corn starch, sherry, mushrooms, Tabasco and salt mixing well. Cook for a few minutes over medium heat then add sour cream and crabmeat. Continue to cook for a few more minutes. Serves 6-8. Serve with small pastry shells or melba toast for a cocktail party.   Kathy Kochansky

SHRIMP TOAST

1 (8 ounce) package frozen, shelled deveined shrimp	2 teaspoons dry sherry
	1 tablespoon cornstarch
4 water chestnuts, finely minced	1 egg, slightly beaten
1 teaspoon salt	6 slices of dry bread, Pepperidge Farm
½ teaspoon sugar	2 cups vegetable oil

Thaw shrimp, and chop very fine. Mix with water chestnuts. Add salt, sugar, sherry, cornstarch and beaten egg. Mix. Trim crusts from bread and cut each slice into 4 triangles. Spread a teaspoon of the shrimp mixture over each triangle. In a saucepan or wok, heat oil to 375°. Gently lower 4-6 pieces at a time into the oil, shrimp side down. After a minute, when the edges begin to turn brown, turn pieces over and fry 5 more seconds. Remove, drain on paper towels. Keep warm in very low oven on cookie sheets until ready to serve. Shrimp toasts can also be fried then frozen. When ready to use, heat in a 400° oven for 10-12 minutes. Yield 2 dozen.   Cristie O. Adams

KING'S CAKE

Brioche Dough:

½ cup lukewarm water (110°-115°)

2 packages dry yeast

4½-5½ cups sifted flour

½ cup sugar

½ teaspoon freshly grated nutmeg

2 teaspoons salt

1 teaspoon grated lemon rind

½ cup lukewarm milk

3 eggs

4 egg yolks

½ cup + 2 tablespoons butter, softened

1 egg lightly beaten with 1 tablespoon milk

1 dime or uncooked dried bean or miniature doll

Sugars:

green, purple and yellow food coloring pastes

12 tablespoons granulated sugar

Icing:

3 cups confectioners sugar

¼ cup strained fresh lemon juice

3-6 tablespoons water

2 candied cherries, halved lengthwise

Soften yeast in water. Combine flour, sugar, nutmeg and salt in mixing bowl. Stir in lemon peel. Make a well in center and pour into it the yeast mixture and milk. Add eggs and egg yolks, and with a large wooden spoon gradually incorporate dry ingredients into liquid ones. Beat in butter and continue beating until dough forms ball. (Mixing of the dough can be done in food processor.) Place ball on floured board and incorporate more flour if necessary, by sprinkling it over ball by the tablespoon. Knead until smooth and elastic. Brush inside of large bowl with 1 tablespoon softened butter. Set dough in bowl and turn it so as to butter entire surface. (At this point you can refrigerate dough overnight.) Cover bowl and set aside for 1½ hours or until doubled in bulk. Brush a large baking sheet with remaining butter. Punch dough down on lightly floured surface. Knead, then pat and shape dough into a cylinder about 14 inches long. Place on baking sheet and form into a ring. Press bean or dime or doll into dough so that it is hidden. Set aside again to rise. When ready to bake brush the top and sides of the ring with the egg-milk mixture. Bake King's Cake in middle of oven at 375° for 25-30 minutes, or until golden brown. Slide cake onto wire rack to cool.

Sugars: Prepare the colored sugars by squeezing a dab of paste in the palm of one hand. Sprinkle 2 tablespoons of sugar over the paste and rub your hands together to color the sugar evenly. Set aside and repeat process with green, then twice with purple and yellow. (Do not mix sugars.)

Icing: When the cake has cooled prepare the icing. Combine the confectioners sugar, lemon juice and 3 tablespoons of water in a deep bowl and stir until the icing mixture is smooth. If too stiff to spread, beat in 1 teaspoonful water at a time, until desired consistency is reached. With a small metal spatula, spread the icing over the top of the cake, allowing it to run down the sides. Sprinkle the colored sugars over the icing immediately, forming a row of purple, yellow and green strips, each about 2 inches wide, on both sides of the ring. Arrange two cherry halves at each end of the cake, pressing them gently into the icing.

Note: Do not use liquid food coloring as it will make the sugar dissolve.

CANDLEMAS DAY

In Acadiana Candlemas Day celebrations on February 2 combine the ancient Catholic tradition of the Blessing of the Candles and the American tradition of Ground Hog's Day. The Acadians added their own special touch to the liturgical rites marking the approach of Spring. Although ground-hogs may sometimes be seen on the prairies on the western edge of the region, their absence in the Delta lands and swamp does not prevent folk predictions concerning the changing of the seasons.

Predominantly Catholic, the Acadians still follow the custom of blessing the year's candles for the churches at early Mass on February 2, or on the nearest Sunday. Formerly, candles were also given to the poor to light their homes. After returning from the church ceremony, the local people prepared Candlemas Day pancakes or crepes, along with other dishes for a festive brunch. The food was served with a special fortune hidden at the bottom of the plate, foretelling the future of each person there during the coming year.

Candlemas Breakfast

Light hearted Bloody Marys
Chicken Livers in Madeira Sauce
Egg Sausage Casserole
Shrimp Crepes
Tomatoes Amilie
Banana Fritters
Wine Peaches with Ice Cream
Wine: Rosé

LIGHT-HEARTED BLOODY MARY

1½ ounces vodka or gin
1¼ ounces lemon juice
3 ounces bloody mary mix

6-8 drops Tabasco or to taste
dash worcestershire
1 ounce soda

Mix all ingredients and serve over ice. The soda adds lightness and the lemon juice adds extra tang. Serves 1.

Bruce Davey

CHICKEN LIVERS IN MADEIRA SAUCE

2 pounds chicken livers
salt and pepper
1 cup flour
4 tablespoons butter

2 tablespoons cooking oil
1 pound fresh sliced mushrooms
1 cup beef bouillon
⅔ cup Madeira

Season livers with salt and pepper and dredge lightly in flour. Melt butter and oil in heavy skillet over moderately high heat. Add chicken livers; toss frequently for 3-4 minutes until livers are lightly browned; add mushrooms and sauté a few minutes longer, pour in beef bouillon and the Madeira; simmer 1 minute. Season to taste. Serve with rice. Serves 8.

Maureen Goldware

SHRIMP CREPES

2 pounds shrimp
2 cans mushrooms, stems and pieces
1 pod garlic
1 large onion
1 cup butter
4 tablespoons flour
1½ cups milk

1½ cups shrimp stock
½ cup cream
2 tablespoons absinthe
2 tablespoons cognac
Parmesan cheese
1 box crepe mix

Peel and clean shrimp. Boil and save stock. Chop shrimp and mushrooms very fine, can use blender. Mince garlic and onion. In a large saucepan melt butter, add flour and stir well. Add milk, stock, cream, absinthe and cognac. Mix well and simmer. Add onion, garlic, mushrooms and shrimp. Season as desired. Mix well and simmer slowly for 15 minutes. Prepare crepes as stated on package. Fill crepes with shrimp mixture and roll. Place in ungreased casserole dish, top with Parmesan cheese. Place under broiler until cheese is melted. Serves 8.

Alonda A. Duos

EGG SAUSAGE CASSEROLE

6 beaten eggs
2 cups milk
1 teaspoon salt
1 teaspoon dry mustard

½ cup green onions, finely chopped
2 bread slices, crumbled
1 pound sauteed sausage, drained
1 cup sharp cheese, grated

Combine all ingredients. Sprinkle cheese on top. Refrigerate overnight. Bake at 350° for 40 minutes. Serves 6-8.   Nell Tolson

TOMATOES AMILIE

2 pounds tomatoes, peeled, seeded
    and halved
¼ teaspoon sugar

salt and pepper to taste
½ stick butter
1 cup heavy cream

In a large skillet, cook tomatoes peeled, seeded and halved with sugar, salt, pepper and butter over low heat for 5 minutes. Stir in 1 cup of heavy cream and cook for 5 minutes more. With slotted spoon transfer the tomatoes to a vegetable dish. Cook sauce over high heat until it is reduced by half. Pour over tomatoes. Season with salt and pepper to taste. Serves 6-8.   Leslie Hayes

BANANA FRITTERS

1½ cups flour
2 teaspoons baking powder
2 tablespoons powdered sugar
¼ teaspoon salt
⅔ cup milk

1 egg
oil
3 bananas, mashed and sprinkled with
    lemon juice
powdered sugar

Measure, sift and mix all dry ingredients. Combine milk and egg, add to dry ingredients. Fold in the mashed bananas. If too thick add milk—too thin add flour. Batter should have consistency to be dropped by teaspoonful in hot oil. Pour enough oil into skillet to a depth of 1 inch. Test heat of oil, when fritters cook in 5 minutes it is ready. Drop by spoonfuls as many as skillet will hold. As it browns on one side turn. Drain on paper towels. Keep warm and just before serving sprinkle with powdered sugar. Serve warm. Serves 10-15.   Marilyn Taylor

WINE PEACHES WITH ICE CREAM

8 firm ripe peaches
1 cup sherry
1 cup port wine

2 tablespoons sugar
1 tablespoon red currant jelly
1 quart vanilla ice cream

Peel peaches, cut in halves and remove pits. Heat wines, sugar, jelly and 4 peach pits. Carefully add peach halves to mixture and simmer gently 30 minutes. Remove pits. Remove peaches and chill in flat dish. Cook liquid down to form a thick syrup. Adding more sugar to taste if desired. Chill. To serve, put 2 peach halves in each compote or serving dish and fill with ice cream. Top with sauce. Chopped pecans or other nuts may be sprinkled over each serving if desired. Serves 8.

MARDI GRAS

In the spirit of *"Laissez les bons temps rouler"* (Let the good times roll) the Cajuns have adopted the New Orleans custom of Mardi Gras. After Twelfth Night, Acadian Krewes begin the festivities with gala balls honoring their own kings and queens. The spirit of celebration continues to heighten until Mardi Gras day itself approaches. The main streets of Acadiana's cities and towns sparkle with the glitter and the revelry of parade floats and maskers as costumed crowds yell "Throw me something, Mister," trying to grab the treasured doubloons thrown by the float riders. The climax of the Mardi Gras activity is the grand ball the night before Ash Wednesday, the first day of the solemn six weeks of Lent. On that night formality reigns in honor of the Acadian Royalty, Queen Evangeline and King Gabriel. Festivity ends and the season closes with midnight buffets held in clubs and private homes throughout the area.

The *joie de vivre* of Mardi Gras is also celebrated in the smaller outlying towns in Acadiana. Mamou has become well-known for its own particular Mardi Gras celebration called *Le Courir de Mardi Gras*—Riding the Mardi Gras. In keeping with Cajun spirit for communal gatherings, the *Courir de Mardi Gras* revolves around the gathering of food for a master gumbo. Led by a Captain carrying a white flag, masked horseback riders appear throughout the countryside demanding of each neighbor chickens, ducks, sausage and other delectables to add to the gumbo or to accompany it. As the riders assemble in each farmyard, the Captain sounds his cow horn and the *Coureurs* sing a traditional refrain in French. The lady of the house is also expected to offer the riders such customary refreshments as *tac-tac* (popcorn), *beignets* (doughnuts) and *gateaux* (tea cakes). At the end of the day all of the gathered condiments are brought into town and everyone enjoys cooking the gumbo and the ensuing celebration.

Mardi Gras

Champagne
English Cheese Chowder
Spinach Salad
Steak and Kidney Pie
Stuffed Oysters
Banana Crepes
Liqueurs

ENGLISH CHEESE CHOWDER

⅓ cup carrots, chopped
⅓ cup celery, chopped
2 cups water
4 ounces butter
1 medium onion, chopped
4 ounces flour

1 quart milk
1 quart canned chicken broth
1 (14 ounce) jar Kraft's Cheez Whiz
salt, pepper, cayenne
1 tablespoon prepared mustard
½ cup chopped green onions

Boil vegetables in water for 5 minutes. Sauté chopped onions in butter for 1 minute. Add flour and blend well. Add boiling milk and chicken broth, stirring briskly. Add cheese, salt, pepper (to own taste), dash of cayenne, mustard and vegetables, including the water in which they were boiled and chopped green onions. Bring to a boil and serve immediately. Serves 12. This freezes well and reheats beautifully.   Mrs. Michael Foreman

SPINACH SALAD

3 packages fresh spinach
24 fresh mushrooms
1 pound bacon

2 11-ounce cans mandarin oranges
2 avocados

Wash and trim spinach. Set aside to dry thoroughly. Slice mushrooms. Fry bacon; drain and crumble. Set bacon aside. May refrigerate these until ready to use. Drain oranges and slice avocado just before tossing salad.

Dressing:
1 cup olive oil
½ cup cider vinegar
½ cup sugar
1 teaspoon salt
1 teaspoon paprika

½ teaspoon dry mustard
½ teaspoon celery salt
¼ teaspoon fresh pepper
1 medium onion, chopped very fine

Combine dressing ingredients. Store in a jar. Refrigerate ahead of time. Shake well before tossing salad. Serves 12.   Ida Baggett

STUFFED OYSTERS

3 dozen oysters
2 large onions, chopped fine
2 ribs celery, chopped fine
½ bell pepper, chopped fine
3 cloves garlic, crushed
¾ stick butter
3 slices bread
¼ cup onion tops, chopped

2 tablespoons parsley, chopped
salt
pepper
1 grated lemon rind
1 tablespoon Worcestershire
2 eggs, beaten
bread crumbs

Preheat oven to 400°. Drain oysters, dry them and chop fine. Cook onions, celery, bell pepper and garlic in small amount of water until tender. Add butter to above mixture. Soak bread in water and squeeze dry. Add to seasoning mixture and mash thoroughly. Add finely chopped oysters, onion tops and parsley, salt and pepper to taste and cook 5-10 minutes. Add grated lemon rind and Worcestershire. Let cook for a few minutes and then add 2 beaten eggs. Place oyster mixture in baking shells, sprinkle with bread crumbs and dot with butter. Bake in hot oven, until hot and brown. Serves 6-8. Recipe easily doubled.
                                        Mrs. St. Paul Bourgeois III

STEAK AND KIDNEY PIE

2 prepared pie crusts, both top and
  bottom
4 pounds round steak
2 pounds veal or young lamb kidneys

Sauce:
2 cans beef broth
2 teaspoons Worcestershire
2 teaspoons salt
2 teaspoons pepper
dash cayenne
2 bay leaves

flour, salt, pepper
½ cup butter, melted
1 large onion, sliced
1 pound fresh mushrooms, sliced
egg white

1 teaspoon thyme
1 teaspoon basil
1 cup water
½ cup red wine
4 tablespoons corn starch

Cut round steak into ½ inch thin cubes and dredge in flour that has been seasoned with salt and pepper. Skin and slice kidney into small, thin pieces. Brown steak and kidney in ½ cup melted butter. Add onion, sliced; continue cooking until onion is yellowish in color. Slice mushrooms, add to meat. To the cans of broth in separate saucepan add seasonings. Make a paste of 4 tablespoons corn starch with a small amount (2-4 tablespoons) of the 1 cup water. Combine remainder of water with wine. Add to broth and seasonings. On medium heat gradually add the flour water paste to hot broth. Cook until thickened, stirring often. Add sauce to meats, mix thoroughly. Place in pie crusts. Add the pie top. Prick well. Glaze with egg white, Place in 450° oven for 10 minutes. Reduce heat, bake 350° for 20-25 minutes. Serves 12.

Sue Alvez

BANANA CREPES

12 dessert crepes
¾ cup sour cream
1 (8 ounce) package cream cheese
3 tablespoons sugar
1 tablespoon vanilla extract
¼ cup chopped pecans

6 medium bananas
½ cup brown sugar
1 teaspoon cinnamon
½ cup margarine
½ lemon

Mix together sour cream and cream cheese until smooth. Add white sugar, vanilla and pecans and mix well. Spoon this mixture evenly on crepes and roll up with the ends left open. Place on a shallow serving tray. This may be done earlier, put in the refrigerator and heated to room temperature in a preheated 350° oven for 5 minutes. Slice bananas crosswise into approximately ½ inch thick pieces and arrange in an oven-proof casserole. Combine brown sugar and cinnamon. Melt margarine and pour evenly over bananas. Squeeze juice of lemon all over this and then sprinkle on the sugar-cinnamon mixture. Bake in a 350° oven for 20 minutes. Remove from oven and spoon bananas and juice over crepes. Serve at once. Serves 6. Recipe easily doubled.

Betty Roy

EASTER

Easter Sunday truly signals the rebirth of *joie de vivre* in the Acadian area after the denials of the Lenten season. Church services begin the day of rejoicing and are followed by family gatherings or reunions for the Easter feasting. Formality is quickly put aside as the time for the egg hunt approaches.

Eggs are often still dyed by the customary method called sack-dying, in which strips of sacking are dipped into juice from fresh berries and laid upon the eggs to create intricate patterns and designs. During the hunt, children rush to find mysteriously hidden eggs to use in the game called "pacqué" which follows. To "pacqué," one grips his egg firmly in his right hand with only the small end showing. The other holds his egg in his right hand with the pointed end down and forcefully taps away at the opponent's egg. The one whose egg cracks first must relinquish his egg. Each victor claims the eggs he has cracked and goes off to present his mother with Monday's egg salad.

Acadian Easter egg customs, like those everywhere, are rooted in ancient fertility rituals thousands of years old. French Louisiana's tradition of "pacqué-ing," however, is unique in the United States and is the central event in the Cajun celebration of the renewal of Spring.

Easter

Bourbon Slush
Squash Bisque
Avocado Appetizers
Leg of Lamb Dijon
Potatoes Amandine
Tomatoes Rockefeller
Charlotte Russe
Cabernet Sauvignon

BOURBON SLUSH

1 cup sugar
1 cup brewed tea
1½ cups bourbon
6½ cups water

1 (6 ounce) can frozen lemonade
  concentrate
1 (6 ounce) can frozen orange juice
  concentrate

Mix together. Freeze overnight. Remove one hour before serving. Serves 8-16.

Charlotte K. O'Flarity

SQUASH BISQUE

½ cup butter
1 large onion, chopped
2 medium potatoes, sliced
2 carrots, sliced
4 cups fresh or 2 packages frozen and
  defrosted yellow sliced squash

1 quart chicken stock, homemade
1 tablespoon salt
¼ teaspoon cayenne
1 cup cream
paprika

Melt butter, sauté onion. Add vegetables, stock, salt and pepper. Cook covered until tender (45 minutes). Puree in blender. (Only fill ½ of blender at a time.) Return to pot and add cream and correct seasoning. Sprinkle each bowl with paprika. (I freeze this before adding cream.) Serve warm in soup bowls or cup as first course. Serves 12.

Sue Billet Dinkins

AVOCADO APPETIZERS

6 small avocados
lemon juice
2 (13 ounce) can jellied chicken
  consommé, chilled

12 tablespoons sour cream
12 teaspoons red caviar
cracked ice for serving
12 lemon wedges

Halve avocados lengthwise; remove pits. Brush cut surfaces with lemon juice. Spoon chilled jellied consommé into avocado centers; then top each with a tablespoon of sour cream, then a teaspoon caviar. Arrange avocados on cracked ice; serve with lemon wedges to squeeze over consommé. This is a colorful and elegant first course. Serves 12.

Mrs. Frank Danna

LEG OF LAMB DIJON

1 (6 pound) leg of lamb
1 jar dijon mustard
2 tablespoons soy sauce
1-1½ cloves garlic, pressed
1 teaspoon rosemary

1 teaspoon thyme
¼ teaspoon ginger
2 tablespoons olive oil
1 teaspoon salt
¼ teaspoon cayenne

Blend all sauce ingredients until of mayonnaise-like consistency. Four hours or more before roasting rub sauce over lamb leg until thickly coated. Place lamb on rack in roasting pan and sear in a 500° oven for 10-15 minutes. Reduce oven to 350° and continue roasting for at least 1 hour for a medium rare leg, 1¼ hours for medium, 2 hours for well done. Let lamb set up before carving. Serves 4-6. Double recipe to serve 12.

Kathryn Leonard

POTATOES AMANDINE

6 large baked Idaho potatoes
6 eggs
½ pound butter
salt and pepper to taste

1 cup flour
2 cups water
2 pounds sliced almonds, toasted

Heat butter in small casserole or pot. Add flour and water and stir briskly until smooth. Remove from fire and add 4 eggs. Heat well really working the whole mixture. Peel the hot potatoes, mash well and season with salt and pepper. Add potatoes to mixture and mix well. This makes a sort of dough. Roll to form a baton. Slice this in pieces about 2 inches long. Dip each piece in flour then in 2 beaten eggs. Roll in almonds. Fry in deep oil in frying pan for about 2 minutes. Should be crispy and crunchy. Drain on paper towels. Serves 12.

Lucille Roy Copeland

TOMATOES ROCKEFELLER

2 packages chopped spinach
2 cups seasoned bread crumbs
6 chopped green onions
6 eggs, slightly beaten
¾ cup melted butter
¼ cup Parmesan cheese
¼ teaspoon Worcestershire sauce

½ teaspoon garlic salt
1 teaspoon salt
½ teaspoon black pepper
1 teaspoon thyme
¼ teaspoon Tabasco
12 thick slices tomato

Cook spinach according to package. Drain. Add remaining ingredients except sliced tomatoes. Mix well. Slice tomatoes, place in buttered baking dish. Mound spinach mixture on top. Bake in 350° oven for 15 minutes or until warm throughout. Freeze what is left in muffin cups. Use as many as needed at a time. Serves 12 or more.

Mary Lou Carmen

CHARLOTTE RUSSE

2 tablespoons gelatin
¼ cup cold water
2 cups scalded milk
½ cup sugar
4 eggs, separated

1 teaspoon vanilla or brandy or other
    strong liqueur to taste
⅛ teaspoon salt
1 pint heavy cream, whipped
24 lady fingers, approximately

Soak gelatin in water. Dissolve this in 2 cups scalded milk. Add ½ cup sugar and stir until dissolved. Pour part of this over 4 egg yolks, return to milk mixture and stir the custard over a very low flame until it begins to thicken. Cool it. Add vanilla or liqueur. Whip egg whites with salt until stiff. Fold egg whites into custard. Fold whipped cream into custard mixture. Line a spring form pan with halves of lady fingers flat side to outside. Fill in center with custard and chill. Can be made ahead. Cover with plastic wrap. Can be frozen. Serves 10-12.

Dottie N. Hopkins

CRAWFISH FESTIVAL

The natural abundance of the Acadian Country is continuously evidenced throughout the year by festivals celebrating the harvesting of such local crops as soybeans, sugar cane, frogs, rice, yams and crawfish. Perhaps the best-known and certainly one of the most popular is the bi-annual Crawfish Festival.

Participants from all over Acadiana flock to the small community of Breaux Bridge to join in the grand celebration of the crawfish. The delicate shellfish is a favored specialty of the region and is featured in every kind of edible form. Crawfish peeling, eating and cooking contests whet the appetites of young and old alike. The crawfish race is a popular event and squeals of delight can be heard as competitors cheer on the first crawfish to crawl slowly backwards to the finish line. Evening begins with the gathering of all to watch beautiful contestants in long formal gowns vie for the coveted title of Crawfish Queen. After the winner is announced, everyone participates in the dancing to the accompaniment of Cajun bands playing age-old folksongs and spirited new music as well on their violins and accordians and harmonicas.

The Crawfish Festival has brought fame to Breaux Bridge throughout Louisiana and outside the state as well. Acadiana is unique in its abundant supply of the tiny lobster-like shellfish and in its culinary creativity with it. Boiled crawfish, simple and unadorned, piled high and steaming on a newspaper-covered table, is a favorite seasonal treat. Dozens of other dishes, ranging from great-grandmother's étouffée to today's new cheesy casseroles, also feature the tasty *écrivisses*. The Crawfish Festival pays just homage to the King of Acadiana's kitchens.

Crawfish Festival—Afternoon Lunch

Beer and White Sangria
Crawfish Boulettes
Bayou Vegetable Salad
Crawfish Bisque
Fried Crawfish
Crawfish Étouffée
Crawfish Maque Choux
Hot Garlic Bread
Grandma's Real Shortcake
Café au Lait

WHITE SANGRIA

½ gallon white wine, Chablis is
  excellent
¼ cup lemon juice
½ cup orange juice

⅔ cup sugar
2 ounces vodka or vermouth, optional
slices of orange and lemon
wedges of apple

Mix all ingredients thoroughly and chill. Float slices of orange and lemon and wedges of apples in the bowl. Note: Best when made the day before. Adjust amount of sugar to suit your taste. Any white or red wine or combination of the two may be used. Cool and refreshing for a hot day. Excellent light drink for a party. Serves 6.

Kim Caldarero
Lake Charles, LA.

BAYOU VEGETABLE SALAD

Spread one layer of each of the following:

1 pound fresh spinach, (torn)
  sprinkled with ½ teaspoon salt,
  ¼ teaspoon pepper and
  ½ teaspoon sugar
½ pound bacon, cooked and
  crumbled
6 hard-boiled eggs, chopped

2 cups grated Swiss cheese
1 head iceberg lettuce, torn in pieces
1 (10 ounce) package frozen peas,
  thawed but not cooked
1 thinly sliced white onion or equivalent
  amount of chopped green onions
sliced radishes for garnish

Optional layers:
bell pepper slivers
thinly sliced celery

sliced black olives
canned mushrooms

Dressing:
2 cups mayonnaise
1 teaspoon sugar
1 cup sour cream

1 package Hidden Valley Ranch
  Dressing

Using a shallow serving platter or tupperware sandwich box, (do not use very deep container) layer spinach, cheese, bacon, eggs, lettuce, peas and onion. Add optional layers.

Mix dressing by mixing mayonnaise with sugar, sour cream and Hidden Valley Ranch Dressing. Spread this on top of layered salad. Garnish with sliced radishes. Cover tightly and refrigerate for 24 hours.

To serve: cut into squares and place on large serving platters in separate squares or place on lettuce leaves. A large flat serving utensil is advised for serving. Serves 10-12.

Karen McGlasson

CRAWFISH BISQUE

20 pounds fresh crawfish
2 cups chopped onions
1 cup chopped celery
½ can whole tomatoes
4 cloves garlic, minced
1 level tablespoon tomato paste

1 cup all-purpose flour
1 cup cooking oil
½ cup green onion tops and parsley,
  chopped
1 gallon cold water
salt, black pepper and cayenne

Scald crawfish: Peel crawfish and save fat in jar. Put crawfish tails in bowl. Set aside.

Make a roux: 1 cup cooking oil and 1 cup flour. Put oil in heavy iron pot over medium heat. When oil is hot, stir flour in gradually. Lower heat. It is very important that you keep stirring constantly. After all of the flour has been combined with the oil, turn fire down very low and cook until golden brown, stirring constantly. Add onions, celery, whole tomatoes, and tomato paste to roux. Cook in uncovered pot over medium heat for about 40 minutes, or until oil separates from tomatoes. Set aside.

Put 1 gallon of water, garlic and the crawfish fat to boil in uncovered pot over medium heat, stirring constantly, until it boils. Season generously with salt, black pepper and cayenne. Add roux mixture. Cook in uncovered pot slowly for 1 hour. Add crawfish tails and continue boiling slowly in uncovered pot for another 20 minutes. Add green onion tops and parsley. Serve in soup plates with cooked rice and Crawfish Bisque Heads.

Don's Seafood and Steak House
Lafayette, La.

CRAWFISH BISQUE HEADS

20 pounds live crawfish
1 cup chopped celery
2 cups chopped onions
½ pound margarine
½ cup green onion tops and parsley,
  chopped

4 eggs
3 stale buns
salt and cayenne to taste
1 cup bread crumbs

Scald crawfish. Peel and clean crawfish tails. Clean and save head shells of crawfish. Save fat from crawfish. Set aside crawfish tails, heads and fat.

Combine margarine or butter, onions and celery in a heavy iron pot. Let cook in uncovered pot over medium heat, until onions are wilted, stirring constantly. Then add crawfish fat and cook slowly for 15 minutes. Season to taste with salt, black pepper and cayenne. Add soaked buns. Mix well. Then add beaten eggs and bread crumbs. Chop half the boiled crawfish tails. Add chopped crawfish tails, green onions and parsley to the cooked mixture. Stuff crawfish heads with the mixture, and serve with crawfish stew made with the remaining crawfish tails. Serve the stew with cooked rice in soup bowls, with about five stuffed crawfish heads in each bowl. Serves 8.

Don's Seafood and Steak House
Lafayette, La.

CRAWFISH BOULETTES

3 tablespoons margarine
1 medium onion, chopped fine
1 cup celery, chopped fine
1 pound crab claw meat, drained
1 pound crawfish tails, ground

¼ cup green onion tops, chopped fine
1 egg, beaten
Progresso bread crumbs
salt and pepper to taste
few teaspoons lemon juice

Sauté onion and celery in margarine until light brown. Drain. To this add 1 pound crabmeat and ground crawfish and onion tops. Stir in egg and add bread crumbs until mixture is meatball consistency. Shape into small balls. Fry until brown in deep fat. Cooks very fast. Yield: 50 cocktail size. You may add lemon juice to give boulettes a slight tartness. Pat Link

FRIED CRAWFISH

1 pound peeled crawfish tails
4 ounces milk
2 eggs
4 teaspoons baking powder

2 tablespoons vinegar
1 cup flour
seasonings to taste

Make a mixture of eggs, milk, baking powder and vinegar. Marinate the crawfish tails in this about 2 hours. Remove and season with salt and red pepper. Dip in flour and fry in hot fat until done. Doesn't take long. Great as an appetizer with various dips, but I prefer it plain. Serves 4 as entrée. Easily doubled.
Virginia Yongue

CRAWFISH ÉTOUFFÉE

2 sticks butter
2 small onions, chopped
2 bunches onion tops, chopped
crawfish fat (optional)

2 pounds crawfish tails
salt and pepper to taste
parsley, chopped

Chop and sauté in butter, onion and onion tops. Add crawfish fat, cover and cook 5 minutes. Add crawfish tails, season with salt and red pepper. Cover and cook about 15 minutes until done. Add parsley just before serving and serve over rice. Serves 6-8. Mrs. Warren Patout

CRAWFISH MAQUE CHOUX

butter to cover bottom of pot
2 large onions, chopped
1 clove garlic, diced or pressed
1 bell pepper, chopped

5 ears fresh corn, cut
1 can Rotel tomatoes
2 pounds crawfish or shrimp tails or
   crabmeat
parsley and onion tops, chopped

Place onions, garlic, bell pepper in medium size heavy pot with butter. Sauté. Add fresh corn with corn milk from corn and season to taste. Stir well. Cover and let simmer stirring occasionally. Add Rotel, a little bit of water, cover and simmer 1 hour on low heat. Add seafood and cook another 15-20 minutes. Can also add parsley and green onions. You may substitute 2 cans whole kernel corn with ⅓ cup evaporated milk. Serves 6-8. Diane Chatelain
Leonard Fontenot

HOT GARLIC BREAD

1 loaf French bread	1 teaspoon oregano
½ cup softened butter or margarin	¼ teaspoon dried dillweed
1 minced garlic clove	Parmesan cheese

Cut a loaf of French bread in ¾ inch slices, not quite through bottom crust. Combine butter with garlic clove, oregano and dried dill. Heat, do not boil in small pot on stove. Spread mixture generously between slices. Sprinkle with Parmesan cheese. Wrap loosely in Reynolds Wrap and heat on grill approximately 15 minutes or oven at 350°. If you like bread a little more crunchy, do not wrap in foil while toasting in oven.   Lucille Roy Copeland

GRANDMA'S REAL SHORTCAKE

2 pints fresh strawberries	1 cup sugar

Cake:	
2 cups flour	1 egg
4 level teaspoons baking powder	3 teaspoons vanilla
1 teaspoon salt	¼ cup milk
3 tablespoons sugar	butter
5 tablespoons shortening	1 carton whipping cream

Prepare strawberries ahead of time. Wash and slice two pints of ripe strawberries, add one cup sugar. Leave out of refrigerator for about an hour, stir well.

Cake: Mix dry ingredients. Cut in shortening. Beat egg. Add milk and 2 teaspoons vanilla to egg, beat well and add to dry ingredients. Mix smooth and spread in a greased pie pan. Bake at 400° for about 20 minutes. When brown, split in half, butter and spread with fresh strawberries. Top with whipped cream that has been sweetened with 1 teaspoon vanilla.

Any fresh fruit or berries can be used, even stewed rhubarb. If peaches are used, add a little almond extract to peaches and 1 teaspoon of nutmeg to the shortcake.

My grandmother used to knead the dough and cut into biscuits and then split them to make individual servings, but in the "rush" age it is faster to make it all in one.   Mrs. L. A. Shelton

CAFÉ AU LAIT

For 2	
1½ tablespoons sugar	1 cup hot coffee
1 cup hot milk	

For 30	
¾ cup sugar, caramelized	15 cups hot milk
15 cups hot black coffee	

Caramelize sugar in heavy iron skillet. Remove from heat. Add hot milk slowly. Add milk to hot coffee and sweeten with sugar.   Adrien Stewart

WEDDING

Acadian wedding traditions range from the simplicity of jumping over a broomstick, the age-old way of joining a couple in marriage until the priest arrived on his yearly visit, to the Charivari, a time-honored ritual usually held after the wedding of a widow or widower. At a Charivari, after a quiet wedding ceremony, close friends of the couple came, bringing food and drink and clanging and banging on pots and pans to announce their arrival.

More often, for first weddings, traditional formal church services were followed by elaborate receptions offering sumptuous refreshments and dancing to Cajun tunes. The *bal de noces*, or wedding dance, during which each male guest took a turn on the dance floor with the bride and graciously pinned to her gown several dollar bills to help the couple off to a happy and easy life, was the highlight of the occasion. Years ago the money collected by the bride was often all the couple had to begin their new life.

Jumping the broomstick is seldom practiced today and Charivaris infrequently occur. Weddings, however, are still occasions for both religious and social celebration. Relatives and friends gather for nuptial mass and gay receptions where elaborate feasts are often served.

Wedding I

Bride's Champagne Punch
Peaches au Champagne
Galantine de Poulet
Jambon Chaud-Froid
Creole Daube Glacé
Oyster Tartlets
Shrimp Remoulade
Fondant Stuffed Dates
Croquembouche

Wedding II

Boneless Brisket
French Style Stuffed Ham
Assorted Breads
Shrimp Duhe
Onion Tarts
Pepper Bread
Liver Paté
Raw Vegetables with Dip
Crab Stuffed Mushrooms
Paradise Cake

BRIDE'S CHAMPAGNE PUNCH

48 ounces lemonade (you may use 4
(6 ounce) cans frozen lemonade
concentrate plus 4 cans only
water)

48 ounces pineapple juice (you may
make your own from fresh
pineapple) or use 4 (6 ounce)
cans frozen pineapple juice
plus 4 cans water

2 quarts gingerale (use 3 quarts if you
plan to omit champagne)

1 quart sparkling water

1 quart dry champagne

block ice

fresh strawberries, carefully selected,
washed but not stemmed

Mix first five ingredients. Pour over block of ice in large punch bowl. Float
strawberries. Serves 50.

Lucille Roy Copeland

PEACHES AU CHAMPAGNE

Peel ripe peaches and place each one in a large goblet. Prick the flesh all over
with fork and pour in champagne to more than cover. Drink the champagne and
eat the wine soaked peach for dessert.

Lucille Roy Copeland

GALANTINE DE POULET

1 large chicken
¼ cup sherry or Madeira

4-5 cups chicken or veal stock

For the Stuffing:
2 tablespoons brandy
2 teaspoons salt, or to taste
freshly ground black pepper
½ pound ground pork
½ pound ground veal
¼ cup pistachio nuts, optional
1 large onion, chopped
2 tablespoons butter

1 teaspoon ground allspice
1 clove garlic, crushed
½ cup white wine
1 egg, beaten to mix
¼ inch slice cooked ham, about ⅓ pound
¼ inch slice cooked tongue
½ cup chicken livers

For the Decoration:
aspic made with 1 quart chicken stock
2½-3 envelopes unflavored gelatin,
softened in ¼ cup Madeira

Vegetables, hard boiled egg whites,
pimento, black olives, cut into
decorative and colorful patterns

Bone the chicken by making an incision down the middle of the backbone and
pulling the skin with one hand while scraping the carcass with a very sharp bon-
ing knife, or paring knife or even a razor blade. Be sure to keep the knife against
the bone and be careful not to pierce the outer skin which will later serve as a
casing. When you have removed all of the bones, then carefully rip the skin from
the meat and reserve.

Cut the pieces of breast into strips, add 2 tablespoons brandy with salt and pepper, mix well and leave to marinate. Work the remaining chicken through the fine blade of a meat grinder, or better still, use a food processor, with the pork and veal. If using pistachios, blanch them in boiling water 1 minute, drain and peel them. Cook the onion in the butter until soft but not browned and add to the meat mixture with the allspice, garlic, white wine, egg and brandy drained from the chicken pieces. Add plenty of salt and pepper. (The mixture should be highly seasoned.)

Spread the chicken skin, cut side up, on a board and fold the leg and the wing skin to close the openings. Spread a third of the stuffing mixture in a rectangle about 3 inches wide, from heat to tail of the chicken, leaving a 1½ inch overlap of skin at the ends and 3-4 inches at the sides. Arrange half the strips of ham, tongue and chicken breast lengthwise down the stuffing and set the chicken livers on top. Build up more stuffing on each side of the livers, then top them with the remaining strips of meat so they are surrounded. Top with the remaining stuffing, shaping it to form a neat brick, and enclose in the chicken skin. Sew the skin with a trussing needle and string to form a neat cylinder and wrap it in a scalded dish towel. (Tie both ends to keep it in shape and fasten the center with a safety pin. (Any creases in the cloth will make wrinkles on the galantine.)

To cook the galantine: Put the galantine in a large stock pot with the chicken bones, Madeira, and enough stock to cover, add the lid and bring slowly to a boil. Simmer 1½-2 hours or until a skewer inserted in the center of the galantine for ½ minute is hot to the touch when withdrawn. Leave it to cool to tepid in the liquid, then drain it, rewrap it in foil, put it on a deep platter, top with a board and a 2 pound weight and chill 5-6 hours or overnight. Strain the cooking stock and chill also.

Crack the fat off the stock and clarify it. Add the gelatin and correct the seasoning. (Be sure that the seasoning will not cloud or float.) The galantine and aspic can be prepared up to 48 hours ahead of time and kept covered in the refrigerator. (Or freeze without the gelatin added.)

To finish the galantine: Unwrap it and cut half to three quarters of the roll in ⅜ inch slices. Put the slices on a wire rack and chill, with the remaining roll. Spoon a layer of aspic in a platter and chill until set. Cool some aspic in a bowl and coat the galantine slices and roll 2-3 times. Chill them thoroughly. Pour most of the remaining aspic into a tray to form a ½ inch layer and chill until set.

To assemble the dish: Set the uncut galantine at one end of the platter and arrange the slices overlapping down the center. Coat once more with aspic and chill thoroughly. Unmold the tray of aspic onto a sheet of wet wax paper, cut out triangles or crescents and decorate the border of the platter. Chop remaining aspic and pile it around the sliced galantine.

Felicia Elsbury

JAMBON CHAUD-FROID
(Ham decorated with a gelatin mayonnaise)

For a 9-12 pound cooked ham, bone in but rind removed.

2 envelopes unflavored gelatin
⅔ cup chicken or beef stock

2 tablespoons vinegar
1 tablespoon prepared mustard, Dijon
1 cup mayonnaise

Dissolve gelatin in stock and vinegar then melt over low heat. When completely cooled, beat mixture into mayonnaise and mustard. Strain. Coat the ham evenly with the mixture and chill. Repeat the coating and chilling 2-3 times until mixture is used up. (If the mixture gets hard before coating the 2nd or 3rd time, place it over a pan of hot water.) The ham is then ready to be decorated with interesting designs; cut hard boiled egg whites, olives, pickles, truffles, grapes, green onion tops, etc.

Felicia Elsbury

CREOLE DAUBE GLACÉ

1 (5 pound) veal roast
6 pig's feet
6 veal knuckles
1 teaspoon whole cloves
2 large onions, chopped
2 cups chopped celery
4 carrots, finely chopped
1 lemon

2 garlic pods
2 cups sherry
salt
red and black pepper
1 cup vinegar
3 bay leaves
thyme

Season meat well and cover with vinegar. Let stand overnight. Remove meat from vinegar. (Reserve liquid.) Brown meat on all sides in a heavy iron pot. Add one onion and half of carrots. Simmer for 10 minutes. Add a quart of water, pigs feet and veal knuckle and reserved liquid. Cover and cook about 3 hours, until meat falls from bones. Remove meats from liquid. Place all remaining ingredients into pot, cook until these fall apart. Strain. Add 2 cups sherry. Discard fat from veal, chop in small pieces. Place in a loaf pan or fancy mold. Strain liquid and pour over veal. Stir. Refrigerate daube overnight until congealed. When ready to serve, unmold and slice.

Lucille Roy Copeland

SHRIMP REMOULADE

1 pound boiled, peeled shrimp
4 tablespoons olive oil
2 tablespoons wine vinegar
1 teaspoon salt
2 tablespoons creole mustard

1 teaspoon hot horseradish
2 teaspoons paprika
2 stalks celery, chopped fine
2 green onions, chopped fine
2 tablespoons parsley, minced

Combine thoroughly oil, vinegar and salt. Add remaining sauce ingredients, mix and refrigerate. Arrange 1 pound of boiled, peeled shrimp on bed of shredded lettuce in 4 individual cocktail glasses and spoon remoulade sauce on top. This sauce keeps well for several days in refrigerator. Serves 4 as an appetizer. Easily doubled.

Betty Billeaud

OYSTER TARTLETS

4 dozen oysters cut in halves
½ cup butter
1 cup minced onion
1 cup minced celery
4 tablespoons flour
1 large can Carnation or Pet milk
¼ cup chopped parsley
¼ cup chopped onion tops

1 small jar chopped pimento
1 small can button mushrooms or
   stems and pieces
red pepper to taste
Salt to taste
Worcestershire to taste
Tart shells

Drain oysters and reserve liquid. Cut oysters in halves. Drop oysters in melted butter and simmer until edges curl. Remove oysters and add onions, celery and flour. Make a roux, stir and cook on low fire until light brown. Add oyster juice, milk, parsley, onion tops, pimento, mushrooms and continue cooking on low fire until thick. Add oysters and season to taste. Simmer a few more minutes. (If too thick, add more milk.) Pour into warm tart shells, decorate center of each tart with a piece of curly parsley and serve immediately. Center each piece of parsley with a dot of pimento for a real festive look. (These oyster tarts freeze beautifully.) Serves 24.

Lucille Roy Copeland

FONDANT STUFFED DATES

4½ cups confectioners sugar
⅔ cup condensed milk
1 teaspoon vanilla extract
1 teaspoon almond extract

1 teaspoon coconut or orange extract
¼ teaspoon salt
½ cup finely chopped pecans
4 dozen pitted dates

Blend sugar, milk and flavorings. Knead fondant until real smooth and creamy. Add finely chopped pecans. Divide mixture into 3 separate bowls and tint one pale green, one pink and leave the other white. Cover bowls with damp cloth and refrigerate overnight. Fill each date with fondant and roll in granulated sugar. Very festive.

Mrs. L. A. Shelton

CROQUEMBOUCHE

The croquembouche is becoming very popular with Acadian brides as a substitute for the more traditional wedding cake. The croquembouche is composed of small cream puffs arranged pyramid style on a baked pastry round. The puffs are glazed with caramel before they are placed on the pastry round.

Custard:

1 cup milk	2 tablespoons cornstarch
½ cup sugar	1 tablespoon flour
¾ cup milk	1 teaspoon vanilla
½ cup sugar	2 egg whites
pinch salt	5 tablespoons sugar
2 egg yolks	

Heat 1 cup milk with ½ cup sugar. In the meantime beat together ¾ cup milk, ½ cup sugar, pinch salt, 2 egg yolks, 2 tablespoons cornstarch and 1 tablespoon flour in a 4 cup pyrex pitcher. Add second mixture slowly to the hot milk and sugar. Cook over low flame until mixture thickens. Cook 2-3 minutes. Fold in meringue made from 2 egg whites and 5 tablespoons sugar. Flavor with 1 teaspoon vanilla. Yield 3 cups. Chill custard.

Puff Pastry (Pastry Round):

2 cups flour	½ cup ice water
½ teaspoon salt	1 ½ sticks sweet butter
2 tablespoons butter	

Into a large bowl sift 2 cups flour with ½ teaspoon salt. Rub in 2 tablespoons butter, cut into small pieces, until the mixture resembles meal. Add a scant ½ cup ice water and incorporate it into the dough. Work the mixture for a few seconds to combine the ingredients and form the dough into a ball. Dust the ball lightly with flour. With a knife cut a deep cross in the middle of the ball and push each quarter of the dough outward to form a 4 inch square. Pat the dough until it is smooth, wrap it in plastic wrap, and chill it.

Let 1 ½ sticks or ¾ cup sweet butter soften slightly. Knead the butter, squeezing it through the fingers, and form into a rough square. Remove the wax paper and dust the butter well on all sides with flour. Wrap it in a clean piece of wax paper and chill it until firm but not hard. On a floured surface roll out the dough to a 7 inch square. Lay the chilled butter diagonally in the center of the square and roll out the 4 visible corners of the dough into 4 inch lengths. Fold each strip of dough over the butter, completely enclosing it, and turn the dough over. Sprinkle the working surface and the dough with flour and roll the dough out to a rectangle about 10 inches long x 6 inches wide. Brush off any excess flour and fold the top third of the rectangle over the center and the bottom third over the top. Turn the folded dough on the board so that an open side faces you. With the rolling pin, flatten the dough with uniform impressions. Roll the dough from the center away from you to within 1 inch of the end. Reserve the strip on the board, flouring the board as necessary, and again roll the dough away from you to make a rectangle about 10 inches long. Do not roll the pin over the ends, or the air and butter will be expelled. Brush off any excess flour from the dough and fold the strip in 3 as before. This completes 2 "turns." Wrap the dough in plastic wrap and chill it for 30 minutes. Make 2 more turns, always starting with an open end facing you.

Wrap the pastry in plastic wrap and chill it for at least 30 minutes or up to 2 days. The pastry is given additional turns before using. Bake as directed.

Prepare 1 piece of pie pastry or puff pastry rolled ¼ inch thick, cut into an 8 inch circle. Prick dough and place on a cookie sheet. Bake at 425° for 12 minutes or until golden. Remove from oven and cool.

Pate À Choux (Puffs):

1 cup water	1 cup flour
1 stick butter	3 eggs
1 teaspoon sugar	

In a heavy saucepan bring 1 cup water, 1 stick or ½ cup butter, cut into pieces, and 1 teaspoon sugar to a boil over high heat. Lower the heat and add 1 cup flour all at once. With a wooden paddle beat the mixture until it leaves the sides of the pan and forms a ball. Transfer the dough to the bowl of an electric mixer. With the mixer at high speed beat in 3 eggs, one at a time, beating well after each addition. The batter should be just thick enough to hold peaks. If it is too stiff, break another egg into a bowl and add enough of it to bring the batter to the right consistency. Chill batter at least 10 minutes before baking. For uniform puffs pipe from pastry bag. You may drop onto greased cookie sheets with 2 spoons to form shape. Keep shape high not flat. Bake at 425° for 10 minutes, then 375° for 10 minutes, then 350° for 10 minutes. Turn oven off, prick puffs, and leave in oven 10 more minutes. Cool thoroughly. Make tiny hole in side of each puff. Now they are ready to be filled with custard.

Caramel Coating:

1½ cups sugar	½ cup water
½ teaspoon cream of tartar	

Blend above ingredients together and bring to boil stirring constantly. When syrup begins to change color turn off heat. Now you are ready to assemble the croquembouche. With tongs pick up one filled puff at a time and dip into caramel, then place on baked pastry round. Cover entire pastry with puffs. Syrup will act as glue. Start second layer ½ inch from the edge. Keep turning the pastry so that you can build the pyramid. Optional: If you are patient enough to wait about 2-3 minutes, the glaze will be cooled off enough for you to spin thread around the pastry. With the tongs, test the syrup. When it starts to become heavy, with the tongs, place a drop of caramel at the bottom side of the pyramid. Gently pull the caramel syrup with the end of the tongs, and you will start spinning threads. Start at the bottom of the pyramid and work your way around. Repeat this procedure. When finished, the croquembouche will be encased in the wispy caramel. Serves 12.

Gourmet Cooking Class
University of Southwestern Louisiana

BONELESS BRISKET

Basic Marinade:

2 teaspoons salt	1 small bottle Italian dressing
3 large bottles soy sauce	½ cup brown sugar
2 small cans pineapple juice	1 bottle Worcestershire
1 boneless brisket	1 tablespoon garlic powder
lemon pepper	

Marinate at least 24 hours. Wipe dry. Place brisket on broiling pan. Season with lemon pepper and garlic powder. Cover entire pan with foil and seal tightly. Cook at 275°-300° until ⅔ done. Take out brisket and place on barbeque pit over low burning coals. Be sure to soak some hickory chips in water for approximately 3 hours and add to coals just before putting brisket on. You will have to watch this closely for 10-15 minutes because fat on the brisket will cause coals to flame. Once the brisket is browned on both sides wrap it in foil and cook on pit for remainder of time. (Figure 30 minutes/pound.) Be sure to save the juice which collects in the foil to pour over the sliced brisket. Marinade can be stored in refrigerator and used several times for any kind of beef—also a good marinade for venison. Serves 12-15.

Lynn Blevins

FRENCH STYLE STUFFED HAM

5 pounds or ½ cooked ham	1 minced clove garlic
1 large onion, sliced	1 teaspoon dark brown sugar
1 teaspoon red hot sauce	3 tablespoons pineapple juice
2 cloves garlic	3 tablespoons water
1 blade celery, chopped finely	1 teaspoon pepper jelly
½ bell pepper, chopped finely	garnish with pineapple rings, whole
½ medium onion, chopped finely	cloves

Place ham in a Dutch oven, cover ham completely with water. Add large onion, sliced; cloves of garlic and hot sauce. Cover and let simmer 2 hours. Remove from water, cool for a short period. Place ham on tinfoil large enough to wrap ham. Make holes in ham, large enough to stuff with dressing made up of celery, bell pepper, onion and garlic. Really push dressing into holes, letting the excess dressing stay on foil. Now make sauce with the sugar, juice and water with pepper jelly. Glaze ham well. Place pineapple rings and 6 whole cloves about ham. Wrap securely with foil, place in loaf pan, bake 2 hours at 350°. Open foil and bake for 10 more minutes. Better if made 1-2 days early. Serves 10.

Mrs. Larry Hebert

SHRIMP DUHE

5 pounds large shrimp
1 pint homemade mayonnaise
¼ cup mustard with horseradish

2 medium yellow onions,
   thinly sliced
lemon juice, salt, red pepper to taste

Fill large kettle ¾ full of water, add small can red pepper, 2 bags crab boil, 3 lemons quartered, ½ box salt, 1 onion quartered and 4 garlic cloves. Bring to a boil. Simmer for 5 minutes. Add shrimp in shells and cook 8 minutes. Peel and place in salad bowl; add other ingredients as listed. Mix well and cover. Allow to marinate at least 24 hours before serving, longer is better. Place in large shallow serving bowl and eat with toothpicks. Can also be served as a salad. Add avocado slices immediately before serving and place on a bed of lettuce. Serves 20.

Doreen Duhe

ONION TARTS

Custard:
3 beaten egg yolks
½ teaspoon salt

cayenne pepper, healthy dash
1 (½ pint) carton sour cream

3 tablespoons butter
2 small onions, minced

½ cup minced ham or cooked, drained
   and crumbled bacon
8 pre-baked, individual pastry shells

Cook custard mixture over simmering water in double boiler for approximately 20 minutes, until thick. Let cool. Melt butter and sauté onions for 2-3 minutes. Stir in ham or bacon. Cook 1 minute more then mix well with custard. Spoon into pastry shells. Bake for 8-10 minutes in a preheated 350° oven. Serves 8.

Mrs. J. L. Beyt, Jr.
New Iberia, LA.

PEPPER BREAD

2 loaves frozen bread dough, thawed
1 pound ground hot pork sausage,
   browned
¼ cup ground bell pepper
½ cup finely chopped onion

¼ cup ground celery
grated sharp cheese
optional: ground ham, sliced or chopped
   jalapenos, chopped mushrooms that
   have been sauteed

Roll out bread dough on 2 cookie sheets. Spread with ingredients. Roll up. Brush with butter. Bake at 350° until golden brown. Slice and serve warm. Delicious with cocktails or in the morning with coffee. Serves 20-25.

Phyllis Ledet

LIVER PATÉ

1 pound pork liver
1 tablespoon vinegar
¾ pound pork fat, sliced
3 tablespoons butter
⅓ cup flour
1 cup milk
8 anchovies

2 medium onions
2½ teaspoons salt
¼ teaspoon ground cloves
1 egg, beaten
1 tablespoon bread crumbs
pepper to taste
2 cloves garlic, minced

Cover liver with cold water and vinegar. Soak one hour. Line loaf pan with very thin strips of pork fat. Put remainder of fat through food processor or chopper once. Melt butter, add flour and milk making smooth white sauce. Add fat and continue cooking slowly 30 minutes. Grind cleaned liver, onions and anchovies in food processor or grinder once using finest setting, twice if necessary. Combine with white sauce, strain through medium sieve. Add salt and spice. Add beaten egg and bread crumbs with pepper and minced garlic. Pour in lined pan. Place pan in larger pan of water and bake at 300° one hour. Chill and serve with crackers and lemon wedges. Serves 25-30.

Mrs. J. C. Chargois, Sr.

DIP FOR RAW VEGETABLES

1 (5 ounce) jar Kraft Roka Blue
    Cheese
1 (3 ounce) package cream cheese,
    slightly softened

1 tablespoon BV meat extract or beef
    flavored extract
1 small grated onion
1 pint mayonnaise, Hellmann's

Mix the above ingredients in order except for the mayonnaise. After they are well mixed add the mayonnaise. Refrigerate for at least 2 hours. Serve with any variety of sliced raw vegetables, carrot sticks, bell pepper, squash, cauliflower. May be made the day before. Yield: 3 cups.

Mrs. Dorothy Verspoor

CRAB STUFFED MUSHROOMS

1 pound fresh mushrooms
1 stick butter or margarine
1 bunch small shallots
juice of ½ lemon
½ pound crabmeat

¼ teaspoon sage
salt and pepper to taste
½ cup seasoned bread crumbs
1 egg beaten plus 1 teaspoon
    cold water

Gently wash and remove stems from mushrooms. Sauté caps in butter. Drain on paper towel. Add finely chopped stems to skillet. Sauté with shallots that have been chopped. Squeeze lemon juice on stems and caps. Add crabmeat to skillet along with seasonings. Add crumbs and mix well. Over low heat, add beaten egg while stirring constantly. Stuff mixture into mushroom caps. (If caps are small, shape into mounds to have more stuffing.) Bake on a cookie sheet for 15-20 minutes in a 325° oven. Serves 6-8.

Marilyn B. Hoffpauir

PARADISE CAKE

½ box powdered sugar
6 eggs
½ pound real butter, softened
1 cup finely chopped pecans
1 cup slivered almonds

1½ dozen macaroons (coconut or almond)
1 teaspoon vanilla
2½ dozen lady fingers, split
1 pint whipping cream

Cream together sugar, butter and 3 eggs, beating after each egg. Crumble macaroons into mixture, add vanilla, almonds, pecans, and 3 egg yolks, beating after each yolk is added. Beat egg whites until stiff and fold into the mixture. Make a ring mold 10 inches in diameter of aluminum foil. Line bottom and sides of mold with lady fingers. Put half of filling into the mold, add another layer of lady fingers, then the rest of the filling. Top with another layer of lady fingers. Place in refrigerator for several hours. Whip cream, adding 2 teaspoons powdered sugar and 1 teaspoon vanilla. Remove aluminum foil mold and frost cake with whipped cream. Garnish with nuts and cherries. Refrigerate until ready to serve. Slice to serve. Servings: 14-16.

LaVerne P. Pozzi
New Orleans, LA.

INDEPENDENCE DAYS

July is a month of festivals. Naturally July 4th is a day for frolic and fireworks as many families gather all along the banks of the bayous to celebrate America's Independence Day. Simple picnic fare which often includes fried catfish, corn on the cob, and Cajun-style homemade ice cream can be sampled from one neighbor's table to the next until the sun sets. The day ends as fireworks flash over bayou waters, making magnificent reflections as they light the moss-draped oaks.

But also true to their French heritage, the citizens of Acadiana celebrate Bastille Day—July 14—the day of the French Independence and establishment of a new French nation. Taking advantage of the lazy days that come with an Acadian summer, the Cajun usually chooses to have another picnic on Bastille Day. More in keeping with French style cuisine, a *Terrine de Poisson des Ecrivisses* might be enjoyed along with cucumber soup, several different types of sandwiches, and a dessert of fresh fig ice cream or a watermelon fruit basket. The festivities conclude with a fais-do-do (go to sleep). Lovers of music and dance, the Cajuns end most of their festivals with this rollicking country dance attended by the entire family. The name *fais-do-do* stems from the olden days when, as the children got sleepy, they were all put down onto a large feather bed while the others danced on and on and on.

Fourth of July

Guacamole Stuffed Celery
Fried Catfish with Dip
Fried Onion Rings
Hush Puppies
Steamed Corn on the Cob
Italian Cake
Chablis

Bastille Day

French '75's
Chilled Cucumber Soup
Terrine de Poisson aux Écrevisses
Caviar Potatoes
Chicken and Watercress Sandwiches
Whole Wheat Bread
Sandwich Surprise
Frog Legs Sauce Picante
Fresh Fig Ice Cream
Gamay Rose or Pinot Chardonnay

GUACAMOLE STUFFED CELERY

1 bunch celery, chilled
2 ripe avocados, mashed
½ cup minced onion
1½ tablespoons lemon juice

1¾ teaspoons salt
3-4 drops hot pepper sauce
1 cup chopped tomatoes

Cut off leaf portions of celery. Separate celery into ribs. Rinse in cold water and dry. Wrap in plastic bag and refrigerate. In a medium bowl combine avocados, onion, lemon juice, salt and hot sauce. Stir in tomatoes. Refrigerate covered if not stuffing celery right away. Use about 3-4 tablespoons guacamole mixture to fill each celery rib. May be served whole or halved or in bite size pieces. Yield: 2½ cups.

Marlene Barry

FRIED CATFISH FILETS

1 jar yellow prepared mustard
salt and pepper to taste
1 box Fish-Fri

fish filets
oil for frying

First coat fish with mustard. Then season. Place some of Fish-Fri in plastic bag and shake the filets. Drop coated fish in hot grease. Cook until light brown, turning once and cook other side. Let drain well over pan before placing on paper towel. Great using bass, catfish and sac-a-lait filets. It seals the flavor in and the oil out. Also the taste of mustard is cooked out. Number of servings depends on amount and size of filets.

Billie White

DIP FOR FRIED CATFISH

1 pint mayonnaise
1 tablespoon chives, minced
1 tablespoon parsley, minced

1 tablespoon horseradish
1 tablespoon mustard
1 large chopped onion

Mix all the above and keep refrigerated. Yield: 1 pint.

Olga Hawley

HUSHPUPPIES

2 eggs, beaten
2 cups milk
6 tablespoons flour
8 teaspoons baking powder

4 cups white or yellow corn meal
4 onions, minced
corn oil

Add onions to your dry ingredients. In a separate bowl, mix eggs and milk. Stir into your dry ingredients. Heat oil to 350°; drop batter by teaspoonsful into hot oil. Fry until golden brown, (approximately 3-4 minutes on each side until done). Drain on absorbent paper. Cover on warm platter until ready to serve.

FRENCH FRIED ONION RINGS

1 cup flour
1 teaspoon baking powder
¼ teaspoon salt
1 egg, well-beaten

1 cup milk
1 teaspoon salad oil
4 large sweet onions
fat for deep frying, heated to 375°

Blend flour, baking powder and salt. Set aside. Combine the egg, milk and oil in a bowl and beat until thoroughly blended. Beat in the dry ingredients until batter is smooth. Cover and set aside while preparing onions. Peel onions, cut off root ends, and slice about ¼ inch thick and separate into rings. Using long-handled fork, dip a few onion rings at a time into batter. Lift out and drain over bowl a few seconds then drop into heated fat. Turn only once as they brown and do not crowd. When golden brown, drain on absorbent paper and salt. Serve hot. Serves 8.

Sally Herpin

ITALIAN CAKE
(Makes about 30 3x3 squares)

1 stick of oleo
½ cup of vegetable shortening
2 cups of sugar
5 egg yolks
2 cups flour
1 teaspoon of baking soda

1 cup of buttermilk
½ cup of chopped nuts
1 small can of shredded coconut
1 teaspoon of vanilla extract
5 egg whites, stiffly beaten

Icing
1 (8 ounce) package cream cheese
½ stick of margarine
1 teaspoon vanilla

1 pound powdered sugar
1 to 2 tablespoons milk
½ cup chopped nuts

Cream the oleo and shortening. Add the sugar and beat until smooth. Add the egg yolks and beat well. Combine the flour and soda and add to the above mixture. Mix well. Then pour alternate portions of milk, nuts, coconut and vanilla into the batter. Stir until well mixed. Finally, fold in stiffly beaten egg whites. Pour into 16x11 roasting pan and bake at 350° for 25-30 minutes.

After the cake has baked and cooled cover with icing.

To make the icing, mix the cream cheese, oleo, vanilla and powdered sugar. Add milk to reach a spreadable consistency. When well mixed add nuts and stir well. The cake may be made ahead of time and frozen. When ready to use defrost and ice.

Mrs. Dorothy Verspoor

FRENCH '75's

1 ounce brandy
1 ounce fresh lemon juice
1 ounce simple syrup

chilled champagne
fresh strawberries

Place all ingredients in a stemmed champagne glass. Stir and top with chilled champagne. Center with fresh strawberry. C'est magnifique. (According to preference, you may substitute gin or vodka for the brandy.)

Chez Pastor Restaurant
Lafayette, La.

CHILLED CUCUMBER SOUP

¼ cup butter or margarine
4 cups chopped, peeled cucumbers
1 cup chopped green onions
¼ cup regular all-purpose flour

4 cups chicken broth
salt and pepper
½ cup light cream
cucumber slices

In a large skillet, in melted butter or margarine, sauté cucumbers and green onions until soft; stir in flour. Gradually add chicken broth, stirring constantly until mixture thickens slightly and begins to boil; add salt and pepper to taste. Simmer, covered 10 minutes stirring occasionally. Refrigerate until thoroughly chilled. At serving time: Pour about 2 cups mixture into electric blender container; cover and puree at medium speed until smooth. Strain mixture into large bowl, discarding seeds. Repeat until all mixture is pureed. Stir in cream. Serve garnished with cucumber slices. Serves 6-8.

Mrs. Richard Kennedy

CAVIAR POTATOES

potato, small new red, as many as
   desired
1 small grated white onion

1 cup sour cream
black caviar

Boil potatoes in salted water until tender, approximately 20 minutes. Remove from water and scoop out about ⅓ of the potato. Salt and pepper lightly. Fill with ¼ teaspoon onion, 1 level teaspoon sour cream, and ½ teaspoon caviar. Can be served as an hor d'oeuvre or as a starch entreé to a meal. Potatoes can be prepared before and kept in refrigerator overnight. Reheat in microwave for 1 minute before filling. Onion and sour cream can be mixed together before also. Add caviar on top of sour cream.

Leslie Hayes

TERRINE DE POISSON AUX ÉCREVISSES
(Fish Paté with Crawfish)

1 tablespoon minced shallots
3 tablespoons butter, unsalted
3 tablespoons flour
1 cup milk
3 dashes Peychaud bitters
Tabasco, salt and white pepper to
    taste, at least ½ teaspoon each

1 pound white fleshed fish, deep water
    catfish is excellent
¾ cup peeled crawfish tails
2 tablespoons vermouth, or dry white
    wine or lemon or lime juice
salt and pepper to taste
4 egg whites

Cook minced shallots in butter for about a minute and then stir in flour. (Don't allow the roux to darken.) Stir in the milk and whisk vigorously. Stirring constantly, add the salt, pepper, Tabasco and bitters and cook until thick and smooth. Chill. Preheat oven to 350°. In a food processor puree fish with vermouth and salt and pepper. Add egg whites one at a time, blending well after each. Add the cold white sauce slowly.

Spoon ⅔ of the mixture into a buttered 1½ quart terrine mold or loaf pan. Make a trench and carefully place the crawfish tails down the center. Cover with the remaining paté. Place on the lid or cover with buttered foil. Put the terrine into a baking pan and add hot water to reach ⅔ up the side of the terrine. Bake for 1 hour or until an inserted knife comes out clean. Cool on a rack.

The paté may be served hot or cold; directly from the mold or unmolded onto a platter. Garnish with fresh dill and/or watercress. To cut neat slices, dip the knife into boiling water.

For dietors: Delete the white sauce, flour, milk. Add 1 cup of skim cottage cheese or 1 eight ounce package diet cream cheese.

Hint: To taste for seasoning: Cook about 1 tablespoon of finished mixture in a small skillet. Serves 6-8 as appetizer.

Felicia Elsbury

CHICKEN AND WATERCRESS SANDWICHES

1 loaf unsliced bread
curry butter
1 bunch watercress

mayonnaise
6 cooked chicken breasts

Freeze an unsliced loaf of white bread in the freezing compartment of the re-frigerator for 2 hours, cut off the crusts, and slice the loaf lengthwise into ¼ inch slices. Spread one side of each slice with curry butter, put half the slices buttered side up on a cutting board, and top them with sprigs of watercress. Spread the sprigs lightly with mayonnaise and arrange thin slices of cooked and skinned chicken breast over them. Spread the chicken lightly with mayonnaise, arrange sprigs of watercress over it, and top the watercress with the remaining sliced bread buttered side down. Stack the sandwiches and chill them, wrapped in a dampened tea towel. Cut the sandwiches crosswise into 1½ inch widths and arrange them on a tray.

Curry Butter: In a small bowl combine 1 stick (½ cup) butter, softened, 1 table-spoon curry powder and salt to taste. Serves 24.

Mrs. Donald Labbé

WHOLE WHEAT BREAD

3 cups milk
⅔ cup honey
3 tablespoons or packages yeast
¼ cup butter or soy or safflower oil
5 cups unsifted, unbleached whole
    wheat flour (stone ground whole
    wheat flour can be used but makes
    a much heavier, darker loaf)

1 scant tablespoon salt
2-3 more cups whole wheat flour or
    enough to make stiff dough

All ingredients should be room temperature. Heat milk and honey to 120° (use candy thermometer) add yeast and let set for 5 minutes. Then mix with butter, 5 cups flour and salt. Beat by hand 100 or more strokes or 7 minutes with electric mixer at low speed. (If dough is not beaten enough, bread will be heavy.) Add and stir well the additional 2-3 cups of flour, or enough to make a stiff dough. Sprinkle about 1 cup flour on bread board or clean counter and turn dough onto it. Knead until dough is smooth and elastic. Use more flour if necessary to prevent from sticking. You'll have to knead about 15-20 minutes. Put into oiled bowl, smooth side down, then turn greased side up, cover and let rise in a warm place 85° about 1 hour. Punch down and let rise again about 30 minutes or until doubled. Then take out, punch down and divide into 2 or 3 portions, depending if you want 2-1½ pound loaves or 3-1 pound loaves. Shape into loaf and put into greased pans. Let rise until dough is up to top of pan, than bake at 350° for about 45 minutes. (We like bread on the light side.) Remove from oven and put on a rack and im-mediately brush with butter. Let cool on rack. Slices better if you let it cool thoroughly but it sure is good hot. If you have a mixer with a dough hook, soften yeast, milk and honey as above, put into mixer with oil, 8 cups of flour and salt. Turn on for 17 minutes. Then put into oiled bowl and proceed as above.

Ann Kernaghan Baron

SANDWICH SURPRISE

2 cups crumbled, crisp bacon
1 cup finely chopped or shaved
  pecans

¼ cup finely chopped or shaved bell
  pepper
mayonnaise

Mix first 3 ingredients together. Add enough mayonnaise to bind the mixture and to make it spreadable on bread. Terrific! Proportions can vary according to individual taste. Yield: 10-12 sandwiches.

Jeanne Loftin Gilley

FROG LEGS SAUCE PIQUANT

6 pairs frog legs
2 tablespoons butter
salt and pepper to taste
4 onions, sliced
6 whole tomatoes, fresh or canned
1 bay leaf

1 sprig thyme
¼ cup chopped parsley
2 garlic cloves, pressed
4 bell peppers, diced
1 cup water or stock

Slowly brown frog legs in butter; add salt, pepper, onions, bell peppers and cook until brown. Add tomatoes, bay leaf, thyme, parsley and garlic. Cover and cook slowly 30 minutes. Add water or stock. Continue to smother until frog legs are tender. Correct seasonings. Serve over rice. Serves 6.

Lucille Roy Copeland

FRESH FIG ICE CREAM

1 quart cream or Half and Half
1 quart homogenized milk
2 level cups sugar
2 teaspoons vanilla

8 eggs
½ teaspoon salt
1 quart fresh peeled figs

Beat eggs in blender until lemon yellow. Blend in sugar. Cook eggs, sugar, milk and cream in a large boiler until custard is thick, stirring all the while it is being cooked. Remove from burner, add vanilla and fold in 1 quart of slightly mashed figs. Place in electric ice cream freezer. This keeps indefinitely in freezer. Serves 15.

Mrs. J. Maxime Roy, Sr.

BOUCHERIE

The Cajun is renowned for his affinity for occasions which bring his family and friends together for fun and feast. The Boucherie, or slaughtering of the pigs, is a picnic which in the past was necessary because of the lack of refrigeration. Each neighbor took his turn selecting a choice pig for the slaughter. The entire community gathered for the day to share in the work necessary to render every part of the animal into delectable repasts. The men butchered the pigs, removing the skin to be crisply deep-fried and then salted for cracklins'. Other men joined the women in making boudin and chaudin, hot, spicy sausages and hogshead cheese, a jellied delicacy made from cooking the head of the pig. Today, pieces of pork and packaged gelatin often substitute for the actual hog's head, but the "cheese" is still a favorite item even for elegant cocktail parties. When the work was done, everyone gathered to sample the products. Music, laughter, beer and festivity accompanied both the day's work and the final feast, which frequently lasted long into the night.

Boucherie

Hog's Head Cheese
Boudin
Gumbo Ya Ya
Country Ribs
Cole Slaw
Sweet Potato Balls
Cracklin' Corn Bread
Bread Pudding with Whiskey Sauce
Les Oreilles de Cochon
Beverages: Beer, Zinfandel

HOG'S HEAD CHEESE

1 fresh pork picnic ham with skin
1 bunch green onions, chopped
1 cup chopped parsley
1 tablespoon paprika

6 fresh pork hocks or pig's feet
4 garlic cloves, minced
salt and pepper to taste

Place all ingredients in a large pot and cover with water. Simmer until meat is tender. Remove meat from broth. Discard fat and bones chop meat into small pieces. Return meat to broth and simmer until thick. Correct seasoning. Pour into long loaf pans and refrigerate until firm. Cut into squares to serve as an hors d'oeuvre.

BOUDIN

2 pounds pork meat
1½ pounds pork liver
salt and pepper to taste
1 large onion, cut up

2 bunches green onions, chopped
6 cups cooked rice
sausage casings soaked in cold water

Cook pork meat and liver and seasonings in water to cover until meat falls apart. Remove meat and reserve some broth. Grind meat, onion, green onions and parsley, saving about ½ cup of green onion tops and parsley. Mix ground meat mixture with the ½ cup of green onions and parsley, rice and enough broth to make a moist dressing. Stuff dressing into casing, using a sausage stuffer. Serves 6-8.

GUMBO YA YA
(Chicken and Andouille Sausage Gumbo)

1 (5 pound) chicken, cut into 10 pieces
salt and freshly ground pepper
cayenne pepper
garlic powder
2½ cups all-purpose flour
1 cup oil
2 cups chopped onion
2 cups chopped green pepper

1½ cups chopped celery
6 cups chicken stock
1 pound andouille sausage or
 kielbasa, diced
1½ teaspoons minced fresh garlic
oysters, optional
steamed white rice

Arrange chicken on a baking sheet and season evenly with salt, cayenne and garlic powder. Let stand 30 minutes at room temperature. Combine chicken pieces and flour in a large paper bag and shake until chicken is well coated. Heat oil in large skillet over medium-high heat. Add chicken (reserve remaining flour) and brown on all sides. Remove with slotted spoon and set aside. Loosen any brown bits on bottom of skillet. Using whisk, add 1 cup reserved flour and stir constantly until roux is very dark brown. Remove from heat and add onions, green pepper and celery, stirring to blend thoroughly and prevent burning. Transfer to large saucepan. Stir in stock and bring to boil over medium-high heat. Reduce heat, add sausage and garlic, and simmer 45 minutes, stirring occasionally. Remove chicken from bones and cut meat into small pieces. Return to saucepan and cook thoroughly. Season with salt and pepper and serve immediately over steamed rice in individual soup bowls. Oysters may be added last 5 minutes of cooking. Serves 8.

COUNTRY RIBS

allow 1 pound country style cut pork ribs per person, plus a couple extra "for the pot"

½ cup soy sauce
1½ tablespoons cornstarch, this amount food for 4½-6 pounds

Sweet and Sour Sauce:
1 cup catsup
1 cup water
¼ cup brown sugar
¼ cup cider vinegar
¼ cup Worcestershire

1 teaspoon chili powder
1 teaspoon salt
dash of pepper
a few drops Tabasco

Place ribs in a large pot with a cover. Add water to cover ribs. Bring to a boil and cook 15-20 minutes. Remove ribs from water and drain well. Brush ribs with soy sauce and cornstarch mixture. Continue to brush both sides of ribs until all soy sauce mixture is gone. This done over a 30-45 minute period in order to allow mixture to penetrate ribs. Place ribs on grill about 6-8 inches from briquettes. Cook about 20-30 minutes, medium to low fire. Every 2-3 minutes ribs should be turned and basted each time with sweet and sour sauce. Serve immediately or put in large pot in oven on "warm" until ready to serve.

To make sauce mix above ingredients and bring to a boil. Use as a basting sauce and serve remainder in individual dishes as a dip for ribs. I have also cooked these ribs in the oven at 350° for about 1-1½ hours and they are almost as good as on the grill. Always good the next day—if any left over.

Pat Guidry

COLE SLAW

1 head cabbage, shredded
1 large apple, peeled and cubed
¼ cup bell pepper, diced
1 tablespoon walnuts, chopped
sprinkle of raisins or diced pineapple, well drained

salt to taste
mayonnaise
paprika

Be sure cabbage is dry before shredding. Mix dry ingredients; toss with mayonnaise—just enough to hold together—not soggy. Chill well. Top individual servings with a bell pepper ring, dab of mayonnaise and sprinkle of paprika.

Mrs. Dwight Andrus

SWEET POTATO BALLS

2 (22 ounce) cans sweet potatoes, drained
1 stick margarine
1 tablespoon brown sugar
1 tablespoon vanilla

1 teaspoon frozen orange juice, more to taste
cornflake crumbs
miniature marshmallows

Preheat oven to 400°. Heat potatoes with margarine and brown sugar; add vanilla and orange juice. Mix with mixer until well blended. Form balls and roll in cornflake crumbs. Add marshmallows to top of each ball. Bake 12 minutes in 400° oven. Yield: 30 balls.

Lou Bivins

CORNBREAD

1 cup yellow corn meal
1 cup white corn meal
1 cup flour
2 eggs
¼ cup sugar

1 cup milk
1 teaspoon salt
8 teaspoons baking powder
2 teaspoons shortening

Mix all ingredients in a large bowl. Beat 1 minute. Grease a 12 inch wrought iron skillet or a 13 inch pyrex dish with oil. Pour mixture in pan and bake at 350° for 30-40 minutes or until golden brown.

CRACKLIN' CORNBREAD

Add 1 cup of crushed cracklins to any good cornbread recipe.

BREAD PUDDING WITH WHISKEY SAUCE

Pudding:
1 quart milk
½ loaf French bread, crumbled
½ cup sugar

4 whole eggs, beaten
2 teaspoons vanilla

Meringue:
4 egg whites
1 teaspoon sugar for each white

dash of cream of tartar

Whiskey Sauce:
4 egg yolks beaten
½ cup sugar
1 stick butter or margarine

6-8 tablespoons bourbon, at least
90 proof

Combine ingredients for pudding and bake at 350° for 30 minutes. Make meringue. Frost pudding with meringue and brown in oven for about 10 minutes. Combine sauce ingredients in saucepan and cook until thickens. When cool add 6-8 tablespoons bourbon and pour over individual pudding servings. Serves 10.

Mrs. J. P. Camos

LES OREILLES DE COCHON

2 cups flour
½ teaspoon baking powder
½ teaspoon salt

½ stick butter
2 eggs
1 teaspoon vinegar

Mix ingredients as for pastry. Divide into separate small pieces, about 2 inches, roll each separately very thin. Fry in hot fat bending one end.

1½ cups cane syrup
½ cup sugar

pinch salt

Mix and cook to soft crack stage, about 275°. Pour 1 tablespoon of this mixture over each "Pig's Ear."

Lois Guilbeaux

HALLOWEEN

The widespread custom of celebrating Halloween has a special meaning in Acadiana. Originally a pagan festival which arose to counteract the Christian practice of honoring the saints on November 1, Halloween in South Louisiana is still closely tied to All Saints' Day and to All Souls' Day, November 2, on which the souls of all the dead are remembered.

The three days marking the transition from Autumn to Winter begin with the festivities of All Hallow's Eve. Trick-or-Treat, a custom relatively unknown in the region until after the Second World War, takes place in the early evening. Acadian superstitions have endured, however, and the ghosts and goblins of the season have a special character. "The Haint," a mysterious light believed to be the soul of an unbaptized child condemned to wander ceaselessly, is said to lure unwary victims into the swamp. "The Crazy Girl" is another well-known spirit who haunts Acadian children with bursts of insane laughter. Many naughty Cajun children think twice before disobeying when reminded that Mrs. Longfingers, an old woman with knotty fingers, will come and pull their toes. Other familiar tales concern the *Couchemar*, or Nightmare, a diabolical creature who suffocates its victims, and the *Tataille*, or Great Beast, a gigantic insect, half-cockroach, half-spider. Mere skeletons and witches seem tame in comparison to Cajun haunts. Formerly, Acadian children and families celebrated Halloween by making decorated boxes, lighted with candles, which they paraded through the evening streets to scare the evil spirits away. Families then gathered for food and drink and ghost stories before bedtime.

All Saints' Day is a church holiday and parochial school children have a day off from school after morning Mass. It is the day on which all families visit the graveyards, cleaning and repairing the graves and placing fresh flowers on them for All Souls' Day on November 2. In many areas lighted candles still illuminate the graveyards during these two evenings. These days mark a very special time for Acadiana's close-knit families. Light-hearted revelry among the living combines with solemn remembrance of the dead to strengthen the bonds in every generation.

Halloween

Hot Buttered Rum
Molded Apricot Salad
Chicken Fricassée
Rice
Eggplant Fritters
Syrup Cupcakes
Molasses Taffy

HOT BUTTERED RUM MIX

1 pint vanilla ice cream	½ teaspoon allspice
2 sticks butter, softened	½ teaspoon cinnamon
1 pound brown sugar	½ teaspoon nutmeg

Mix all ingredients well by hand and store in freezer. Yield 1 quart.

To mix 1 cup of drink use: 1 jigger rum
1 cup hot water
2 tablespoons mix
Janelle Juneau

MOLDED APRICOT SALAD

32 apricot halves	3 packages peach jello
½ cup vinegar	6 ounces cream cheese
1 teaspoon whole cloves	¼ cup pecans, finely chopped
3 sticks cinnamon	

Drain apricots, reserving juice. Add enough water to the apricot juice to make 6 cups. Pour into saucepan and add viengar, cloves, and cinnamon sticks. Let come to a boil and simmer 3 minutes. Strain liquid and add to jello, stirring until dissolved. Set aside to cool. Cream the cream cheese with a fork until smooth, adding a teaspoon or two of juice to thin mixture. Add pecans. Fill cavity of one apricot half with the cream cheese mixture and place a second apricot on top making a "stuffed apricot." Arrange the 16 stuffed apricots in a 8x8x2 inch pyrex dish. Pour jello over. Refrigerate until firm. (To keep the apricots from floating pour ½ jello over fruit, chill until partially set and then add remainder of jello.) Good for a luncheon or buffet supper. May be molded in custard cups and served on cranberry jelly slice. Serves 16.   Sarah Young Beacham

CHICKEN FRICASSÉE

⅔ cup cooking oil	seasonings to taste (salt, red and
½ cup flour	black pepper)
2½ pound fryer	2 quarts warm water
2 large onions, chopped fine	½ cup chopped bell pepper
2 pods garlic, minced	2 tablespoons chopped parsley
½ cup chopped celery	2 tablespoons chopped onion tops
2 tablespoons sugar	1 small can mushrooms

In a six quart heavy stainless steel pot, make a roux with the oil and flour. Stir roux constantly until dark brown over medium heat. Add cut up chicken pieces. Stir until chicken is well coated with roux. Add chopped onions stirring until onions are transparent, Add garlic, celery, sugar, seasonings to taste and warm water. Cover and cook 30 to 40 minutes. Add bell pepper and cook until chicken is very tender but not leaving the bone. Add parsley, onion tops and mushrooms. Cook 5 more minutes.

If gravy is too thick to your liking, add more water. If not thick enough, add a little cornstarch paste (1 tablespoon cornstarch and a little water). Serves 6-8.
Mrs. L. A. Shelton

EGGPLANT FRITTERS

1 egg	2 teaspoons sugar
½ cup milk	1 teaspoon salt
1 cup flour	1 cup cooked and mashed eggplant
2 teaspoons baking powder	

Beat together egg and milk. Mix dry ingredients. Mix eggplant with liquids. Add this to dry ingredients and mix. Drop fritters into deep fat with large spoon and cook until brown. Serves 6.

Truman Hawes, Sr.

SYRUP CUPCAKES

1½ cups sugar	1 teaspoon nutmeg
1¼ cups Steen's syrup	1 cup boiling water with 2 teaspoons
1¼ cups oil	soda
3 eggs	2¾ cups flour
1 teaspoon cinnamon	

Mix first 6 ingredients in large mixing bowl and then add: 1 cup boiling water with 2 teaspoons soda added to it. Stir well, then add gradually 2¾ cups flour.

Bake in 9x13 inch pan at 350° for 40-45 minutes.
Bake in 2 round pans—at 350° for 30-35 minutes.
Bake as cupcakes—at 325° for 20-25 minutes.

Cupcakes are delicious in lunch boxes and are really better after second day. Everyone loves these.

Mrs. Robert M. Andrus

MOLASSES TAFFY
(Pull Candy)

2 cups molasses	3 tablespoons butter
1 cup sugar	¼ teaspoon soda

Combine all ingredients and boil until hard ball stage. Wet a shallow pan and pour in candy. When cool enough to handle, pull until as light a color as desired is reached. Twist and cut into sticks.

THANKSGIVING

Perhaps more than any other seasonal holiday, the celebration of Thanksgiving reveals the Cajun's amalgamation of American and local tradition. While harvest festivals mark the season elsewhere in the United States, Acadiana's Thanksgiving festivities are associated most particularly with the regional fascination with hunting.

Cajunland lies directly on the route followed by millions of ducks and geese flying South from Canada to Mexico. The region also abounds in rabbits, squirrels, turkeys, doves and deer, which add to the huntsman's quarry. Even today, when wildlife is no longer necessary to fill the winter pantry, hunting preoccupies most of the male population in November, December and January. Thanksgiving feasts usually feature game from the hunter's bag.

Hunting camps dot the Louisiana marshland. Some are elegant and palatial, others mere wooden shacks. Male camaraderie begins the evening before the hunt as sportsmen gather in the camps to cook a hearty gumbo or spicy *sauce piquante*, which prepares them for the cold and wet weather they will face when they rise before dawn to travel to the blinds. Heavily clothed in hip boots or waders for protection against the marshy waters, the hunter takes his decoys—formerly exquisitely carved wooden models, now usually rubber or plastic—his shotgun, his gamebag and ammunition, and travels to the blind. Duck blinds—most often simple boat-blinds made of two-by-fours with a platform and camouflaged with marsh grasses into which the pirogue can be secured or cast-iron barrels sunk deep into the marsh and also camouflaged with weeds—shelter him from sight of the waterfowl. All through the winter, waterfowl, venison steaks, sausages and roasts, and gumbos of infinite variety will fill Cajun homes with irresistible aromas. At Thanksgiving meals throughout Acadiana, gratitude is expressed not only for the successful harvest, but equally for the abundance of game which enriches the Cajun table.

Thanksgiving

Wild Goose Quenelles–Truffle Sauce
Fish Courtbouillon
Iced Sorbet
Deep Fried Quail with Pepper Jelly
Andrus Baked Wild Duck
Wild Rice
Squash Pecan Casserole
Caesar Salad
Pumpkin Praline Pie
Chateauneuf de Pape

WILD GOOSE QUENELLES
(This requires a food processor)

1 lb. breast of goose
   cut into chunks
½ lb. veal, cut into chunks
6 egg whites
1 c. whipping cream

⅛ teaspoon Chinese 5 spice
   powder (optional)
½ teaspoon salt
⅛ teaspoon white pepper
Several good dashes of Tabasco

Puree the goose, veal and add the seasonings in a processor or blender. Add the egg whites one at a time, mixing well after each. Chill for 30 minutes while you make the sauce. Incorporate the whipping cream in a steady steam into chilled mixture. Chill again until very thick.

Heat at least 2 inches of water in a large skillet to boiling; reduce heat to low and do not allow it to bubble profusely again. Shape the goose mixture into an oval little dumpling or quenelle, by using two wet spoons. Poach the quenelles about 10 minutes, turning after 5 minutes. Remove the quenelles with a slotted spoon. Serve with truffle sauce.   Felicia Elsbury

TRUFFLE SAUCE

3 cups veal or chicken stock
2 teaspoons arrowroot dissolved in
   1 tablespoon cold water
½ cup whipping cream

2 egg yolks
1 truffle, minced
1 teaspoon lemon juice
Salt and white pepper to taste

Heat stock in small saucepan and reduce liquid to 1½ cup. Combine arrowroot and water; stir into stock; cook until thickened. Mix cream and egg yolks in a small bowl. Add ¼ cup of the thickened sauce to the egg mixture and then whisk the egg mixture into the remaining sauce. Add salt, pepper and lemon juice to taste. Stir in truffle. Keep warm but do not let it boil.   Felicia Elsbury

RED FISH COURTBOUILLON

4 pounds red fish, or any firm fish,
   (catfish, goo, large sac-a-lait)
¼ cup flour
½ pound butter
2 tablespoons green onions, chopped
2 large onions, finely chopped
½ cup celery, chopped
1 large green pepper, chopped
1½ quarts water

1 tablespoon parsley, minced
1 large can stewed tomatoes
salt to taste
red pepper to taste
2 bay leaves
¼ cup dry sherry
1 teaspoon rosemary, optional
lemon slices

Melt butter and blend in flour. Sauté onions slowly until light brown, stirring constantly. Add all ingredients except fish. Cook about 20 minutes. If thicker consistency is desired thicken with a little cornstarch. Filet and skin fish and cut into 2½ inch squares. Add fish to mixture and cook slowly, stirring gently so as not to break fish. Cook about 20 minutes longer. Just before serving garnish fish with lemon slices and add sherry. Serve with rice. Serves 6.   Lucille Roy Copeland

ICED SORBET

lemons, oranges, limes, tangerines
3 egg whites plus ¼ teaspoon cream of
  tartar plus pinch of salt
1¼ cups sugar

⅓ cup water
optional: 1 jigger of sweet liqueur, added
  after first freezing

Cut a small strip from bottom of fruit so that it will stand upright. Scoop out the pulp and juice. Remove the seeds and run through the blender. Add enough liquid to fill a 4 cup measure. (You must account for the sugar on a ratio of not more than 1 to 4 as too much sugar will keep it from freezing.) Beat the egg whites until foamy, add cream of tartar and salt and beat until stiff. Beat the egg whites on slow speed while you prepare a syrup of:

1¼ cups sugar   ⅓ cup water

Boil without stirring to soft-ball, 238°.

Dribble the hot syrup into the egg whites at moderate speed until the egg whites are cool and form stiff peaks. Beat in the fruit flesh and juice. Freeze until mushy. Beat again with whisk or mixer and add liquor if you choose. Spoon into fruit shells. Wrap individually and freeze. To serve remove at least 30 minutes before serving. (Lemons and limes fit very nicely in an after dinner coffee saucer and are easily eaten with an after dinner coffee spoon.) Serves 6-8.

Felicia Elsbury

DEEP FRIED QUAIL

8 quail
salt and pepper
milk

flour
2 eggs plus 1 tablespoon oil
fresh bread crumbs

Salt and pepper quail and if you have time soak them in milk for 1 hour. Drain. Dip them in flour, then eggs beaten with oil, then in fresh bread crumbs. (Make the bread crumbs from the inside part of stale French bread.) Fry in deep fat 375° until brown, about 6 minutes. Fry only 2-3 at a time. Serves 8.

Felicia Elsbury

PEPPER JELLY

⅓ cup hot red or green peppers
1⅓ cups bell peppers
6½ cups sugar
1½ cups wine cider vinegar

1 small bottle Certo
2-3 tablespoons green or red
  food coloring

Seed peppers and grind or chop. Mix peppers with sugar and vinegar. Bring to a boil and boil 1 minute. Cook about 5 minutes; then add Certo and food coloring. Put in jelly glasses. Important! Wear rubber gloves while cleaning and preparing peppers.

Mrs. Frank Myers
Beaumont, Texas

ANDRUS' BAKED WILD DUCK

6 ducks (mallard, pintail or
    American widgeon)
salt, red and black pepper

1 bell pepper, quartered
6 ribs celery, 3-4 inches
12 pods garlic, 4 slices per pod

Cooking Ingredients:
2 bell peppers, quartered
2 pods garlic, diced

cooking oil
Sauterne, Christian Brothers

Day Before:
Wash and clean ducks inside and out; making sure that cavity is thoroughly clean. Drain well and pat dry with cloth or paper towel. Make 2 slits on each side of breast of each bird and insert slice of garlic in each slit. Using salt, red and black pepper, season the cavity generously and then stuff with 1 quarter bell pepper, 1 rib celery and 4 additional slices garlic. After cavity is stuffed; sew with large cotton twine or close with poultry clamps. Re-dry outside of ducks and then season with salt, red and black pepper. After seasoning, use hands and rub ducks well so that seasoning will adhere to duck's skin. Place in glass or plastic container with tight fitting cover, or wrap tightly in aluminum foil. Refrigerate overnight.

Cooking:
Preheat oven to 500°. Cover bottom of roaster with oil, add ducks and place in oven uncovered. Brown for approximately 40 minutes, turning often to brown evenly. Remove from oven, add remaining bell pepper, diced garlic, ½ cup water and ¼ cup Sauterne. Lift and rotate roaster to mix liquids together. Cover and return to 300° oven and bake for 3-4 hours, or until tender. During this period the ducks should be checked and basted every ½ hour, adding water to gravy if needed. (Never add more than ¼ cup water at a time.) Remove ducks from roaster, cover with foil and allow to cool.

Place roaster on top of stove and skim excess oil from gravy, reserving this oil to spoon over the ducks before serving. At this time, the gravy usually needs ¼ cup water and ¼ cup sauterne to make right consistency for serving.

To serve, remove legs and arrange on platter. Slice breast thinly off of carcass and add to platter. Spoon oil that has been reserved over ducks and serve. Serves 4-6 (½ duck per person, plus 2 ducks lagniappe).

Nedra & Dwight Andrus, Jr.

WILD RICE

small box wild rice
1 stick butter
1 chopped onion
½ bell pepper, chopped

garlic, minced
2 cups chicken broth
¼ cup sherry
fresh mushrooms

Wash box of wild rice cover and cook in salted water 20 minutes or until ½ done. Drain water. In heavy skillet melt butter. Sauté chopped onion, bell pepper and garlic. Add rice and stir. Add chicken broth and sherry and sauteed fresh mushrooms. Simmer, covered until done. Serves 6.

Joan Guidry Hill

SQUASH PECAN CASSEROLE

2 pounds yellow squash, cooked
2 teaspoons sugar
2 eggs, beaten
½ cup grated cheddar cheese

1 stick butter, melted
salt to taste
buttered cracker crumbs
1 cup chopped pecans

Preheat oven to 400°. Mix all ingredients except nuts and crumbs. Pour into large buttered casserole dish. Top with nuts and cracker crumbs. Bake for 20 minutes at 400°. Serves 12. Proportions easily increased or decreased.

Tolley Odom

CAESAR SALAD

1 large clove garlic
1 tin flat anchovy fillets
1 teaspoon capers
½ teaspoon salt
¼ teaspoon black pepper
¼ teaspoon dry mustard
1 whole egg
2 tablespoons Worcestershire

6 tablespoons salad or olive oil
4 tablespoons tarragon vinegar
juice of 1 lemon
2 large or 4 small bunches Romaine lettuce
¼ cup Parmesan cheese, freshly grated if possible
1½ cups plain croutons

Rub bowl with garlic clove. With a spoon, mash the anchovies to a pulp in bottom of bowl. Mash capers in bowl. Add salt, pepper, dry mustard, mixing well. Break egg into bowl and mix in well. Add Worcestershire, oil, vinegar, and juice of 1 lemon. Allow this mixture to sit for about 30 minutes. When ready to serve, tear lettuce into bowl, if leaves are large; put in whole if lettuce is small. Add cheese, croutons, and toss. Serve on salad plates. Serves 6-8.

Tommy Godfrey
Monroe, LA.

PUMPKIN PRALINE PIE

1 unbaked 9″ pie shell

Filling:
⅓ cup white sugar
⅓ cup brown sugar
¼ teaspoon salt
1 teaspoon cinnamon

½ teaspoon ground nutmeg
1 cup cooked pumpkin
2 eggs, beaten
¾ cup hot milk

Topping:
½ cup brown sugar
¼ cup butter

¾ cup pecans, chopped

To make filling: combine sugars and spices. Mix in pumpkin and eggs. Add the hot milk slowly mixing well. Pour into pie shell and bake at 370° for 25 minutes. While pie is baking assemble topping by blending brown sugar, butter and pecans. After 25 minutes distribute topping evenly over pie and continue to bake for 30 minutes. Remove from oven and cool to room temperature before serving. Serves 8.

Karen McGlasson

CHRISTMAS

Strong religious values, as well as strong family ties, have distinguished Cajun culture since the eighteenth century and still do so today. Christmas, a major festival of the liturgical year, is perhaps the region's most joyous holiday and an occasion for family gatherings and religious ritual. Attending Mass in reverence for Christ's nativity is necessary for all; but everyone who can attends Midnight Mass on Christmas Eve. Churches are filled with poinsettias, winter-blooming camellias and candles. In many places it is still the custom to carry lighted candles and foodstuffs for the less-privileged to the nativity scene, which is always prominently set near the main altar.

Presents decorate Christmas trees in Cajunland as elsewhere, although snow is nowhere found. Families congregate Christmas morning to open their gifts. Christmas Dinner, served at mid-day, nearly always features such specialties of the region as an oyster soup, a Creole bread dressing, or a Bûche de Noël—Christmas Cake.

The Christmas season lasts through New Year's Day which is the occasion for serving customary foods which ensure health, wealth, and happiness for the coming year. Although Americans elsewhere must eat cabbage on New Year's Day, the Cajuns always have black-eyed peas as well, sometimes cooked with a silver dime. The lucky one who finds the dime in his serving is assured of a financially happy year.

Christmas

Cranberry Vodka Punch
Chicken Glacé
Oyster Soup
Cranberry Wine Salad Mold
Prime Rib Roast
Petit Pois a la Menthe
Carrot Baskets
Rice or Cornbread Dressing
Nannie's Date Cake
Buche de Noel
Christmas Lizzies
Holiday Ambrosia
Spiced Sugared Pecans
Hermitage

CHICKEN GLACÉ

1 fryer, 2½-3 pounds
1 large onion, minced
1 pod garlic, minced
3 stalks celery and leaves, minced
1 bell pepper, minced

4 cups broth
2 small packages unflavored gelatin
½ cup green onion tops, minced
½ cup parsley, minced
salt and pepper

Place chicken with all ingredients except onion and parsley in enough water to cover. Cook until meat comes off bone, about 1 hour, and save broth, about 4 cups. Debone meat. Chop chicken fine. Heat 3 cups broth with onion and parsley. Dissolve gelatin in that 1 cup broth that is left. Add gelatin plus chicken to the 3 cups broth. Pour in greased mold and refrigerate. Can be frozen. Defrost in refrigerator 4-5 hours. Tastes like hogs head cheese. Yield: 1 large mold or 2 small. Serve with toast or crackers.

Connie Gauthier

OYSTER SOUP

2 quarts whole milk
2 sticks butter
8 dozen oysters with liquid,
    unwashed preferred
salt

cayenne
½ cup parsley, finely chopped
½ cup shallots, finely chopped
fresh cracked black pepper

Put milk, butter and oyster liquid in large saucepan and cook over medium heat until butter has melted. Add oysters. Salt to taste depending on saltiness of oysters. Add cayenne. Cook slowly until edges of oysters begin to curl. Add parsley and shallots and simmer for 5 minutes. Serve in bowls and sprinkle cracked black pepper on top. This as a main dish serves 8 or serves 16 as a soup course.

Mrs. J. J. Burdin

CRANBERRY WINE SALAD MOLD

2 (3 ounce) packages raspberry jello
1 (16 ounce) can cranberry sauce with
    whole cranberries
1 (8½ ounces) can crushed pineapple,
    undrained

½ cup burgundy wine
½ cup chopped pecans
1 (3 ounce) package cream cheese

Dissolve jello in 2 cups boiling water. Stir in cranberry sauce, undrained pineapple and burgundy. Chill until partially set. Fold in nuts. Pour into lightly greased 6 cup mold and chill until firm. Meanwhile, freeze the cream cheese; and when the salad has been unmolded, finely grate the cheese over the mold. It makes a festive garnish that resembles snow. Serves 10-12.

Maureen Goldware

CRANBERRY VODKA PUNCH

¼ cup sugar
½ cup water
1 cup frozen lemon juice
1 cup frozen orange juice

1 pint cranberry juice
1 quart gingerale
1 pint vodka

Boil sugar and water for 5 minutes. Let cool, add frozen juices, cranberry juice and mix well. Add vodka. Freeze overnight. Remove 1 hour before serving. Add gingerale. Mix until slushy. Sometimes called a Red Rooster. Yield: 2 quarts.

Sandy Hamilton
London, England

PRIME RIB ROAST

3-6 pound prime rib roast
salt

cayenne
black pepper

Right before time to cook, remove roast from ice box and season generously with salt, cayenne and black pepper. Place on rack in pan and set in oven preheated to 500°. Sear roast for 10 minutes and reduce temperature to 325°. Continue to roast for 35 minutes for rare roast, longer for desired doneness. Remove from oven and let stand before carving. This recipe never fails me. You may serve with a side sauce prepared with horseradish and sour cream. Serves 4-6. Increase the size of roast for more servings.

Kathryn Leonard

PETIT POIS A LA MENTHE

Cook frozen green peas as directed. (Or cover with several lettuce leaves instead of the lid.) Do not overcook and do not let them sit with the lid on while hot, or they will lose the pretty bright green color. Drain. To serve: Quickly stir minted butter into the drained peas; heat, drain and scoop into carrot or potato baskets.

Minted Butter: Mash and mix 1 fresh mint leaf per teaspoon butter. Heat until butter is melted and then strain through a fine mesh strainer.

Felicia Elsbury

CARROT BASKETS OR NESTS

4 cups grated carrots
deep fat heated to 400° (peanut oil)

double nested wire baskets (from
gourmet shops or use 2 twin sieves)

Dip the whole basket into the deep fat first to prevent sticking. Line the largest basket with ⅜ inch layer of carrots and clamp on the insert. Dip and turn the carrot nest in the deep fat until wild bubbling subsides, then submerge it and fry about 3 minutes until brown. Drain, knock off protruding bits from outside and let cool 2-3 minutes. Carefully remove insert basket; unmold nest by turning upside down and knocking gently. These may be reheated in the oven or frozen and reheated. They are lovely served as a case for plain vegetables, seafood or fried potatoes. (You may also substitute raw potatoes for the carrots.)

Felicia Elsbury

RICE OR CORNBREAD DRESSING

1½ pounds chicken livers,
   finely ground
3 pounds chicken gizzards
   finely ground
¼ cup oil
3 cups raw rice, cooked, or 6 cups
   cornbread, crumbled

2 onions, finely chopped
2 bell peppers, finely chopped
salt and pepper to taste
¼ cup parsley
¼ cup onion tops

In large pan brown ground livers and gizzards in ¼ cup hot oil. When well browned add onions and bell peppers, salt and pepper and cook slowly until vegetables wilt. Continue to cook slowly stirring often and adding water to get a medium consistency. Cook for approximately 2 hours. When mixture is cooked add onion tops and parsley, correct seasoning and mix with hot cooked rice or cornbread. Yield: 12-14 servings.

Elsie Pickney

NANNIE'S DATE CAKE

Step 1:
1 cup boiling water
1 stick butter, melted

1 8-ounce package whole dates

Step 2:
1½ cups flour, sifted
1¼ cups white sugar
¼ cup packed brown sugar

1 teaspoon soda
1 teaspoon nutmeg
1 teaspoon cinnamon

Step 3:
1 beaten egg
2 cups toasted pecans—salt and bake
   in 400° oven for 5 minutes

3 teaspoons vanilla

Combine ingredients in step 1. In a separate bowl, combine ingredients in step 2 and then mix with those in step 1. To this mixture add ingredients in step 3. Pour into a greased tube pan and bake for one hour at 325°. (When straw comes out clean it is done.)

Mrs. L. A. Shelton

BÛCHE DE NOËL
(A Christmas or Holiday Log Cake)

Cake:

5 egg yolks	1 teaspoon vanilla
¼ cup flour, sifted	5 stiffly beaten egg whites
3 tablespoons cocoa, sifted	¼ teaspoon cream of tartar
1 cup sifted confectioners sugar	(375° oven, preheated)
½ teaspoon salt	

Beat egg yolks until thick and form the ribbon. Add sifted dry ingredients and beat until well blended. Add vanilla. Beat egg whites in copper or stainless bowl until stiff, adding cream of tartar when they are foamy. Fold yolk and chocolate mixture into egg whites. Spread evenly into a jelly roll pan which has either been prepared with: parchment paper or greased, waxed paper, greased and floured with cocoa. Bake in 375° oven for 12 minutes, or until it pulls away from sides. Remove from oven, sprinkle heavily with sifted powdered sugar, cover with a tea towel and invert. Cool about 8 minutes.

Peel off the parchment or waxed paper and spread on the filling. (If you choose to fill it with a flavored whipped cream, then you must roll it first with the tea towel inside and cool completely. It must be rolled while it is still warm or it will crack.) Roll it up and let it cool.

Suggested filling and icing:

2 sticks butter	pinch salt
2 packages confectioners sugar, sifted if using electric mixer	1 teaspoon instant coffee, optional
	2 teaspoons vanilla
6 tablespoons cocoa, Dutch chocolate is best	2 tablespoons corn syrup
	2-4 tablespoons cream or milk

(For electric mixer) Beat butter until soft, beat in sugar, cocoa, salt and coffee until crumbly. Add milk, corn syrup and vanilla. Beat until mixture is smooth and spreadable.

(For food processors) This must be made in two batches. Start with confectioners sugar and run machine until sugar is free of lumps. Add cocoa, salt and coffee. Run machine. Add butter, cut in pieces. Run. Add milk, syrup and vanilla.)

To Assemble: Cut off about 4 inches of the end of the roll at a diagonal slant. Dig a hole in the roll and stick in this piece to resemble a branch on a tree. Frost the log with the icing. (Leave the ends unfrosted.) Rake fork across the icing to resemble the bark. Decorate with real leaves, flowers and especially meringue mushrooms if you have them.

Felicia Elsbury

CHRISTMAS LIZZIES

1 cup brown sugar
1 stick butter
4 eggs, well beaten
1½ cups bourbon whiskey
2 pounds fruit cake mix
2½ cups pecans
2 small boxes raisins

3 tablespoons milk
3 cups flour
1 teaspoon cloves
1 teaspoon cinnamon
1 teaspoon nutmeg
3 scant teaspoons soda

Cream butter and sugar. Add eggs and milk which have been mixed. Sift flour once then add dry ingredients and sift again. Reserve enough flour at first to dredge nuts and fruit. Add flour slowly to batter then add nuts and fruit. Lastly add whiskey. Drop by afterdinner coffee spoonful on lightly greased cookie sheet. Bake in 300° oven until brown. Make six weeks before Christmas and keep in tightly covered tins.

Mabel Hawkins

HOLIDAY AMBROSIA

6 navel oranges, cut in pieces
1 large can crushed pineapple
1 can angel flake coconut
½ teaspoon salt

½ cup confectioners' sugar
1 jar maraschino cherries and juice
1 teaspoon almond extract
1 teaspoon coconut flavoring

Cut oranges in small pieces and mix with all the above ingredients in a large mixing bowl. Use the juice from the cherries. Refrigerate and serve. I serve in individual dishes and use as a salad with Christmas dinner. Can also substitute ½ cup sherry wine for extract flavoring. Serves 10-12.

Mrs. Eugene Cella

SPICED SUGARED PECANS

3 cups shelled pecan halves
1 large or 2 small egg whites,
    unbeaten

1 cup sugar
3 level teaspoons cinnamon

Mix the egg whites over pecans until absorbed. Sift sugar and cinnamon over all until covered. Place in a shallow pan in preheated oven 300°, about 35 minutes. Toast until light brown. To keep crispness, let cool before packing.

Mamou Roy

MARDI GRAS IN LAFAYETTE

Mardi Gras is the celebration which takes place the day before the beginning of the season of Lent. This is a French and Spanish tradition which has been kept alive in South Louisiana. Although the New Orleans Mardi Gras is the best known throughout the rest of the country, there is also a celebration of a different type in the area known as "Acadiana".

The early Lafayette Mardi Gras was a day of singing and dancing in the streets. Early accounts show that there was not much masking and costume dressing as we have now. One of the first men to costume was Lawrence Butcher. I have shown him in three of his most colorful costumes which he wore in the '30's. Today Lafayette has several weeks of activities and balls and parades.

BEVERAGES, APPETIZERS, HORS D'OEUVRES

FUNNY FRUIT DRINKS

2½ cups pineapple juice
1 or 2 bananas
1 box or bag frozen strawberries, not sweetened
½ of 14 ounce can cream of coconut
grenadine syrup to taste
rum

Fill half of blender container with pineapple juice then add bananas, strawberries, cream of coconut and grenadine syrup. Blend well, pour half of this mixture into another container and reserve. To remaining mixture, add desired amount of rum, then fill blender with cracked ice. Blend and serve, repeat with reserve. Yield 10 cups. Keeps well in freezer.

Linda Nelson

VITAMIN C LEMONADE

½ tespoon powdered or granular vitamin C, ascorbic acid
8 ounces water
sugar or honey
ice

Put ½ teaspoon of powdered vitamin C in a cup of ice water, stir and sweeten to taste. So much better for you than Koolaid. Powdered vitamin C is usually about 1000 milligrams per ¼ teaspoon. This is especially good for someone who has a cold or recovering from an illness and it can't ever do anything but help, even if you're not sick.

Anne Kernaghan Baron

MINT JULEP

1 fifth Jack Daniel Black Bourbon
6-7 stems of mint leaves
simple syrup
Anjelro rum
fresh sprigs of mint
orange slices

Crush mint leaves and marinate overnight with bourbon. When ready to serve, float 2 ounces of bourbon marinade over a 6-8 ounce glass of crushed ice and ½ ounce of simple syrup. (Equal amounts of sugar and water simmered until sugar is melted.) Stir until frosty. After the mixture settles down, float 1 teaspoon of Anjelro rum and serve with 2 straws, an orange slice and fresh mint sprig.

Putsy Beyt
New Iberia, LA.

FROZEN DACQUIRIS

1 (6 ounce) can limeade
1 limeade can light rum
1 large banana or equal amounts of
 strawberries or peaches

6 teaspoons confectioners sugar
ice

Place all ingredients in blender. Add ice to top. Blend quickly and serve. Serves 6-8. Can be made ahead and frozen. Remove from freezer prior to serving.

Odon Bacqué, Jr.

PIÑA COLADA

12 ounces sweetened coconut milk
24 ounces pineapple juice

18 ounces rum

Mix coconut milk and pineapple juice together. Combine 2 parts fruit juices to 1 part rum. Mix well again. Pour over ice and serve. Serves a crowd.

Charles Chatelain

ARTILLERY PUNCH

1½ fifths rye whiskey
1½ fifths claret
6 cups strong black tea
1½ pints dark Jamaican rum
¾ pint gin

¾ pint cognac
3 ounces Benedictine
3 cups orange juice
1½ cups lemon juice

Mix all ingredients together in a large container. Let stand for 2 hours to develop full flavor. Pour over large block of ice into large punch bowl. Serves 25.

Peggy Guidry Comeaux

WINE PUNCH

½ gallon dry red wine
32 ounces water
12 ounces simple syrup, bottled

1 sliced lemon
8 cinnamon sticks
15 cloves

In a one gallon container, heat above ingredients, but do not boil. After two hours, remove lemons and cinnamon sticks. Serve while hot. Festive holiday punch!

Audrey Leonard

WHISKEY SOUR

½ cup water
1 cup sugar
1½ cups fresh lemon juice

2 cups straight bourbon whiskey
2 tablespoons maraschino cherry juice
orange slices

Add water to sugar in saucepan. Cook over medium heat until clear and syrupy. Add lemon juice and cook until frothy. Cut off fire and add bourbon and cherry juice. Refrigerate and serve over chipped ice or cubes. Put orange slice and cherry in glass. Will keep in refrigerator for months. Serves 8-10.

Doreen S. Duhe

BRANDY ICE

8 servings vanilla ice cream   3 ounces brandy
2 ounces creme de cacao

Place half of ingredients in blender. Blend one minute. Pour into 4 champagne glasses. Repeat. May be prepared and stored in freezer in advance. Remove from freezer approximately 30 minutes before serving. Serves 8.

MILK PUNCH

15 ounces brandy   1½ cups simple syrup, bottled
½ cup white Creme de Menthe or   3 quarts milk
  green Creme de Menthe

Mix all ingredients and put in 1 gallon freezer container. Place in freezer at least overnight. Remove 1 hour before serving; in summer ½ hour. Keeps several weeks in freezer. Serves 32 (4-ounce) servings.

Marlene Dauterive

VIENNESE COFFEE

1 gallon vanilla ice cream   brandy or coffee flavored liqueur
4 cups café au lait (2 cups strong black   to taste
  coffee and 2 cups hot milk)

Alternately mound balls of ice cream in a large metal bowl. Store in freezer. At serving time, bring bowl of ice cream to the table and carefully pour the cafe au lait over ice cream. Stir gently. When the hot coffee has sufficiently melted the ice cream, add the brandy. Yield: 20 cups.

from the files of
Mrs. Jean Williams

RUTHIE'S COFFEE PUNCH

1½ gallons vanilla ice cream   bourbon to taste
3 cups strong coffee

Put all in a blender until smooth. Serves 15.

Earlene McCallum

HOT EGGNOG

1 quart milk
5 egg yolks
⅓ cup sugar
¼ teaspoon salt

3 egg whites
3 tablespoons sugar
½ cup bourbon, brandy or rum
freshly grated nutmeg

Scald milk. Beat egg yolks with ⅓ cup sugar until thoroughly blended. Add salt and milk and stir well. Return mixture to medium heat and cook stirring constantly until mixture thickens, do not boil. Beat egg whites until foamy. Add 3 tablespoons sugar gradually beating until stiff peaks form. Fold beaten whites into hot milk mixture. Blend in liquor of choice and serve hot sprinkled with freshly grated nutmeg. Serves 8.

Joan Guidry Hill

GIN PUNCH

Fifth 90 proof gin
1 (12 ounce) can orange juice
   concentrate
1 (6 ounce) can pure lemon or lime
   concentrate

18 ounces water
⅓ cup grenadine syrup
1 quart gingerale

Combine ingredients. Keeps indefinitely in refrigerator if well sealed. Pretty in punch bowl with dry ice, makes a steaming effect. Yield: 1 gallon.

Mrs. Vera Hardcastle

HOT CRANBERRY CIDER

2 quarts cranapple or 1-2 quarts
   cranberry drink
5 cups strong tea, unsweetened

4 sticks cinnamon
3-4 slices orange
1 cup sugar

Heat all to boiling. Strain and serve. Serves 12-14.

Mrs. Jon E. Riseden

STUFFED MUSHROOMS

12 fresh large mushrooms or
   20-24 smaller
2 tablespoons butter
1 medium onion, chopped
2 ounces pepperoni, chopped
¼ cup chopped green pepper
1 small clove minced garlic or
   garlic salt

½ cup crushed saltines
3 tablespoons Parmesan cheese
1 tablespoon parsley
½ teaspoon salt
¼ teaspoon oregano
⅓ cup chicken broth
dash pepper

Wash mushrooms—remove stems and chop. Melt butter—add onion, pepperoni, pepper (green), garlic and stems. Cook till tender. Add crumbs, cheese, parsley, salt, pepper and oregano. Stir in broth. Spoon stuffing on caps—make rounded. Place in shallow pan with ¼″ of water. Bake at 325° about 25 minutes. (Less if mushrooms are smaller.) Serve hot as appetizer.

Mary Lou Carman

CRABMEAT REMICK APPETIZER

1 pound lump or backfin crabmeat
¼ stick butter
1 teaspoon dry mustard
½ teaspoon paprika
½ teaspoon celery salt

⅛ teaspoon Tabasco
½ cup chili sauce
1 teaspoon tarragon vinegar
1 pint jar mayonnaise
6 slices bacon crisply cooked

Butter 6 ramekins and fill with crabmeat. Bake in 350° oven for 5 minutes. Blend mustard, paprika, salt, Tabasco, chili sauce, vinegar and mayonnaise. Top each ramekin with crisp bacon and spread some sauce generously over all. Broil under broiler until glazed and serve hot. Serves 6.

Kathryn Leonard

CRABMEAT AU GRATIN

3 tablespoons butter
3 tablespoons flour
⅛ teaspoon pepper
½ teaspoon salt
¼ teaspoon paprika
1½ cups thin cream

½ cup grated cheddar cheese
1 tablespoon Worcestershire
1 cup crabmeat picked over and flaked
   (canned, frozen or fresh)
2 tablespoons dry sherry
⅓ cup bread or corn flake crumbs

Melt butter in a saucepan, stir in flour, pepper, salt, and paprika. Gradually blend in cream, stirring constantly until the sauce is smooth and velvety. For a thinner sauce add ½ cup more cream. Add to the sauce the cheese, Worcestershire and crabmeat, stirring until cheese is melted. Add the sherry and pour into 4 individual small ovenproof casseroles that have been buttered. Top with crumbs and bake 15-20 minutes in a hot oven, 400°, or until golden brown. Serves 4.

Sandy Hamilton
London, England

CRAWFISH BIENVILLE I

1¾ stick butter or margarine
¾ cup flour
3 cups milk
1 medium onion, chopped fine
4 medium cloves garlic, crushed
2 ounces mushrooms, stems and
  pieces, drained
1 cup shallots, tops and bottoms,
  chopped fine
¾ pound cooked crawfish tails for
  sauce*

1½ teaspoons salt
½ teaspoon red pepper
2 tablespoons lemon juice
3 tablespoons dry sherry
1 tablespoon absinthe
2 tablespoons chopped parsley
rock salt
oyster shells
¾ pound cooked crawfish tails
Parmesan cheese

Make thick white sauce using 1½ sticks butter, flour and milk and remove from heat. In another pan, sauté onions and garlic in ¼ stick butter until onions are clear. Add mushrooms, shallots and cook 5 minutes more. Put half of white sauce, crawfish, onion and mushrooms mixture into blender for a few seconds, only until all is coarsely chopped. Return to pot of white sauce and add all other ingredients. Put rock salt in shallow baking pan and place oyster shells on salt. Put 2-3 crawfish in each shell and cover with sauce. Sprinkle with Parmesan cheese. Broil until sauce browns and serve immediately. *Left over boiled crawfish may be used or raw crawfish can be sautéed in butter and seasoning. Serves 6.

Mrs. Warren Patout

CRAWFISH BIENVILLE II

1 large white onion, finely chopped
2 celery stalks, finely chopped
½ pound butter
2 pounds peeled crawfish tails, no fat

4 tablespoons flour
1 large plus 1 small can Carnation milk
2 egg yolks
salt and red pepper

Sauté onions and celery in butter until soft. Add crawfish tails and cook for 10 minutes uncovered and 10 minutes covered. Remove crawfish tails. Add flour to butter mixture and blend. Add milk and blend. Remove from heat and add egg yolks and blend. Add crawfish, salt and red pepper. Bake at 350° for 30 minutes uncovered. Serves 6 as main course in individual dishes or 12 as an appetizer.

Jacqueline D. Bouligny

ESCARGOTS À LA BOURGUIGNONNE
(Snails in Garlic Butter)

2 dozen snails
1 stick butter, no substitute
2-4 cloves garlic

2 tablespoons minced fresh parsley
salt, pepper and lemon to taste
2 dozen mushroom caps

For food processor users: Put parsley in container with blade. Be sure that the bowl is dry and the parsley not moist. Run the machine until it is finely minced. If it is not minced enough, it will be when you add other ingredients. Add the garlic and run machine. Add the butter, cut into chunks and the salt, pepper and lemon juice. Run the machine until mixed; you may have to scrape down the sides, but do not overmix. Fill mushroom caps with butter mixture and escargots. Run under broiler until hot. Serves 4.

Felicia Elsbury

OYSTERS BIENVILLE I

4 tablespoons butter
8 shallots, finely chopped
2 tablespoons flour
1 cup chicken broth
1 cup cooked shrimp, chopped
1 (7 ounce) can mushrooms
2 egg yolks

½ cup white wine
salt and pepper to taste
½ cup bread crumbs
2 tablespoons Parmesan cheese
paprika
2 dozen oysters on the half shell

Heat butter in pan. Add shallots and sauté until soft. Add flour and stir until slightly brown. Stir in broth until blended. Add shrimp and mushrooms. Beat egg yolks with wine and add to mixture, stirring until blended and slightly thickened. Remove from heat and season with salt and pepper to taste. Arrange 6 shells on each of 4 pie pans, ½ filled with rock salt. Heat in 450° oven for 10 minutes. Remove and add oysters. Top with spoon of prepared sauce. Combine bread crumbs and cheese. Sprinkle on tops. Add paprika. Bake at 450° for 15 minutes. Serves 4.

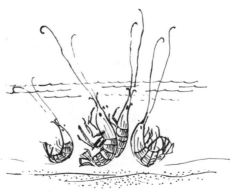

OYSTERS BIENVILLE II

1 ounce bacon
1 cup boiled shrimp, seasoned,
    ground
2 ounces mushrooms, grind coarsely
2 cloves garlic, crushed
1 cup green onions, chopped finely
1 stick butter
½ cup flour
1 quart hot milk
1 (6 ounce) bottle clam juice

2 tablespoons dry sherry
¼ cup lemon juice
¼ cup parsley
2 tablespoons Anisette
1 tablespoon Worcestershire
salt and red pepper
3 dozen oysters
1 box rock salt
1 cup buttered bread crumbs

Cut bacon into small pieces and fry. Remove and grind with shrimp. Put mushrooms in pan and cook until almost brown, add garlic and cook until almost
brown, add green onion and cook until wilted. Add butter and melt. Add flour
and blend with wire whisk. Cook 5 minutes. Add hot milk slowly at first, stirring
with whisk until mixture thickens. Add shrimp, clam juice, sherry, lemon juice,
parsley, anisette and other seasonings. Cook slowly for 15 minutes. Fill 6 pie tins
with rock salt. Arrange six oysters on half-shell in bed of salt. Put under broiler
until oysters bubble and curl up. Drain off juice. Cover each oyster with Bienville
mixture. Sprinkle bread crumbs on each and return to broiler. Cook until bubbly
around edges and slightly brown on top. Serves 6.

Doreen S. Duhe

OYSTERS ROCKEFELLER

1 stick butter
½ cup flour
2 cups oyster liquid, drain oysters and
    reserve
½ tube anchovy paste
salt and cayenne pepper to taste
1 cup green onion tops

½ cup parsley
2 tablespoons chopped garlic
4 boxes frozen chopped spinach, cooked
    according to box directions
¾ cup Pernod
4 dozen large oysters

Melt the butter over moderate heat, add flour and mix well. Stirring constantly
with a wire whisk, pour in oyster liquid in a slow, thin stream, cook over high heat
until the sauce comes to a boil, thickens heavily and is smooth. Stir in anchovy
paste, pepper and salt. Remove from heat. Put green onions, parsley, garlic and
spinach which has been boiled and squeezed, into food processor or blender.
Blend until mixture is smooth. Add this to the sauce mixture. Simmer uncovered
for 10 minutes or until the sauce is thick enough to hold its shape. Remove from
fire and stir in the Pernod and taste for seasoning. Put oysters on a cookie sheet
and place under broiler about 5 minutes, to cook oysters slightly, and remove
some of the liquid. Use oyster plates, six oysters to a plate, and arrange oysters on
plate. Cover with spinach sauce and sprinkle with bread crumbs. Put a wedge of
lemon on center of plate. Place under broiler about 2 minutes. Microwave oven
can be used instead of broiler. Serve immediately. Serves 8.

Mrs. Warren Rush

OYSTERS À LA LUCILLE

3 cloves garlic minced
2 tablespoons olive oil
4 tablespoons bread crumbs
½ cup bechamel sauce
2 tablespoons cream
6 tablespoons Madeira

2 strips bacon
1 cup lump crabmeat
rock or kosher salt
1 dozen oysters with shells
lemon

To make topping: mix 2 cloves garlic, minced, 2 tablespoons olive oil and 4 tablespoons fresh bread crumbs. Set aside. In a saucepan combine bechamel sauce,
cream and Madeira. Stir and bring to a boil. Preheat oven to moderately hot,
375°. Mince 2 strips bacon and 1 garlic clove. In a hot skillet sauté until bacon is
crisp. Drain off fat and combine with crabmeat.
Presentation: In 2 ovenproof dishes place a layer of kosher or rock salt forming a
bed. Place 6 large opened oysters on the half shell on each bed of salt. Top each
oyster with a generous mound of crabmeat mixture. Sprinkle each with the fresh
bread crumbs and on each place 1½ inch square of uncooked bacon. Place in a
moderately hot oven and bake for 15-18 minutes, depending on your oven, or
until bacon is crisp and crumb topping is browned. Serve at once with lemon
wedges and green salad and hot buttered French bread when served as a meal.
Delightful as an appetizer. Serves 2.   Lucille Roy Copeland

GARLIC BUTTER SHRIMP

2 pounds shrimp, peeled with tail
   left on
1 stick butter

1 toe garlic, pressed
salt and red pepper to taste
juice of ½ lemon

Place peeled shrimp in buttered baking dish. Season generously with salt and
cayenne. Press garlic on top of shrimp and mix well together. Cut butter in pieces
and dot all over to melt evenly. Squeeze lemon over all and bake at 400° for about
10 minutes. You should stir shrimp to insure all being well cooked and may have
to cook longer. Serve with heels of French bread to dip in sauce. Serves 4.
                    Kathryn Burdin Leonard

BACON WRAPPED SHRIMP

5 pounds large shrimp
1 cup olive oil
5 tablespoons wine vinegar
1 tablespoon garlic powder

2 tablespoons Beau Monde Seasoning
salt and pepper
2 pounds bacon

Shell and devein shrimp. Wash and pat dry. Combine oil, vinegar and seasonings. Pour over shrimp. Marinate 3 hours at room temperature. Slice bacon
strips in thirds. Take only a few pieces of bacon out at a time. It is much easier to
work with when cold. Wrap each shrimp with bacon strip. Fasten with toothpicks
which have been soaked in water for 1 hour to prevent charring. Broil 6 inches
from heat until bacon is crisp. Turn occasionally. Serves 16.

                    Mrs. Bill Davis

ACAPULCO SHRIMP

12 jumbo shrimp
1 (8 ounce) block jalapeno cheese
6 slices bacon
1½ cups flour

1 cup milk
salt and cayenne to taste
toothpicks
oil for frying

Peel, devein and split (butterfly) shrimp down the back. Season well with salt and pepper. Cut cheese into ¼ inch cubes. Insert 1 slice of cheese into back center of each shrimp. Wrap shrimp with bacon and secure with toothpick. Double dip shrimp in milk and flour and deep fry until golden and crisp. Serves 4.

Ron Ray

SHRIMP ROCKEFELLER

2½ cups spinach, drained and
   chopped
12 slices bacon, crisply cooked and
   crumbled
1½ cups minced onion
½ cup chopped parsley

2 bay leaves, crumbled
1 teaspoon celery salt
1 cup butter or margarine
1 cup fine dry bread crumbs
2 pounds shrimp, cooked, shelled and
   deveined

Preheat oven to 400°. Combine spinach, bacon, onion, parsley, bay leaves and celery salt. Melt butter; add spinach mixture and cook, stirring constantly until heated thoroughly. Stir in bread crumbs and let bubble 1 minute. Grease 8 one cup ramekins or a casserole. Arrange shrimp, cover with spinach sauce, top with more shrimp. Bake just until heated. Serves 6 as a main course, or 8 as an appetizer.

Carrie Isoltz
New Orleans, LA

SHRIMP WITH INDONESIAN SAUCE

3 dozen large shrimp in shells
1½ cups peanut oil
5 cloves garlic, minced
2 tablespoons dried chopped mint
2 teaspoons chili powder

1 tablespoon turmeric
1 tablespoon basil
2 tablespoons vinegar
salt and pepper to taste

Slit shrimp down the back, deveining, but leaving in shell. In a shallow, 3 quart casserole, place oil, garlic, mint, chili powder, turmeric, basil, vinegar, salt and pepper. Mix well. Place shrimp into marinade, coating each one. Marinate 6-8 hours. Place shrimp on a broiler pan, baste with marinade and broil 6 minutes on each side. Serve with additional marinade. This can also be an excellent appetizer for 12 people. Watch out for turmeric as it stains cabinets. Serves 4.

Mrs. Richard R. Kennedy

SEAFOOD REMOULADE SAUCE—WHITE

1 cup mayonnaise
½ cup salad oil
2 tablespoons dry mustard
1 tablespoon chopped green onion
1 tablespoon chopped celery
1 tablespoon chopped parsley
1 tablespoon horseradish
2 tablespoons tarragon vinegar

2 tablespoons tomato catsup
2 tablespoons paprika
½ teaspoon salt
½ teaspoon Worcestershire
dash of hot sauce
fresh cooked, peeled shrimp or
    crabmeat
shredded lettuce

Combine all ingredients except shrimp or crabmeat and lettuce in blender container. Blend until smooth. Chill thoroughly, serve with peeled, cooked shrimp or crabmeat on a bed of lettuce. Yield 2 cups.

Ramona Mouton

SHRIMP REMOULADE—RED

4 tablespoons oil
2 tablespoons wine vinegar
½ teaspoon salt
2 tablespoons creole mustard
1 teaspoon hot horseradish

2 teaspoons paprika
2 stalks celery, finely chopped
2 green onions, finely chopped
2 tablespoons parsley, minced

Combine thoroughly oil, vinegar and salt. Add remaining ingredients, mix and refrigerate. Arrange 1 pound boiled, peeled shrimp on a bed of shredded lettuce in 4 individual cocktail glasses. Spoon sauce on top. Keeps well for several days in refrigerator. Serves 4.

Betty Billeaud

PEPPERONI DON SALVATORE

4 large green peppers
8 tablespoons olive oil
3 tablespoons red wine vinegar
¼ teaspoon salt
⅛ teaspoon pepper
⅓ teaspoon sugar

⅓ teaspoon paprika
1 teaspoon lemon juice
dash Worcestershire
1 clove garlic, mashed
2 fillets of anchovies, mashed

Preheat oven to 450°. Wash green peppers. Place on baking sheet and bake in oven for 20 minutes, or until skins blister. Remove, cool slightly then peel. Cut in half, discarding stems and seeds, and place flat on a serving platter.
Dressing: Combine olive oil, vinegar, salt, pepper, sugar, paprika, lemon juice and Worcestershire sauce. Mash garlic and anchovies and stir into dressing. Pour dressing over peppers and marinate for 15 minutes. Put in refrigerator for several hours and serve chilled. Serves 4. This recipe is from the Blue Fox Restaurant in San Francisco. It is very good and easy to prepare. It makes a great appetizer for an Italian dinner.

Stephanie Bacqué
Lake Charles, LA

EGGPLANT APPETIZER

No. 1 Step
3 cups cubed eggplant
½ cup chopped bell pepper
1 medium onion, chopped

2 cloves garlic, pressed
½ cup olive oil

No. 2 Step
1 cup tomato paste
1 (4 ounce) can mushrooms, chopped
¼ cup water
½ cup stuffed olives, chopped
1½ teaspoons sugar

½ teaspoon oregano
1 teaspoon salt or to taste
½ teaspooon pepper
1 teaspoon Worcestershire

Combine No. 1 in skillet, cover and stir. Cook for 10 minutes. Add No. 2, all ingredients. Mix well, cover and simmer until tender. Serve hot on toast or crackers, or chill and serve the same way. Freezes well. Will keep in the refrigerator, well covered, for about 1 week. Serves 8.

Helen Biddle Beaullieu

RATATOUILLE

2 medium eggplants cut into 1 inch
   unpeeled chunks
½ cup olive oil
2 large onions, thickly sliced
2 large cloves crushed garlic
3 medium green peppers cut in strips
6 zucchini cut into unpeeled slices
1 small head cauliflower (optional)
4 tablespoons catsup
2 teaspoons salt

½ teaspoon freshly ground pepper
1 teaspoon basil
1 pound fresh mushrooms, trimmed and
   left whole
1 cup pitted black olives
2 tablespoons capers
½ cup chopped parsley
1½ pounds cheese, (Swiss or Monterey
   Jack)

Salt eggplant chunks. Let stand 1 hour then rinse and pat dry. Set aside. In a heavy Dutch oven heat oil. Add onions, garlic and sauté until soft. Add peppers, eggplant, zucchini and cauliflower. Cook for 15 minutes over medium heat stirring occasionally. Add catsup, salt, pepper, basil and continue simmering another 15 minutes. Add mushrooms, olives and capers. Simmer 10 minutes. Add chopped parsley. Turn into large 6 quart casserole or individual servings. Top with a thick layer of cheese. Bake at 350° for 40 minutes or until cheese melts. Can be frozen before baking. Allow extra time for frozen casserole to thaw before baking. Yields 2 quarts.

Lillian Nugent

SPINACH BALLS

2 packages frozen chopped spinach
2 cups herbed bread stuffing mix
2 medium onions, chopped fine
½ cup chopped celery or water
　　chestnuts
6 eggs, beaten

¾ cup margarine, melted
½ cup Parmesan cheese
1 tablespoon garlic salt
½ teaspoon thyme
½ teaspoon pepper
Tabasco to taste

Cook spinach and drain well. Mix all ingredients together. Shape into small bite size balls. Bake at 350° for 20 minutes. Can be frozen before baking. Yields: 60-70 balls.

Billie M. White

SPINACH DIP

1 package frozen, chopped spinach
¼ cup green onion tops, chopped
　　finely
1 teaspoon red pepper

1 teaspoon salt
2 cups mayonnaise, homemade or
　　prepared

Cook spinach, do not salt spinach. Drain well and cut up with scissors. Mix all ingredients together. Serve hot with crackers. Delicious. Serves 6-8.

Marie Goodhue

ASPARAGUS SANDWICHES

1 (16 ounce) can asparagus, or fresh
　　if in season

1 loaf thinly sliced white bread

Spread
¾ cup mayonnaise
¼ cup olive oil
1 garlic clove, mashed

½ teaspoon paprika
salt
few drops Tabasco

If using fresh asparagus cook until tender. Drain asparagus well on paper towels. Cut crusts from bread and flatten with rolling pin. Spread with mayonnaise mixture. Place asparagus spears on slices of bread and roll up tightly. Cover and refrigerate until ready to serve. Yield: 25 sandwiches.

Katherine Lipsey

MARINATED ARTICHOKE HEARTS

1 package frozen or 1 can artichoke
   hearts
¼ cup vinegar
½ cup salad oil

1 clove garlic, chopped
1 tablespoon white onion, chopped
1 tablespoon parsley, chopped
salt and pepper

Cook frozen hearts or heat canned artichoke hearts. Drain and place in shallow dish. Mix other ingredients and pour over warm artichoke hearts. Marinate for 4 hours. (Marinade can be used for other vegetables, cooked cauliflower or cooked green beans) Serves 4.

Sally Brockschmidt Herpin

MARINATED MUSHROOMS

1 cup oil
4 tablespoons vinegar
1 can anchovies, mashed flat,
   reserve oil
2 pods garlic, pressed

black pepper
paprika
2 or 3 large cans button mushrooms,
   drained

Mix oil and vinegar. Pour oil from anchovies into this. Add mashed anchovies and 2 large pods garlic to above and put through a garlic press. Season with pepper and add mushrooms and enough paprika to color. Refrigerate covered at least 1 day stirring occasionally. Add more garlic if desired. Serves 10-12.

Lou Bivins

MUSHROOM FRITTERS

½ cup all-purpose flour
1 egg
1¼ tablespoons olive oil
⅝ cup milk

salt and pepper to taste
3 cups fresh mushrooms
Parmesan cheese, optional
oil

Prepare fritter batter by beating together until smooth, flour, egg, olive oil, milk, salt and pepper. Prepare mushrooms, clean and drain. Coat mushrooms in batter and fry in deep hot oil until crisp and golden. Drain on paper towels and add more salt and pepper if desired. Mushrooms may also be sprinkled with Parmesan cheese. Serve hot. This is an Italian dish, Fritella De Funghi. Small pieces of fillet fish may be fried in this batter also. Zucchini and artichoke hearts are good this way too. Serves 4.

Carolyn Richard

CUCUMBER BOATS WITH CAVIAR

1 large, long cucumber
1 small jar caviar, either black or red
1 small carton sour cream
2 large cabbage leaves, purple ones
    are very pretty

2 long wooden skewers
6-8 small green onions, trimmed neat

With a zigzag movement, cut a cucumber into 2 long pieces. Scoop out the seeds and some of the pulp. Drain the two boats on paper towels until ready to serve. When ready to assemble: Slice off a very thin strip from the bottom of the boats, so that they will not dump over. Fill the boats with sour cream and then top with caviar. Spear cabbage leaves with the wooden skewers so that they resemble sails. (Cut them with scissors if necessary.) Stick the sails into the front half of the boat. Let the green onions dangle from the sides as if oars. Garnish with lemon slices and sliced cucumbers and cabbage leaves.

Felicia Elsbury

CUCUMBERS IN YOGURT

3 cucumbers
1 clove garlic
1 teaspoon salt

2 cups yogurt
pinch of dry mint

Peel and slice cucumbers thinly. Mash garlic with salt in bottom of bowl. Mix in yogurt. Fold cucumbers into yogurt and chill. Sprinkle with dry mint before serving. Serves 6-8.

Mrs. Norris Landry
Royal Catering

PICO DE GALLO

3 medium sized avocados, chopped
2 medium size ripe tomatoes, chopped
1 medium size orange, chopped
2 cups diced jicama
½ cup chopped onion
¼-½ cup chopped chili peppers,

amount of chili peppers depends on
    how hot you want to serve it
2 tablespoons chopped cilantro
salt to taste
sour cream

In a mixing bowl, add all ingredients except sour cream. Mix well. Transfer to serving bowl. Garnish with sour cream. Pico de Gallo can be served by rolling into soft tortillas. Fold the filled tortilla on one end and eat as a finger food. Also very good served with corn chips as a dip. Serves 6-8.

LaFonda's Mexican Restaurant of Lafayette

MEXICAN HOT SAUCE

1 (14 ounce) can whole tomatoes
1 (12 ounce) can jalapeño peppers,
   seeded and de-stemmed

2 tablespoons vinegar
pinch sugar

Use juices of tomatoes and peppers and run through a meat grinder. Grind the tomatoes fine and the peppers coarse. Add vinegar and sugar. Especially good with bean dip. Yield: Approximately 3 cups.

Lou Bivins

CRABMEAT AND BACON BALLS

1 pound fresh crabmeat
¼ teaspoon dry mustard
½ cup dry sherry

1 cup dry bread crumbs
pinch salt
12 slices lean bacon

Sauce:
3 tablespoons prepared mustard

1 cup mayonnaise

In a large bowl place crabmeat, dry mustard, sherry, salt and crumbs and mix well. Form into 24 small balls the size of a walnut. Wrap each ball with half a slice of lean bacon and secure with a toothpick. Place on cookie sheet and broil 3 inches from flame for 10 minutes, turning once. Drain off fat and transfer to platter. Keep warm in 200° oven until ready to serve. Serve with a mustard sauce made by combining the prepared mustard and mayonnaise. Yield: 2 dozen.

Sandy Hamilton
London, England

CRABMEAT DIP

1 (4 ounce) can mushrooms
3 tablespoons chopped onion
3 tablespoons butter, melted
¼ cup flour
½ teaspoon salt
¼ teaspoon dry mustard

dash pepper
1¼ cups milk
1 cup grated cheddar cheese
1 pound crabmeat
Tabasco to taste

Sauté mushrooms and onion in butter. Blend in flour and seasoning. Add milk gradually and cook until thick, stirring constantly. Add cheese and stir until melted. Stir in the crabmeat and check seasoning. Serves 10-12.

Mrs. John Tolson, III

HOT CRAB DIP

¾ stick margarine or butter
1 large onion, finely chopped
1 stalk celery, finely chopped
2 tablespoons parsley, chopped
1½ pounds crabmeat
1 small can evaporated milk
1 pound Velveeta cheese

½ teaspoon garlic powder
½ can cream of mushroom soup
½ teaspoon powdered thyme
salt and pepper to taste
Kitchen Bouquet, optional
bread crumbs, optional

In large pot melt butter and wilt onions and celery. Add the rest of the ingredients in order given. Cook approximately 15 minutes or until cheese has melted on low heat with lid on pot. Stir occasionally to prevent sticking. Kitchen Bouquet may be added to darken dip. Bread crumbs may be added to thicken. Can be made a day in advance. Serve heated with desired crackers. Serves 20-25.

John Daigre

HOT STUFFED MUSHROOMS

24 large fresh mushrooms
3-4 tablespoons butter or margarine, melted
2 tablespoons minced onion
1 toe garlic, minced
½ pound crabmeat, cooked and flaked
2 eggs, lightly beaten
2 tablespoons bread crumbs, Progresso Italian

2 tablespoons mayonnaise
2 tablespoons finely chopped green onions
1 teaspoon lemon juice
red and black pepper and garlic salt to taste
Parmesan cheese

Clean mushrooms and remove stems. Dip caps in melted butter or margarine. Chop stems in a blender and sauté with minced onion and garlic in remaining melted butter. Combine with crabmeat, eggs, breadcrumbs, mayonnaise, green onions, lemon juice and seasonings. Stir well and simmer for a few minutes. Fill caps, not too full, and top with Parmesan cheese. Place in well buttered shallow baking dish and bake in preheated 400° oven for 10-15 minutes until mushrooms are tender and tops are brown. Yield: 2 dozen.

Alonda Duos

CRAWFISH DIP

½ cup Wesson oil
3 green onions, chopped
2 small bell peppers, chopped
1 cup crawfish tails
½ pound grated Swiss cheese

½ pound grated American cheese
3 teaspoons sweet pickles, chopped
1 jar pimento, chopped
1 can tomato soup
1 small can ripe olives, chopped

Sauté onion and bell pepper in oil, add crawfish, and cheese. When cheese is melted add other ingredients, simmer for 10 minutes and serve. Serves 10-12.

Pat Link

OYSTERS IN PATTY SHELLS

3 dozen oysters, well drained and
  chopped
½ stick butter
2 bunches green onions, chopped
½ bunch parsley, chopped

2 cans cream of mushroom soup
1 large can chopped mushrooms or ½
  pound fresh mushrooms, sautéed
juice of 1 lemon, dash Tabasco
4 dozen patty shells, cocktail size

Curdle oysters in own juice. Drain, reserve juice. Melt butter and sauté onions and parsley. Add soup, mushrooms, lemon juice and some of the oyster juice for flavor. Cook stirring constantly until very thick. Add oysters. Fill warmed patty shells. Also may be used as a dip. Yields 48.

Jean Frazell

SHRIMP MÉLANGE

3 tablespoons bourbon or brandy
1 tablespoon dried celery leaves
1 tablespoon dried green pepper
  flakes
2 tablespoons butter or margarine
⅓ cup finely chopped onion
1 can cream of shrimp soup, less 3
  tablespoons
1 (4½ ounce) can medium shrimp,
  well drained and mashed with fork
¾ cup finely chopped mushrooms,
  well drained

½ teaspoon dijon mustard
½ teaspoon Worcestershire
½ teaspoon garlic powder
1 teaspoon paprika
¼ teaspoon salt
½ teaspoon Tabasco
1 tablespoon bread crumbs
¼ cup chopped pecans or other nut
2 tablespoons minced fresh parsley

Soak celery and pepper flakes in bourbon until reconstituted. In medium sized heavy saucepan, sauté chopped onion in butter until soft, but not browned, about 15 minutes. Add bourbon soaked vegetables, shrimp soup, shrimp, mushrooms, mustard, Worcestershire, garlic powder, paprika, salt and Tabasco. Combine well and heat to a boil, lower flame, and stirring often, cook 15 minutes. Remove from fire; add bread crumbs, pecans and parsley. This should be kept warm when served, either in chafing dish or over candle warmer. Serve with melba rounds or small party shells. This recipe makes 2 cups or 64 one teaspoon servings. For luncheon serve in ramekins topped with bread crumbs and brown in oven. More shrimp should be added if served this way. This mixture freezes well. Reheat in double boiler.

Mrs. Warren L. Butcher

SHRIMP DIP

1 medium onion, grated
2 cloves garlic, minced
1 tablespoon parsley
3 (8 ounce) packages cream cheese
juice of 1 lemon

2 tablespoons Worcestershire
red pepper and salt to taste
liquor from 1 can cleaned and deveined
  shrimp
3 cans well drained shrimp

Grate onion, mince garlic and parsley. Place first 8 ingredients in mixer and beat until light and fluffy. Add shrimp and mix lightly. Can be served cold but is best heated. Serve with Fritos. Do Not Freeze. Serves 25.

Tolley Odom

SHRIMP ÉTOUFFÉE DIP

1 stick butter
1 large onion, chopped fine
½ large bell pepper, chopped fine
3 pods garlic, chopped

1 teaspoon salt
1 tablespoon flour
1 pound shrimp tails, chopped well
1 can Rotel tomatoes with chili peppers

Sauté onion, bell pepper and garlic in butter. Add salt and flour, blending well. Add shrimp tails, cooking over low fire. Add can of Rotel tomatoes which has been pureed in blender. Cook 15 minutes. Serve in chafing dish with individual bite-sized pastry shells or Melba toast. Pastry shells may be filled with shrimp preparation and frozen for 3-4 weeks. To serve, merely heat in oven until hot and serve immediately. Yields 75 bite-sized pastry shells.

Mrs. Richard R. Kennedy

MARINATED SHRIMP

2 pounds cooked, peeled shrimp
2 lemons sliced thinly
1 pint sour cream
½ cup mayonnaise

3 teaspoons salt
1 teaspoon cayenne pepper or Tabasco
  to taste

Line 1½ quart casserole with shrimp, cover with lemon slices—alternate layers. Mix sour cream, salt and pepper and mayonnaise. Pour mixture over shrimp and lemons. Cover and place in refrigerator. Stir once in a 24 hour period. Serves 6 to 8.

Olga Hawley

HOT CLAM DIP

1 stick butter
1 bunch green onions, chopped
4 tablespoons flour
3 (8 ounce) cans clam and liquid
2 (8 ounce) packages cream cheese
1-2 cans cream of mushroom soup
1 (8 ounce) can mushrooms, stems
   and pieces

3 cloves pressed garlic
2-3 teaspoons lemon juice
1-2 tablespoons Worcestershire
salt, pepper, Tabasco to taste
2 tablespoons fresh parsley, chopped

Set aside two tablespoons onion tops for garnish. Sauté remaining onion tops and bottoms in butter until tender. Add flour and stir until smooth. Add clam juice and stir until slightly thick. Cream cheese in blender and stir into sauce until melted. Add desired amount mushroom soup. (Second can stretches recipe.) Stir in clams, drained mushrooms, garlic, lemon juice, Worcestershire sauce and seasonings and heat thoroughly. Serve in chafing dish garnishing with chopped onion tops and parsley. Serve with melba rounds, potato chips or fritos. Serves 20-25.

Janice Ryder Roy
Alexandria, LA

SMOKED SALMON MOUSSE

1 pound smoked salmon
¼ cup lemon juice or to taste
⅓ cup chopped onion
½ pound butter
1 cup sour cream

¼ teaspoon dill weed
salt and pepper
Garnishes: Lemon slices, capers,
   snipped fresh dill

Pureé salmon, onion and lemon juice in blender or food processor. Melt butter and add in a steady stream while blending. Remove to a bowl, fold in sour cream and season to taste. Place the mousse in a mold or serving dish and refrigerate. Unmold, garnish and serve with Melba toast or party rye. Serves 25-30.

Carola Bacqué

PATÉ

½ pound chicken livers
4 ounces butter, do not substitute
4 cloves garlic

⅛ teaspoon thyme
salt and black pepper to taste
2-3 ounces brandy or port

Put liver in skillet with 3½ ounces of butter and cook gently 5 minutes or until centers are pink. Add brandy or port and simmer 10 minutes. Add garlic and seasonings and put through mix-master, liquidizer or cuisinart. Pour into tureen, melt rest of butter, skim and pour over to seal paté. Chill before serving and serve on small crackers, wheat thins, etc. Serves 12-14.

Adrien A. Stewart

MONA'S OYSTERS DUNBAR

1 stick butter
1 large onion, chopped fine
1 bunch green onions, chopped
3 toes garlic, mashed
1 14 ounce can artichoke hearts,
    quartered
2 pints oysters, quartered
2 cans cream of mushroom soup
½ cup dried parsley
2 tablespoons Worcestershire sauce

1 tablespoon poultry seasoning
1 teaspoon salt
½ teaspoon black pepper
dash of Tabasco sauce
½ cup sherry
1 (4 ounce) can sliced mushrooms,
    chopped fine
1 small jar pimentos, sliced
1 cup seasoned Italian bread crumbs

Melt butter, fry onions, green onions, and garlic until glazed. Add quartered artichoke hearts and cook for 10 minutes. Strain oysters, reserving liquid. Cut oysters into quarters or finer. Add oysters, liquid and all ingredients except pimento and bread crumbs. Simmer 15 minutes; add pimento and bread crumbs. Add more bread crumbs if sauce is too thin. Pour into a 2 quart pyrex casserole and bake in 350° oven until hot and bubbly. Serves 25 as dip with crackers; 12 in pastry shells.

Ramona Mouton

FRIED WON TON

1 pound ground pork
½ cup chopped bamboo shoots
¼ cup chopped green onions
1 teaspoon salt

1 teaspoon monosodium glutamate
½ teaspoon sesame oil
package of egg roll skins

Mix all ingredients for ground pork mixture. Cut egg roll skins into 4 squares. Place 1 teaspoon ball of meat mixture in center. Fold over skin once. Fold as for a diaper, dampen edges to hold, and invert ball of meat. Fry slowly in deep fat until brown or drop into soups for Won Ton Soup. Yield: 40.

Mrs. W. T. Black, Jr.
Quitman, TX

PORK APPETIZER

1 pound ground pork
½ cup grated cheddar cheese
¼ cup chopped onions
¼ cup chopped pimento olives

1 egg
salt and pepper to taste
1 pound bacon

Mix all ingredients except the bacon and shape into bite-sized balls. Cut bacon strips in half. Wrap each ball with ½ strip of bacon and secure with a toothpick. Bake on rack at 400° for 30 minutes or until bacon is cooked. Keep warm in chafing dish or crock pot and serve. Serves 10-15.

Mrs. Easton Hebert

HUNGARIAN SURPRISES

1 pound bulk pork sausage
1 pound ground round steak
1 pound Velveeta cheese
½ teaspoon garlic powder

½ teaspoon Worcestershire
1 teaspoon oregano
2 loaves Pepperidge Farm party rye
paprika

Brown sausage and steak in separate skillets. Drain in colander. Put both meats in a saucepan. Break up cheese into meat. Slowly melt cheese and then add seasonings. Spread on bread slices and sprinkle with paprika. Freeze on cookie sheets and then package in bags. Bake frozen at 350° for 15-20 minutes. Yield: 50.

Karen V. McGlasson

SWEET AND SOUR SAUSAGE

1 package Lipton Onion Soup
1 bottle Russian salad dressing

1 (8 ounce) jar apricot preserves
1 pound Oscar Mayer little wieners

Preheat oven to 350°. Simmer soup mixture, salad dressing and preserves on stove top for 5 minutes. Cool. Put sausage in one quart casserole. Pour cooled mixture over them. Marinate over night. Bake uncovered at 350° for 1¼ hours. Yield: 1 quart.

Pat Martin Hance

SWEET AND SOUR MEATBALLS

1 pound ground beef
1½ teaspoons salt
½ teaspoon pepper
1 (5 ounce) can water chestnuts,
    chopped fine
¼ cup milk
2 tablespoons cornstarch

½ cup sugar
¼ cup wine vinegar
2 tablespoons soy sauce
1 medium green pepper chopped in ½
    inch pieces
½ cup celery, chopped in ½ inch pieces
1 small can pineapple cubes with juice

Mix beef, seasonings, water chestnuts and milk. Work and form into balls. Place in large flat pan and place in a 350° oven until done. Shake pan occasionally so the meatballs won't stick. They don't have to get dark. The sauce will darken them. Combine remaining ingredients in saucepan and bring to boil. Reduce heat and simmer a few minutes. Add meatballs. Serve in chafing dish. Serves 15-20. 15-20.

Jeanne Gilley
Mrs. Stan McEacharn

CHINESE SWEET AND SOUR SPARERIBS

4-5 pounds meaty spare ribs
soy sauce
salt

black pepper
red pepper

Have butcher break the end bones of the ribs and slice them lengthwise. Brush them lightly with soy sauce and season with salt, black pepper and red pepper. Place ribs in flat, uncovered pan and roast them in a moderate oven, 350° for 1¼-1½ hours, or until they are brown, and crisp, turning them once during the roasting. Cut the spareribs into finger pieces, separating each rib. Serve on a platter with this sweet and sour sauce.

Sauce
1 cup sugar
1 cup vinegar
½ cup Madeira wine
2 tablespoons soy sauce
1 green pepper, cut into strips

2 tablespoons corn starch
red food coloring, optional
½ cup pineapple chunks
¼ cup chopped sweet pickles

Heat first 5 ingredients together. Bring to a boil and add cornstarch mixed with a little cold water, stirring until thick and transparent. (You may at this point add a drop of red food coloring.) Two minutes before serving, add pineapple chunks and sweet pickles. Spoon the sauce over the spareribs. Serve with hot Chinese mustard and soy sauce. Serves 6.

Mrs. C. B. Billeaud, Jr.

SWEET AND HOT MUSTARD

2 cans dry mustard
1 cup apple cider vinegar

3 eggs
1 cup sugar

Mix mustard and vinegar and let sit overnight. Beat eggs, add sugar and add to mustard mixture and cook in double boiler until thick. This is especially good served as an hors d'oeuvre type dip with pastrami and salami cubes. Yield: 1 pint.

Lynn Wilson Blevins

SHRIMP PATÉ

1 pound cooked, peeled, deveined
   shrimp
½ cup butter or margarine
2 tablespoons dry sherry
1 tablespoon lemon juice

1 tablespoon minced onion
¼ teaspoon mace
¼ teaspoon dry mustard
¼ teaspoon cayenne pepper

Cream butter, blend in sherry, lemon juice, mace, mustard and pepper. Mince shrimp and onion together and add to butter mixture. Place in an oiled, 3 cup mold and refrigerate until firm. To unmold, dip mold in warm water and invert on serving platter. Makes 2½ cups paté.

Frances Wallace

NUT AND CHEESE LOG

1 cup pecans, ground
1-2 cloves garlic, ground
6 ounces cream cheese
⅛ teaspoon salt

⅛ teaspoon Worcestershire
⅛ teaspoon soy sauce
4 drops Tabasco
1½ teaspoons chili powder

Put pecans and garlic through medium blade of food chopper. Blend next 5 ingredients in a bowl. Mix in ground nuts. Shape in a roll 1½ inches in diameter. Sprinkle chili powder. Wrap tightly in wax paper. Chill log at least 4 hours. Slice before serving or leave as log. Allow to soften at room temperature. Serve with crackers. Very good to serve as a dip. Yield: 1 log.

Barbara Spraker

CHEESE-CORNMEAL CIGARS

2 cups boiling water
1¼ teaspoons salt

1½ cups cornmeal
1 cup grated sharp cheese

Add salt to boiling water in saucepan. Add cornmeal and stir until mixture leaves sides of pan. Remove from fire and stir in cheese. Take out in large teaspoonsful and form into balls. Then roll in shape of cigars. Fry in deep fat for 2 minutes. Yield: 25-30.

Grace Cox Black
Quitman, TX

SPICED NUTS

1 cup sugar
½ teaspoon salt
1 teaspoon cinnamon
¼ teaspoon cloves
2 tablespoons butter

¼ teaspoon nutmeg
1 teaspoon vanilla extract
2 tablespoons water
1 cup pecans, or any mixture of pecans,
  cashews and walnuts, toasted

Combine sugar, salt, cinnamon, cloves, nutmeg, butter, vanilla and water in saucepan. Cook stirring constantly, until a small amount dropped into cold water forms a soft ball. Stir in toasted nuts. Remove from heat and stir until no longer glossy. Pour into buttered baking sheet and spread thinly. Cool, and break into pieces.

Mrs. L. A. Shelton

GALA PECAN SPREAD

1 (8 ounce) package cream cheese,
  softened
2 tablespoons milk
1 package sliced dried beef, cut into
  small pieces

¼ cup finely chopped green pepper
2 tablespoons dried, minced onion
½ teaspoon garlic salt
¼ teaspoon pepper
½ cup sour cream

Topping:
½ cup coarsely chopped pecans
2 tablespoons margarine

1 teaspoon salt

Combine cream cheese and milk, mixing well. Stir in sliced, dried beef, green pepper, onions, and seasonings. Mix well, fold in sour cream. Spoon into baking dish. Heat and crisp pecans in butter and salt. Remove pecans from butter and salt mixture with slotted spoon and sprinkle over cream cheese mixture. Bake at 350° for 20 minutes. Serve hot with wheat thins and knife. Crackers will break if dipped into casserole. Served in a silver chafing dish, this is delicious and good looking for cocktail parties. Serves 8-10.

Mrs. Frank P. Danna

INDIENNE CASHEW SPREAD

½ cup chopped cashews
5 tablespoons Major Grey Chutney,
  chopped

½ teaspoon lemon juice
1 (8 ounce) package cream cheese
¼ teaspoon curry powder

Mix all together. Spread on cool, unpeeled apple rings or triscuits. This covers about 15 apple rings.

Allene Mayo
Tulsa, OK

Louisiana Strawberries

TANTE 'GITE'S GUMBO

America might like baseball, hot dogs, apple pie, and Chevrolet, but if you don't give a Cajun his gumbo, he won't be happy at all. A gumbo can be made with chicken, okra, shrimp, oysters, crabs, sausage, or almost anything, and a Cajun always serves it with rice. This soup-like dish is as unique as the Cajun culture and is served often to the Cajun family.

I have spoken about the Cajun's culture not being absorbed into the mainstream of American life, but as you know, this is not completely true, for no culture in America has remained totally isolated. I show this fact by making some of the clothes of the Acadians become parts of the trees and ground. Tante 'Gite symbolically holds her famous gumbo in her lap, but her dress has become part of the earth, and the gumbo has become part of her.

BREADS, CHEESE, EGGS
SOUPS AND GUMBOS

BANANA NUT BREAD

3 medium or 2 large bananas
lemon juice
½ cup butter or 1 stick margarine
1 cup white sugar
2 whole eggs, beaten lightly

½ teaspoon salt
2 cups all-purpose flour
1 teaspoon soda
2 teaspoons vanilla
1 cup pecans, finely chopped

Preheat oven to 350°. Mash bananas and sprinkle with lemon juice. In a separate bowl, cream butter and sugar, add eggs and salt. Then add flour and soda sifted together. Beat well, then add vanilla, pecans and mashed bananas. Grease and flour loaf pan, 9x5x3 inches. Pour batter into pan and bake for 45 minutes or until toothpick comes out clean. I stress that this must not be over-baked. Turn out on rack to cool. This freezes well. You can use 2 smaller loaf pans for this recipe. Rule to successfully slice nut breads: cool bread several hours, or over night and it can be sliced without crumbling. If in a hurry, partly freeze loaf, then slice.

Helen Patey
Knoxville, Tennessee

SWEET POTATO BREAD

⅔ cup shortening
2⅔ cups sugar
4 eggs
1 can (16 ounce) sweet potatoes,
    mashed
⅔ cup water
3⅓ cups flour

2 teaspoons soda
1½ teaspoons salt
½ teaspoon baking powder
1 teaspoon cinnamon, ground
1 teaspoon cloves, ground
⅔ cup coarsely chopped nuts
⅔ cup raisins

Preheat oven to 350°. Grease 2 (9x5x3 inch) loaf pans. In a large bowl, cream shortening and sugar until fluffy. Stir in eggs, sweet potato and water. Blend in flour, soda, salt, baking powder, cinnamon and cloves. Stir in nuts and raisins. Pour into pans. Bake about 70 minutes until wooden pick inserted in center comes out clean.

Mrs. George Sobiesk

PUMPKIN BREAD I

3½ cups all-purpose flour
2 tablespoons cinnamon
2 tablespoons nutmeg
3 cups sugar
1 teaspoon salt
2 teaspoons baking soda
4 eggs

1½ cups fresh mashed pumpkin or 1 (16 ounce) can solid pack pumpkin
½ cup water
1 cup oil
¾ cup raisins
1 cup pecans or walnuts, chopped

Preheat oven to 350°. Sift together dry ingredients then add and mix remaining ingredients. Fill 4 greased and floured coffee cans about half full and bake for 1½ hours.

Jeanette Dugas

PUMPKIN BREAD II

3 cups sugar
1 cup salad oil
4 eggs, beaten
1 (16 ounce) can pumpkin
3½ cups all-purpose flour
2 teaspoons soda
2 teaspoons salt

1 teaspoon baking powder
1 teaspoon nutmeg
1 teaspoon allspice
1 teaspoon cinnamon
½ teaspoon ground cloves
⅔ cup water
pecans if desired

Preheat oven to 350°. Cream sugar and oil together. Add eggs and pumpkin. Mix well. Sift together dry ingredients. Add water. Mix all ingredients together. Pour into two well greased and floured 9x5 inch loaf pans. Bake for 1½ hours or until tested done. Let stand 10 minutes. Remove from pan to cool. Variation: Use ¾ cup orange juice instead of water.

Mrs. Ben Klemmer

SUGARLESS CAKE

½ cup butter
1½ cups unsweetened applesauce
1 cup chopped dates
1 large egg or 2 small
1 teaspoon vanilla
1½ cups flour (whole wheat is delicious)

1½ teaspoons soda
½ teaspoon ground cloves
½ teaspoon cinnamon
½ teaspoon salt
1 cup chopped pecans

Preheat oven to 350°. Mix butter, applesauce and dates. Bring to boiling, stirring constantly. Cool to lukewarm, add beaten egg and vanilla. Sift together flour, soda, salt and spices. Add to first mixture. Beat until blended. Stir in nuts. Bake in well greased and lightly floured loaf pan for 1 hour. Test after 45 minutes.

Sandy Brewer Holbert

HOMEMADE FRENCH BREAD

1 package yeast	1½ tablespoons melted butter
¼ cup water warm (110°)	3 cups sifted flour
¾ cup milk, scalded	2 egg whites
¾ cup ice water	2 cups flour
1 teaspoon salt	3 egg whites
2 tablespoons sugar	3 teaspoons water

Dissolve 1 package yeast in ¼ cup warm water. Add scalded milk, ice water, salt, sugar, butter, sifted flour. Fold in 2 egg whites beaten until they cling to the side of the bowl. Add 2 cups flour. Turn onto kneading surface, knead eight minutes. Place in greased bowl. Let rise until doubled 45-60 minutes. Punch down. Let rise again until double. Punch down and divide into 3 equal parts. Form into 8x16 inch rectangle. Roll up jelly roll style. Make slashes across the top with a knife. Bake for 1 hour and 15 minutes at 325°. Wash every 20 minutes with 1 egg white and 1 teaspoon water. Reheat when ready to use. Can be frozen. Serves 8-10.

Linda Roy

TOASTED GARLIC BREAD

Garlic Butter:

1 cup soft butter or margarine	¼ cup grated Parmesan cheese
¼ cup chopped parsley	1 clove garlic, crushed

2 loaves French bread, about 14 inches long

Several hours before dinner, combine the ingredients for garlic butter. Mix well. Cut each loaf in half lengthwise. Spread cut sides with garlic butter. Cut each half, on the diagonal, not quite all the way through, into 1 inch thick slices. Set the bread aside on a cookie sheet, loosely covered. Just before serving, bake bread at 450° until lightly toasted. Yield: 3 dozen slices.

Marcella Y. Lecky

YORKSHIRE PUDDING

2 eggs	1 teaspoon salt
1 cup milk	grease—preferably from standing rib
1 cup flour	roast, but any beef flavored fat will do

Preheat oven to 350°. Beat eggs, add milk and beat hard. Add this slowly to 1 cup flour and 1 teaspoon salt. Beat hard again and pour into hot drippings (grease) in a hot iron skillet. Bake about 30 minutes in a moderate oven. Take pudding from oven when it is light brown and dry underneath. Cut into serving size pieces. Eat immediately either plain or with a little butter or salt. Serves 4.

Mrs. Carroll Pooler, Jr.

ASPHODEL BREAD

5 cups biscuit mix
¼ cup sugar
½ teaspoon salt
2 cups warm milk

1½ envelopes yeast
4 eggs
¼ teaspoon cream of tartar

Sift into large mixing bowl biscuit mix, sugar and salt. Soften yeast in milk which has been warmed to 125°. Beat eggs with cream of tartar. Combine yeast, milk, and eggs and pour into dry mixture. Stir and set aside in warm place. Cover. When doubled in bulk, punch down. Fill two greased and floured pans about ½ way; set aside until doubled. Bake at 350° for approximately 30 minutes. Makes two loaves. This is the recipe used at Asphodel Plantation.

Fran Barbato

SWISS TYPE BREAD

2 tablespoons yeast
4 cups water
9 cups flour, unbleached

2 tablespoons salt
2 large boiled potatoes, boiled the day
before and finely grated

Preheat oven to 450°. Melt yeast in 2 tablespoons of lukewarm water; then mix in some of the 4 cups water. Add flour, salt and grated potatoes. Knead for 12-15 minutes, adding water in small amounts. Let rise for 1½ hours. Make into loaves and place in lightly greased trays. Let rise again for ½-¾ hour. Bake for ½ hour at 380°, lower to 360° for last 20 minutes. Total baking time 50 minutes. Our Swiss ski instructor in Idaho told us about the way his wife made all their bread at the beginning of every week and that it didn't dry out. They hang it in the attic in wintertime in Switzerland, so he said, until it's all eaten. Anyway, I asked him for the recipe and here it is. It is inexpensive, rather bland not so many calories as our bread. As it lay on the counter, covered, it did harden as the days went by, but I sliced it very thin and toasted it, buttered, to eat with marmalade for breakfast. It was all gone after a week at our house. This makes a lot of bread, so you may cut it in half for small families. Yield: 4 loaves.

Walter Hofstetter

French Bread..... Our Staff of Life

MAMA KIM'S BISCUITS

2 cups sifted self-rising flour   1 cup buttermilk
½ cup shortening

Sift flour into large mixing bowl. Add shortening and cut in with 2 knives or a
pastry blender. Make a well in center of flour and shortening mixture; add buttermilk. Mix well. Knead slightly, not more than 3 times. Roll out on floured
surface to ½ inch thick; cut with desired biscuit cutter. Bake at 400° for 25 minutes or until brown. This recipe comes from North Georgia from my great
grandmother who of course never measured a thing. Yield: 1 dozen.

Eva B. Kimsey

SUPPER MUFFINS

½ cup dairy sour cream   ¼ cup chopped onion
½ cup shredded process American   1 tablespoon butter or margarine
  cheese   1 (14 ounce) package corn muffin mix

Mix sour cream and cheese in small bowl; reserve. Sauté onion in butter in small
skillet over low heat until limp, about 5 minutes. Prepare corn muffin mix according to package directions; stir in onion. Spoon batter into greased 2½ inch muffin
cups, filling each ⅔ full. Top each with 1½ teaspoons of the reserved cheese
mixture. Bake as directed on package until tops are bubbly and edges golden,
15-20 minutes. Yield: 1 dozen.

Micro Directions: Prepare supper muffins through stirring in onion. Let batter
stand 10 minutes to reduce leavening. Spoon 2 tablespoons of the batter into
paper-lined 2½ inch microwave muffin or custard cups. Top each with 1 teaspoon
of the reserved cheese mixture; microwave 6 at a time 1½ minutes on full power.
Let stand 2 minutes. Yield: 1½ dozen.

Mrs. Edwin Preis, Jr.

COUCH-COUCH—ACADIAN STYLE

2 cups corn meal   1½ cups milk or water
1½ teaspoons salt   ½ cup oil
1 teaspoon baking powder

Mix thoroughly corn meal, salt, baking powder, milk or water and add to hot oil
in hot skillet over high heat. Let a crust form. Give a good stir and lower heat to
low. Cover and cook about 15 minutes; stir often. Serve with milk and sugar as a
cereal, or with cane syrup and crisp bacon.

Mrs. Gladys Begnaud

EASY BREAD

2 packages yeast
2 cups warm water
2 teaspoons salt
⅓ cup oil
⅓ cup honey or sugar
⅔ cup nonfat dry milk

2 eggs, beaten
½ cup wheat germ
½ cup soy flour, optional
2-3 cups white flour, use larger amount if
   soy flour is omitted
3 cups whole wheat flour
Sprinkle of sugar

Have all ingredients at room temperature. Dissolve yeast in water with a sprinkle of sugar. Add salt, oil, honey, nonfat dry milk, eggs, and wheat germ. Mix with electric mixer, gradually adding 3 cups of flour. Mix 10 minutes. Add 2 more cups flour, mixing it in by hand. Sprinkle rest of flour on kneading surface. Turn out dough and knead until dough stiffens up with extra flour. Knead 10 minutes until elastic. Cover and let rest 20 minutes. Punch down by kneading a few times. Divide into equal portions. Roll out into rectangle on oiled surface. Roll up like jelly roll and place in greased loaf pan. Cover and refrigerate from 2 to 24 hours. Remove from refrigerator 10 minutes before baking, puncture any air bubbles with oiled toothpick. Bake at 350-375° for 45 minutes. May also be made into cloverleaf rolls. Yield: 2 loaves.

Merilyn Istre

HOMEMADE ROLLS

½ cup milk
3 tablespoons sugar
2 teaspoons salt
3 tablespoons butter

1½ cups warm water
2 packages active dry yeast
6 cups all-purpose flour, sifted
   (approximately)

Scald milk; stir in sugar, salt and butter. Cool. Dissolve yeast in warm water. Add cooled milk mixture and 3 cups flour. Stir until smooth. Add enough flour to make a soft dough. Put mixture on a lightly floured surface and knead until smooth and elastic. Add any additional flour if necessary. Place mixture into a buttered bowl and butter top of dough. Cover and let rise in a warm place until doubled in bulk, approximately 1 hour. When ready punch down dough. Let it rest about 10 minutes. With buttered hands squeeze pieces of dough, about the size of a golf ball, and form dough into a ball. Put rolls close together in 2 (9x5x3 inch) bread pans. Cover, let rise in a warm place until double in size. Place rolls in oven at 400° and bake until light brown, approximately 20-30 minutes. Variation: Cheese Rolls: add 1 cup grated cheese before you knead dough.

Mrs. Carroll Pooler, Jr.

REFRIGERATOR ROLLS

1 cup scalded milk
1 cup mashed potatoes
⅔ cup shortening
½ cup sugar
1 teaspoon salt

2 eggs, well-beaten
1 cake yeast in lukewarm water
flour to stiffen (when dough no longer
    sticks to hands)

Add potatoes, sugar, shortening, and salt to warm milk. Let cool. Then add eggs and yeast and enough flour to stiffen. Put in refrigerator overnight. Take out desired amount of dough and make into desired shape (Parker house, cloverleaf). Let rise two hours or until double in size. Bake at 425° for approximately 10 minutes. Keep remaining dough in refrigerator and use as needed. A very good hot roll recipe which my mother got from the mother of her childhood friend in Pittsburgh.

Sally Brockschmidt Herpin

CARIBBEAN TOAST

5 eggs
3 ounces rum
2 ounces cream
1 medium can sliced peaches,
    liquid reserved

¼ cup sugar
1 dash cinnamon
8 slices bread

Whip eggs and add 1 ounce rum with 1 ounce peach juice from can and cream. Place peach slices and remainder of juice and rum in small saucepan and bring to a boil. Add sugar and cinnamon and bring to a simmer stirring occasionally. Dip bread in egg mixture and place on hot buttered griddle, cook until lightly brown on each side and serve hot, pouring peach sauce proportionately over toast. Developed to cure the morning after. A delicious pick me up or just a pleasant breakfast. Serves 4.

Roger T. Hendrix

DON'S FAMOUS FRENCH TOAST

5 eggs
3 tablespoons sugar
⅔ cup milk
1 tablespoon vanilla extract

¼ teaspoon cinnamon
1 teaspoon butter, approximately
8 slices bread

Heat skillet to medium high. Mix first five ingredients well with whisk. Coat skillet with light film of butter. Thoroughly soak bread in batter, remove to skillet and cook until golden. Serves 4.

Odon Bacqué, Jr.

LUMBERJACK GRANOLA

A:

6 cups Quick Quaker Oats

1 cup shredded coconut

1 cup natural wheat germ

½ cup sunflower seeds

¾ cup cashews, halved

1 cup raisins

B:

½ cup cooking oil

½ cup honey

⅓ cup water

1½ teaspoons salt

1½ teaspoons vanilla

Preheat oven to 350°. Combine all of "A" in a large bowl. Put all of "B" into a jar. Cover and shake well. Pour "B" into bowl with "A"; toss to mix well. Spread granola onto greased cookie sheet or sheets and bake 20-30 minutes at 350°. Stir while baking. Allow to cool thoroughly before storing. Good to eat while hiking, skiing, playing tennis, etc. I find it is good to nibble on when I don't have time for breakfast. It is good for quick energy. Children should love it.

Jean Ellen Smith
Friendswood, TX

RICE PANCAKES

3 eggs, separated

3 cups cooked rice

½ cup milk

4 tablespoons flour

⅛ teaspoon salt

⅛ teaspoon pepper

Beat egg yolks; stir in cooked rice, milk, flour, salt and pepper until well combined. Beat egg whites until stiff peaks form; fold into batter. Bake in hot, lightly greased skillet or griddle until edges start to dry. Turn and bake other side until golden brown. Serve immediately with touch of butter on top. Serves 6-8.

Owen B. Hawes

BUTTERMILK PANCAKES

1 cup sifted flour

1 teaspoon baking powder

¼ teaspoon salt

1 tablespoon sugar

1 egg

1 cup buttermilk

½ teaspoon baking soda

3 tablespoons melted margarine

Sift flour with baking powder, salt, and sugar. In another bowl, beat the egg well. Add the soda to the buttermilk, mix well, and add to beaten egg. Slowly add this mixture to flour mixture. Add melted butter last. Bake on hot griddle. Turn pancakes when bubbles on top form and start to pop. Cook on other side until slightly brown. If thinner pancakes are desired, batter may be thinned with small amounts of regular milk. I always make extra batter and freeze in containers large enough for one meal. Serves 2-3.

Sally Brockschmidt Herpin

YEAST WAFFLES

1 cup milk	1 cup lukewarm water
2 tablespoons sugar	2 tablespoons melted shortening
1 teaspoon salt	2 eggs
1 package yeast	2½ cups flour

Scald milk, add sugar and salt. Dissolve yeast in water and add to lukewarm milk. Add shortening, eggs and flour. Cover, let rise in warm place until light, about 1 hour. Stir well and bake on hot waffle iron. Can also be used for pancake batter. This also can be made the night before and it will be ready for breakfast the next morning. If you do this use only ¼ package of the yeast and add an additional ½ teaspoon salt. Cover and refrigerate overnight. Serves 3.

Liz Sargent

SOUR DOUGH PANCAKES

1 package dry yeast	⅔ cup water
2 cups buttermilk biscuit mix	1 egg, beaten at room temperature
2 cups milk	

Place undissolved yeast in blender container, then add biscuit mix. Heat milk and water in saucepan until liquids are warm. Pour over dry ingredients. Cover and stir at mix speed for 1 minute. Scrape sides. Add egg; cover and stir 1 more minute.

Pour batter into bowl. Cover; let stand at room temperature for 3 minutes. Stir down batter. Cook on slightly greased griddle or skillet using ¼ cup batter per pancake. Makes 14 pancakes. Delicious with homemade maple syrup!

Ramona Mouton

RAISIN BRAN MUFFINS

1 (15 ounce) box raisin bran cereal	4 teaspoons cinnamon
3 cups sugar	4 eggs, beaten
5 cups flour: 2 white, 3 whole wheat	1 quart buttermilk
5 teaspoons baking soda	1 cup corn oil
2 teaspoons salt	

Mix dry ingredients. Add liquids. Combine. Refrigerate covered. When ready to use fill muffin cups ½ full and bake 15 minutes at 400°. Keeps in refrigerator for 6 weeks. Add more raisins if you wish. Can microwave on high for 2 minutes and 10 seconds.

Betty Hukill

WALNUT ROLLS

Filling:

2 cups ground walnuts
½ cup sugar

½ cup raisins
1½ teaspoons cinnamon

Dough:

1 package dry yeast
¼ cup lukewarm water
pinch sugar
4½ cups flour
¼ cup sugar
½ teaspoon salt
3 egg yolks

¾ cup butter, well softened
¼ cup sour cream
2 teaspoons grated lemon rind
¾ cup milk
⅓ cup sieved apricot jam
6 tablespoons melted butter
1 egg beaten with 1 tablespoon milk

Preheat oven to 400°. In a small bowl, proof yeast in water and pinch of sugar for 10 minutes. Into a large bowl sift flour with sugar and salt. Add egg yolks, butter, sour cream, and lemon rind. Combine yeast with milk and add it to flour mixture. Form dough and turn it out on lightly floured board and knead for 5 minutes. Cut the dough in half. On a lightly floured board roll out half the dough about ½ inch thick and fold it into thirds. Roll it out again into a rectangle 15x10 inches. Spread the rectangle with the jam leaving a ¾ inch border on all sides. Sprinkle jam evenly with half the walnut filling and half the melted butter. Roll the dough up tightly lengthwise and pinch the ends together. Transfer the roll to a buttered cookie sheet, seam side down. Prepare the second roll in the same manner with the remaining filling, dough, jam and butter. Let the rolls stand in a warm place for 30 minutes. Brush rolls with egg and milk. Bake in preheated oven for 10 minutes and reduce heat to 350° and bake 25 minutes longer. Let cool and cut the rolls diagonally into ¾ inch thick slices. Yield: 3 dozen rolls.

Mrs. Robert F. Tarpy

PECAN BUNS

¼ cup warm water
1 package active dry yeast
¾ cup lukewarm milk
3½ to 3¾ cups flour
¼ cup sugar
1 teaspoon salt
1 egg
¼ cup corn oil

3 tablespoons soft margarine
¼ cup brown sugar
½ cup pecan halves
2 tablespoons soft margarine
⅓ cup brown sugar
1 teaspoon cinnamon
⅓ cup light corn syrup

In mixing bowl dissolve yeast in warm water. Stir in milk, half of flour, sugar, salt, egg, and corn oil. Mix with spoon until smooth. Add remaining flour; mix with hand. Turn onto lightly floured board. Knead until smooth and blistered, about 5 minutes. Round up in greased bowl; bring greased side up. Cover with damp cloth and let rise in warm place, 85°, until double in bulk, about 1½ hours. Punch down; round up; let rise again until almost double, about 30 minutes. Spread margarine on bottom of pan. Sprinkle brown sugar and pecans over margarine. Pat or roll dough into rectangle about ¼ inch thick. Spread with rest of margarine, brown sugar, and cinnamon. Bake at 375° for 25-30 minutes. Yield: 1 dozen buns.

Mrs. Robert F. Tarpy

MONKEY BREAD

3 medium cans buttermilk biscuits	1 stick margarine
½ cup sugar	¾ cup sugar
½ teaspoon cinnamon	¾ teaspoon cinnamon

Preheat oven to 350°. Quarter the biscuits and roll each quarter in mixture of ½ cup sugar and ½ teaspoon cinnamon. Pile in a greased and floured Bundt pan. Melt 1 stick of margarine in a saucepan. Add ¾ cup sugar and ¾ teaspoon cinnamon. Heat until sugar melts. Pour over biscuits. Bake at 350° for 30-35 minutes. Remove from oven, let stand 10 minutes and invert on cake plate. Pull apart pieces with fingers. My kids love to make this! They dig right in with their little grubby hands.

Mrs. George Malagarie

MEXICAN CORNBREAD

1 cup corn meal	½ teaspoon soda, added to milk
1 cup milk	2 eggs
½ teaspoon salt	½ cup oil
1 cup yellow cream style corn	3 jalapeno peppers, minced
1 cup grated cheddar cheese	

Mix all ingredients and bake in large skillet at 350° for about 40 minutes.

Kathe Haxthausen
Houston, TX.

TOMATO BREAD

large loaf of French bread or 6 little Frenchies	garlic powder to taste
	2-3 large sliced tomatoes
¼ pound margarine or butter	1 pound sliced mozzarella cheese

Preheat oven to 450°. Slice Frenchies in half lengthwise or large loaf lengthwise, then each of these into 6 equal portions. Add garlic powder to melted butter; then spread garlic butter over cut portions of bread. Cover bread with slices of tomato, then slices of mozzarella. Bake until cheese melts. May be used as sandwich substitute for lunches, suppers, late night snacks and, if cut into smaller pieces, as hors d'oeuvres. Serves 6 — 2 slices per person.

Helen Nugier Sobiesk

PIZZA CRUST

2½ to 3¼ cups flour
1 package dry yeast
1 tablespoon sugar

1½ teaspoons salt
2 tablespoons salad oil
1 cup warm water (120-130°)

Combine 1½ cups of the flour and the rest of the dry ingredients. Then add oil and water. Mix with electric mixer for 3-5 minutes. By hand, gradually add the rest of the flour. However, all may not be needed. Some can be saved to flour the kneading surface. When dough is stiff and easy to handle, knead for about 5 minutes. Let rise in a greased bowl for about an hour, until doubled in size. Punch down, divide in half and roll out to fit 2 (13-inch) pizza pans. Bake 10 minutes at 350°. Top with favorite ingredients and bake 20 minutes at 425°. Serves 2 pizzas.

Mrs. Easton Hebert

CORN DODGERS

1 cup corn meal
½ cup flour
boiled water

2 level teaspoons baking powder
½ tcaspoon salt

Sift all ingredients together. Have water boiling hot and add mixture until thoroughly damp. Fry in hot grease in black iron skillet. Be sure to have the mixture hot because if it gets cold you will not get the same effect when you fry it.

Marianne A. Ruffin

CORNMEAL DUMPLINGS

1 quart of juice saved from baking a
   ham, approximately
2 cups yellow or white cornmeal

½ teaspoon black pepper
boiling water

If the ham broth is too strong add some boiling water. Some hams are not salty enough and a little salt may have to be added for flavor. Bring broth to rolling boil. Mix cornmeal to which pepper has been added, with enough boiling water to make the meal stick together. Shape into balls about 1 inch in diameter. Drop in boiling, rolling, broth. Shake the saucepan, occasionally, do not stir. Cooking time about 15 minutes. Reduce heat after the balls have set. I always sprinkle a little more pepper on top when ready to serve.

Grace Cox Black
Quitman, TX

APPLESAUCE NUT BREAD

1 cup sugar	1 teaspoon baking soda
1 cup applesauce	1 teaspoon baking powder
¼ cup oil	½ teaspoon salt
3 egg whites	½ teaspoon cinnamon
3 tablespoons skim milk	¼ teaspoon nutmeg
2 cups sifted enriched flour	½ cup chopped walnuts

Preheat oven to 350°. In a large bowl, combine sugar, applesauce, oil, egg whites and skim milk. Mix thoroughly. Add flour, baking soda, baking powder, salt, cinnamon and nutmeg. Combine until all ingredients are well blended. Stir in chopped walnuts. Spread batter in oiled and floured 9x5x3 inch loaf pan. Bake for 45 minutes or until toothpick comes out clean.

Ann F. Martin

ORANGE BUTTER

4 tablespoons undiluted frozen orange juice concentrate	1 tablespoon grated orange rind
1 pound butter	½ pound confectioners sugar, sifted

Thaw orange juice concentrate. Soften butter. Add juice, rind and sugar. Blend thoroughly. Place in mold and refrigerate. Great on hot rolls and toast.

Doris Y. Ottinger

MAYHAW JELLY

3 pounds fresh mayhaws	1 box Sure-Jell
4 cups water	5½ cups sugar
4 cups mayhaw juice	

Bring berries and water to boil. Cover and simmer rapidly 10-12 minutes. Remove cover and mash berries with a potato masher until pulpy. When mixture is cool enough to handle, place in bag (a pillow case will work nicely) and squeeze out juice.

Mix Sure-Jell with juice in an 8-quart saucepan. Bring quickly to a hard boil, stirring occasionally. Add sugar at once. Cook and stir. When mixture returns to a full rolling boil (cannot be stirred down), cook and stir 1 full minute. Remove from heat; skim off foam with metal spoon. Pour into scalded jars and allow to cool before sealing with lids. If you seal the jelly with hot paraffin, do so while it is still hot. Makes 6 (8-ounce) glasses.

Margaret Chambley

EASY QUICHE

1 can crescent dinner rolls
1 egg, beaten
1 cup evaporated milk
½ teaspoon salt
1 teaspoon Worcestershire

1 cup Swiss cheese, grated
1 (3½ ounce) can French fried onion
   rings
9 slices crisp bacon, crumbled

Preheat oven to 325°. Arrange 8 inch pie pan crust by pressing rolls into pan. Beat egg, milk, salt, and Worcestershire. Add grated cheese to mixture. Sprinkle ½ of the onions on unbaked crust. Add egg mixture and layer bacon and remaining onions. Bake at 325° for 25-30 minutes. Serves 5-6.

Mary T. Miller

CRAB QUICHE

1 (9 inch) pastry shell (partially
   baked or unbaked)
1 tablespoon butter
2 tablespoons minced shallots
1 cup crabmeat
1 tablespoon flour
1½ cups shredded Swiss cheese,
   divided

3 eggs
1 cup Half and Half cream
½ teaspoon salt
dash white pepper or hot pepper sauce
dash nutmeg
minced parsley

Have a 9 inch pastry shell, partially baked or unbaked. Sauté shallots in butter until tender, about 2 minutes; mix with crabmeat and flour; set aside. Sprinkle half the cheese in pie shell, then spread with crab mixture. Sprinkle with remaining cheese. Beat eggs, cream, salt, pepper, nutmeg, and parsley until mixed. Pour into shell. Bake for 25-30 minutes at 350°. Serves 6-8.

Mrs. Warren D. Rush

BEEF-MUSHROOM QUICHE

1 unbaked 9 inch pie shell
½ pound ground beef
1 (10¾ ounce) can condensed cream
   of mushroom soup
½ cup milk
2 eggs lightly beaten

2 tablespoons chopped chives
¼ teaspoon salt
dash of Tabasco
1 (4 ounce) can of mushroom pieces,
   drained
¾ cup shredded Swiss cheese

Preheat oven to 450°. Prick bottom and sides of pie shell with fork. Bake 12-15 minutes. Remove from oven. Reduce oven temperature to 350°. In a small skillet cook ground beef until browned, stirring often. Remove with slotted spoon and set aside. In a medium bowl mix mushroom soup, milk, eggs, salt, spices, and Tabasco. Add ground beef, mushrooms, and cheese. Pour into partially baked pie shell. Cover edges of pie shell with foil. Bake for 60 minutes or until knife inserted in center comes out clean. Quick, easy and delicious. Serves 3-4.

Karen Nims Keller

MARGARITA'S QUICHE

2 (9 inch) pie crusts, deep
5 eggs
¼ cup milk
8 ounces Swiss cheese

1 small can green chilies
1 (16 ounce) container sour cream
1 cup mushrooms, ham, shrimp or
    crawfish

Preheat oven to 500° and bake 2 (9-inch) pie crusts for 10 minutes. Sprinkle cooked meat or mushrooms in bottom of crust. In blender, combine eggs, cheese, chilies and milk and add sour cream. Pour mixture over meat in pie crusts. Dot with butter. Bake at 450° for 35-40 minutes or until brown. Serves 8-12.

Altixco, Puebla, Mexico

CRAB AND MUSHROOM QUICHE

4 eggs, well beaten
2 cups half and half
½ cup minced onion
1 teaspoon salt
½ teaspoon pepper

1 pound crabmeat
1 cup fresh mushrooms, sauteed in
    butter
1 cup shredded mozzarella cheese
2 unbaked pie shells

Preheat oven to 400°. Combine eggs, half and half, onion, salt and pepper. Drain crabmeat until dry. Sprinkle crabmeat, mushrooms, and cheese over bottom of pie shells. Pour in egg mixture over top. Bake at 400° for 15 minutes; reduce heat to 300° and bake 30 more minutes. Let stand 10-15 minutes before serving. Yield: 2 quiches.

Mrs. Henry W. Busch, Jr.

SHRIMP QUICHE

Pastry:
2 cups minus 2 tablespoons flour
2 tablespoons cornmeal
1 teaspoon salt

⅔ cup shortening
⅓ cup milk

Filling:
1 pound coarsely chopped, cooked
    shrimp
½ pound sliced Swiss cheese
1 small can evaporated milk and
    homogenized milk to equal 1¾ cups

3 tablespoons flour
3 eggs
¼ teaspoon white pepper
dash salt

Preheat oven to 375°. Pastry: Mix dry ingredients and salt. Cut in shortening to form mealy mixture. Add milk, stirring just until ball is formed. Roll out pastry and fit into individual dishes. Filling: Distribute shrimp evenly among casseroles. Top with Swiss cheese. Mix remaining ingredients and pour over shrimp and cheese. Bake about 35-40 minutes or until knife inserted in center comes out clean at 375°. Good with green salad and white wine. Serves 4.

Merilyn Istre

INDIVIDUAL QUICHES

pastry for 2 crust pie
¾ cup chopped, cooked shrimp
½ cup sliced green onion
1 cup shredded Swiss cheese
½ cup mayonnaise

2 eggs
⅓ cup milk
¼ teaspoon salt
¼ teaspoon dried dill weed

Preheat oven to 400°. On floured surface roll out ½ of pastry into a 12 inch circle. Cut 6 (4 inch) circles from it. Repeat with remaining pastry. Fit into 12 (2½ inch) muffin pan cups. Fill each with some shrimp, onion, and cheese. Beat remaining ingredients. Pour over cheese. Bake in 400° oven 15 minutes or until browned. Serves 12.

Mary Lenny Perrin

CREPE CUPS

12 cooked crepes
4 slices bacon
1 cup grated Gruyère cheese
2 tablespoons flour

¼ teaspoon salt
dash Worcestershire sauce
2 eggs beaten
1 cup milk

Line greased muffin pan with cooked crepes. Cook bacon until crisp; drain and crumble. Sprinkle in crepe shells. Top with cheese. Mix flour, salt, Worcestershire sauce, and eggs with milk; pour over cheese. Bake at 350° for 15 to 20 minutes or until firm. Cool 5 minutes before removing from pan. Serve hot. Serves 12.

Crepe Batter:
2 eggs
⅛ teaspoon salt
1 cup flour

1⅛ cups milk
⅛ cup melted butter

In medium mixing bowl, combine eggs and salt. Gradually add flour alternately with milk, beating with an electric mixer or whisk until smooth. Beat in melted butter. Refrigerate batter at least 1 hour. Cook on upside down crepe griddle or traditional pan. Makes about 16-18 crepes.

Mable Hoffman

LES OEUFS EN GELÉE
(Poached Eggs In Aspic)

Preparing the eggs for poaching:
Pierce a pinhole ⅜ inch deep in the large end of each egg. Lower the whole unbroken eggs into slowly boiling salted water and time 10 seconds. Remove immediately.

Preparing the poaching water:
There should be about 2 quarts salted water about 2½ inches deep. Pour about ⅓ cup vinegar into the boiling water to reduce heat to simmer.

Sharply crack egg on side of pan, then holding egg as close over the water as you dare, with your fingers almost in the water, swing the shells open fast and wide to let the egg slide into the simmering water. Set timer for 4 minutes. Rapidly continue with the other eggs adding them clockwise around edge of pan.

Regulate heat so poaching water remains at hardly a bubble and when 4 minutes are up carefully remove first egg with perforated spoon and slide it into a bowl of water. Remove the other eggs in turn.

Aspic:
1 package unflavored gelatin   1½ cups clarified stock
3 tablespoons Madeira wine

Soften gelatin in wine and stir in stock. Stir over ice until cool and spoon into individual molds. Chill until set up.

Decorate with designs of olive or truffle or other colorful goodies. Brush with more gelatin and let set up. Drain poached egg on paper towel and arrange on top of gelatin. Spoon on more gelatin and chill for at least 30 minutes.

Felicia Elsbury

OEUFS AU CHAVELLE

sharp cheddar cheese   white vinegar
thin sliced bread   herbs (marjoram, thyme, basil)
eggs   Angostura bitters

For each serving, suggest 2 eggs per person, cut cheddar cheese in thin, long pieces approximately pencil size and place around edges of sliced bread forming a levee. To water, add white vinegar flavored with marjoram, thyme and/or basil and poach eggs until about half cooked. Remove egg with slotted spoon, place on sliced bread and broil in oven until cheese melts on outside and egg finishes cooking on inside. Serve immediately with dash of angostura bitters on top of egg.

Bob Copeland

EGGS A LA CREME WITH MUSHROOMS

8 eggs
1 cup sliced mushrooms
squeeze of lemon juice
1 tablespoon butter

1 cup heavy cream
salt and pepper
pinch of grated nutmeg
1 cup grated Gruyere cheese

Sauté mushrooms with lemon juice in butter for 3-4 minutes or until tender. Pour half the cream into the buttered ramekins (8), then break the eggs on top carefully and cover with mushrooms. Season the remaining cream, add nutmeg and spoon it over the mushrooms. Cover each dish with a thick layer of grated cheese, stand in a water bath of very hot water and bake at 350° for 10 minutes or until the eggs are lightly set. Serves 8.

Judy Fuller

EGGS FLORENTINE

1 (10 ounce) package frozen
   chopped spinach
2 tablespoons grated Parmesan
   cheese

2 tablespoons dijon mustard
½ small onion, sauteed in butter
salt and white pepper
1 egg

Cook spinach until tender and drain. Combine warm spinach with 2 tablespoons grated cheese, mustard, and sauteed onion. Season to taste with salt and pepper. This part can be made ahead and refrigerated until ready to use. Spoon into individual casserole, spread evenly on bottom and up sides. Carefully break one egg into dish. Bake in 350° oven for about 20 minutes or until egg sets. Serves 1.

Clarice Burch

BAKED EGGS À LA SUISSE

butter or margarine
1 slice fresh bread
2 slices Swiss cheese
1 thin slice tomato
thyme

3 tablespoons heavy cream
1 or 2 eggs
salt and pepper
Parmesan cheese, grated

Preheat oven to 325°. Butter bottom and sides of 6 inch au gratin dish. Remove bread crust and break up remainder into small pieces to line the bottom of the dish. Place 2 slices of Swiss cheese over bread arranged to cover bottom and sides of dish. Make slight indentation in center and place a thin tomato slice in it. Add a dash of thyme and 1 tablespoon of heavy cream. Break eggs into center and cover with 2 tablespoons of heavy cream. Salt and pepper lightly and sprinkle generously with Parmesan cheese. Bake uncovered 15-20 minutes or just until eggs are set. Let stand at least 10 minutes before serving. Serves 1.

Stephen P. Engelbrecht

ASPARAGUS WITH EGGS

½ **pound fresh asparagus or**   1 tablespoon butter
   10 ounces frozen   4 eggs
3 **tablespoons Parmesan cheese**

Tie up ½ pound of fresh asparagus, or 9 ounces frozen, in a bundle and cook in boiling salted water for 15 minutes, covered loosely. (If frozen asparagus are used, follow directions on package.) Drain and place in flat casserole dish. Stir together 3 tablespoons of Parmesan cheese, 1 tablespoon of softened or melted butter and dot over asparagus. (If butter is melted, dribble over asparagus.) Broil for about 3 minutes. Should be crisp and bubbly. Fry eggs in butter and place over asparagus. Multiply ingredients by number of servings.

Bob Copeland

BRUNCH BAKED EGGS

Cheese Sauce:
2 heaping tablespoons butter   salt and pepper
2 tablespoons flour   dash Worcestershire sauce
1 cup plus 2 tablespoons milk   dash Tabasco
½ cup cheddar cheese

Layers:
butter   salt and pepper
6 slices of ham, sliced thin   ½ cup grated American cheese
   and into wide strips   ¼ cup bread crumbs Italian style
2 tomatoes sliced medium thick   butter dots
8 eggs (2/person)

Melt butter in pan and blend in flour; add milk gradually, stirring constantly. When smooth and thickened, add bits of cheese, salt, pepper, dash of each Worcestershire and Tabasco. Line buttered baking dish with ham. Lay tomato slices flat on ham. Break eggs over tomatoes. Salt and pepper. Cover with cheese sauce. Top with grated cheese, bread crumbs and butter dots. Bake in pre-heated 325° oven for 20 minutes. Serves 4.

Judy McEacharn

BRUNCH CASSEROLE

2 cups plain croutons
4 ounces shredded cheddar cheese
  (1 cup)
4 beaten eggs
2 cups milk
1 teaspoon salt

½ tablespoon prepared mustard
¼ teaspoon onion powder
⅛ teaspoon pepper
4 slices bacon
hot spices, optional

Preheat oven to 250°. Combine croutons and cheese and put into greased baking dish, 10x6x2 inches. Mix and blend eggs, milk, and seasonings and pour over croutons in casserole. Cook bacon until crisp—drain and crumble over mixture. Bake at 250° for 55 minutes or until eggs set. Garnish with bacon curls. Can be made the night before if needed and cooked before serving. Serves 6-8.

Cynthia Dunlap

HUEVOS RANCHEROS

Sauce:
2 tablespoons butter
3 tablespoons chopped onion
1 clove minced garlic
2 tablespoons chopped bell pepper
pulp of 2 green pod peppers, chilies

½ teaspoon leaf oregano
1 large ripe tomato, chopped
salt and pepper to taste
½ cup beef stock or water

Serve over tortillas, fried eggs.

Melt butter and cook onions and garlic in it until golden, but not brown. Add bell pepper, chilies, oregano, tomato, and salt and pepper. When well mixed, add liquid and cook until the vegetables are tender and the sauce has thickened. Serve sauce over a warm tortilla topped with fried egg. Note: I use hot jalapeno peppers but milder ones could be used by those who prefer. Serves 4-6.

Sally Brochschmidt Herpin

EGGS RANCHEROS

2 tablespoons margarine
1 can Ro-tel tomatoes, cut up whole
  tomatoes
salt and pepper to taste

1 onion, chopped
1 pod garlic, mashed
2 whole jalapeno peppers
6-8 eggs, poached

Melt margarine in skillet. Add can of Ro-tel tomatoes and slice all whole tomatoes in skillet. Slightly rinse can with water and add to tomatoes. Season with salt and black pepper. Add chopped onion, garlic, and pepper. Simmer on low a few minutes and spoon on top of poached eggs. Eggs can be placed on top of toast and sauce over both. This is highly seasoned!!! Serves 6-8.

Mrs. John Tolson, III

SCRAMBLED POTATOES

4 eggs lightly beaten
4 tablespoons butter
1-2 cloves garlic, optional, finely
    chopped
¼ cup onion, chopped

1 large potato, diced
    ⅜ inch square
1 tablespoon water
salt to taste
Tabasco to taste

Beat eggs lightly and add water, salt, and Tabasco, set aside. Chop onions and garlic, set aside. Melt butter in skillet, add cubed potatoes; sauté in butter until soft and very lightly brown on edges over medium heat, do not let butter burn; add onions and garlic and let wilt slightly; pour eggs over and scramble. Serves 2-3.

Susan Powers

JO ANN'S CHEESE CASSEROLE

½ cup finely chopped onions
¼ cup finely chopped bell pepper
1 cup grated sharp cheddar cheese
2-4 finely chopped jalapeño peppers,
    to taste

1 teaspoon sugar
salt and pepper
6 eggs

Preheat oven to 350°. Mix the first 6 ingredients together. Place in a buttered pyrex dish. Beat 6 eggs until foamy and pour over mixture. Bake in 350° oven about 15 minutes. A great luncheon dish that can be served with a tossed salad. Serves 4.

Mrs. Edward Stuart, Jr.
Beaumont, TX

CHEESE STRATA

16 slices white bread
1 pound sharp cheddar cheese
2 teaspoons dry mustard
2 teaspoons salt
1 teaspoon pepper

1 small can chopped green chilies,
    seeded
4 cups milk
6 whole eggs

Preheat oven to 350°. Trim bread, cut into cubes. In a 3 quart baking dish, put half of bread cubes, cheeses, dry mustard, salt, pepper, and green chilies. Repeat a second layer. Pour beaten eggs and milk over the layers. Bake in 350° oven for 30-40 minutes or until bubbly and slightly brown on the top. Freezes very well. Serves 8-12.

Mrs. Joe Fisher
Beaumont, TX

CHEESE SOUFFLE

1 can mushroom soup
2 cups shredded cheddar cheese,
  (sharp or mild to taste)

6 eggs, separated

Preheat oven to 400°. Put soup in pot and heat. Add grated cheese and stir until melted. Beat egg whites stiff. Beat egg yolks until light in color. Fold soup/cheese into yolks mixing thoroughly. Fold in whites. Pour into a 2 quart souffle casserole and bake for 30 minutes in 400° oven. Serve at once. For variations, 1 pound of fresh lump crabmeat thoroughly drained may be gently folded after folding in the soup/cheese mixture into yolks for a more elegant company souffle. Delicious with hot rolls, green salad and chilled glass of white wine for a Sunday night supper. Serves 4-6.

Adrien A. Stewart

MACARONI AND CHEESE

1 package shell macaroni
1 large jar Cheese Whiz or 1 pound
  rat or hoop cheese
2 cans mushroom soup

1-2 cans Rotel tomatoes, depending on
  how hot you like it
salt and pepper

Preheat oven to 350°. Cook macaroni according to instructions. If using rat cheese, grate and add it to cooked macaroni, if using Cheese Whiz, pour it into warm cooked macaroni. To this add rest of ingredients and bake at 350° covered for 1 hour. Serves 12-15.

Connie Gauthier

BACON SOUR CREAM MACARONI CASSEROLE

½ pound bacon
2 ¼ cup cooked macaroni
1 cup (4 ounces) grated American
  cheese
½ cup sour cream
¼ cup milk
1 can (2 ounce) mushroom stems and
  pieces

2 tablespoons chopped green pepper
1 tablespoon chopped pimento
½ teaspoon onion salt
¼ teaspoon salt
dash pepper

Cook bacon over low heat until crisp. Drain and crumble. Combine all ingredients. Place in 1 or 1½ quart casserole. Bake for 30 minutes at 350°. Serves 4.

Judy Cole

RICOTTA CROQUETTES

½ pound of macaroons
1 pound ricotta cheese
3 eggs

dash cinnamon
bread crumbs

Crush macaroons and press the crumbs through a fine sieve. Add to the crumbs, cheese, eggs, lightly beaten and a dash of cinnamon and mix well. Shape the mixture into small balls, dip into beaten egg and roll in bread crumbs. Sauté in butter until golden on all sides. Serves 6.

Peggy Guidry Comeaux

PASTA SCUITTA (POOR MAN'S PASTA)

3 large white sweet onions
2-3 large pods garlic
1 stick butter
¼ cup olive oil
2 cans tomato sauce

1 (2 pound) box Velveeta cheese
2 teaspoons salt
Parmesan cheese to sprinkle top
1 (1 pound) box spaghetti

Slice onions, mash garlic in press. Melt butter in frying pan. Add olive oil to butter. Place onions and garlic in butter/oil on low heat; cook until onions are yellowish in color. Add tomato sauce; heat thoroughly. Add Velveeta cheese cut into chunks; until thoroughly melted, stir cheese into onion mixture. Add salt. Cook spaghetti in boiling, salted water until tender (about 10 minutes). Drain thoroughly.

Add cheese and tomato sauce to cooked spaghetti. Remove to hot dish for serving. Sprinkle with Parmesan cheese before serving. Serves 4-6.

Mrs. Sue Alves

ASPARAGUS SOUP

1 can cream of asparagus soup
1 can cheddar cheese soup
1 cup milk
1 cup water

2 tablespoons butter or margarine
salt, black and red peppers to taste
1 can asparagus

Heat soups, milk, water, butter and seasonings slowly in a heavy pot. Add asparagus. Heat and stir occasionally. Serves 6.

Susan Quoyeser

CHILLED AVOCADO SOUP

3 medium size avocados, peeled and
   cut in chunks
1 cup commercial sour cream
juice of 1 lemon
1 cup light cream

¼ teaspoon chili powder
2 cups chicken broth
salt, red and black pepper to taste
paprika and onions for garnish

Place all ingredients except chicken broth in processor or blender and process until smooth. You will have to do this in 2 batches and empty into a 2 quart bowl. Then stir in chicken broth, correct seasoning and chill well. Serve in clear soup bowls garnished with paprika and chopped onions. Serves 6.

Mrs. C. B. Billeaud, Jr.

APPETIZER BROCCOLI SOUP

2 (10 ounce) packages frozen,
   chopped broccoli
2 cans condensed cream of mushroom
   soup

2 soup cans milk
½ cup dry white wine
4 tablespoons butter or margarine
dash of pepper

In a large saucepan, cook broccoli according to package directions; drain. Add soup, milk, wine, butter or margarine, and pepper. Heat through and serve. DO NOT BOIL OR THE LIQUID WILL SEPARATE. Serves 8.

Mrs. Easton Hebert

ARTICHOKE SOUP

2 cans artichoke bottoms
4 egg yolks
2 cans of undiluted chicken broth
salt and pepper to taste

8 tablespoons flour
8 tablespoons butter
2 cartons whipping cream (1 pint)
2 cans artichoke hearts, mashed

In a blender combine the artichoke bottoms, egg yolks, chicken broth and seasonings using a medium speed until smooth. Leave this mixture in the blender for later use. In a pan heat the butter, flour and whipping cream until very hot, but not boiling. Add this mixture to the blender and mix well. Pour the entire contents of the blender in the saucepan and reheat. When hot add the mashed artichoke hearts and serve. May be made the day ahead. Serves 8.

Mary S. Jeansonne

BLACK BEAN SOUP

1 pound black beans
¼ cup chili powder
½ cup chopped onions
2 cloves garlic
4 ounces salt pork or ham

1 quart chicken or beef stock
enough water to cover beans
salt to taste
½ cup chopped green onion tops
corn chips

Cover beans with water and soak over night. Change water before putting on stove to cook. Sauté onions and garlic until the onions are soft, add salt meat and cook a few minutes longer. Add onions and salt meat to beans, bring ingredients to a boil, add salt and chili powder, reduce fire and cook beans slowly adding more water as necessary. Stir often to keep from sticking. Cook beans until they are very well done. When beans are cooked, remove one cup of whole beans from pot and set aside. Remove salt meat. Take remaining beans with broth and puree in a blender or food mill adding enough chicken or beef stock until you have your desired consistency. Reheat and serve in bowls, adding a few whole beans to each bowl. Garnish each bowl of soup with chopped onion tops and serve with corn chips. Yield: 2 quarts.

LaFonda's Restaurant
Lafayette, La.

BROWN STOCK

2 pounds beef and veal bones
½ cup celery
½ cup onions
½ cup carrots
8 cups water
¼ teaspoon thyme
1 teaspoon salt

¼ teaspoon marjoram
1 cup red wine or ¼ cup vinegar
3 cloves
1 bay leaf
¼ teaspoon parsley
1 teaspoon red pepper

Use large Dutch oven or soup pot. Brown beef and veal bones, try to get a mixture of bones with marrow and knuckles. Add remaining ingredients. Simmer for 3-4 hours with lid cracked a bit. Strain and refrigerate overnight with meat in separate container. Crack up fat the next day. Freeze in small containers, use fat in sauces or to brown mushrooms or shallots, etc. Use as base for soup or sauces. Yield: 2½ quarts.

Helen Gankendorff

LUSCIOUS CHICKEN SOUP

⅓ cup butter
¾ cup flour
6 cups chicken stock

1 cup warm milk
1½ cups finely diced chicken
season highly with salt and pepper

Melt butter, add flour and cook over low heat until well blended. Add 2 cups hot chicken stock, do not use bouillon cubes, and the warm milk and blend. Cook slowly, stirring frequently, until thick. Add remaining 4 cups of chicken stock and the chicken and heat to boiling. Season. Though white soups are relatively uncommon in Louisiana, this recipe seems to be enjoyed before a formal dinner. Serves 6-8 small servings.

Judy Cole

CHICKEN SOUP WITH RICE AND MUSHROOMS

1 stewing hen, about 5 pounds
6 quarts water
1 whole onion, stuck with 1-2 cloves
2 whole stalks celery
2 tablespoons salt
½ teaspoon Tabasco
¼ teaspoon green hot
　sauce
2 medium onions, chopped

3-4 cups celery, chopped
2 large carrots, grated
1 pound fresh mushrooms, sliced,
　canned mushrooms may be
　substituted
1 cup rice, uncooked
1 teaspoon leaf thyme
salt and pepper to taste
fresh chopped parsley to garnish

Simmer hen, whole onion stuck with cloves, and whole stalks celery in pot of water for at least 3 hours. Season water with salt, Tabasco and green hot sauce. Remove hen, onion and stalks of celery. You should have only chicken broth remaining in pot. Discard whole onion and whole stalks of celery. To broth add chopped onions, chopped celery, grated carrots, mushrooms, rice, thyme, salt and pepper and simmer about 10 minutes. Finally add chicken which has been skinned, deboned, and cut into bite-sized pieces. Adjust the seasoning to taste. Freezes exceptionally well, however, I prefer to freeze it without the parsley. Add fresh sprigs only to that portion being served. Yield: 1½-2 gallons.

Mrs. Catherine Haydel Mouton

CHICKEN VEGETABLE SOUP

½ cup chopped onion
½ cup chopped celery
½ cup chopped carrots
1 tablespoon chopped parsley
boney pieces, backs, necks and wings
    of 2 chickens
1 can stewed, seasoned tomatoes

1 quart water
1 tablespoon salt
¼ teaspoon pepper
½ cup narrow noodles, broken up
1 teaspoon monosodium glutamate,
    optional
1 tablespoon Beau Monde seasoning

Place chopped vegetables, chicken, tomatoes, water, salt, and pepper in Dutch oven. Bring to boiling. Reduce heat, and simmer, covered for 50 minutes. Remove chicken, add noodles, continue simmering 10 minutes. Remove skin and bones from chicken, return meat to soup. Taste, then if desired add more seasoning. I like both thyme and sweet basil, even a little more Beau Monde seasoning. If desired at this time add monosodium glutamate, heat and serve. Yield: 2 quarts. Can be cooked in a slow cooker for 8½-10½ hours. Can be frozen.

Frances Wallace

CLAM CHOWDER

4 medium potatoes, pared and sliced
¼ pound bacon or 3 tablespoons
    bacon drippings
1 cup chopped onion
1 cup chopped celery
5 tablespoons margarine or butter
5 tablespoons flour

3 cups milk
1 cup bottled clam juice or substitute
    additional cup of milk
3 (6 ounce) cans minced clams,
    undrained
½ teaspoon thyme
salt and pepper to taste

Using a 3 quart pot, cover potatoes with salted water, boil until done, 10-15 minutes and drain. While potatoes cook, fry bacon in large pot until crisp. Set bacon aside on toweling to drain and retain drippings to wilt, do not brown, onions and celery over medium heat. When onions and celery are soft, add butter, mix in flour, add milk and clam juice and stir constantly until thickened. Add boiled potatoes, clams, thyme, salt and pepper. Heat thoroughly. DO NOT BOIL. Serve hot and garnish with bacon bits. Serves 4-6.

Helen Nugier Sobiesk

CREAMY CORN SOUP

3 tablespoons unsalted butter
1 medium onion, chopped
1 tablespoon flour, sifted slowly
1 large package frozen corn

1 half-pint whipping cream
1 pint Half and Half
chopped parsley
seasoning to taste

Brown the first three ingredients slowly, about 10 minutes. Add frozen corn, simmering long and slow until corn is quite soft. Add cream and Half and Half, cooking until well blended. Then put in parsley and salt and pepper. Again cook until well blended. Put mixture in blender and puree. Pour mixture through strainer to remove corn husks. Reheat and serve warm as an appetizer. Skimming the corn husks from the soup makes all the difference in the world, both in taste and consistency of the dish. Serves 5-6.

Joel Lafayette Fletcher

CREAM OF GREEN BEAN SOUP

2 cups finely cut, French cut, green
  beans
1 tablespoon minced onion
3 tablespoons butter or margarine
1 teaspoon salt
dash pepper

dash cayenne
2 tablespoons flour
2 cups boiling water
2 cups (14½ ounce can) evaporated milk
¼ cup grated American cheese

Add beans and onions to butter and season. Simmer covered about 10 minutes, stirring occasionally. Stir flour into vegetables, gradually add water and cook 5 minutes stirring constantly until thick and smooth. Add milk and heat thoroughly. Sprinkle portions with cheese. Serves 6.

Sallie Sorrell

CREAM SOUP WITH VEGETABLES

Soup Base:

3 tablespoons butter
3 cups sliced leeks (white part only) or
    onions or combination of both
3 tablespoons flour
6 cups chicken broth

1 tablespoon salt (or less to taste)
3 cups chopped potatoes
pepper to taste
1 cup cream
your favorite cooked vegetables

Melt butter over moderate heat in a 3-4 quart heavy pan. Stir in leeks and/or onions, cover and cook slowly for 5 minutes without browning. Blend in flour and cook about 2-3 minutes. Remove from heat—cool several minutes, then gradually beat in 1 cup hot chicken broth. Blend thoroughly, then stir in rest of hot chicken broth, 6 cups in all. Add salt and pepper and diced potatoes. Bring to a boil then simmer partly covered for 40 minutes until vegetables are tender. Place in blender to make smooth mixture. Soup base may be completed days ahead to this point. When cool—cover and refrigerate—reheat before proceeding.

Vegetable Addition: Heat soup base. Add cooked vegetables such as squash, brussel sprouts, broccoli, cauliflower, peas, artichoke hearts. Simmer 5 minutes. Puree in blender, return to pot, add cream—a little butter if desired. Correct seasoning to taste. Serves 6-8.

Kathryn Breaux

CUCUMBER VICHYSSOISE

⅓ cup white of leeks, sliced
1 small onion, sliced
2 tablespoons butter
3 cups potatoes, peeled and sliced
5 cups chicken stock
1 large cucumber, peeled, seeded and
    sliced

1½ cups heavy cream or half and half
¼ teaspoon mace or nutmeg
salt to taste
white pepper to taste
3 tablespoons chives, minced

Sauté leeks and onions briefly in butter. Simmer potatoes in stock, covered 20 minutes or until tender. In two equal amounts, put vegetables and stock into blender or food processor fitted with steel blade, add cucumbers and blend until smooth. Stir in cream, add mace or nutmeg, salt and pepper to taste and chill thoroughly. Adjust seasonings and serve garnished with minced chives. Yield: 10-11 cups.

Mrs. Richard D. Chappuis, Sr.

LIME SOUP

1 (3-3½ pound) chicken
10 cups water
6 peppercorns
3 parsley sprigs
1 stalk celery
1 medium onion, quartered
2 teaspoons salt
½ teaspoon dried thyme leaves
2 tablespoons vegetable oil
1 medium onion

1 medium green pepper, chopped
2 cups tomatoes, fresh or canned,
    chopped
2 limes, halved
3 tablespoons fresh parsley or coriander
salt and pepper to taste
tortilla chips
lime slices
Parmesan cheese, optional

Place chicken in Dutch oven with next seven ingredients. Heat to boiling, reduce heat, simmer until chicken is cooked, approximately 1½ hours. Remove film occasionally. Remove chicken from broth cool, and debone. Strain broth. While chicken is cooling, heat oil in Dutch oven. Sauté onion and pepper until tender. Add tomatoes; cook five minutes. Add reserved broth, juice from two limes, and ½ squeezed lime. Stir in coriander; simmer 20 minutes. Add chicken, heat until hot. Taste and adjust seasoning. Serve in soup bowls garnished with tortilla chips and lime slices. You may also sprinkle lightly with Parmesan cheese. Yield: approximately 3 quarts.

Carola Bacqué

CREAMY ONION SOUP

¾ cup butter or margarine
2 cups sliced white onion
¾ cup all-purpose flour
6 cups beef stock
salt to taste
½ teaspoon cayenne pepper

1 egg yolk
2 tablespoons cream
croutons
Parmesan cheese
buttered bread crumbs

Melt butter in a 3 quart soup kettle. Add onions, reduce heat to very low, and cook until onions are clear and transparent. Do not brown onions. Add flour and cook 5-10 minutes longer, stirring occasionally. Blend in beef stock, salt, and cayenne and bring to a boil. Reduce heat and simmer about 15 minutes. Remove from heat. Beat egg yolk and cream together; add a little of the soup to this mixture and blend quickly; then add to the soup kettle. Serve in soup cups with croutons. Sprinkle with Parmesan cheese and buttered bread crumbs. Brown under broiler and serve hot. Yield: 1½ quarts.

Ramona Mouton

FRENCH ONION SOUP

6 purple onions
¾ stick butter
3 tablespoons flour
8 beef bouillon cubes
6 cups water
2 tablespoons Kitchen Bouquet

2 tablespoons cornstarch
½ cup water
salt and pepper to taste
Brie cheese
croutons
Swiss cheese

Thinly slice onions. Sauté onions in butter in large covered pot until brown. Add flour to onions and continue to simmer. Dissolve bouillon cubes in water and add to onions. Add Kitchen Bouquet for color and simmer 30 minutes. To thicken soup, dissolve cornstarch in ½ cup water and add to soup. Add more for thicker soup. Season with salt and pepper. When serving put a wedge of Brie cheese at the bottom of each cup. Place some croutons on top of soup and top that with a slice of Swiss cheese. To melt cheese, pass in a microwave or standard oven just long enough to soften cheese. Serves 8.

Connie Gauthier

WILLIAMSBURG STYLE PEANUT SOUP

3 cups chicken broth or bouillon
¼ cup chopped celery
¼ teaspoon salt
1 small onion, chopped fine
2 tablespoons butter
½ cup smooth peanut butter

1 cup milk
¼ cup flour
¼ cup water
¼ cup chopped peanuts, optional
parsley for garnish, optional

Combine stock and next four ingredients and cook 2-3 hours on low fire. Add milk, flour and water, mixed together and peanut butter to above ingredients and cook on high for 15 minutes. Stir constantly with wire whisk until smooth. Serve in bowls and sprinkle with chopped peanuts and parsley if desired. Serves 4.

Mrs. C. Earl Weber, Sr.
New Orleans, LA

CREAM OF SPINACH SOUP

½ cup boiling water
2 cups frozen spinach
¼ cup finely chopped onion
4 tablespoons butter
4 tablespoons flour

4 cups milk
1 teaspoon salt
a dash of Accent
Provolone cheese, grated

Add water to the spinach and allow to stand until spinach is heated through. Put in the electric blender until smooth. Brown onion in the butter and stir in the flour. Cook until bubbly; add the milk; stirring rapidly until thickened. Add spinach, salt and Accent. Let stand at least 15 minutes before serving. When serving, put a teaspoon of Provolone cheese on top. Serves 6.

Mrs. William Eggart

SPINACH AND OYSTER SOUP

2 boxes frozen chopped spinach
5 ounces sour cream
4 tablespoons butter or margarine
2½ cups milk
2 cans cream of chicken soup

½ cup shallots
¼ teaspoon white pepper
2 jars oysters, drained
salt to taste

Prepare spinach as shown on box; drain and mix sour cream and butter with spinach in a separate bowl. In soup pot add milk, canned soup, shallots, and white pepper. Stir and cook for 20 minutes on medium fire. Then stir in spinach mixture. Cook for 15 minutes on simmer. Add oysters and simmer 15-20 minutes. Salt to taste. Delicious as an appetizer soup or a main dish. Serves 8 one cup servings.

Karen Nims Keller

COLD STRAWBERRY CREAM SOUP

3 cups fresh strawberries, washed
    and stemmed
1½ cups water
1½ cups white wine
½ cup sugar

2 tablespoons fresh lemon juice
1½ tablespoons cornstarch mixed in
    1½ teaspoons cold water
3 teaspoons lemon zest, grated
½ cup sour cream

Slice all but 6 strawberries. Combine sliced berries, water and wine and simmer in a covered saucepan about 10 minutes. Add sugar, lemon juice and cornstarch, heat to a boil and stir until thickened. Transfer mixture in 2 equal amounts to an electric blender, add 1½ teaspoons grated lemon zest and ¼ cup sour cream, and blend until smooth. Cool, taste for sugar, and chill thoroughly. Serve in crystal soup bowls and top each portion with a whole strawberry. Serves 6.

Mrs. Richard Chappuis, Sr.

VEGETABLE SOUP

2-3 pounds tender soup meat
flour, enough to dredge meat in
1 cup vegetable oil
2 large onions, chopped
2 cans peeled whole tomatoes
1 (8 ounce) can tomato sauce
large, fatty and meaty soup bone
1½ quarts hot water
salt and pepper to taste

Tabasco to taste
4 cubes beef bouillon, dissolved in ½ cup
    hot water
1 large bag frozen corn
1 large bag frozen string beans
1 large bag frozen small lima beans
1 large bag frozen sliced carrots
3 Irish potatoes, peeled and cubed
1 teaspoon Worcestershire

Cut meat in bite-size pieces and dredge in flour to coat heavily. Heat oil and add meat and onions. Brown meat. Add tomatoes, with their juice, tomato sauce, soup bone and water. Cover and simmer for 1 hour. Season with salt, pepper, Tabasco and beef bouillon. Add vegetables and simmer for a couple of hours. Add Worcestershire before serving. Serves 10-12.

Marjorie Bray

TURTLE SOUP

2 pounds turtle meat
2 tablespoons oil
2 tablespoons flour
½ cup minced green onion tops
2 tablespoons tomato paste
1 cup chopped onion
1 cup chopped celery
2 cloves minced garlic

2 quarts water
½ lemon, sliced thinly
salt and pepper to taste
dash of Worcestershire
dash Tabasco
2 hard-boiled eggs, sliced
parsley
½ cup sherry

Cut turtle meat into small pieces and lightly brown in hot oil in large pot. Remove from pot and add flour to pot. Brown. To this roux, add celery and onions. Sauté until limp. Add tomato paste, green onions and garlic. Cook for a few minutes, stirring frequently so as not to burn roux. Return meat to mixture, add 2 quarts of water, seasoning, and lemon slices. Simmer in covered pot until meat is very tender and broth is smooth, about 1 hour, stirring occasionally. Just before serving remove lemon slices and add sherry, parsley and Worcestershire sauce. Place slices of hard boiled eggs sprinkled with paprika in soup plates before serving. Additional sherry may also be added at table. Serves 6.

Lucille Copeland

BOUILLABAISSE

1 (3-5 pound) red fish sliced in
  2 inch strips
3 onions, finely chopped
2 bell peppers, finely chopped
4 sticks celery, finely chopped
1 can tomatoes, chopped
2 cups fish stock

6 crabs, par-boiled, cleaned and halved
1 pint oysters
1 pound shrimp
1 pound crabmeat
½ cup onion tops, chopped
¼ cup parsley
lemon

In a large heavy soup pot make layers of chopped vegetable, then fish meat and repeat layers until all is used up. Set on low heat and begin cooking covered for at least ½ hour. Add tomatoes and stock, continue cooking covered for 1 hour. Occasionally shake or twist pot to blend ingredients but *never never stir.* Add crab halves, cover and cook for ½ hour longer, then add the last 5 ingredients. Cook for 30 minutes more. Squeeze juice from one lemon over top of pot. Serve over rice in soup bowls. Serves 6-8.

Stock: Boil fish head and bones with carrot stick, celery stick, bouquet garni for 1 hour. Strain and reserve.

Kathryn Leonard

ROUND STEAK OKRA GUMBO—OKRA GUMBO VIALA

2 pounds beef round steak, defatted and cubed
1 small ham steak, cubed or left over ham
2 tablespoons cooking oil

2 pounds okra, finely sliced
2 medium onions, finely chopped
2 tablespoons flour
2 tablespoons bacon drippings
2-3 quarts boiling water

Brown round steak in large Dutch oven in oil. When almost brown add ham. Remove from pot. Add okra and onions to drippings in pot. Cook slowly about 45 minutes, stirring occasionally. When okra is no longer ropey add meat, salt and pepper, and red pepper. Then add boiling water. Bring to boil, lower heat and cover. Make a roux with flour and bacon drippings. When dark brown add to meat-okra mixture. Simmer covered for 1 hour or more. Serve with rice. Filé may be added at table if desired. Serves 8-10.

Dorothy Green
Beaumont, Texas

COURTBOUILLON

5 teaspoons salt
1 cup sugar
8 cups whole tomatoes
3 cans Rotel tomatoes
4 teaspoons minced garlic

7 slices bacon, chopped
1 cup chopped celery
6 cups chopped onions
4 tablespoons Kitchen Bouquet
1 gallon shrimp stock

Bring all ingredients to a boil and add:

2 cups roux

Lower fire and cook for 2½ hours if mixture cooks down, add more shrimp stock. Add to this basic soup any seasoned seafood such as fish, shrimp, crab, oyster. This is truly a "soup of the court." Yield: 2 gallons.

Chez Pastor Restaurant
Lafayette, La.

ROUX

The typical Cajun roux is a blend of equal parts flour and fat cooked together in a heavy pot over slow heat until a medium brown color is reached. You must stir any roux constantly to avoid burning.

The French roux is usually a blend of equal parts flour and butter cooked slowly until bubbly and well blended, but not browned.

Some people prefer a roux made with approximately one-fourth cup more oil than flour.

Most of the time when a Cajun roux is called for, the addition of finely chopped onion and bell pepper are added to the browned roux to arrest the cooking temperature and prevent the scorching of the roux. This step begins the cooking of the desired dish.

CRAWFISH GUMBO

¾ cup oil
¾ cup flour
2 medium onions, chopped fine
8 ounces tomato sauce
3 quarts stock, any kind
1½ bell peppers, chopped fine

2 large cloves garlic, mashed
1 tablespoon salt
1 teaspoon red pepper
2 pounds peeled crawfish and fat
¼ cup chopped parsley
¼ cup chopped green onion

Make roux. Add onions and cook until clear. Add tomato sauce and cook on low heat about 15 minutes. Add stock slowly at first and mix well. (It should be hot before adding.) Add bell pepper, garlic, salt, and pepper. Bring to boil and cook hard for 20 minutes. Add fat and continue to simmer for 40 minutes or until it is thickness desired, making allowance for water in crawfish. Add crawfish and simmer 15 minutes until done. Adjust seasoning and sprinkle with green onion and parsley. Serves 8-10.

Doreen S. Duhe

MOM'S SHRIMP GUMBO

4 strips bacon
1 bunch green onions, chopped
2 bell peppers, chopped
4 tablespoons oil
4 tablespoons flour
2 (10 ounce) packages frozen okra
2 pounds cleaned shrimp
3 quarts water

1 (16 ounce) can tomatoes
1 (8 ounce) can tomato sauce
2 bay leaves
1 teaspoon thyme
2 teaspoons salt
½ teaspoon black pepper
1 teaspoon red pepper

Fry 4 strips of bacon. Eat bacon and use the fat to sauté 1 bunch of green onions and 2 bell peppers. Make a roux with oil and flour. Brown roux, add peppers and onions, frozen cut-up okra, shrimp, cut in halves, water, tomatoes, tomato sauce, bay leaves, thyme, salt, black pepper, 1 teaspoon (more or less) red pepper. Bring to a boil, then turn heat down and simmer 1½ hours. Serve over rice. Serves 12 (It just isn't right unless you stand up there and "eat the bacon" while sautéing the onions and pepper.)

Jean Gill Larsen

TURKEY AND SAUSAGE GUMBO

1 turkey carcass
½ cup salad oil
½ cup all-purpose flour
1½ large onions, chopped
½ green pepper, chopped
1 stalk celery, chopped
1½ pounds smoked sausage, cut into
   2½ inch pieces

salt
red and black pepper
¼ cup chopped parsley
¼ cup chopped green onion tops
hot cooked rice
filé (optional)

Use a turkey carcass with a little meat left on it; a smoked turkey is best. Cover carcass with water and boil until meat leaves bones (about 1 hour). Reserve broth, and remove meat from carcass; discard bones. Combine salad oil and flour in a large iron pot; cook over medium heat, stirring constantly, until a medium brown roux is formed. Add onion, green pepper and celery; cook about 5 minutes or until tender, stirring constantly. Add sausage, turkey and 2-3 quarts broth (add water to make 2 quarts if necessary). Simmer 1 hour. Season gumbo to taste with salt and peppers. Stir in parsley and green onion, cook 10 minutes longer. Serve over rice. Thicken with filé, if desired. Serves 8-10.

Mrs. Pat Cashman

WILD DUCK, SAUSAGE AND OYSTER GUMBO

1 cup flour
1 cup oil (bacon drippings if desired)
4 onions chopped
4 celery stalks chopped
1 bell pepper chopped
3 garlic pods minced
¼ cup parsley minced
1 pound Andouille or smoked
   sausage (cut in ¼ inch slices)

4 wild ducks (cut for frying)
4 quarts warm water
2 bay leaves
2 teaspoons salt
black pepper to taste
cayenne pepper to taste
3 pints oysters
filé
green onions (top and bottom chopped)

Make roux in black pot with oil and flour. Brown until very dark. Add next 5 ingredients and cook until tender. Add sausage and duck pieces and cook until browned. Stir in water, add bay leaves, salt, and peppers. Cover and simmer for about 2 hours or until duck is tender. Add oysters and ½ of oyster liquid. Cook uncovered for about 30 minutes. Serve over rice with green onions and filé as compliments. Can be frozen without oysters. Serves 8.

Mrs. Vernon M. Ventress, Jr.

CHICKEN AND SAUSAGE GUMBO

2 large chickens	1 tablespoon black pepper
2 large onions	1½ tablespoons red pepper
1 cup chopped celery	2-3 pounds smoked sausage, hot
2½ cups oil	parsley
2½ cups flour	onion tops
2 (10 ounce) packages frozen,	4 chicken bouillon cubes
chopped okra	filé
2½ tablespoons salt	

Rinse chicken. Put in a large roaster about half full of water with some salt and pepper added. Bring to a boil. Cover and simmer about 1 hour until chickens are tender. Strain and save the broth to use as your liquid in the gumbo. Debone the chicken.

Cut up the onions and celery. Make the roux in a heavy black iron skillet as follows: heat the oil for 3 minutes on medium-high heat and then add the flour slowly, stirring constantly. Cook on medium-high heat until brown. Turn heat to low, add onions and celery and cook until soft. Transfer roux, onions and celery to a large roaster or gumbo pot. Measure broth. Add 1½ gallons of liquid—broth and water to make up the difference; bring to a boil. Add the okra, salt, black pepper and red pepper, sausage (cut into bite size pieces), and bouillon cubes. Cook 1 hour on simmer; then skim the fat off the top. Add the deboned chicken. Simmer for 30 minutes. Add some parsley and onion tops and cook about 5 minutes. Serve over rice. Add filé (½ teaspoon) to each bowl as served. Serves 17 adults.

Use this same recipe with your leftover turkey, smoked turkey or ducks. Smoke the ducks instead of boiling for an extra delicious flavor.

Linda Larsen Billeaud

pot of gold at the End of the rainbow

THE MUSIC MEN

The Cajun cuisine reflects the Cajun culture, but the true Cajun gets all of his energy from his music. Our culture has many unique customs and traditions. The music of the French people of South Louisiana is the closest thing to a true art form which the culture has produced. This music which is played primarily with a fiddle and an accordian, and is sung in Cajun French, reflects the life style of its people. The fun-loving Cajun who worked hard all week found time to dance and sing his heart away every Friday and Saturday night.

SALADS AND DRESSINGS

MARINATED CARROTS

5 cups sliced carrots (2 1-pound
   packages)
1 small green pepper
1 medium sweet onion
½ cup salad oil
1 can tomato soup

¾ cup vinegar
1 cup sugar
1 teaspoon prepared mustard
1 teaspoon Worcestershire sauce
1 teaspoon salt
1 teaspoon pepper

Cook carrots until just tender, do not overcook. Drain and cool. Slice pepper and onion. Mix oil, soup, vinegar and sugar. Add seasonings and mix well. Shake in a jar. Layer carrots, onion and pepper in container with a cover. Pour the oil mixture over this. Let marinate for 12 hours in refrigerator. Drain to serve. Serves 6.

Elizabeth D. Corrigan

CUCUMBER BOATS

cucumbers
onions
celery
bell pepper

tomatoes
red onion
vinegar
sugar

Peel cucumbers, cut lengthwise. Scoop out inside and throw away scooped out seeds. Set cucumber aside. Chop onions, celery, bell pepper, cucumbers, tomatoes and a little red onion. Marinate this in vinegar, sugar and a little water for 2-3 hours. Drain mixture and then place mixture in the scooped out cucumbers. Very pretty on luncheon plate. Cut into smaller pieces and use for a diet hors d'oeuvres using artificial sweetener; you can't tell the difference.

Jeanne Gilley

MARINATED TOMATOES

1 teaspoon salt
¼ teaspoon pepper
½ teaspoon thyme
¼ cup chopped parsley

¼ cup chopped chives
⅔ cup oil
¼ cup tarragon vinegar
1 pint cherry tomatoes (peeled)

Combine all ingredients but tomatoes. Pour over peeled, cherry tomatoes. Marinate overnight. Serve on lettuce leaves or may be served alone. (I usually marinate mine in a quart jar in refrigerator. These keep well.) Serves 4-6.

Jean G. Frazell

VEGETABLE SALAD I

1 can French cut beans
1 small can peas
1 sliced onion
1 green pepper, sliced thin
1 can water chestnuts, sliced thin
1 can mushrooms, sliced or stems and
  pieces, amount depends on your
  preference
1 can shoe peg corn

2-3 raw carrots, shredded
cauliflower pieces (a small whole one)
1 cup celery, cut fine
1 can bean sprouts
2½ cups vinegar
2 cups sugar
6 teaspoons salt
pepper
1 cup corn oil

Mix altogether. Store very well covered in refrigerator. Serves a large group of people (16-20).

Mrs. Wallace Stroud
Elton, LA

VEGETABLE SALAD II

1 box frozen, chopped broccoli,
  cooked
1 box brussel sprouts, cooked
1 box cauliflower, cooked
1 can artichoke hearts

1 avocado, chopped
1 pound cherry tomatoes
green onions, chopped
Wishbone Italian Salad Dressing

Boil first 3 vegetables until tender. Drain. Mix all vegetables together. Add dressing and marinate overnight. Serves 10-12.

Phyllis Ledet

ORIENTAL SALAD

2 bunches spinach
2 cans water chestnuts, sliced
4 hard boiled eggs sliced

1 can bean sprouts, well drained
½ pound bacon, fried crisp and
  crumbled

Sweet and Sour Dressing:
1 cup salad oil
¼ cup vinegar
1 medium onion, minced

½ cup sugar
1 tablespoon Worcestershire
⅓ cup catsup

Chill spinach in refrigerator until crisp. Break leaves into small pieces. Combine all ingredients except bacon. Chill. When ready to serve pour on dressing. Sprinkle with bacon. For salad dressing combine all ingredients and shake thoroughly. Serves 12.

Diane Hamsa

BROCCOLI SALAD I

2 bunches broccoli, use only the
    flowerettes and cut into bite size
    pieces
5 hard boiled eggs, chopped fine

¾ cup stuffed olives, sliced
¼ cup green onion tops, chopped
⅓ pound crisp bacon, crumbled

Dressing:
1 cup mayonnasie
½-¾ cup Parmesan cheese

Wishbone Italian salad dressing

To make the dressing, add the Parmesan cheese to the mayonaise. Thin out the dressing with the Wishbone Italian. Begin with 3 ounces then if you like a thinner dressing, add more of the Wishbone. Toss dressing through all the other ingredients except the bacon, which is put on top of the tossed salad. Serves 8.

Mrs. Dan Bereba

BROCCOLI SALAD II

2 boxes chopped, frozen broccoli
1 cup sour cream
¾ cup mayonnaise
1 teaspoon dry mustard
1 small onion, sliced thin

3 tomatoes
salt and pepper
lettuce

Cook broccoli and drain well. Add next 4 ingredients and mix well then refrigerate overnight. Serve on lettuce with sliced tomatoes. Serves 6-8.

Pat McBride Naumann

CAULIFLOWER IN MUSTARD SAUCE

3 large heads cauliflower
salted water
1 cup mayonnaise
1 cup sour cream

2 tablespoons prepared mustard
2 tablespoons lemon juice
½ teaspoon salt
¼ teaspoon white pepper

Cook cauliflower in salted water until tender. Cool in refrigerator. Combine remaining ingredients. When cauliflower is cool, pour sauce over and refrigerate until serving time. Serves 10-12.

Lydia Bacqué

MUSHROOM SALAD IN AVOCADO HALF SHELL

3 avocados
4 boiled egg yolks
4 tablespoons white part only of green
  onion, minced finely
4 teaspoons minced parsley

4 tablespoons olive oil
4 teaspoons red wine vinegar
1 clove garlic, crushed
salt, pepper
1 pound sliced mushrooms

Cut avocados lengthwise, remove seed, and peel. Mash one avocado and egg yolks finely. Blend gently with other ingredients. Add salt and pepper to taste. Pour over mushrooms and mix thoroughly. Place remaining avocado halves on lettuce leaves and fill each with mushroom mixture. Cherry tomatoes make a pretty garnish. You may put avocado, egg yolks, and rest of dressing ingredients with exception of mushrooms through food processor. Serves 4.

Carola Bacqué

RED, WHITE AND GREEN SALAD

5 cups broccoli flowerettes, 2 bunches
2½ cups cauliflower flowerettes,
  1 head

1 onion, chopped
½ pound sliced mushrooms
2 cups cherry tomatoes

Dressing:
1 cup mayonnaise
½ cup sour cream

2 tablespoons vinegar
2 tablespoons sugar

Mix all together except tomatoes. Pour dressing over and mix together. Add salt and pepper to taste. Chill 6 hours. Add tomatoes before serving. Serves 8.

Marianne Schneider

TABBOULEH
(Parsley and cracked wheat salad)

½ cup Number 1 Burghul, crushed
  wheat
3 chopped tomatoes
1 cup finely chopped parsley
1 cup finely chopped onion

⅓ cup freshly squeezed lemon juice
2 teaspoons salt
⅓ cup olive oil
2 tablespoons chopped fresh mint

Wash wheat several times. Squeeze dry or press dry in colander lined with cheese cloth. Add to dry wheat other ingredients. Serve as a salad on leaf of lettuce. Serves 6-8.

Mrs. Norris Landry
Royal Catering

RICE SALAD

4 cups cooked brown rice
¼ cup diced green pepper
2 tablespoons finely chopped green
  onion
3 tablespoons finely chopped radishes
½ cup finely chopped celery

½ cup hot chow chow
1 minced garlic clove
¾ teaspoon nutmeg
1 tablespoon curry
⅛ teaspoon cloves, ground
¼ cup mayonnaise
salt

Combine all ingredients. Mold into bundt pan and chill for 3-4 hours. Serve well chilled. Serves 4-6.

Mrs. E. H. Vallee
Beaumont, TEXAS

TOMORROW FRUIT SALAD

1 (number 2) can pineapple chunks
  drained, reserve juice
1 (11 ounce) can mandarin oranges,
  drained

1 pound large purple grapes
6 ounces miniature marshmallows
1 (1 cup) carton whipping cream
nuts, optional

Dressing:
3 egg yolks
1 teaspoon salt
1 tablespoon white vinegar

2 tablespoons sugar
2 tablespoons pineapple juice

Cook dressing in small saucepan until it thickens. Cool completely. Cut grapes in half and remove seeds. Mix marshmallows, grapes, oranges and pineapple together and keep cold. Whip cream and fold cool dressing into whipped cream. Fold this mixture into fruit combination. Refrigerate overnight. This salad goes well with chicken, pork or ham for buffet dinners. Serve with chicken salad finger sandwiches for a luncheon. Serves 6-8.

Cynthia Dunlap

POTATO SALAD FOR SIXTEEN

8 medium red potatoes, boiled in
  jackets
1½ cups mayonnaise
1 cup sour cream
2 teaspoons horseradish
½ teaspoon salt

½ cup chopped parsley
½ cup diced celery
12 ounce package bacon, fried and
  chopped
1 cup chopped green onions
pepper

Peel and slice potatoes into thin slices and set aside. Mix parsley, onion, celery. In a third container mix mayonnaise and sour cream and horseradish. Now layer potatoes, parsley, onion-celery mixture and then ice layer with the dressing mixture. Top with crumbled bacon. Continue until finished then garnish with remaining bacon. Best when allowed to refrigerate in a tightly covered container for 24 hours. Salt and pepper layers of potatoes. Serves 16.

Mrs. Russell Theard

MOLDED ASPARAGUS SALAD

1 can cream of asparagus soup
3 tablespoons lemon juice
1 tablespoon gelatin
pinch of salt
¼ cup cold water

1 (3 ounce) package cream cheese
¾ cup sour cream
1 (10 ounce) can cut asparagus
¾ cup or more sliced almonds
celery salt, black and red pepper to taste

Heat soup. Stir in lemon juice, gelatin, salt and water. Beat in cream cheese and sour cream. Add celery salt, black and red pepper to taste. Chill. Fold in asparagus and almonds and pour into molds. Let chill until set. Serves 12-16.

Missy Abendroth

RED APPLE SALAD

6 apples
1 cup sugar
½ cup water

1 package cinnamon candy, Red Hots
red food coloring

Stuffing:
1 small package cream cheese
¼-½ cup fine chopped pecans
¼-½ cup fine chopped raisins

few drops lemon juice
milk

Peel and core apples. In saucepan boil sugar, water and candy until all candy melts. Add red food coloring and 2-3 apples at a time at slow boil until tender. Set aside in large pyrex dish to cool. Pour extra syrup over all to glaze. Mix stuffing ingredients with small amount of milk to desired consistency. Stuff each apple and refrigerate. Serve on lettuce. Serves 6.

Mrs. John Tolson, III

RED, WHITE AND GREEN CONGEALED SALAD

Bottom Layer:

1 package raspberry Jello
1 package frozen raspberries, thawed

1 cup boiling water
¾ cup raspberry juice

Second Layer:

1 cup coffee cream
½ cup sugar
1 package gelatin-¼ cup water

1 cup sour cream
1 teaspoon vanilla

Third Layer:

1 package lime Jello
1 cup boiling water
1 small can crushed pineapple,
   juice reserved

1 banana sliced
2 heaping tablespoons sour cream

Dissolve raspberry Jello in 1 cup boiling water and scant ¾ cup raspberry juice drained from thawed raspberries. After cool, add raspberries; pour in mold and when set, heat together cream and sugar, but do not boil. Dissolve 1 package plain gelatin in ¼ cup cold water. Add to warm cream and stir. When cool, add 1 cup sour cream, 1 teaspoon vanilla and beat well. Pour this on top of bottom layer. Let set. Dissolve lime Jello in 1 cup boiling water and scant ¾ cup pineapple juice drained from can of pineapple and then pineapple. Beat in sour cream, add sliced banana. Add this third layer and let set. Serves 8.

Priscilla Shepherd

CRIMSON CREME SALAD

Creme Jello Layer:

1 (3 ounce) package lemon Jello
1½ cups boiling water
1 (8 ounce) package cream cheese,
   room temperature

1 teaspon vanilla
3 tablespoons powdered sugar

Crimson Jello Layer:

1 (3 ounce) package strawberry Jello
1 cup boiling water
1 pound fresh cranberries
2 cubed, seeded, unpeeled oranges, or
   other fruits if preferred

2 (10 ounce) packages canned or frozen
   cranberry orange relish may be substituted for cranberries and oranges

In a small container dissolve lemon Jello in water. Cool. With electric mixer, in large bowl, mix cream cheese, vanilla and powdered sugar. Beat on low setting the cooled Jello (not set) mixture into cheese mixture and mold until firm. After creme layer is set, 4-5 hours, dissolve strawberry Jello in water. Cool. Make cranberry orange relish or use thawed 10 ounce package by grinding oranges and cranberries in blender, ½ cup at a time. Add to cooled Jello mixture and pour over creme layer and allow to set 5-6 hours or overnight. Serves 8-10.

Helen Nugier Sobiesk

CRANBERRY SALAD

1 package Knox gelatin
2 small or 1 large package cherry jello
1 large can crushed pineapple
1 can Royal Ann cherries
juice from canned fruit plus enough orange juice to make 4 cups, if needed

½ cup chopped pecans
juice from 1 lemon and 1 orange
dash of salt
1½ cups sugar
1 pound fresh cranberries

Dressing:
2 beaten egg yolks
½ cup sugar
½ teaspoon salt
¼ cup lemon juice

1 teaspoon grated lemon rind
1 tablespoon vinegar
1 tablespoon butter
1 cup whipping cream, whipped

Dissolve gelatin in ½ cup of canned fruit juice. Heat remaining of liquid and pour over jello. Add dissolved gelatin. Grind cranberries in blender with lemon and orange juice. Cook cranberries with sugar and dash of salt for about 10 minutes. Add chopped pecans and mix all ingredients together and pour into 4 foil Christmas tree molds or large dish and congeal.

Dressing: Cook egg yolks, sugar, salt, lemon juice, lemon rind, and vinegar in double boiler or heavy saucepan until thick. Add butter. Cool. Add whipped cream. Decorate top of salad with dressing. If serving from large dish, cut squares and place on lettuce leaves and garnish with cherry. Serves 10-12.

Marianne Schneider

BLACK CHERRY MOLD

1½ (3 ounce) packages cream cheese
few drops lemon juice
cream and salt
1 (number 2) can black cherries
½ cup cherry juice
3 tablespoons unflavored gelatin

½ cup sherry or port
1 (3 ounce) package black cherry Jello
1 cup boiling water
1 cup pecan halves

Soften cream cheese with lemon juice and cream. Season with salt. Drain cherries reserving liquid. Pit and stuff with cream cheese. Dissolve Jello in 1 cup boiling water. Add cherry juice and sherry. Chill. Just before gelatin is set, add cherries and pecans. Use medium salad mold. Serves 6.

Brenda B. Hawes

BING CHERRY SALAD

1 (3 ounce) package lemon jello
½ cup boiling water
1 cup evaporated milk
¼ cup celery, chopped
1 (8 ounce) package cream cheese

1 (3½ ounce) package black cherry jello
½ cup boiling water
1 can black pitted bing cherries plus
    juice
½ cup chopped pecans

Dissolve lemon jello in boiling water; add milk, chopped celery and cheese. Beat with mixer until smooth. Pour into dish and refrigerate until firm. Dissolve cherry jello in boiling water then add cherries with juice and pecans. Pour this mixture over first very carefully. Let chill until firm then cut into squares. This is delightful for any holiday menu. Children love it. Serves 8.

Mrs. E. B. Mercer, III

TOSTADO SALAD

1½ pounds ground meat
½ teaspoon salt
½ teaspoon pepper
1 tablespoon Pickapeppa Sauce
pinch garlic
1 (1 pound) can undrained kidney
    beans

1 head lettuce, shredded
2 tomatoes, coarsely chopped
2 avocados, coarsely chopped
2 onions, coarsely chopped
3 cups shredded cheddar cheese
1 large bag Doritos, crushed

Dressing:
1 cup Thousand Island

1 cup chili sauce

Season beef with next 4 ingredients and sauté in large skillet until brown, add undrained beans and simmer covered for 10 minutes. Set aside to cool. Place lettuce in large salad bowl. Arrange tomatoes, avocado and onions and cheese attractively around edge of lettuce in mounds. Heap cooled meat mixture in center. Just prior to serving toss with dressing and crushed Doritos. (Blend Thousand Island and chili sauce.) May vary amount of dressing to suit taste. Leftovers very good the next day. We serve this with Nachos made from homemade bean dip—1 can refried beans, ¼ cup chili sauce, 2 dashes of Tabasco. We reserve some of the flat, unbroken chips from the above recipe. Top with slice of jalapeno pepper, bean dip and shredded cheese. Bake at 350° until cheese melts. Top with sour cream just before serving. Serve hot. Serves 10-12.

Marcee Hoffpauir

CRAWFISH OR SHRIMP SALAD

1 pound cooked shrimp or crawfish
  tails
4 hard-cooked eggs
2 stalks celery, chopped
6 midget gherkins, chopped
6 green olives, chopped, optional

1 cup homemade mayonnaise
1 tablespoon Coleman's dry mustard
1 teaspoon salt
½ teaspoon cayenne
1 teaspoon Worcestershire
½ teaspoon onion salt

Combine all ingredients in order listed and blend well. Correct seasoning and serve on bed of lettuce or in tomatoes or avocados. Serves 4-6.

Kathryn Leonard

CRAB SALAD OR SPREAD

2 (7½ ounce) cans crabmeat, drained
  (frozen will do, drained)
1 package small frozen peas, cooked
  according to directions and drained
1 cup cooked rice, you may add up to
  two cups of rice

½ cup green onion, chopped
3 stalks celery, chopped
½ cup sour cream
1 cup mayonnaise
1 tablespoon Salad Supreme seasoning
1 tablespoon fresh lemon juice

Mix all ingredients together and salt and pepper to taste. Prepare and refrigerate at least 24 hours before serving. Serve with crackers or on lettuce as a salad. Serves 6-8.

Mrs. Frank Annweiler
Houston, TX

SHRIMP SALAD

2 hard-cooked eggs
½ cup mayonnaise
1 tablespoon lemon juice
dash Worcestershire
3 cups cooked, cleaned shrimp, cut
  into pieces

1 cup chopped celery
1 cup grated apple
1 teaspoon chopped chives
1 teaspoon salt
lettuce leaves

Chop 1 hard-cooked egg; reserve other egg for garnish. Blend mayonnaise, lemon juice and Worcestershire sauce in bowl. Add chopped egg and all remaining ingredients except the lettuce. Toss lightly. Serve in lettuce lined bowl. Garnish with hard-cooked egg. Serves 6-8.

Mrs. Owen B. Hawes

MARINATED SHRIMP SALAD

1 head raw cauliflower, broken up
3 pounds cooked shrimp, peeled
3 onions, sliced
1 can drained mushrooms
1 cup cooking oil

¼ cup vinegar
3 teaspoons yellow mustard
2 tablespoons lemon pepper
2 tablespoons season-all
2 tablespoons garlic powder

Pour hot shrimp over onions and mushrooms. Let cool slightly. Add remaining ingredients. Refrigerate overnight, stirring 2-3 times. Serve over lettuce leaf. Serves 6-8.

Brenda Trahan

CREAMY SHRIMP MOLD

1 cup cream of mushroom soup,
    undiluted
2 (3 ounce) packages cream cheese
1 envelope gelatin, softened in 3
    tablespoons water
4 shallots, minced
3 pounds shrimp, cooked, peeled
    and coarsely chopped

1 cup finely chopped celery
1 cup mayonnaise
1 tablespoon lemon juice
Tabasco to taste
1 pound crabmeat, optional

Heat soup, mix in softened cream cheese until melted. Remove from heat. Stir in softened gelatin until dissolved. Add remaining ingredients and blend thoroughly. Turn into greased mold and chill until firm. Serves 6 for lunch. Can be used as party dish and served with crackers.

Tolley Davis

MOLDED TUNA SALAD

2 (6 ounce) cans tuna
2 hard-cooked eggs, chopped
½ cup chopped stuffed olives
1 tablespoon minced onion or chives

2 tablespoons plain gelatin
½ cup cold water
2 cups mayonnaise
red pepper to taste

Lightly grease fish mold or individual molds with salad oil and drain. Mince tuna with eggs, olives and onion. Soften gelatin in water for 5 minutes. Dissolve over hot water and add mayonnaise, gradually, stirring constantly. Fold into fish mold. Turn mold and chill until firm. Unmold on lettuce. Serves 6-8.

Mrs. Paula Maxwell

CRAWFISH SALAD

¾ jar (5¾ ounce) Louisiana Creole
   Mustard
¾ cup oil
½ cup vinegar
2 tablespoons paprika

6 green onions, chopped fine
4 teaspoons horseradish mustard
3 pounds crawfish, cooked
3 pounds crawfish tails, peeled
   and cooked
lettuce

Mix all ingredients. Pour over the crawfish and let stand in the refrigerator over-night. Serves 8.

Mrs. John Tolson, III

SEATTLE SALAD

4 ribs celery, cut Chinese style
1 can heart of palm, sliced

2 heads bibb lettuce, torn
½ jar chopped macadamia nuts

Dressing:
⅓ cup salad oil
2 tablespoons lemon juice
1 teaspoon sugar
½ teaspoon salt
½ teaspoon bitters

¼ teaspoon paprika
2 tablespoons chopped green olives
1 tablespoon chopped onions
2 tablespoons poppy seeds

Combine celery, hearts of palm, lettuce and macadamia nuts and toss with dressing. Serves 10-12.

Paula Palmer

DIFFERENT POTATO SALAD

1 cup sour cream
2 tablespoons wine vinegar
1 tablespoon prepared mustard
2 teaspoons granulated sugar
1½ teaspoons salt
½ teaspoon pepper

½ teaspoon caraway seeds
4 cups diced, cooked potatoes, about 4
   medium potatoes
½ small cucumber, chopped
2 small onions, chopped

In a large bowl, blend sour cream, vinegar, mustard, sugar, salt, pepper and caraway seeds. Add remaining ingredients; toss gently until well mixed. Refrigerate to develop flavors until serving. Serve on crisp greens. The caraway seeds and sour cream give new flavor to this potato salad recipe. Serves 8.

Mrs. Frank P. Danna

ORANGE DRESSING

2 tablespoons orange juice, fresh
1½ tablespoons wine vinegar
½ teaspoon fresh lemon juice
2 teaspoons sugar
½ teaspoon salt

¼ teaspoon prepared mustard
½ teaspoon prepared horseradish
1 teaspoon grated fresh orange rind
2 tablespoons olive or salad oil
½ clove garlic

Beat ingredients in bowl. Let stand 30 minutes and remove garlic. Good on any fruit salad, but "special" with ½ papaya filled with pineapple and crabmeat or shrimp.

Patricia T. Olson

CREME DE CASSIS FRUIT SALAD DRESSING

1 cup sour cream
1 (8 ounce) package cream cheese
½ cup creme de Cassis

¼ cup powdered sugar or more to taste
1 cup heavy cream, whipped

Mix first 4 ingredients and fold in whipped cream. Yield: 3½ to 4 cups.

Marilyn Tarpy

DRESSING FOR GREEN SALAD

2 hard boiled eggs, chopped
1 cup mayonnaise
2 tablespoons ice water
1 tablespoon Parmesan cheese

¼ teaspoon creole seasoning
¼ teaspoon garlic salt
1 teaspoon chopped parsley

Mix ingredients in order given. This may be mixed by hand or in a blender. After the dressing is mixed, store in a jar or covered container in refrigerator. Keeps about a week. Serve on mixed greens. Seasoning may be altered according to taste. Serves 6.

Sally M. Chappuis

ONION-SOUR CREAM DRESSING

1¾ cups sour cream
½ teaspoon sugar
⅛ teaspoon pepper
2 tablespoons cider vinegar

1½ teaspoons prepared mustard
½ cup grated onion, or pureed
½ cup sliced ripe olives

Combine all ingredients and refrigerate. Yield: 2½ cups.

Lydia Bacqué

POPPY SEED SALAD DRESSING

1 cup honey
⅓ cup wine vinegar
⅓ cup fresh lemon juice
1 teaspoon salt

2 teaspoons prepared mustard
½ of 1 medium onion
2½ cups vegetable oil
5 teaspoons poppy seeds

Combine honey, vinegar, lemon juice, salt, mustard and onion in electric blender. Blend until onion is well grated. Stir in oil very slowly until well blended. Add poppy seeds. Store in covered container in refrigerator. Yield: 4 cups.

Ramona Mouton

ROQUEFORT CHEESE DRESSING

½ clove garlic, minced
1 cup mayonnaise
1¼ ounces Roquefort cheese
¼ cup lemon juice

¼ teaspoon Worcestershire
¼ teaspoon pepper sauce
1 (6 ounce) can evaporated milk, chilled
    and icy

Combine all ingredients except milk. Chill 30 minutes. Beat milk until peaks form. Fold into cheese mixture. Yield: 2½ cups.

Carole H. Bond
Baton Rouge, LA

HOMEMADE MAYONNAISE

3 eggs
3 teaspoons Coleman's dry mustard
3 teaspoons salt
3 teaspoons sugar

½ teaspoon cayenne
¼ teaspoon Tabasco
38 ounces oil
juice of 1 lemon

Blend first six ingredients in processor or electric mixer. Slowly add ½ of the oil and blend thoroughly. Add lemon juice and then continue to slowly blend remaining oil until mayonnaise consistency is reached. Correct seasoning and refrigerate. Yield: 1½ quarts.

Kathryn Leonard

HOT BAKED CHICKEN SALAD

1 stick butter
1 cup chopped shallots or green
   onions
1 cup sliced fresh mushrooms (may
   use canned)
1 cup chopped pecans or almonds
salt
1 teaspoon lemon pepper marinade
1 cup chicken broth
4 cups chopped, cooked chicken
½ cup mayonnaise
1 (12 ounce) package Philadelphia cream
   cheese

Sauté mushrooms and onions or shallots in butter. Add pecans and salt and lemon pepper. Add chicken broth, saved from boiling chicken. Add chopped chicken and mayonnaise. Add cream cheese and blend well. Spoon into casserole and bake at 350° for 30 minutes. May use a topping such as French fried onion rings or crushed chips of your choice. May be served hot or cold. Good for ladies luncheon. Serves 6-8.

Marilyn Hoffpauir

CHICKEN SALAD A LA PÊCHE

½ cup herb seasoned stuffing mix
¼ cup Italian salad dressing
1 clove pressed garlic
1 cup diced cucumber or celery
¼ cup mayonnaise
½ cup sour cream
½ teaspoon thyme
¼ teaspoon basil
¼ teaspoon salt
2 cups diced, cooked chicken
8 peace halves or pineapple rings

Combine first 3 ingredients and cook in small skillet and chill. Mix remaining ingredients and chill. When ready to serve, combine all ingredients and serve on peach halves or pineapple rings. Keep separate until ready to serve. Serves 8.

Marjorie S. Bray

MAYONNAISE

1 egg
1 teaspoon salt
1 teaspoon sugar
1 teaspoon prepared mustard
dash Worcestershire
1 pint vegetable oil
2 tablespoons lemon juice

Into a medium-size bowl put first 5 ingredients. Stir just to mix well. With mixer on medium speed, slowly add all of oil, beating until real thick. Delicious on fresh summer tomatoes. Yield: 1½ pints.

Mrs. John A. Bolin

FISH FRYING AT PIERRE PART

The Acadians came from Canada to South Louisiana with many skills such as hunting, fishing, and trapping. They thrived on the fresh-water and salt-water fish found along the coast of Louisiana. Little has changed in methods of finding and catching fish, but a lot has changed in the methods of preparation.

A modern fish fry is much like a Bar-B-Que in other parts of the United States. The Cajun of today has a butane burner and all the equipment for frying fish as well as boiling crawfish and crabs. As I show, this is usually a meal prepared by the men of the family. One of the major items necessary for a good fish fry, is an ice chest full of beer.

FRUITS AND VEGETABLES

HOT FRUIT CASSEROLE

butter
8 bananas, sliced
3 cans pear halves, drained
1 can stewed apples
1 can whole berry cranberry sauce

2 cups brown sugar
1-2 teaspooons cinnamon or curry
  powder
½ stick butter, melted
1 teaspoon lemon juice

Preheat oven to 350°. Rub casserole with butter. Place all fruit in a 3 quart casserole. Mix sugar with cinnamon or curry powder. Add to melted butter with lemon juice. Pour over fruit. Bake at 350° for 25-30 minutes. Serves 14.

Marion M. McDade

SPICED CHERRIES

1 (28 ounce) jar maraschino cherries
⅔ cup white vinegar
1½ cups sugar
½ teaspoon powdered ginger

1 tablespoon whole cloves
½ lemon, cut in slices
2-3 sticks cinnamon

Drain cherries, reserve syrup. Place syrup and next 3 ingredients in a saucepan and boil for approximately 15 minutes. Cool. Pour syrup in jars, add cherries, lemon slices, cloves and cinnamon sticks. Cover tightly. Let stand at least a week before using. Serve with orange slices as a garnish for Old Fashions. Pretty as a decoration for poultry, veal or pork.

Mable Roy Hawkins

PEACHES AND CARROTS

2 jars whole baby carrots
1 jar spiced peaches
½ cup brown sugar

¼ cup brandy
½ cup pecans
parsley

Drain carrots—set aside. Drain peaches and reserve liquid and blend it with brown sugar. Bring this to a slow boil and cook until reduced and thickened. Add brandy. Arrange carrots and peaches in 13 inch casserole. Sprinkle pecans over all. Pour liquid over dish and bake at 350° for 30 minutes. Garnish with parsley. Serves 6-8.

Margaret Leonard
Redlands, California

CRUDITES

broccoli—tiny flowerettes
carrots—slivers or iced curls
cauliflower—tiny flowerettes
celery—slivers, long slim fingers or
  iced curls
Chinese cabbage—halved, stalks or
  rolled up leaf sections
cucumbers—peeled, long fingers or
  sliced
mushrooms—fresh sliced lengthwise

green onions—tiny ends trimmed only
kohlrabi—peeled, sliced
radishes—lengthwise quarters
snow peas—whole and crisp
squash—yellow crookneck summer, tiny,
  thick unpeeled slices
tomatoes—cherry, or tiny pear whole
turnips—tiny peeled or not, sliced thin
zucchini—small, thick unpeeled slices

Bleu Cheese Sauterne Spread:
½ pound Danish bluc cheese,
  crumbled
1 (3 ounce) package cream cheese
¼ cup Sauterne

1 teaspoon Worcestershire
¼ peeled and chopped clove garlic
¼ cup chopped parsley

Place Danish and cream cheese in blender. Blend until smooth. Add other ingredients. Blending well. Refrigerate covered up to 3 days, if desired. Remove from refrigerator 1 hour before serving. Serve with fresh vegetables.

Mayers Caterers

ARTICHOKE CASSEROLE

1 large onion, chopped
½ cup olive oil
5 cloves garlic
2 cans French style green beans

2 cans artichoke hearts
1 cup Parmesan cheese
1½ cups Italian Progresso bread crumbs
salt and pepper

Sauté onions in oil, add garlic. Drain beans, rinse in hot water. Chop artichokes and beans, mix. Add other ingredients. If dry add more olive oil. Put in casserole and sprinkle with bread crumbs. Bake at 350° for 30 minutes. Serves 8-10.

Sue Billet Dinkins

BROCCOLI-ARTICHOKE MARINADE

3 boxes broccoli, cooked according to
  package directions
3 cans artichoke hearts, heated
  and drained
1 medium jar pimento pieces,
  heated and drained

make a dressing of olive oil, vinegar, salt
  and pepper; or use bottled Italian
  dressing
2 hard cooked eggs, sliced for garnish
paprika

Arrange hot vegetables in casserole dish. Heat dressing and pour over vegetables, mix gently. Garnish with egg slices and sprinkle with paprika. Serve immediately. If prepared early in the day, reheat in 325° oven for 25 minutes. Serves 12-14.

Marion M. McDade

STUFFED ARTICHOKES

8-10 artichokes, washed and drained
2 cups ground ham
2 cups Italian bread crumbs
1 cup grated Romano cheese
1 bunch parsley, chopped
3 cloves pressed garlic

1 lemon, sliced
water
2 teaspoons salt
2 teaspoons lemon juice
2 teaspoons olive oil

Mix ground ham, bread crumbs, parsley, cheese and garlic. Stuff each leaf and middle. Take lemon slices and twist on top. Place artichokes in Dutch oven with about 1 inch water. Season water with salt, olive oil and lemon juice. Dribble each one with water and cover and let water come to a boil. Simmer, still covered for 1 hour. Fill cooking syringe with liquid from Dutch oven and dribble 3-4 times while cooking for 30-45 minutes longer. Mixture can be stored in the freezer and used as needed. Serves 8-10.

Bern Lank

ASPARAGUS HANEMANN

Asparagus, cooked
bacon strips

sharp cheddar cheese

Figure on 5 thin or 3 thick cooked asparagus. (Canned is fine.) Make bunches of asparagus by wrapping 3 or 5 with one strip of lean bacon. Put one fine strip of sharp cheddar cheese across bacon on each bunch. Heat in 350° oven for 25 minutes. Serve two bunches per plate.

Louis Hanemann

GREEN BEANS TURKISH STYLE

2 pounds green beans, fresh
2 onions, finely chopped
2 tomatoes, chopped
salt to taste

1 cup (8 ounce) olive oil
6 cups water
1 teaspoon sugar

Wash and trim beans. Put beans, onions, tomatoes and salt in pan and stir well. Add olive oil and 1 cup water. Cover and cook over high heat for 30 minutes, stirring occasionally. Add 5 cups water and 1 teaspoon sugar and continue cooking until beans are tender. Let cool in pot and serve. Serves 8-10.

Pat Ferris Vickery

GREEN BEANS IN SOUR CREAM

2 cans drained green beans
1 (8 ounce) Wishbone Italian dressing
1 teaspoon salt
1 teaspoon pepper
1 large chopped onion
1 (8 ounce) carton sour cream

½ cup mayonnaise
1 teaspoon lemon juice
2 teaspoons chopped chives
¼ teaspoon dry mustard
1 tablespoon horseradish
1 small grated onion

Marinate overnight—green beans in Italian dressing along with salt, pepper and chopped onion. Cover. Next day drain beans and cover with the remaining ingredients. Serves 4-6.

Sally Chow

BARBECUE GREEN BEANS

2 cans whole green beans
8 strips bacon

toothpicks
barbecue sauce

Barbecue Sauce:
1 small can tomato paste
¼ cup butter
2 tablespoons brown sugar
¼ teaspoon garlic
½ teaspoon liquid smoke
2 tablespoons Worcestershire

2 teaspoons prepared mustard
1 teaspoon onion juice
½ teaspoon salt
¼ teaspoon black pepper
dash Tabasco

Drain beans. Wrap ½ strip of bacon around bundle of beans. Secure bacon with toothpick. Place in flat casserole or skillet.
Barbecue Sauce: Combine all ingredients and cook slowly for 10 minutes. Pour barbecue sauce over beans and cook 20-25 minutes on medium heat. Serves 6-8.

Patricia D. Low

DILL BEAN CASSEROLE

2 cans string beans, undrained
1 teaspoon dill seed

2 strips bacon
cracker crumbs

Sauce:
1 stick margarine
6 tablespoons flour
1½ teaspoons black pepper
2 teaspoons salt

2-3 drops Tabasco
1 cup milk
1 cup dill seed juice from beans

Cook beans, dill seed and bacon together for 30 minutes. Drain beans, reserve liquid. Make sauce as follows: Place all sauce ingredients in pot. Stir over low heat until well blended. Mix with beans and pour into casserole. Top with cracker crumbs and bake at 350° for 30 minutes. Serves 8-10.

Mrs. Virginia C. Naremore
Baton Rouge, LA

RUBY BEETS

4 tablespoons cornstarch
2 tablespoons sugar
¼ teaspoon salt

1⅓ cups cranberry juice
1 can sliced beets, drained

Mix first 3 ingredients together over medium heat. Add cranberry juice and cook until thickened. Pour over drained beets and marinate overnight. Serve warm or cool. Serves 4.

Margaret Leonard
Redlands, California

EASY BROCCOLI MOLD

2 packages frozen chopped broccoli,
    cooked and drained well
1 cup mayonnaise
1 tablespoon butter

1 tablespoon flour
3 eggs
1 cup light cream
2 teaspoons salt

Preheat oven to 350°. Mix cooked broccoli, mayonnaise and butter while broccoli is still hot. Sprinkle the flour over the top. Beat 3 eggs until light and add to the above. Add light cream and salt. Mix all ingredients thoroughly and pour into greased ring mold or casserole dish. Place in a pan of water and bake uncovered for 30-40 minutes or until knife inserted in center comes out clean. Serves 6.

Mrs. Chelsea Brindley
Oakdale, La.

BROCCOLI CASSEROLE

2 boxes chopped broccoli or 6 cups
    cubed zucchini
1 medium onion, chopped
1 can cream of chicken soup
1 carton sour cream, 8 ounces

2 cups shredded carrots
1 (8 ounce) package herb seasoned
    stuffing
½ pound butter, melted

Cook broccoli with onion in salted water. Fold together broccoli, soup, cream and carrots. Check seasoning; mix stuffing and butter; put ½ mixture in bottom of casserole, 9x12 inch, then all of broccoli mixture. Top with other half of stuffing. Bake for 25-30 minutes at 350°. Freezes beautifully. Serves 8-10.

Annelle Heckert

PASTA WITH BROCCOLI AND PINE NUTS

Sauce:
1 bunch broccoli (flowerets)   3 cloves garlic, minced
salt   ½ teaspoon basil
1 (2 ounce) can anchovies with oil   ½ cup pine nuts
½ cup olive oil

Pasta:
1 pound spaghetti, linguine or   ¼ cup freshly grated Parmesan cheese
    noodles of your choice
3 quarts salted, boiling water, to
    which 1 teaspoon olive oil has been
    added

Preheat oven to 350°. Cook broccoli in boiling water until just tender. Refresh under cold running water and set aside. Heat olive oil and oil from anchovies. Add anchovies. Stir until anchovies dissolve. Add garlic and cook for 3 minutes. Add basil and stir a few minutes more, being careful not to brown garlic. Set aside. Place pine nuts in 350° oven for 15 minutes or until nuts are golden brown. Remove from oven and set aside. Cook pasta until al dente or about 10 minutes. Reheat sauce and add broccoli to mixture. Drain and rinse pasta and combine with broccoli mixture. Season to taste. Sprinkle with pine nuts and cheese and serve. Serves 6 generously.

Carola Bacqué

BRUSSEL SPROUTS

1 package frozen Brussel sprouts   ½ cup Parmesan cheese
1 cup heavy cream, unwhipped   salt and pepper

Cook and drain the sprouts. Heat the cream and add the cheese. Pour over the sprouts and serve. Serves 2-4.

Pat Lindsey

DELICIOUS COOKED CABBAGE

4 cups cut cabbage   1 teaspoon paprika
½ cup bacon fat   1 tablespoon minced onions
1 teaspoon salt   ½ cup sour cream

Preheat oven to 350°. Sauté cut cabbage in bacon fat for 5 minutes. Add all other ingredients except the sour cream. Pour in baking dish. Pour sour cream over the top. Bake at 350° for 30 minutes. This is delicious! Serves 5-6.

Mrs. Frank P. Danna

LOOSE CABBAGE ROLLS

1½ pounds ground beef
1 large onion, chopped
½ bell pepper, chopped
2 ribs celery, chopped
½ cup raw rice

salt
pepper
1 head cabbage, sliced
1 (12 ounce) can V-8 juice, more for more
   tomato taste

Sauté first four ingredients until meat is brown. Remove from heat; add rice; salt and pepper heavily. Layer sliced cabbage, meat mixture in a 2 quart casserole. Pour V-8 juice over top. Cover and cook in a 350° oven for 1½ hours. Great food processor recipe. Serves 8.

Lesleen C. Owen

GREEK CARROTS

1 pound carrots
butter

6 ounces sour cream
chopped chives or parsley

Cut one pound of carrots into julienne strips. Sauté in butter until slightly soft. When soft, fold in sour cream and sprinkle with finely chopped chives or parsley. Garnish with parsley. Serves 4-6.

Louis Hanemann

CARROT CASSEROLE

1 large cooking onion
1 large green pepper
3 bunches carrots
1 teaspoon sugar

½ cup cream, Half & Half
seasoning salt to taste
½ pound American cheese, grated

Preheat oven to 350°. Saute onion and green pepper, chopped very fine in frying pan. In another pot cook carrots, chopped and mash. Mix all ingredients and mix in ½ pound of American cheese. Bake in the oven at 350° for about 20 minutes. Serves 4-6.

Mrs. John H. Crump

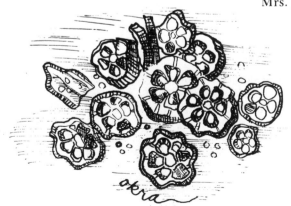

CARROTS ELEGANTE

2 pounds carrots, pared, cut
   crosswise into thin slices
½ cup butter or margarine
1 tablespoon sugar

1 teaspoon celery seeds
½ teaspoon salt
½ cup orange juice

Heat all ingredients except orange juice in 2 quart saucepan over medium heat until butter melts; reduce heat. Simmer covered, stirring occasionally, 10 minutes. Stir in orange juice; simmer covered until carrots are tender, about 5 minutes.

Micro directions: Place carrots, ⅓ cup butter and the sugar in a 2 quart glass baking dish; microwave covered on full power, stirring after 5 minutes. Add ½ teaspoon celery seeds, the salt and orange juice. Let stand covered 3 minutes. Serves 8.

Mrs. Edwin Preis, Jr.

DILL CARROTS

2 tablespoons salt
1 teaspoon sugar
½ teaspoon red pepper, more if
   desired
2 teaspoons dill seed

1 large onion sliced in rings
2 large garlic buds, crushed
6 carrots
1 cup water
1 cup vinegar

In a quart jar mix first 6 ingredients. Clean, wash and dry carrots and pack tightly in jar. Boil water and vinegar together. Pour over carrots and mix well. Cool in refrigerator. Serves 2, as a vegetable or 6-8 as a crudite.

Bill Fuller
Kinder, LA

CAULIFLOWER AND BROCCOLI CASSEROLE

1 small cauliflower or ½ large one
1 small bunch of broccoli or ½ large
   one
1 cup water
½ cup milk

½ stick butter
2 tablespoons flour
½ cup to ¾ cup grated cheese
salt and pepper to taste
Hi Ho or Ritz crackers

Cut cauliflower into flowerettes and cook. Cook and drain cut up broccoli. Place vegetables in casserole dish. Make a cream sauce with water, milk, flour, salt, butter and cheese. Cook until it comes to a boil and pour over vegetables. Add pepper and crush crackers on top. Heat at 350° for 20-25 minutes and serve. Serves 6-8.

Mrs. Eugene P. Cella

CAULIFLOWER AU GRATIN

1 large or 2 small to medium heads
   of cauliflower
2 tablespoons butter
2 tablespoons flour
1 pinch each of thyme, nutmeg, salt
   and cayenne pepper

1 bay leaf
2½ cups milk
4 tablespoons grated Parmesan cheese
1 cup grated Gruyere cheese
½ cup bread crumbs

Prepare bechamel sauce by melting the butter in a saucepan and adding the flour off the heat and stirring until butter absorbs flour. Add a pinch of thyme, nutmeg, salt and cayenne pepper to taste. Return to heat and add milk and bay leaf. Stir over medium heat until the sauce boils. Reduce heat and allow sauce to simmer for 45 minutes or until it is reduced by about one-half. Remove bay leaf and strain through a fine-meshed strainer. Prepare the cauliflower by removing the flowerettes and boiling in salted water for 8-9 minutes. Drain in a colander and cool by running cold water over. Place the finished bechamel sauce, the cooked cauliflower and the cheeses in a bowl and mix thoroughly. Place the mixture in a buttered souffle dish or casserole, sprinkle top with bread crumbs, dot with butter and bake at 375° for 45 minutes. Serves 6.

CORN FRITTERS

1 cup cream style corn
¾ cup flour
1 teaspoon sugar
dash of pepper

2 teaspoons baking powder
½ teaspoon salt
1 tablespoon melted butter
1 egg, beaten
oil for frying

Add all measured, sifted and mixed dry ingredients to corn in a bowl. Add beaten egg then melted butter. Pour an inch or so of oil into skillet and heat to frying temperature. Drop batter by teaspoonful into oil. Turn to brown. Drain on a paper towel and serve hot. This makes a nice puffy corn dish to any meal. Yield 10-15 fritters.

Marilyn Tankersley Taylor

CORN DELIGHT

margarine
1 small onion, minced
½ bell pepper, minced
1 can cream style corn
1 can whole kernel corn, drained

1 can Rotel tomatoes, drained
1 cube chicken bouillon
½ teaspoon Accent
dash of sugar

Grease saucepan, sauté onion and bell pepper, then add rest of ingredients. Break Rotel tomatoes into pieces and add to corn. Cook down over medium-low heat at least ½ hour or more until thick. Serves 6-8.

Karen G. Jones

HOT CORN CASSEROLE

1 medium onion, chopped fine
margarine
1 ½ tablespoons onion soup mix, dry
⅓ can Rotel tomatoes

2 cans white corn or shoe peg
1 small can cream style corn
pinch of sugar
½ cup grated cheddar cheese

Sauté onion in small amount of margarine. Add onion soup. Add ⅓ can of Rotel tomatoes. Stir well and add corn. Simmer about 5 minutes. Add pinch of sugar. Put in casserole and top with grated cheese. Cook for 20-25 minutes in 300° oven. This can be frozen. Good with Mexican food. Serves 6-8.

Mrs. Gladys Martin
Oakdale, LA

CORN AND OKRA CREOLE

⅓ cup bacon drippings
1 cup chopped green peppers
½ cup chopped green onion
1 clove garlic, chopped finely
1 cup corn

1 cup sliced okra
2 tomatoes, peeled, seeded, chopped
¼ teaspoon thyme
salt and pepper
Tabasco

Sauté pepper, onion and garlic until soft. Add rest of ingredients and simmer, mixture covered, for 20-30 minutes. Serves 4. May garnish with chopped bacon.

Carola Bacqué

BRAISED CUCUMBERS

¼ cup margarine or butter
1 tablespoon sugar
½ teaspoon salt
2 large cucumbers, peeled and cut
   into 2 inch pieces
1 medium onion, chopped

2 tomatoes, quartered
¼ cup water
1 teaspoon lemon juice
¼ teaspoon dill weed
½ cup sour cream

Melt margarine in large sauce pan. Add sugar and salt; cook until lightly browned. Add cucumbers and onion. Cook, stirring constantly, until onions are transparent. Add water, tomatoes, lemon juice, and dill weed. Cook 10-12 minutes. Stir in sour cream. Serve immediately. Serves 4.

Mrs. Dennis J. Vidrine

EGGPLANT PARMIGIANA

2 tablespoons butter
½ cup chopped onion
1 clove garlic, crushed
1 pound ground chuck
1 can (17 ounce) Italian style or
    stewed tomatoes
1 (6 ounce) can tomato paste
2 teaspoons dried oregano leaves
1 teaspoon dried basil
1½ teaspoons salt
¼ teaspoon pepper

1 tablespoon brown sugar
1 cup water
1 large eggplant (1½ pounds)
2 eggs, slightly beaten
1 tablespoon water
½ cup Progresso bread crumbs, Italian
1¼ cups grated Parmesan cheese
¼ cup olive oil
1 (8 ounce) package Mozzarella cheese,
    sliced

In hot butter in large skillet, sauté onion, garlic, and ground chuck until meat is no longer red—about 5 minutes. Add tomatoes, tomato paste, oregano, basil, salt, pepper, brown sugar and 1 cup water. Bring to boil. Reduce heat and simmer uncovered 20 minutes. Add seasonings to taste if necessary. Meanwhile, preheat oven to 350°. Lightly grease a 13x9x2 inch baking dish. Wash eggplant, *do not peel.* Cut crosswise into slices ½ inch thick. In a pie plate combine eggs and 1 tablespoon water, mix well. On a sheet of wax paper combine bread crumbs with ½ cup Parmesan cheese. Mix well. Dip eggplant slices into egg mixture coating well. Then dip into crumbs mixture coating evenly. Sauté eggplant slices a few at a time in 1 tablespoon hot olive oil until crisp and both sides are golden brown. (Add more olive oil as needed.) Arrange half the eggplant slices in bottom of baking dish. Sprinkle with half of remaining Parmesan cheese. Top with half of Mozzarella cheese covered with half of tomato mixture. Repeat layer with tomato sauce on top. Bake uncovered 20 minutes. Arrange remaining Mozzarella over top and bake 20 minutes more or until cheese is melted and slightly brown, contents hot and bubbly. Delicious. Serve with green salad and hot French bread. Delicious served as a vegetable. Serves 6.

Lucille Copeland

SPIRITED BLACK EYED PEAS

1 pound dried black eyed peas,
    washed
1 can beer
½ pound cubed salt pork
1 small can Snap-E Tom

fresh ground black pepper
salt
1 large chopped onion
1 tablespoon Worcestershire
1 teaspoon dry mustard

Soak peas overnight in beer. Do not drain. Add salt pork, Snap-E Tom, black pepper, salt, chopped onion. Worcestershire and dry mustard. Cook over low heat covered for 1½ hours. Keep adding beer as needed. Add dash or two of Tabasco to taste. Never add water. Serves 6-8.

June Dunkerly
Seagrove Beach, Florida

HENRY'S FIELD PEA CASSEROLE

2 cans field peas
3 large tomatoes, sliced
3 bell peppers, sliced
3 large white onions, sliced

½ cup Parmesan cheese, optional
6 slices bacon
salt and pepper to taste

In a casserole dish add a layer of field peas, a layer of tomatoes, a layer of bell peppers and a layer of white onions. Repeat until all ingredients are used. Sprinkle with cheese and place bacon strips on the top. Bake covered at 400° for 1 hour. Remove cover and broil until bacon is crisp. Serves 8.

Henry L. Mayer, Jr.

SAUTEED MUSHROOMS

½ pound fresh mushrooms
½ stick butter or margarine
1-2 cloves garlic
2-3 green onions
3 tablespoons Italian flavored bread
    crumbs

3 tablespoons grated Parmesan cheese
2 tablespoons sauterne or any dry wine
2 dashes Tabasco
2 dashes Worcestershire
salt, black pepper to taste

Chop onions, press garlic, and sauté in butter. Slice mushrooms; begin cooking on low heat with onions and garlic. Cook approximately 3-5 minutes or until mushrooms are tender. Add all other ingredients; cook for approximately 3-5 more minutes. Serve immediately. (Use more butter if mushrooms absorb all liquid.) Serves 2.

Robert Bray

SAUTEED CHANTERELLES

¼ cup butter
1 pound chanterelles
1 large clove garlic, pressed

⅛ teaspoon tarragon
3 capfuls vermouth
salt and pepper to taste

In ¼ cup butter over medium high heat sauté chanterelles about 3-5 minutes. Add rest of ingredients and cook about five minutes longer, stirring often. Serves 4

Chanterelles are wild mushrooms, well known in France and Germany. We are fortunate because we have access to a growing place and we get a year's supply of these mushrooms every June. We blanch and freeze them. They can be used in many ways. They also can be found canned in some grocery stores and gourmet restaurants.

Carola Bacqué

MUSHROOM VEGETABLE CASSEROLE

Sauce:

1 stick margarine	1 can mushroom soup
1 large onion, chopped	¾ roll jalapeno cheese, sliced
2 stalks celery, chopped	¾ roll garlic cheese, sliced
1 pint fresh mushrooms	2 teaspoons salt
1 package artichoke bottoms, fresh or frozen	1 package Brussel sprouts, fresh or frozen

If fresh, cut the stems off and remove a layer of the bottom leaves of the artichokes and Brussel sprouts. In a separate pan soak vegetables for 1 hour then boil in salted water. Boil Brussel sprouts for 10 minutes or until easily pierced with a fork. Drain. Artichokes can be boiled with 1 onion sliced and 1 stalk of celery broken into pieces along with 2 teaspoons salt. Boil for 1 hour or until leaves can be removed easily. Remove artichoke bottoms and drain. Prepare sauce. Sauté onion, celery and mushrooms in margarine until mushrooms are dark. Add soup and cheese. Pour over drained vegetables. Cook for 30 minutes in 350° oven. Other vegetables may be substituted such as broccoli or spinach. Fresh vegetables are much better, but frozen can be used. Serves 8.

Leslie Owen Hayes

MUSHROOMS SUPREME

1 pound fresh mushrooms	⅓ cup grated cheddar cheese
2 tablespoons all-purpose flour	1 (8 ounce) carton sour cream
1 teaspoon salt	1 tablespoon dry sherry
⅛ teaspoon red pepper	1 tablespoon finely chopped parsley
1-3 tablespoons melted margarine	buttered toast

Wash mushrooms and drain on paper towel. Remove stems. In paper bag, mix flour, salt and pepper. Add mushroom buttons and shake until well coated. Chop stems. Sauté mushroom buttons and stems in margarine over low heat, stirring frequently, until tender, about 10 minutes. Add cheese and sour cream and stir until cheese is melted. Add sherry and stir until mixture is well blended. Do not overcook or boil. Serve on buttered toast with parsley sprinkled on top. Serves 4

Joe L. Whitterbery

SMOTHERED OKRA

3 pounds fresh okra or 3 bags frozen, cut okra
salt, red and black pepper to taste
3 heaping tablespoons oil
3 tomatoes, peeled and chopped

1 bell pepper, minced
2 onions, minced
2 pods garlic, minced (optional)
1 tablespoon butter
fresh hot pepper (optional)

If fresh okra is used wash and dry each piece and slice very thin. If okra is frozen, be sure to defrost the okra thoroughly, until all is separated, as though it was just cut. Season okra well with salt, red and black pepper. Into a heavy Dutch oven or heavy skillet, put in oil and heat. Add okra and simmer for 15-20 minutes, until it is no longer "ropey." Then add tomatoes, bell pepper, onions and garlic. Let all simmer well, partly covered, stirring often so as not to stick or burn. Continue cooking until all looks cooked and oil comes to the top and okra shrinks from sides of pot. Add the butter to the top of okra. Hot fresh peppers can be minced and added to okra before taking it up. This can be put in a pyrex dish and kept warm in the oven on 200°. Serves 6-8.

Mrs. Dwight Andrus, Sr.

BAKED POTATO STUFFING

1 pint sour cream
1 (8 ounce) package cream cheese
5 slices crisp bacon, crumbled

3 tablespoons chives
salt and pepper to taste

Blend sour cream into cream cheese with fork. Add bacon and chives and seasonings. Use as stuffing in baked potato, dip or on top of green beans. Serves 4.

Brenda B. Hawes

ELISE GREENWOOD'S ONION PIE

½ pound (1 cup) sliced onions
3 ounces (scant ⅓ cup) lard
1⅔ ounces (¼ cup) butter
2 ounces (¼ cup) flour
1 pint cream, light

salt, pepper, grated nutmeg
2 egg yolks
4½ ounces streaky bacon, cut into small sticks
1 pie crust

Cook onions in lard until golden. In another pan, melt the butter, add flour, stirring until smooth, but don't let it brown. Add the milk or light cream, stirring well, and the seasonings and cook a bit. Take off the burner and add the egg yolks (beaten) and onions. Adjust the seasonings. Blanch the bacon, (or if preferred, fry briefly and drain). Pour the filling into an uncooked pie crust, 8½ inches or 9½ inches and drop the bits of bacon on top (they will sink in). Bake for 20-25 minutes in a hot, 400°, oven. Serves 6-8.

Elise Greenwood

FLO'S POTATO CASSEROLE

6 potatoes, peeled and sliced
½ pound grated cheese, cheddar or
   American
salt and pepper

1 large onion, diced
1 green bell pepper, diced
1 can cream of mushroom soup

In baking dish, place layers: raw potatoes, cheese, soup and seasonings. Cover tightly with lid and place in 350° oven for 1½-2 hours. Makes a delicious and easy dish to serve with beef. Serves 4-6.

Mrs. J. Alfred Mouton, Jr.

SPINACH STUFFED POTATOES

2 baking potatoes
butter
1 package frozen spinach souffle,
   thawed

2 slices American cheese

Cut potatoes in half. Butter cut sides. Bake until slightly tender. Remove a small amount of potato in center to make a slight indentation. Spoon ¼ spinach into each potato half. Place on baking sheet in 375° oven for 30 minutes. Remove, grate cheese on top of potato, return to oven for 5 minutes or until cheese is melted. Serves 4.

Suzanne Arceneaux Dupuis

RICE DRESSING

½ cup roux	1 hot pepper
3 pounds ground beef	1 mild pepper
1 pound lean ground pork	2 stalks celery
1 pound chicken livers (chopped fine)	1 cup water
1 pound chicken giblets (chopped fine)	4 dozen oysters
	1 quart green onion tops
1 bell pepper	3 cups raw rice, cooked
5 medium onions	salt to taste

Make approximately ½ cup roux. Add onions, bell pepper and celery to roux until wilted. Add pork and beef, let cook on low heat for approximately two hours. Add liver and giblets, let cook for one half hour. Add about one cup of water (you want to keep it moist, but not too watery).

When you are ready to serve, add oysters and green onion tops, let cook until oysters are done, about five minutes. Add the cooked rice to the mixture gradually, as you want to keep the dressing very moist.

The above mixture without oysters and rice can be frozen for months. You may also cut the recipe in half. The chicken livers and giblets may be left out, if you so desire. Serves: 16.

Mrs. Charles Barras
Mrs. Dennis J. Vidrine

CHINESE FRIED RICE

2 tablespoons oil	2 eggs
2 cups onions, chopped coarsely	1 tablespoon soy sauce
2 cups cold cooked rice	½ teaspoon salt

Heat pan, add oil, and fry onions until brown. Add rice and sauté. Mix together eggs, stirred slightly, soy sauce and salt, then add to mixture; sauté until done. Serves 4-6.

Variations: add 2 cups chopped, cooked meat (ham, shrimp, bacon, or leftovers), green peppers. Heat thoroughly. More soy sauce may be added if desired.

This dish can be served as a main dish or a side dish with any meat or fish. A great way to use leftovers. (I learned how to make this from my maid when I lived in Japan.)

Cynthia Dunlap

CHILI RICE

1 cup raw rice cooked by package
   directions
1 cup sour cream
1 can chopped green chilies

½ pound Monterey Jack cheese,
   shredded
salt to taste
butter

Mix cooked rice, sour cream and salt. Put one-half of the mixture in baking dish. Put layer of chilies and the shredded cheese. Layer the rest of rice on top of cheese. Dot with butter. Bake 30 minutes at 350°. Serves 4-6.

Mrs. Frank P. Danna

RAISIN BARBECUE RICE

½ cup seedless raisins
1 teaspoon chili powder
3 tablespoons butter
3 cups hot cooked rice

½ teaspoon salt
2 tablespoons chopped green onions
2 tablespoons pimento
pecans, optional

Heat raisins in chili powder and butter until glazed. Toss with rice, salt, green onions, pimento and pecans. Tastes great with chicken or spareribs. Serves 6.

Lucille Roy Copeland

RICE AND NUT LOAF

1½ cups rice
2 cups medium white sauce
¾ cup finely chopped onion
1 egg, slightly beaten
1½ cups chopped nuts

½ teaspoon poultry seasoning
1 teaspoon salt
¼ teaspoon black pepper
fine bread crumbs

Cook rice. Add remaining ingredients and pack into a well greased loaf pan which has been sprinkled with fine bread crumbs. Bake at 375° about 30 minutes. Turn onto heated platter. Goes well with wild ducks. Serves 6-8.

Mrs. Bill Davis

SPINACH MUSHROOM ARTICHOKE CASSEROLE

2 (15 ounce) cans leaf spinach
6 tablespoons butter
1 (6 ounce) can button mushrooms
1 tablespoon flour

½ cup milk
1 (1 pound) can artichoke hearts
½ teaspoon salt
½ teaspoon pepper

Topping:
½ cup sour cream
½ cup mayonnaise

2 tablespoons lemon juice

Cook spinach then drain. Sauté mushrooms in butter, remove and drain. Add flour to melted butter and cook until bubbling. Add milk and stir until smooth. Add spinach, mushrooms, drained artichoke hearts and seasonings. Place in a 2 quart casserole dish. Prepare topping. Mix ingredients and warm. Pour over casserole. Bake in a 350° oven for 30 minutes. Serves 8.

Mrs. Brit Busch

DUTCH SCALLOPED SPINACH

1 pound spinach
1 egg, beaten
1 cup milk
1 cup toasted bread crumbs

½ cup melted butter
⅓ teaspoon salt
dash of pepper
¼ cup chopped bacon

Cook and chop spinach. Add all other ingredients except bacon and ½ cup bread crumbs for topping. Mix and put in 1 quart casserole. Sprinkle on topping. Bake at 350° for 35-40 minutes. A favorite from Anna Maud Cafeteria in Oklahoma City. Serves 4-6.

Sarah M. Fambrough

SQUASH CASSEROLE I

5 peeled and sliced yellow squash
1 stick butter or margarine
3-4 corn muffins, crumbled

1 small onion, minced
salt and pepper to taste
1 cup grated cheddar cheese

Preheat oven to 350°. Boil squash until tender. Drain. Mash and stir with fork. Add butter. Add crumbled corn muffins. Add onion, salt and pepper. Put in greased 1 quart casserole. Sprinkle with cheddar cheese. Bake at 350° for 30 minutes. Serves 4-6.

Cristie Adams

PIZZA ZUCCHINI

3 zucchini squash
4 mushrooms
3 tablespoons butter
3 tablespoons diced onion

½ cup grated Parmesan cheese
½ (8 ounce) can tomato sauce
1 clove garlic, minced
½ teaspoon oregano

Preheat oven to 350°. Slice zucchini and mushrooms in thin slices. In large skillet sauté zucchini, onions and mushrooms in melted butter. Cover and simmer for 15 minutes. Add Parmesan cheese, tomato sauce, garlic and oregano. Blend well. Pour into 1 quart casserole dish and bake 30 minutes in 350° oven. Serves 5.

Sandry Brewer Holbert

RICE AND ZUCCHINI PIE

2 zucchini
⅓ cup chopped onion
2 tablespoons butter
1 clove garlic, minced
¼ pound mushrooms
¼ teaspoon oregano
¼ teaspoon basil

salt and pepper to taste
1½ cups cooked rice
3 eggs, lightly beaten
⅓ cup grated Parmesan cheese
more grated Parmesan cheese
2 tablespoons softened butter

Preheat oven to 350°. Quarter 2 zucchini, scrub and trim and cut into thin slices. In a skillet sauté onion and garlic in 2 tablespoons butter until onion is soft. Stir in zucchini, mushrooms, oregano, basil and salt and pepper to taste. Cook this mixture over moderate heat until vegetables are tender and moisture has evaporated. Transfer to a large bowl and add cooked rice, eggs and grated Parmesan cheese. Toss this mixture and add salt and pepper to taste. Transfer to buttered 8 inch pie pan. Sprinkle with Parmesan cheese and dot with 2 tablespoons softened butter. Bake in lower third of 350° oven for 15 minutes. Transfer to upper third of oven and continue baking 10-15 minutes until it is set and cheese is golden brown. Serves 4.

Carolyn C. Richard

ZUCCHINI WITH SOUR CREAM

5-6 medium-small zucchini squash
½ stick butter
1 large onion, ringed thinly
2 pods garlic, chopped
2 slices Swiss cheese

½ carton sour cream
salt, pepper, celery salt, Tabasco
1 small package Mozzarella cheese,
    grated
bread crumbs

Cut zucchini into ¾ inch pieces. Simmer until tender in small amount of boiling, salted water (10-15 minutes). Drain and set aside. In skillet, melt butter, simmer onions and garlic until clear and tender. Add drained zucchini. Fold in Swiss cheese in pieces or grated on low fire until melted. Add sour cream and remove from fire. Season with salt, pepper, celery salt, and a dash of Tabasco. Put into a rectangular casserole dish, top with Mozzarella cheese and bread crumbs. Bake at 350° for 15 minutes or until bubbly. Serve immediately and enjoy. Serves 5-6.

Ann Humphries LeJeune

ZUCCHINI CASSEROLE

2½ pounds zucchini, washed and
  sliced
½ cup diced green peppers
½ cup chopped onions
3 tablespoons margarine
3 large tomatoes, diced

3 tablespoons flour
1½ teaspoons salt
¼ teaspoon pepper
¼ teaspoon sugar
¾-1 cup cheddar cheese, grated
½ cup buttered bread crumbs

Preheat oven to 350°. Cook squash in small amount of water about 8 minutes. Drain well and put in 2 quart casserole. Sauté pepper, onion in margarine until limp. Add tomatoes. Sprinkle with flour and stir well. Cook 2 minutes longer. Season with salt, pepper and sugar. Spoon mixture over squash. Put cheese over top, then sprinkle with bread crumbs. Bake about 30 minutes at 350°. Freezes well. Serves 8.

Marge Pfeuffer

TOMATOES ITALIANO

4 medium-size, ripe tomatoes
4 tablespoons margarine
salt and pepper to taste
3 strips bacon, fried crisp and
  crumbled

2 green onions with tops, chopped fine
1 (4 ounce) can mushrooms, chopped
fine
1 (4 ounce) package shredded
  Mozzarella cheese

Cut thin slice off top of each tomato and discard. Slice tomatoes into thirds and place on a cookie sheet. Melt margarine in a small saucepan and brush on top of each tomato slice. Salt and pepper to taste. Cook tomatoes for 15 minutes at 350° and remove from oven. Mix together bacon, onion, mushrooms and cheese. Heap this mixture on each slice and return to oven still at 350° for about 10 minutes or until cheese is bubbly. Serves 4-6.

Betty Bray Roy

STUFFED TOMATOES WITH RICE

6 large tomatoes
1 bell pepper, cut up
1 large onion, chopped
1 jalapeno pepper, chopped

1 cup raw rice, cooked
6 slices bacon, fried and crumbled
seasonings
bread crumbs

Cut off top of tomato and scrape pulp out of inside. Add pulp to skillet with the bell pepper, onion and jalapeno pepper. Cook covered under low heat for about ¾ hour. Add rice and bacon and season to taste. Stuff this back into the tomatoes and sprinkle with bread crumbs. Place tomatoes in a casserole or baking dish with a slight amount of water to keep from sticking. Cook in oven at 425° for 15-20 minutes or until tomatoes are tender. Serves 6.

Henry L. Mayer, Jr.

TURNIP GRATIN

1 clove garlic
3 tablespoons butter
1½ pounds turnips, peeled and cut in ⅛ inch slices, parboiled for 2-3 minutes and drained
salt
freshly ground pepper

1 teaspoon fresh or dried herbs, parsley, tarragon, thyme, oregano
½ cup Gruyere and Parmesan cheese, grated and mixed
½ cup heavy cream
¼ cup bread crumbs

Rub a small gratin dish with garlic, butter well and arrange the turnip slices in a layer. Sprinkle with salt and freshly ground pepper, herbs and ⅓ of the cheese, making three layers, finishing with the cheese on top. Pour the cream over the turnips, sprinkle with breadcrumbs and bits of butter. Bake 45 minutes in a 400° oven. Serves 4

Judy Fuller
Kinder, LA

BLENDER HOLLANDAISE SAUCE

½ cup butter
3 egg yolks
2 tablespoons lemon juice

¼ teaspoon salt
dash white pepper
½ teaspoon prepared mustard

Heat butter in a small saucepan until bubbly but not browned. Put egg yolks, lemon juice, seasonings and mustard in an electric blender. Cover and blend on speed 2 for about 5 seconds. Add butter very, very slowly blending on speed 2, then switch to high and blend for 30 more seconds. This makes an easy base for Bearnaise Sauce. Yield: ¾ cup.

Ramona Mouton

MEDIUM WHITE SAUCE

2 tablespoons butter
2 tablespoons flour

1 cup milk
salt to taste

Melt butter over low heat. Add flour and stir well. Add milk gradually, and cook until thick and smooth. Add salt. Yield 2 cups.

Mrs. Bill Davis

SAUCE EXTRAORDINAIRE

1¾ cups mayonnasie (homemade is
  best with a little olive oil)
2 tablespoons anchovy paste
¼ cup green onions, cut in pieces
1 clove garlic, pressed or chopped

1 teaspoon dried tarragon
½ cup parsley sprigs
2 tablespoons tarragon vinegar
⅛ teaspoon red pepper

Combine all ingredients in food processor and process until mixture is fairly smooth. This sauce is great with artichokes, asparagus, broccoli, and as tartar sauce with fish. Yield: approximately 2 cups.

Carola Bacqué

CHOW CHOW

2 cabbages
1 cauliflower
1 quart white onions
9 cucumbers, peeled and large seeds
  removed
6 bell peppers
3 stalks celery (1 bunch)
1 tea cup salt

2 quarts cider vinegar
1 cup flour
3-4 cups sugar
1 tablespon turmeric
6 tablespoons dry mustard
6 tablespoons mixed spices, put in a bag
1 teaspoon red pepper

Chop up vegetables. Cover with a tea cup of salt to a half gallon of water overnight, soak. In the morning put on fire. When it comes to a boil, take off fire and drain thoroughly. Sift sugar, flour, turmeric and mustard. Add this to 1 quart of vinegar. Stir until smooth. Add other quart of vinegar which must be boiling with bag of spices. Stir well and add vegetables. Bring to a boil. (One can of chopped pimentos may be added for color.) Remove spice bag. Can at once. Yield 11 pints.

Yolande Toups Kaplan

LIME PICKLES

7 pounds cucumbers
2 cups distilled (pickling) lime
2 quarts vinegar
8 cups sugar

2 teaspoons pickle mix
1 teaspoon celery seed
2 teaspoons whole cloves

Slice cucumbers. Put into crock (Do not use metal). Cover with water. Add lime and soak 24 hours. Stir with wooden spoon several times. Pour off water and wash clean. Soak in clear water 3 hours. Drain and add remaining ingredients which have been mixed together. Soak for 12 hours. After soaking, bring mixture to boil, lower heat and simmer for 45 minutes. Seal in sterilized jars.

Eugenia Somervell Yeates
El Dorado, Arkansas

REFRIGERATOR PICKLES

4 cups sugar
4 cups white vinegar
¼ cup salt
2 teaspoons dill seed
1 teaspoon celery seed

1 teaspoon dry mustard
1 teaspoon turmeric
3 cloves garlic, sliced thin
3 onions
8-10 medium cucumbers, sliced thin

Mix well, put in jars and refrigerate. Let stand at least 1 week before using.

Jimmie Ruth Procter
Beaumont, TX

WATERMELON PICKLES

4 pounds prepared watermelon rind
Lime water (about 2 tablespoons lime
  in 2 quarts of cold water)
2 tablespoons whole allspice
2 tablespoons whole cloves

10 2-inch pieces stick cinnamon
1½ quarts white vinegar
1 lemon, sliced thin
1 quart water
4½ pounds sugar

To prepare melon, pare skin and pink flesh. Cut into 1½ to 2 inch squares. Soak for 2½ hours in lime water. (Lime of calcium oxide can be purchased from drug store.) Drain, cover with fresh water, and cook until tender (about 1½ hrs), adding more water as needed. Let stand several hours or overnight. Drain. Put spices in cheesecloth bag, tying loosely. Bring to boil the spices, vinegar, lemon, water, and sugar. Add rind and boil slowly for two hours, or until syrup is fairly thick. Remove spice bag. Pack pickles in clean hot jars, fill with boiling syrup and seal.

Margaret Helen Chambley
Oakdale, LA

MIRLITON PICKLES

6-8 mirlitons
2 onions sliced
1 bell pepper sliced
1 clove garlic, sliced
¼ cup salt

1 cup sugar, less if desired
¾ tablespoon mustard seed
1 teaspoon turmeric
2 cups white vinegar, 4% acidity
red pepper, if desired

Slice mirlitons very thin. Add sliced onions, bell pepper, garlic and sprinkle salt all over. Cover with cracked or cubed ice. Let stand for 3 hours. Drain well. Boil remaining ingredients. Add vegetable mixture. Turn fire very low. Cook 5 minutes on simmer. Seal in sterilized jars. If you intend to store for any length of time, process jars in hot water as for canning. Yield: 1 quart.

Mrs. Walter Johnston
New Orleans, LA.

RAY HAY'S CAJUN PO-BOYS

Cajun food and Cajun cooking are making their way around the country. You can find "Cajun Wharf" restaurants in Little Rock, Arkansas; and Nashville, Tennessee. Crawfish is served in New York and Washington, D.C., and in Houston you'll find not only crawfish, but Cajun boudin, cracklins, gumbo, and Cajun Po-Boys at the famous "Ray Hay's Cajun Restaurants".

This painting portrays Ray Hay holding his Cajun Po-Boy sandwich, and beside him is Bud Petro of Lafayette, Louisiana. The two are discussing one of the new items on the menu, Petro's juicy fried rabbit. The preparation of the rabbit is so secret, that Mr. Petro was flown in to Houston to teach the cooks how to prepare this Cajun delicacy.

MEAT

RARE ROAST BEEF

beef roast up to 10 pounds, rump
  or sirloin tip
1 clove garlic

5 teaspoons kosher salt, regular salt may
  be used, but isn't as good as kosher

In a small bowl, put garlic through a press and mix with salt. Rub mixture on each end and on exposed fat. Cook at 190-200° 1 hour per pound for roasts under 4 pounds or ¾ hour per pound for roasts over 4 pounds. Do not open oven door until ready to test for doneness. Do not baste or turn. The roast should be rare at the appointed time. If necessary it may stay in oven 1 more hour and still be rare. Use a meat theremometer to double check your time. There can be a difference between individual ovens. There will be no gravy in the pan because all juice stays in the roast. Make your own gravy or use an au jus mix. Serves 8-10.

Melinda Woods Jones

BEEF WELLINGTON

1 (5 pound) filet, or 2 smaller ones
1 teaspoon dry mustard
larding pork to cover filet
1 tablespoon butter
½ pound mushrooms, chopped
¼ pound chopped ham
½ clove garlic, crushed with salt

⅓ cup sherry
4 chopped chicken livers
1 tablespoon tomato puree
1 tablespoon beef extract
pastry to cover filet
1 egg yolk
1 teaspoon water

Sprinkle filet with dry mustard. Secure larding pork over filet. Roast in 400° oven for 25 minutes. Chill. In butter, sauté mushrooms until dark brown. Add chopped ham, garlic and salt. Add sherry. Sauté 4 chopped chicken livers in mixture. Next, add tomato puree, then beef extract. Mix well and remove from heat. Shape pastry (pie, puff, brioche, or premade pie crust) to fit meat, laying cold filet in center. Pile mushroom, ham and liver mixture on and around filet. Wrap dough around entire mixture and filet, turning in ends and pressing all seams together. Lay filet seam side down on baking sheet. Brush with egg yolk beaten in teaspoon water. Cut swags from remaining pastry and decorate dish. Bake at 425° for 25-30 minutes. Serves 10-12.

Mrs. Robert F. Tarpy

CABES' CHUCK ROAST

meat tenderizer
1 (3-4 pound) chuck roast, 2 inches
   thick
1 (5 ounce) bottle soy sauce
1½ cups water

½ cup bourbon
2 tablespoons brown sugar
2 tablespoons Worcestershire
juice of 1 lemon

Tenderize meat with tenderizer overnight. Combine remaining ingredients in shallow baking pan. Put meat in the marinade and marinate for 3 hours on each side. Barbecue on grill approximately 20 minutes on each side for medium. Baste with left over marinade. Something a little special for a meat and potatoes man. Serves 4.

Robert Cabes

SAUERBRATEN

2 onions, sliced
2 bay leaves
1 teaspoon black peppercorns
1 clove garlic crushed
1 cup lemon juice

2½ cups water
½ cup sugar
4 pound rump roast
cooking oil
12 gingersnap cookies, crushed

Combine and heat all ingredients except roast and cookies. Pour mixture over meat and marinate 24-36 hours, turning meat occasionally. Remove meat and wipe dry. Brown in hot oil. Add marinade, cover and simmer in 325° oven for 2 hours or until tender. To make gravy combine ¾ cup strained marinade, ¼ cup water and gingersnaps. Cook until thickened. Serves 4-6.

Lydia Bacqué

BRISKET

1 (4-5 pound) brisket with fat trimmed
½ teaspoon salt
½ teaspoon red pepper

½ teaspoon garlic powder
paprika

Sauce:
1 carton sour cream
1 tablespoon horseradish

1 teaspoon lemon juice

Sprinkle brisket with seasonings. Coat with paprika. Pound both sides of meat with fists. Wrap in foil. Bake fat side up, 4 hours in 300° oven. Serve with sauce. Serves 6-8.

Pat Lindsey

FILET STEAKS FLAMBÉ

¾ stick margarine
4 beef filets
salt and pepper to taste
1 cup, minimum, sliced fresh
  mushrooms

3 ounces brandy
10 ounces brown mushroom gravy
½ cup dry white wine

In a large flambé pan, melt ½ stick margarine, butter will burn too easily. Season the filets with salt and pepper. Be sure to remove bacon, if wrapped with it, and use toothpicks if needed to hold filets together. Brown filets over medium flame on both sides, 2-3 minutes/side. Cook over low flame until firm to touch, for medium rare, turning frequently to prevent sticking. This usually takes about 15 minutes, but will vary with thickness of meat. Move filets to the outer edges of pan and raise flame to medium. Add ¼ stick margarine and when melted add sliced mushrooms. Sauté briefly. Move filets back to center of pan and spoon on the sauteed mushrooms. Raise flame to high and move pan around to evenly heat the bottom of the pan. Hold away from flame for a few seconds and then add brandy, pouring directly over filets. (If the liquor should start to bubble or boil vigorously, continue to hold away from flame until it subsides. If you ignite it when it is overheated, eyebrows flambé will result.) Now move pan back over high flame and ignite brandy by tilting pan slightly and letting the flame lap over the edge of the pan. Shake gently to prolong the blue flame which will result. Add brown mushroom gravy carefully as flames die down, and stir gently. When flames are gone add wine and continue stirring. Serve immediately. Serves 4
Stepehn P. Engelbrecht

STEAK DIANE

4 rib eye steaks ½ inch thick
salt
freshly ground pepper
4 tablespoons butter
¼ cup brandy

2 small shallots, minced
3 tablespoons chopped chives
½ cup dry sherry
cherry tomatoes and celery leaves for
  garnish

About 20 minutes before serving:
On cutting board, with meat mallet, edge of plate or dull edge of French knife, pound steaks until about ¼ inch thick, turning occasionally. Sprinkle meat with salt and pepper. In 10 inch skillet over high heat, in 1 tablespoon butter cook one steak until both sides are just browned. Pour 1 tablespoon brandy over steak and with match, set aflame. (brandy must be slightly warmed before doing this). When flaming stops stir in ¼ amount of shallots and chives; cook, stirring constantly, until shallots are tender, about 1 minute. Add 2 tablespoons sherry, heat through. Place steak on a warm dinner plate and pour sherry mixture over it. Garnish with cherry tomatoes cut partway through and celery leaves. Repeat with remaining steaks. Serve immediately. Serves 4.
Sandy Hamilton
London, England

TOURNEDOS KATHALEEN

1 (4 ounce) filet mignon
2 ounces fresh crabmeat, warmed

2 ounces bearnaise sauce

Cut filet into ⅛ inch medallions. Broil to desired doneness. Put warmed crabmeat over meat and top with bearnaise sauce.

Bearnaise Sauce:
¾ cup Hollandaise sauce
1 tablespoon tarragon vinegar
1 teaspoon chopped fresh parsley

1 teaspoon chopped fresh tarragon
1 teaspoon chopped fresh chevril

Mix all ingredients together. (If fresh herbs are not available, use ¼ teaspoon each of the dried herbs.) Serve with broiled or baked fish and meats. Yield: ¾ cup.

Hollandaise Sauce:
¾ cup (1½ sticks) butter
3 large egg yolks, well beaten

4 teaspoons lemon juice
dash of each salt and cayenne

Break butter into 3 pieces. Put 1 piece into the top of a double boiler. Add egg yolks and lemon juice. Beat well with a wire whisk constantly while cooking over hot water (not boiling) until butter is melted. Add the second piece of butter, continue beating and cooking until the mixture thickens, never allowing the water to boil. Then add the last piece of butter. Stir and cook until sauce has thickened. Remove from heat and stir in salt and cayenne. Serve with fish, shellfish and vegetables.

Should the Hollandaise mixture curdle, add 1½ tablespoons boiling water, beating constantly, to rebuild the emulsion. Yield: ¾ cup.

Jacob's Restaurant

L'ENTRECOTE LOUISIANNE

1 large flank steak with membrane
   removed

½ cup clarified butter

Sauce:
4 anchovy fillets
4 tablespoons onion tops, green
4 tablespoons parsley
1 clove garlic
2 teaspoons lemon juice

3 teaspoons cognac
2 sticks softened butter
4 tablespoons sage
1 teaspoon black pepper
3 teaspoons French Dijon mustard

Puree first 6 ingredients of sauce. Add softened butter, sage, pepper and mustard. Mix all together in bowl until well blended. Heat drawn butter in a heavy skillet. Brown steak on both sides until desired doneness, 4-6 minutes on each side for medium. Remove steak to warm serving platter. Spread sauce onto steak and let it melt. To serve cut steak against the grain into ½ inch strips. Surround steak with crisp French fries. Serves 4-6.

Blair Bowden Cabes

FLANK STEAK

6 tablespoons oil
6 tablespoons Worcestershire
6 tablespoons mustard

sprinkle of garlic salt
2 medium to large flank steaks

Mix oil, Worcestershire, mustard and garlic salt. Marinate 2 flank steaks in mixture. Cover and refrigerate overnight. Turn once or twice. Broil 6 inches from heat for about 6 minutes on each side or until cooked. Slice thin on an angle. Delicious when barbequed. Serves 6-8.

Mary Lou Carman

FLANK STEAK MARINADE

¼ cup soy sauce
3 tablespoons honey
2 tablespoons vinegar
1½ teaspoons garlic powder

1½ teaspoons ground ginger
¾ cup salad oil
1 green onion, chopped

Mix all ingredients in blender and marinate scored flank steak all day or overnight. Broil close to flame 5 minutes on each side. Serves 4-6.

Elizabeth Childs Crockett

BROILED FLANK STEAK ROLL

1 (8 ounce) can sliced mushrooms
2 tablespoons butter or margarine
1 (1½-2 pound) beef flank steak
1 teaspoon salt

¼ teaspoon pepper
¼ teaspoon dried marjoram leaves
4 slices bacon, cooked and crumbled
fresh snipped parsley

Sauté mushrooms in butter in small skillet over medium heat, stirring occasionally, until mushrooms are light brown, about 3 minutes. Trim excess fat from meat. Pound with meat mallet or side of cleaver until meat is slightly flattened. Score meat diagonally on both sides. Rub entire surface of meat with mixture of salt, pepper and marjoram. Distribute mushrooms and bacon evenly over meat. Roll up meat from short end; secure with skewers. Place meat roll on aluminum foil-lined broiler pan. Broil meat roll 3-4 inches from heat to medium doneness, about 20 minutes, rotating meat a quarter turn every 5 minutes. Garnish with snipped parsley.
Micro directions: Prepare bacon slices in microwave oven according to manufacturer's instructions. Microwave mushrooms in butter in glass baking dish, 10x6x1¾ inches, on full power stirring every 30 seconds, until mushrooms are tender, about 2 minutes. Proceed with recipe. Serves 4.

Elizabeth Preis

A LA GORDY'S MUSHROOM STEAK SAUCE

In a medium size stew pot with cover, melt ¼ stick of margarine or butter. When hot, add a medium size onion chopped fine together with the chopped bottoms of a bunch of green onions. (Save green onion tops for later.) Stir and cook onions until soft, 6-8 minutes, and add following:

8 tablespoons tomato catsup
4 tablespoons Heinz 57 steak sauce
4 tablespoons savory steak sauce
4 tablespoons Pickapeppa steak sauce
4 tablespoons A-1 steak sauce

4 tablespoons H. P. Steak sauce
2 tablespoons Kitchen Bouquet
2 dashes each Tabasco and Louisiana
   Red Hot Sauce
1 teaspoon sugar

Stir to blend and allow the above to simmer on slow fire in covered pot for 10-15 minutes and add following:

1 (16 ounce) can mushroom stems
   and pieces, including liquid

salt, red and black pepper to taste
⅓ cup dehydrated parsley flakes

Stir and bring to boil. Cover pot and simmer for 20 minutes. Add:
⅔ cup chopped green onion tops. Simmer for 10 more minutes. Cut fire off, add:
2 tablespoons Worcestershire sauce
Now ready to spoon on pre-cooked steaks. Note: For ½ pound can mushrooms cut above exactly in half. Yield: approximately 3½-4 cups.

Mat Gordy

ROLADEN

8 slices sandwich steak, ¼ inch thick
8 teaspoons yellow mustard
4 slices bacon, halved
2 medium onions, chopped
2 medium green peppers, chopped

8 small dill pickles, chopped
salt, pepper and garlic powder to taste
oil to cover bottom of pan
water

On each sandwich steak smear 1 teaspoon mustard, and top with bacon and onions, bell peppers and dill pickles. Sprinkle with salt, pepper and garlic powder to family's likes. When all ingredients are on top of meat roll each slice and tie with a string to keep closed while cooking. Cover bottom of roaster pan with oil. Brown roladen on all sides, adding a little water at a time to make a gravy. Add the remaining onions and bell peppers. Let simmer until done, checking occasionally to be sure gravy doesn't get dry. Gravy won't be very dark. This recipe was given to me by a German family we lived with while in the service in Germany. Serves 8.

Bootsie Cella Arceneaux

GRILLADES

1½ pounds veal steak
flour, salt, pepper
2 tablespoons oil
⅓ cup onion, chopped
⅓ cup celery, chopped

⅓ cup bell pepper, chopped
1 (8 ounce) can tomato sauce
¼ teaspoon thyme
1 bay leaf
seasonings to taste

Take a tender veal steak and cut into cutlets about 4 inches long and 4 inches wide. Flour, salt and pepper very lightly and fry to a golden brown. Set aside. Using fat cutlets were fried in, fry the following seasonings with tomato sauce: onion, celery, and bell pepper. Return cutlets to pan and spoon sauce over. Add water until they are covered; let simmer until meat is tender and gravy is brown. Serve with rice, spaghetti or yellow grits. In sauce for grillades, put a little thyme and bay leaf for flavoring. Serves 4-6.

Mrs. Richard D. Chappuis, Sr.

ITALIAN STYLE ROUND STEAK WITH OLIVES

1 round steak, trimmed and cut into
  6 serving portions
½ cup flour
1 teaspoon salt
¼ teaspoon pepper
¼ cup salad oil
2 cloves garlic, pressed

2 large or 4 medium tomatoes or 1 (1
  pound) can whole tomatoes, reserve
  liquid
½ cup dry red wine
12 olives, ripe
6 sprigs parsley

Coat squares of steak with mixture of flour, salt and pepper. Heat oil in skillet, add meat and brown on both sides. Add finely chopped or pressed garlic after turning meat. Chop tomatoes into small pieces. When meat has formed a brown crust on both sides, add tomatoes to skillet. Allow to sauté for about 5 minutes. Pour wine over meat and tomatoes. Cook for about 3 minutes (If canned tomatoes are used, the liquid in the can should be added at this point.) Cover and cook over low heat for 30-40 minutes. Add sliced olives. Serve on platter of cooked noodles and garnish with parsley. This is also delicious served over rice. Serve with green salad and crusty French bread. Serves 4-6.

Mrs. Kenneth N. Lacaze

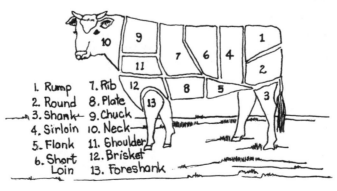

1. Rump   7. Rib
2. Round 8. Plate
3. Shank 9. Chuck
4. Sirloin 10. Neck
5. Flank 11. Shoulder
6. Short 12. Brisket
   Loin   13. Foreshank

PIGS IN A BLANKET

1 (4-4½ pound) beef sirloin, sliced as
   thinly as possible
1 cup finely chopped onion
2 pounds finely chopped bacon
toothpicks

3 tablespoons oil
6 cups water
salt and pepper to taste
½ teaspoon Kitchen Bouquet
3 tablespoons flour

Pound slices of meat. Combine onion and bacon. Place approximately 2 heaping tablespoons in the middle of each slice of meat, roll and secure either end with toothpicks. Brown rolls in oils. Add 6 cups of water. Season with salt and pepper and ½ teaspoon Kitchen Bouquet. Simmer for ½ hour. Dissolve flour in small amount of water and add to gravy to thicken. Simmer 10 minutes more. Serves 6.

Helen Nugier Sobiesk

STEAK AND POTATO CASSEROLE

1 round steak, cut in serving pieces or
   4 thin steaks of choice
seasonings: salt, black and red
   pepper
oil
flour
3 potatoes
1 bell pepper

2 onions
4 carrots
cherry tomatoes
1 can water chestnuts, quartered
½ cup cognac, optional
1 teaspoon Kitchen Bouquet
water
parsley

Season steaks as desired, coat lightly with flour. Brown in well greased baking pan in pre-heated oven, 350°. Peel and slice potatoes, carrots and onions. Slice bell pepper and tomatoes, add water chestnuts. Season this mixture as desired and add to meat. Add cognac and Kitchen Bouquet and cover meat with water. Cover pan tightly with foil and continue to bake until vegetables are tender, about 1 hour. When cooked, garnish with parsley and serve over rice. Serves 4-6.

Mrs. Dwight Andrus, Sr.

ORIENTAL BEEF SUPREME

2 tablespoons oil
½ pound lean beef, cut into strips
1 onion, sliced
1 green pepper, sliced
1 cup sliced celery
1 cup cut green beans, fresh
1 can sliced water chestnuts

1 can drained fancy Chinese vegetables
4 teaspoons cornstarch
3 tablespoons soy sauce (or more
   according to how much you like this
   flavor)
¾ cup water
4 ounces sliced fresh mushrooms

Brown beef in oil, add vegetables and cook 3-5 minutes. Combine cornstarch with soy sauce and water. Add to pan with mushrooms and cook 10 minutes stirring until liquid is clear and shiny and beans are tender. Salt to taste. Serve over rice. Serves 6.

Betsy Wild

BEEF STROGANOFF

2 pounds sirloin or top round
salt and pepper
Kitchen Bouquet
3 tablespoons butter
½ pound sliced mushrooms
3 tablespoons butter

3 tablespoons flour
2 cups beef stock
1 tablespoon tomato paste (or ketchup)
2 teaspoons Kitchen Bouquet
1 carton sour cream

Cut steak into thin strips and sprinkle generously with salt, red pepper and Kitchen Bouquet. Sauté meat and mushrooms in a large skillet with 3 table-spoons butter until brown. Remove from heat. Blend 3 tablespoons butter and flour in saucepan over low heat until roux is smooth and golden. Add beef stock gradually—stir and blend after each addition. Cook and stir until sauce is thick and smooth. Blend in tomato paste and Kitchen Bouquet. Pour sauce over meat in skillet. Return to low heat and cook uncovered for 15 minutes. Ten minutes before serving, blend sour cream into stroganoff—simmer gently 5-10 minutes. Serve over boiled rice or noodles. Serves 4-6.

Kathy Leonard

BEEF CURRY FROM INDIA

2 pounds round steak cut in cubes
¼ cup oil
1 cup chopped onion
2 cloves garlic, chopped
4 tablespoons curry powder

4 cups water
salt and pepper to taste
1 small can tomato paste
1 small can Pet milk
juice of 1 lemon

Brown onion and meat in oil, add garlic, when slightly wilted, add tomato paste and water and curry powder, salt and pepper. Simmer for 1½ hours uncovered. Five minutes before serving, add pet milk and lemon juice. Serve over rice.

Condiments: (Pile these on top.) Chopped green onions, chopped tomatoes, sliced cucumbers, raisins, crushed pineapple, sliced bananas, shredded coconuts, chutney. Beer is a good beverage to serve with curry. This recipe was given to me by our family cook in Kuwait—his name was Razario and he was from Pakistan. Serves 4 (For serving more people, allow ½ pound meat per person.)

Beth Bickham Mouton

CHINESE STIR-FRIED BEEF

1 pound beef tenderloin sliced in thin strips
4 tablespoons vegetable oil
½ cup coarsely chopped onion
2 cups (½ pound) sliced fresh mushrooms
1 cup sliced celery
2 cups fresh bean sprouts, or 1 No. 2 can mixed Chinese vegetables, rinsed and drained
2 beef bouillon cubes dissolved in 1½ cups hot water

1 small can (8 ounce) bamboo shoots, drained
1 small can (8 ounce) water chestnuts, drained and sliced
2 teaspoons cornstarch
1 teaspoon sugar
3 tablespoons warm water
3 tablespoons soy sauce
2 cups chow mein noodles
1 teaspoon salt
1 teaspoon pepper

Heat 2 tablespoons vegetable oil in wok over medium high heat. Stir fry beef slices in hot oil until browned. This should take about 5 minutes. Remove meat and juices and set aside. Heat remaining 2 tablespoons vegetable oil until hot. Add chopped onion and stir fry about 1 minute. Continue stirring and in fairly quick succession add fresh sliced mushrooms, celery slices and fresh bean sprouts. Stir fry until the vegetables begin to turn clear and become slightly tender. This process should take about 5-7 minutes. Remove vegetables and set aside with meat. To bouillon cubes dissolved in water add 1 teaspoon salt and ¼ teaspoon pepper. Place this liquid in the wok and add the bamboo shoots, sliced water chestnuts and any other canned vegetables. (If canned bean sprouts are used, add them now.) Stir lightly. Bring to a boil, covered. Combine cornstarch, sugar, warm water and soy sauce. Stir until cornstarch is dissolved. Add this to the hot bouillon and vegetables now in the wok. Then add the stir fried beef and vegetables which have been set aside. Stir until thoroughly mixed. Then simmer covered 1-2 minutes, or until liquid has slightly thickened. Taste for seasoning. Stir in 2 cups chow mein noodles and serve immediately on a bed of hot rice. Serves 4-6.

Beth Hollier Engelbrecht

TERIYAKI STEAK SUPREME

½ cup red wine
¼ cup teriyaki sauce
1½ pounds round steak
2 tablespoons butter
1 (10½ ounce) can mushroom gravy

2 tablespoons currant jelly
1½ cups sliced bell pepper
2 tart apples
3 cups cooked rice

Combine wine with teriyaki sauce. (You may buy prepared teriyaki sauce or make your own with 2 tablespoons pineapple juice and 2 tablespoons cooking oil plus 1 tablespoon soy sauce.) Pour over steak. Set aside to marinate. Slice bell peppers, core and slice apples. Drain and reserve marinade from meat. Sauté meat in butter, high heat so as to quickly brown meat. Stir in mushroom gravy, jelly and marinade. Bring to boil. Place sliced peppers and apples on top, cover and simmer 5 minutes. Serve over cooked rice. Serves 6.

Sue Alves

BEEF CUBES IN MUSHROOM SAUCE

1 pound beef chuck, cut in 1 inch
  cubes
4-6 tablespoons cooking oil
2 tablespoons flour
½ teaspoon monosodium glutamate
  or Accent
1½ teaspoons salt
½ teaspoon red or black pepper

1 medium onion, chopped
1 clove garlic, crushed
1 can (1¼ cups) beef gravy
1 (3 ounce) can broiled, sliced
  mushrooms, undrained
¼ teaspoon basil
¼ cup claret or other light, dry red wine

Trim excess fat from meat. Heat 4 tablespoons oil in skillet. Dredge meat in a mixture of flour, Accent, salt and pepper. Brown meat in oil, adding more oil as needed. Push meat to side of pan. Add onion and garlic and cook 3 minutes. Add gravy, mushrooms with juice and basil. Cover and simmer 45-60 minutes or until tender. Add a little water at a time to prevent sticking. Add claret. Serve on hot rice. Serves 3-4.

Karen Veillon McGlasson

BEEF BURGUNDY

3 pounds lean beef chuck, cubed
1 (10½ ounce) can consomme
1 (10½ ounce) can onion soup
1 (4 ounce) can V-8
1 cup burgundy
½ cup light brown sugar, packed

½ teaspoon garlic powder
1 teaspoon oregano
½ teaspoon celery salt
2 bay leaves
3 tablespoons cornstarch
⅓ cup water

Combine all ingredients except the cornstarch and water. Cover and simmer 2 hours, stirring occasionally. Then combine the cornstarch and water, add to stew, and cook until it thickens. Serve in soup bowls with garlic bread and green salad. My children like this over rice. Serves 6.

Betsy Wild

BOURGUIGNONNE VERON

2½ pounds stew meat	2-2½ teaspoons Bovril broth and
1½ cups teriyaki sauce	seasoning base
1 large onion, chopped	2 tablespoons tomato paste
1 large bell pepper, chopped	1½ cups burgundy
1 stick butter	¾ cup dry sherry
3 tablespoons brandy	¾ cup ruby port
½ pound small white onions, peeled,	1 (10½ ounce) can beef bouillon,
(about 12)	condensed
½ pound small fresh mushrooms	⅛ teaspoon pepper
2½ tablespoons flour	1 bay leaf

Marinate beef in teriyaki sauce 1½-2 hours with chopped onion and bell pepper. Heat 4 quart Dutch oven with tight lid. In hot butter over high heat, brown beef cubes, onions and peppers, about ¼ beef at a time, just enough to cover bottom of Dutch oven. Continue until all beef is browned, adding more butter as needed. Return all beef to Dutch oven. In small saucepan heat 2 tablespoons brandy, until hot. Ignite and pour over beef. When flame is out remove all beef. Set aside. Add 2 tablespoons butter to Dutch oven, heat slightly, add onions and cook over low heat, covered, until onions are slightly browned. Add mushrooms, cook for 3 minutes while stirring. Remove onions and mushrooms from oven. Stir in flour, Bovril and tomato paste until well blended. Stir in burgundy, sherry, port and bouillon. Preheat oven to 350°. Bring wine mixture to boiling, stirring, remove from heat, add beef, pepper and bay leaf, stir and mix well. Bake, covered and stirring occasionally 1½ hours or until beef is tender, adding remaining brandy a little at a time. Serves 6.

Terry Veron

MULLIGAN STEW

½ cup oil	2 quarts water
2 tablespoons flour	1½ cups diced raw potatoes
1 small can tomato paste	1 large can green giant peas
1 large onion, minced	left over roast and gravy
3 cloves garlic	salt and pepper to taste
1 stalk celery, chopped	3 tablespoons sugar
½ cup bell pepper, chopped	3 tablespoons chopped parsley
1½ cups sliced carrots	3 tablespoons chopped onion tops

Heat oil, add flour, make a light brown roux. Add tomato paste, stirring constantly over low heat for a few minutes, then add onions, stirring well; now add carrots and water. Cover and cook until carrots are almost tender. Now add potatoes and all remaining ingredients, except parsley and onion tops. Cover and cook slowly for 35-40 minutes. If not thick enough, add a little flour and water paste, or add water if too thick. Add onion tops and parsley and cook about 2 minutes more. Serves 6-8.

Mrs. L. A. Shelton

SHORT RIBS WITH HORSERADISH SAUCE

6 beef short ribs, seasoned with salt
    and pepper
2 cans beef broth
5 carrots, cut in quarters

5 onions, cut in quarters
8 new or small potatoes, peeled
12 large mushrooms

Horseradish Sauce:
1 tablespoon butter
1 tablespoon flour
2 cups broth from stew

½ cup sour cream
3 tablespoons horseradish
salt and pepper to taste

Brown short ribs. Season with salt and pepper. Add broth and enough water to cover. Simmer 1½ hours covered. Add vegetables and simmer another 20 minutes.

Sauce: Melt butter in saucepan, add flour and cook 5 minutes over low heat. Remove from heat. Add slowly 2 cups of broth from stew. Return to heat, stirring constantly. Add sour cream and horseradish and salt and pepper to taste. Add more broth if needed. Serve horseradish sauce on top of ribs and vegetables. Serves 4.

Brenda B. Hawes

STUFFED PEPPERS

2-4 cups cooked rice
10 green bell peppers
4 pounds ground beef
3 cups chopped onions
2 beef bouillon cubes

¾ can mushroom soup
salt, garlic powder, red pepper, black
    pepper to taste
seasoned bread crumbs
2 eggs

Cook approximately 2 cups of raw rice until dry and fluffy. Halve bell peppers lengthwise, cut out seeds and pulp and wash. Parboil pepper halves for about 10 minutes, until they are slightly pliable, remove and drain on paper towel. Brown ground meat in heavy pot. Add onions before meat is completely browned and cook down until onions are clear. Dilute bouillon cubes in small amount of water, add bouillon to mixture and add other seasoning except salt. Do not salt until you have added all other seasoning as the bouillon is salty. Add rice to desired consistency and then add mushroom soup and ½ cup seasoned bread crumbs. Mixture at this time should have the consistency of moist rice dressing. Beat eggs and add to mixture. Stuff pepper halves with beef and rice mixture and top with bread crumbs and a pat of butter. Place peppers in a pan or glass casserole dish containing about ⅛ inch water. Bake at 350° for 45 minutes to 1 hour. These are excellent to keep in the freezer—wrap individually in foil. Can be placed in oven still frozen—cover pan with foil for about 30 minutes and then uncover for about 30 minutes more until heated throughout. Serves 10-20.

Lynn Wilson Blevins

PIONONOS-STUFFED PLANTAIN RINGS

Meat Mixture:

2 ripe plantains
3 tablespoons oil
4 slices white bread
¼ cup milk
½ pound lean ground pork
¼ pound lean ground beef
1 cup finely diced ham
½ cup finely chopped onion
⅓ cup finely chopped green onion

1 small green pepper, finely chopped
2 tablespoons oil
1 cup drained canned or 3 fresh peeled
    chopped tomatoes
⅛ teaspoon allspice
salt and pepper to taste
beaten egg
⅓ cup oil

Salsa roja—red sauce:

1 onion, diced
2 stalks celery, diced
2 chili peppers, minced
1 (16 ounce) can tomatoes, chopped
    and drained

4 garlic cloves, minced
⅛ teaspoon ground cloves
salt to taste
1 cup dry red wine

Peel plantains and cut each one into four strips. In a skillet sauté plantains in three tablespoons oil over low heat, adding more if necessary. Cook for about 4 minutes on each side or until golden brown. Transfer plantains to paper towels to drain. While still warm shape plantains into rings and secure with toothpicks. Soak bread in milk and squeeze out most of liquid. Combine meats and bread and blend until smooth. In a large skillet sauté onion and green pepper for a few minutes. Add meat mixture stirring until meat is cooked. Add tomatoes after browning meat—add allspice. Remove pan from heat, and let mixture cool. While meat mixture is cooling, prepare sauce. Sauté onion, celery and chili peppers until soft. Add tomatoes, garlic cloves and salt. Cook over moderate heat about 4 minutes or until thick. Add wine, cook 10 minutes more and correct seasoning. Makes about 2 cups.

Stuff plantain rings with ⅓ cup meat mixture. Pat meat firmly into place and gently press top as flat as possible. Brush rings generously with beaten egg and brown in oil on both sides. Transfer to platter, remove picks, and serve with sauce. Serves 4.

Carola Bacqué

RICE EGGPLANT DRESSING

2 cups rice
3 eggplants
5 slices bread
3 pounds ground beef
2 onions, chopped finely
1 bell pepper, chopped finely
5 stalks celery, chopped finely

1 can tomatoes, chopped with liquid
1 tablespoon garlic salt
1 tablespoon salt
1 tablespoon black pepper
½ tablespoon red pepper
Parmesan cheese
bread crumbs

Cook 2 cups rice. Peel and cut up eggplants. Boil for 20 minutes in a little water with salt added. Add 5 slices of shredded bread to soak up. Brown ground meat. Add onions, bell pepper and celery to meat and cook until soft. Add the meat mixture to the eggplant along with a can of tomatoes, garlic salt, salt, black and red peppers. Add the rice. Top with Parmesan cheese and bread crumbs. Bake for 30 minutes at 350°. I've started using this dressing instead of cornbread dressing or rice dressing at Thanksgiving and Christmas. Fills two 2 quart casseroles. Freezes well. Serves 16.

Linda Larsen Billeaud

EGGPLANT DRESSING

1 pound Owens hot bulk sausage
½ pound ground meat
2 large eggplants, peeled and cubed
½ teaspoon oregano
½-1 cup Progresso Italian bread
  crumbs
1 large onion, chopped
2-3 stalks celery, chopped

½ bell pepper chopped
1 clove garlic, chopped
1 egg, slightly beaten
1 teaspoon Worcestershire
seasonings to taste
green onion tops and parsley
Parmesan cheese

Brown sausage meat and ground meat. Add eggplant and chopped vegetables. Let cook until eggplant is tender, stirring often. Season with oregano. Add Italian bread crumbs until moisture is absorbed. Add Worcestershire, green onion tops and parsley and salt and pepper to taste. Beat a small amount of dressing mixture into egg in order to prevent egg from cooking. Then add to dressing mixture. Pour into 1½-2 quart casserole. Sprinkle with cheese. Bake at 350° until heated thoroughly. Serves 8.

Judy Griffin

ST. LOUIS HAMBURGER

1 pound ground round
1 can deviled ham
salt, pepper

roquefort or blue cheese
dry red wine
butter

Blend ham spread with ground round. Add salt and freshly ground pepper to taste. Mold hamburgers about 1½ inch squares of cheese and put in a crock. Cover hamburgers with red wine and let stand covered in fridge for about 3 hours. Butter skillet adding a little of the marinade, and pan broil hamburgers to taste. Remove but keep warm. Add a little more butter and marinade to the pan. Let boil and pour sauce over hamburgers. Delicious served with hot biscuits and crisp green salad. Serves 4.

Eleanor Hall Lasseigne

BAKED KIBBIE

1 pound lean ground round
1 pound cracked wheat
1 medium onion
1 teaspoon salt

1 teaspoon pepper
1 cup butter
ice water

Stuffing:
1 pound chili ground meat
2 medium onions
¾ cup pine nuts

¼ teaspoon pepper
½ teaspoon salt

Wash cracked wheat and squeeze out the water. Add meat, onion and seasoning, put through fine blade of grinder, adding ice water as required for smoothness. Set aside, making stuffing.

Stuffing:
Chop onions, add to meat and seasoning, sauté. In a skillet on the side, saute pine nuts with a little butter and add to filling. Cook until brown. Butter 8x8 inch pan, make a layer of kibbie, spread stuffing, add another layer of kibbie, score top layer with knife, pour melted butter on top. Bake at 400° for 20-30 minutes. Serves 6-8.

Mrs. Norris Landry
Royal Catering

UPSIDE DOWN MEAT LOAF

½ cup brown sugar
½ cup catsup
1½ pounds ground beef
¾ cup milk
2 eggs beaten

1½ teaspoons salt
¼ teaspoon pepper
1 small onion, chopped
¼ teaspoon ginger
¾ cup crushed cracker crumbs

Butter a 9x3x5 inch loaf pan well. Press the brown sugar in bottom of pan and spread catsup over the sugar. Mix all remaining ingredients together and shape into a loaf. Put on top of catsup. Bake at 350° for 1 hour. Turn upside down to serve. Serves 6.
Variation: A little vinegar or lemon juice may be added to catsup to give sauce some tartness.

Billie Morgan White

MEAT LOAF

1 pound ground beef
¼ pound ground pork or sausage
2 tablespoons chopped onions
1 tablespoon chopped celery
1 teaspoon salt
1 teaspoon pepper
1 teaspoon sage

1 teaspoon mustard
1 teaspoon poultry seasoning
2 slices soft bread cubed and soaked in ½
    cup warm milk
1 beaten egg
2 teaspoons Worcestershire

Mix all together and bake 1 hour at 325°-350°.

Mrs. Robert S. Hatfield
Redlands, CA

TAMALE PIE

oil to cover bottom of pan
1 pound ground beef
salt
pepper
chili powder
3 pods garlic, minced

½ large bell pepper, chopped
2 stalks celery, chopped
4-6 bags, individual size, Fritos crushed
2 cans tomatoes
1 onion, sliced
½ cup grated Velveeta

Season meat and brown with garlic, bell pepper and celery. Layer 2 or 2½ quart casserole with crushed Fritos, then meat, then squeezed tomatoes, then finely sliced onions. Repeat layers. Put final layer of crushed Fritos on top. Grate Velveeta cheese over Fritos. Bake in 350° oven until cheese melts. Use juice of tomatoes in each layer when squeezing tomatoes. Serves 4-6.

Mrs. J. C. Chargois, Sr.

LASAGNA

Meat Sauce:
⅛ cup olive oil
¼ cup margarine
3 medium onions, finely chopped
1½ pounds ground beef, regular
8 garlic cloves, finely chopped
6 tablespoons wine, Chianti

6 tablespoons finely chopped parsley
2 (6 ounce) cans tomato paste plus 4
    tablespoons water
2 (8 ounce) cans tomato sauce
6 stalks celery, finely chopped
salt and pepper to taste

Lasagna:
3 tablespoons salt
3 tablespoons olive oil
9 quarts boiling water
2 (12 ounce) packages curly edge
    lasagne
1 recipe meat sauce

3 (6 ounce) packages mozzarella cheese,
    sliced
18 slices American cheese
3 (12 ounce) packages cottage cheese or
    Ricotta

Meat Sauce:
In saucepan, heat olive oil and margarine together. Add onion and ground beef, sauté until brown, stirring occasionally. Add garlic and parsley. Cook over low heat 10 minutes. Stir in wine; cover and steam for 2 minutes. Add tomato paste and water and tomato sauce. Bring to boiling point and add celery, salt and pepper. Cover and cook over low heat for 1 hour, stirring occasionally.

Lasagna: Add 3 tablespoons salt and 3 tablespoons olive oil to rapidly boiling water. Gradually add lasagna so that water continues to boil. Cook uncovered, stirring occasionally until tender. Drain in colander. Cover bottoms of 3 rectangular baking dishes or foil lasagna pans with ⅓ meat sauce. Place ⅓ mozzarella, 1⅓ slice in each dish divided into 4 long strips over sauce and place 2 slices American cheese, divided, in each dish between mozzarella and over sauce. Top each with ⅓ of 1 (12 ounce) cottage cheese. Add a layer of half the lasagna, 4 pieces each dish, cover with ⅓ meat sauce, ⅓ mozzarella and American cheese and ⅓ cottage cheese. Add remaining lasagna, 4 slices each dish. Cover with remaining meat sauce and cheeses. Makes 3 dishes of lasagna. Bake 1 in moderately hot oven 375°, for about 30 minutes. Cover 2 with foil and freeze for future use. To prepare frozen lasagna, put covered frozen lasagna on a pan in oven at 350° for about 1 hour. Uncover the last 10 minutes of baking time to let the moisture escape. Serves 12.

Mrs. Joseph Giglio, Sr.

MOM'S MANICOTTI OR CANNELLONI

8 manicotti or cannelloni noodles

Filling:
4 ounces chopped Mozzarella cheese
½ cup chopped green onion tops
¾ cup Ricotta cheese or cottage cheese
½ cup Parmesan cheese

1 package fresh or frozen spinach, cooked 5 minutes and drained
¼ cup Italian bread crumbs
dash of garlic powder
1 egg, slightly beaten

Sauce:
1 tablespoon cooking oil
2 onions, chopped
salt and pepper to taste
2 cans stewed tomatoes

1 can tomato paste
2 bay leaves
1 teaspoon oregano
1 pound ground meat

Topping:
¼ cup Parmesan cheese

Boil noodles 10 minutes; drain.
Filling: Mix all ingredients together and stuff noodles with filling.

Sauce: Sauté onions in oil, add remaining ingredients and cook covered, on a low heat until sauce is thick—at least 1 hour. Put one thin layer of sauce in baking dish, then stuffed noodles. Spread rest of sauce on top and sprinkle with Parmesan cheese. Cover with foil and bake at 325° for 1 hour. Serves 4.

Mrs. J. R. Romero, Jr.

FANTASTIC CANNELLONI

1 (8 ounce) package manicotti or cannelloni shells
1¼ pounds Italian sausage
1 (10-ounce) package frozen chopped spinach, thawed
2 eggs, lightly beaten
8 ounces mozzarella cheese, shredded

1 cup creamed cottage cheese, small curd
¼ cup grated Parmesan cheese
½ cup bread crumbs (optional)
salt and pepper to taste
1 (32-ounce) jar Hunt's Prima Salsa Sauce

Boil cannelloni shells in a large amount of salted water to which 2 tablespoons cooking oil have been added. Drain and rinse thoroughly; separate to prevent them from sticking together. Remove Italian sausage from casing and brown in heavy skillet, stirring to break up pieces. Place in bowl and add thawed spinach, mozzarella cheese, cottage cheese, Parmesan cheese, bread crumbs and eggs. Season to taste with salt and pepper and mix thoroughly. Stuff mixture into prepared cannelloni shells and place in a single layer in a well-greased baking dish. Cover with Prima Salsa Sauce; you may not need the whole jar, but do be generous. Bake in a pre-heated 350° oven for 30 minutes. Additional Parmesan or mozzarella cheese may be strewn on top of the sauce during the last 10 minutes of baking. Servings: 6.

Margaret A. Blumberg

CREOLE SPAGHETTI

Sauce:

6 tablespoons cooking oil	4 cans water
3 large onions, chopped	3 (15½ ounce) cans tomatoes, include
3-4 cloves garlic, chopped	juice
2-2½ teaspoons salt	1 tablespoon Worcestershire
4 small cans tomato paste	bag crab boil

Meatballs:

1½ pounds ground meat	¾ cup grated Parmesan cheese
1 teaspoon salt	3 unbeaten eggs
¼ teaspoon black pepper	2 tablespoons chopped parsley
⅛ teaspoon garlic powder	1 cup Redi-flavored bread crumbs
2 teaspoons finely chopped green	1 cup milk
onion tops	dash Worcestershire

Sauce: (Day ahead of meatballs) Cook onions and garlic in oil. Cover and do not brown. When onions are soft, mash to a fine pulp with potato masher. This must be done slowly, takes about 25 minutes. Add salt, tomato paste, tomatoes, Worcestershire. Drop in full bag of crab boil. Be careful not to break bag when stirring. Now you are ready for a whole morning of simmering. Cover pot—slow and long cooking is the key. The sauce made ahead and reheated is best. After 2 hours simmering, you should taste. Sauce may be getting too hot, you may want to remove bag, need to add salt, garlic powder or more Worcestershire. This is where you go creative. Place bag in bowl, you may want a little of the juice to give your meatballs a piquant flavor.

Next Day: Meatballs:
Mix all the ingredients and shape into small round balls. This is a messy job. Fry slowly in deep oil until firm, not too brown. As you brown meatballs, drop into sauce. Remember, sauce is still on slowest heat. The meatballs are supposed to absorb sauce. Leave them all day if you wish, but don't cook. Two packages of Capellini Number 1 is needed for this amount. You should have approximately 39 quarter size meatballs. Serves 8.

From the files of Mable Lewis Kitt

CHILI

small amount cooking oil	2 tablespoons whole cumin seeds
1 large onion, chopped	1 tablespoon brown sugar
½ cup bell pepper, chopped	1 bay leaf
2 pounds lean ground beef	2 tablespoons catsup
1 small can tomato paste	1 teaspoon Accent
1 (6 ounce) can tomato juice	dash Tabasco
1 (1 pound) can kidney beans	salt and pepper to taste
3 tablespoons chili powder	1 cup water

Sauté onions and green pepper in small amount of oil. Add ground beef and brown. Add rest of the ingredients and simmer for 2 hours. This can be frozen. Serves 4-8.

Mrs. E. B. Mercer, III

DON'S CHILI

2 pounds ground chuck
2 white onions, diced
2 cloves garlic, chopped finely
1 (16 ounce) can whole tomatoes
1 (10 ounce) can enchilada sauce
2 teaspoons salt
2 tablespoons black pepper
3 teaspoons cumin seeds

3 teaspoons chili powder
1 jalapeno pepper, chopped
1½ cups boiling water
½ teaspoon cayenne pepper
1 can pinto beans, added last 15 minutes
   cooking time
4 tablespoons butter

Sauté onions in butter until tender. Add ground meat, sauté until well done. Add remaining ingredients, cook slowly for 2 hours. Serves 4-8. Variations: May substitute Rotel tomatoes for regular if you like it hot and spicy. Freezes well.

Don Burts

COONY FRIED RICE

1½ pounds ground beef/pork
   mixture
1 large onion, coarsely chopped
2 stalks celery, chopped
½ teaspoon garlic powder
2 tablespoons soy sauce

salt and pepper to taste
1½ cups water
1 large bell pepper cut in large squares
2 cans LaChoy fried rice
green onions tops, chopped
parsley, chopped

Brown meat. Add onions, celery, garlic powder, soy sauce, salt and pepper. Cook for 10 minutes. Add water and simmer for another 5-10 minutes. Add bell pepper and rice. Cover and cook slowly until rice is fluffy and soft. Add onion tops and parsley. Great with plain meats or fried chicken. Beef/pork mixture can be substituted with sausage. Serves 10.

Wally Romero

DRIP BEEF SANDWICHES

1 (6-7 pound) chuck roast
1 bay leaf
1 bouillon cube
1 teaspoon each—cracked pepper,
   salt, oregano, rosemary, summer
   savory, garlic salt

enough water so roast is covered from
   bottom of pan to middle
your favorite bun

Put roast in pan. Season roast while in pan. Fill pan with water until roast is ½ submerged. Add bayleaf and bouillon. Bake in 200° oven overnight (10 P.M. to 8 A.M.) Remove roast and let cool. Meanwhile put roaster with drippings on the stove on low heat. Cook for at least 3 hours. Taste the gravy. Add another bouillon cube and more salt if necessary. Shred roast into small pieces. Arrange on your favorite bun and serve with small bowls of gravy for dunking. Great for cold weekends at home. Can be frozen. Serves 10.

Melinda Jones

PUERTO RICAN PIG ROAST

1 pig, 50 pounds dressed with breast
  and pelvic bones left intact
seasoning mixture: 1½ cups salt, 4-5
  large heads garlic, mashed (use
  food processor), ½ cup coarse black
  pepper, ½ cup red pepper, ½ cup
  oregano

olive oil and lemon juice
100 pounds charcoal, twine, nails
annatto oil—made from simmering
  achiote seeds (available in speciality
  shops) in vegetable oil, then
  discarding seeds
salt water for basting

Wash pig well inside and out with lemon juice. With sharp knife make slits all over pig approximately 1½-2 inches apart. Fill slits with seasoning mixture. Rub pig well with mixture of olive oil and lemon juice. Refrigerate overnight. This is done by placing pig in large garbage bag.

Make annatto oil. In 1 quart hot vegetable oil simmer 2 cups achiote seeds for 10 minutes. Remove from heat, cool oil, and strain into jar. Discard seeds. Refrigerate. This oil may be kept for several months. It is used to redden and mildly flavor meat, poultry and seafood sauce in many Latin American countries.

Day before pig roast, dig a shallow pit about 4 feet long and 3 feet wide. Cut a sapling one to two inches in diameter and 8-10 feet long. Also cut 2 fork sticks about 2½-3 feet long. Drive fork sticks into ground 6-10 inches at opposite ends of pit. Early in morning line both sides of pit with foil. Place 10-15 pounds of charcoal on foil and light. (You will add more charcoal every 30-40 minutes.) It will take about 30 minutes to be ready. At this time drive sapling through mouth and tail of pig. Make 3 slits along either side of backbone evenly spaced from shoulder to rump. Run twine through these slits around pole and tie securely. Drive one nail through snout into pole, the other at base of tail. Tie front legs to the sapling at the chest cavity. Tie hind legs behind tail. Place pig on 2 fork sticks over fire and rotate to cook evenly. After eight hours start basting pig with annatto oil every 20-30 minutes. The last hour baste pig with salt water, which is very salty to crisp skin. Pig should be ready in 12 hours. This is a very festive meal, and although the cooking period is long a good time can be had by all while assisting the chef. Serves 30.

Odon Bacqué, Sr.

OVEN PORK CHOPS

4 butterfly pork chops, ¾-1 inch thick
salt, red and black pepper
margarine—softened

Italian bread crumbs
oil

Season pork chops with salt and peppers to your taste. Coat each side of the chop with softened margarine, then with bread crumbs. Place in well greased baking pan and put in preheated 350° oven. Cover tightly with foil. Cook for about 1½ hours, turning once at midway point and adding a little water to the bottom of the pan. Cover again and continue cooking until chops are tender. Make a gravy from pan drippings if desired. Serves 4.

Mrs. Dwight Andrus, Sr.

PORK CHOP CASSEROLE

4-5 (1 inch thick) pork chops
2 tablespoons melted shortening
1½ cups uncooked regular rice
1 (6 ounce) can tomato wedges,
    undrained
1 (10½ ounce) can beef consomme

1 (1⅜ ounce) package dry onion soup mix
1 teaspoon thyme
1 teaspoon oregano
salt and pepper to taste

Brown chops in shortening in heavy skillet. Place rice in a greased shallow 2 quart casserole, lay chops on top. Combine tomatoes, consomme, onion soup mix, thyme, oregano, salt and pepper. Pour over chops. Cover and bake at 350° for 1¼ hours. Rich but good. Serves 4-5.

Annette Myers

PORK CHOP BAKE

4 medium potatoes
1 tablespoon oil
4 thick pork chops
1 tablespoon butter
1 large onion, cut in rings

1½ tablespoons flour
1 cup chicken or beef bouillon
2 teaspoons vinegar
dash garlic salt
1 cup sour cream

Peel and quarter potatoes and boil just until tender. Season and brown chops; place in a shallow baking dish along with boiled potatoes. Sauté onions in butter, remove and add to the chops. Stir flour into butter remaining in pan. Add more butter if necessary. Cook flour slowly for 2-3 minutes, but do not allow to brown. Add bouillon, vinegar and garlic salt and season to taste with salt and pepper. Remove from heat and add sour cream, stirring until blended. Pour over potatoes, chops and onions. Bake at 375° covered for ½ hour and uncovered for ½ hour. Serves 4.

Margart A. Blumberg

PORK CHOPS AND CABBAGE

1 teaspoon oil
salt and pepper
8 pork chops
2 teaspoons water
½ teaspoon salt
2 whole cloves
1 bay leaf
1 medium head cabbage, sliced thinly

1½ cups diced tart apples, about 2
    cooking apples
½ large onion, chopped
¼ cup sugar
1½ teaspoons flour, all-purpose
2 teaspoons vinegar
2 teaspoons water

Heat oil in skillet at 350°. Salt and pepper meat; brown chops. Add 2 teaspoons water, ½ teaspoon salt, cloves, bay leaf; cover and simmer 30 minutes. Remove chops. Discard cloves and bay leaf. Add cabbage, apple and onion. Mix sugar, flour, vinegar and water; pour over cabbage. Cover and simmer 5 minutes. You may stir, return chops to top of cabbage; cover and cook 20 minutes or until all is tender. Serves 4-8.

Brenda Fuselier

PINEY-WOODS PORK CHOPS

6 pork chops
salt, pepper to taste
6 pineapple rings, reserve juice
1 (4 ounce) can mushroom stems and
    pieces

sherry wine
paprika
oil
1 cup water

Have pork chops cut 1 inch thick. Season both sides with salt and pepper. Brown both sides in skillet with small amount of oil. Reduce heat and add 1 cup water. Place 1 pineapple ring on top of each pork chop. Pour pineapple juice from can into skillet. Fill hole of pineapple with mushroom stems and pieces and add mushroom juice to skillet. Add any additional seasoning desired. Keep liquid in skillet about ¼ inch deep. Cover skillet with lid and cook slowly for 2 hours. Pour a little sherry wine over chops 4 times while cooking and baste frequently. Ten minutes before serving, sprinkle paprika on pineapple rings and place under broiler long enough to slightly brown the pineapples. This is an original recipe. Serves 6.

Bill Fuller
Kinder, LA

LULU'S PORK CHOPS AND SPAGHETTI

6-8 center cut pork chops
flour
2 large onions, chopped
1 cup celery, chopped
1 cup chopped bell pepper
1 can drained tomatoes
2 small cans tomato paste
water

8 ounces spaghetti
salt and pepper to taste
2 cloves chopped garlic
2 tablespoons parsley, chopped
2 tablespoons onion tops, chopped
Parmesan cheese
4 tablespoons oil

Heat 4 tablespoons cooking oil in skillet. Salt and pepper pork chops, flour and fry until almost cooked. Put aside on kitchen toweling to drain excess oil. Put spaghetti on to cook. Now cook onions, celery, bell pepper in same skillet and oil you fried pork chops in. Cook until soft and drain off excess oil. Add tomatoes and tomato paste. Cook 5 minutes. Add water, a cup at a time until you have a nice thick gravy. Add chopped garlic and salt and pepper to taste. Now place pork chops in this gravy and cover and cook on a low fire for 30 minutes, until chops are tender. Put cooked spaghetti in a large casserole dish and mix most of gravy into it, mixing well. Place pork chops on top of dish and put rest of gravy over them. Add parsley and onion tops to casserole. Top with Parmesan cheese and bake at 350° until hot. Serves 6-8.

Mrs. Eugene P. Cella

STUFFED PORK CHOP SAUCE PIQUANT

oil
8 stuffed pork chops (if stuffed not
   available, chops about ¾ to 1 inch
   thick may be used)
4 large white onions, chopped
2 bell peppers, cut into silver dollar
   size pieces

2 cans Rotel tomatoes
2 (1 pound) cans regular tomatoes
1 (12 ounce) can tomato sauce
1 tablespoon roux
1 bunch onion tops, chopped

With small amount of cooking oil, brown the chops in a large black iron pot or Dutch oven. Remove chops; add onions and sauté. Add other ingredients except the onion tops and cook covered on low heat for about 1½ hours. Add chops and cook for an additional hour or until chops are tender. Turn off heat and allow to sit until oil comes to the top. Skim off all oil, put in onion tops and reheat. Serve with rice. Serves 8.

Henry L. Mayer, Jr.

PORK PATTIES

1 pound ground pork
½ cup dry bread crumbs
1 egg
1 tablespoon minced onion

½ teaspoon salt
⅛ teaspoon pepper
1 tablespoon vegetable oil

Mix all ingredients except oil. Shape into 4 patties. Fry patties in hot oil in 10 inch skillet over medium heat, turning once, until brown on both sides, about 15 minutes.

Micro Directions: Prepare patties as directed. Reduce vegetable oil to 1 tablespoon; microwave vegetable oil in 9 inch glass pie plate on full power until hot, about 2 minutes. Add patties; microwave on full power until light brown, about 5 minutes. Turn patties, rotate plate a half turn. Microwave until light brown, 4 minutes. Serves 4.

Elizabeth Preis

PLUM BARBECUED SPARERIBS

1 (10 ounce) jar Damson plum jelly
⅓ cup dark corn syrup
⅓ cup soy sauce
¼ cup chopped green onions
2 cloves garlic, crushed

2 teaspoons ground ginger
2 pounds spareribs, separated into
   individual ribs or cut into bitesize
   pieces

Mix together jelly, corn syrup, soy sauce, green onions, garlic and ginger in small sauce pan. Heat over medium heat until jelly is melted. Pour into 11¾x7½x1¾ inch dish. Add ribs, cover and marinate in refrigerator overnight. Remove from marinade and place in shallow baking pan. Bake in preheated 350° oven for 1 hour. Baste with marinade last ½ hour. Serves 4.

Mrs. William Bacqué
Lake Charles, LA

SAUCE FOR PORK CHOPS OR RIBS

⅛ cup salad oil
½ cup chopped onions
1 chopped garlic clove
1 cup honey
½ cup wine vinegar
½ cup ketchup

¼ cup Worcestershire
1½ teaspoons dry mustard
¾ teaspoon salt
½ teaspoon oregano
½ teaspoon pepper
¼ teaspoon thyme

Heat oil and add onion and garlic. Cook until tender not brown. Add other ingredients and bring to a boil. Turn down heat and simmer for 5 minutes. Baste meat last 10 minutes of cooking time with this sauce. This can be stored in refrigerator for several weeks. Yield: 1 quart, enough for 3-4 pounds pork chops or ribs.

Marilyn Tankersley Taylor

PORK CHOP DINNER

1 large can peas, reserve juice
2 large potatoes, peeled and sliced in thin rounds
cracked black pepper, salt to taste

1 stick butter
garlic powder, onion powder to taste
6-8 pork chops, may use stuffed ones also

Grease pyrex dish with oil or use Pam. Layer and season above ingredients in order except pork chops. Dot with 1 stick butter then add juice from peas to cover bottom of pan. Add seasoned pork chops and bake covered with foil for 1¼ hours. Open foil 10 minutes at end of cooking time. This is good to make in advance. You may also debone chops to fit more in recipe. Add this to a salad and bread and you have a good meal. Serves 6-8.

LaNien Clark Theard

BAKED BEANS WITH PORK CHOPS

Serves 6-8

1 pound Michigan Whites (navy beans)
1 clove garlic
1 teaspoon salt
2 tablespoons molasses or cane syrup
½ teaspoon dry mustard

1 medium onion, diced
2 tablespoons catsup
Water to completely cover beans
6-8 pork chops

Boil the beans gently until just barely cooked. Add the rest of the ingredients, except pork chops. Brown pork chops and place on top of beans in a large baking dish. Bake covered for 1 to 1½ hours at 350 degrees. Be sure there is enough water so that it doesn't become dry. Serves 6-8.

Lorraine Usner

CHERRY ALMOND PORK

salt and pepper
1 (4 pound) pork loin, rolled, boned
   and tied
1 (12 ounce) jar cherry preserves
2 tablespoons light corn syrup
¼ cup red wine vinegar
¼ teaspoon salt
¼ teaspoon cinnamon
¼ teaspoon nutmeg
¼ teaspoon cloves
¼ cup slivered almonds, toasted

Rub roast with a little salt and pepper. Place on a shallow baking pan. Roast uncovered in 325° oven for about 2-2½ hours. Meanwhile, combine remaining ingredients except for almonds. Heat to boiling, stirring frequently; reduce heat and simmer 2 minutes. Add toasted almonds. Keep the sauce warm. Spoon enough sauce over the roast to glaze; return to oven for 30 minutes more or until meat thermometer registers 170°. Baste the roast several times during the last 30 minutes. Pass the remaining sauce with the roast. Serves 8.

Maureen Goldware

APRICOT GLAZED PORK LOIN

1 (5-6 pound) pork loin roast
2 large cloves garlic, slivered
2 cloves garlic, pressed
½ cup soy sauce
½ cup catsup
¼ cup lemon juice
½ teaspoon black pepper
2 cups apricot preserves
spiced crab apples and parsley for
   garnish

Make small slits in roast and insert garlic slivers. Combine next 5 ingredients. Place roast in 13x9 inch baking dish and pour soy sauce marinade over roast. Let roast marinate overnight turning 3-4 times. Place roast in shallow open roasting pan on rack. Baste with marinade. Place in oven which has been heated to 325°. Roast about 2 hours basting with remaining marinade every 30 minutes. Melt apricot preserves. Remove roast from oven and brush ¾ cup of melted preserves over top of roast. Return to oven and continue baking for 30 minutes. Place roast on large platter and garnish with parsley and crab apples. Serve roast with remaining heated apricot preserves. (Note: This recipe calls for no salt. Soy sauce makes roast brown very rapidly, making it necessary sometimes to cover top with foil to prevent burning.) Serves 10.

Mrs. Bill Davis

NEVA'S JAMBALAYA

2 cups chopped onion
Butter
1 (1 pound) can whole tomatoes with
  juice
½ pound salt meat, parboiled, cubed
1 pound smoked sausage, cut in
  bite-size pieces

1 pint oysters and juice
2 cans chicken consommé
Salt and pepper to taste
3½ cups uncooked rice
½ cup finely chopped onion tops
½ cup finely chopped parsley
½ stick butter, melted

Sauté onions in a large, heavy metal saucepan. Add tomatoes with juice, break-ing up tomatoes. Add parboiled salt meat and sausage pieces, oysters and oyster juice, consommé, and salt and pepper to taste. Remember the salt meat and sausage will make dish salty, so be careful not to oversalt. Bring this mixture to a boil. Add raw rice, turn heat down low, cover and cook slowly 30-40 minutes, until rice is tender. Stir in onion tops, parsley and melted butter. Serves 10.

Marion M. McDade

WHITE SQUASH AND HAM CASSEROLE

3 medium white squash
1 large minced onion
1 clove garlic, optional
½ cup chopped bell pepper
2 tablespoons butter
1½ cups cooked rice
1 cup cubed, cooked ham
2 strips crisp bacon, crumbled

1 teaspoon chopped parsley
1 teaspoon chopped onion tops
1 tablespoon sugar
salt to taste
red and black pepper to taste
cracker crumbs
Parmesan cheese

Peel squash and remove large seeds, cut and parboil until tender. Drain all but a little water from the squash and set aside. Now, in a skillet, sauté onions, garlic, bell pepper in 2 tablespoons butter. Mash squash, add to skillet and cook a little more. Add cooked rice, ham and bacon, parsley and onion tops and seasonings. Put mixture in buttered casserole dish. Top with cracker crumbs, bits of butter and sprinkle with Parmesan cheese. For variations: Use ½ pound of crabmeat or 1 pound shrimp instead of ham. Add to skillet after onions are sauteed and cook a little while. Serves 6.

Mrs. Eugene P. Cella

HAM AND CHEESE CASSEROLE

3 cups cubed French bread
3 cups cubed cooked ham
½ pound cheddar cheese
3 tablespoons flour
1 tablespoon dry mustard

3 tablespoons melted butter or
  margarine
4 eggs
3 cups milk
Tabasco

Make a layer of ⅓ of bread, ham and cheese in a buttered 8 cup baking dish or souffle dish. Mix flour and mustard, sprinkle about 1 tablespoon of this mixture over first layer. Drizzle 1 tablespoon melted butter over first layer. Repeat with remaining ingredients to make 3 layers total. Beat eggs with milk and Tabasco. Pour over layers in baking dish. Cover, chill 4 hours or overnight. Bake uncovered until puffed and golden at 350° for 1 hour. Serves 6.

Barbara Ringham

COMPANY HAM IN SOUR CREAM

3 cups cooked ham in julienne strips
½ cup chopped onion
4 tablespoons butter or margarine
4 tablespoons white flour
2 cups dairy sour cream

1 (8 ounce) can broiled, sliced
  mushrooms, drained
hot, cooked rice or patty shells
⅛ teaspoon cayenne pepper

Cook ham and onion in butter until onion is tender but not brown. Sprinkle with flour, gradually stir in sour cream. Add mushrooms, cook over low heat stirring constantly, just until mixture thickens, 2-3 minutes. Serve over rice or in patty shells. Season to taste. Garnish with parsley. Serves 4.

Karen Veillon McGlasson

BRUCCIALUNA

Veal Birds:

2 tablespoons onion tops, finely
  chopped
2 tablespoons parsley, chopped
2 cloves garlic, pressed
2 hard-boiled eggs, mashed
2 raw eggs

½ cup Parmesan cheese
1 teaspoon salt
½ teaspoon cayenne
2½ cups bread crumbs
6-8¼x2½ inch slices veal or round steak
1 stick butter

Mix all ingredients except meat and butter until well blended. Pound meat until thin and tender. Spread 1 tablespoon of mixture on each piece of meat—roll up and tie with string or secure with tooth picks. Brown birds well in butter or oil and add to tomato gravy and cook slowly about 2 hours. (Birds or sauce can be prepared a day or so ahead of time.)

Sauce:

½ cup oil
½ cup flour
1 onion, finely chopped
1 bell pepper, finely chopped
2 (15 ounce) cans tomato sauce

1 can mushroom pieces
1 can cream of mushroom soup
1 cup water
salt and cayenne to taste

Make a golden roux with oil and flour, add onions and bell pepper and cook until tender. Add sauce, mushrooms, soup and water, salt and pepper. Cook slowly for 1 hour. Adjust seasoning and add water as needed. After birds are added cook an additional hour or more. Serve over spaghetti. Serves 4-6 generously.

Kathy Leonard

STUFFED VEAL CUTLETS

6 veal cutlets
1½ cups herb stuffing mix
½ pound fresh mushrooms, chopped
¼ cup celery, chopped finely
¼ cup onions, chopped finely

1 stick butter
¼ cup water
1 can cream of mushroom soup
½ can water
½ cup sour cream

Sauté vegetables in ½ stick butter, reserve ½ the chopped mushrooms for gravy. Mix sauteed vegetables with stuffing mix and ¼ cup hot water. Divide stuffing into six portions and form into balls. Place on cutlets, roll and secure with toothpick. Using ½ stick butter, sauté cutlets in a skillet. Add soup, remaining mushrooms and ½ can water. Cover and cook on low heat until tender, about 1 hour. Stir occasionally. Three minutes before serving, add ½ cup sour cream to hot gravy. Spoon gravy over cutlets when serving. Serves 6.

Jo Ann Broussard

VEAL ITALIANO

4 tablespoons butter
2 tablespoons olive oil
½ cup shallots or green onions,
　chopped
1 clove garlic, chopped
½ pound mushrooms
½ pound fresh tomatoes, peeled and
　chopped

½ cup dry sherry wine or Marsala
½ teaspoon sugar
¼ teaspoon oregano
¼ teaspoon basil
¼ teaspoon pepper, coarse ground
6-7 thin veal scallops, about 1½ pounds
1 tablespoon grated Parmesan cheese

Sauté onions and garlic in 2 tablespoons butter and 1 tablespoon olive oil for about 3 minutes. Add mushrooms and cook until golden brown. Add chopped tomatoes, wine, oregano, sugar, basil and pepper. Simmer for 30 minutes. In another skillet, brown veal in remaining butter and olive oil on both sides and cook for about 5 minutes. Pour sauce over veal and simmer for 5 minutes. Sprinkle with Parmesan cheese and serve. Serves 4-5

Rita Durio

DELICIOUS VEAL CHOPS

8 rib chops ½ inch thick
2 sticks salted butter
2 (4 ounce) cans button mushrooms
　with liquid
2 teaspoons prepared mustard

¼ teaspoon pepper
1 cup seasoned bread crumbs
salt to taste
green onion tops

Marinate chops: Melt butter over low heat. Don't let the butter brown. Combine butter with liquid from mushrooms, mustard and pepper. Spoon marinade over chops that are placed in a skillet. Place skillet over a pilot light on stove or turn electric burner on lowest heat possible. Marinate for at least 1 hour. Bread chops, save marinade. Salt to taste. Broil chops 3 inches from heat, 15 minutes on each side. Baste every 5 minutes with marinade. Sprinkle with mushrooms, onion tops and marinade in the last 10 minutes. Serves 4.

Cristie O. Adams

EASY VEAL CORDON BLEU

4 slices young veal cutlets, lightly
　salted
4 slices thin, boiled ham
4 slices Swiss cheese
½ cup flour

1 egg, beaten
1 cup dry bread crumbs
2 tablespoons cooking oil
2 tablespoons olive oil

Pound veal slices until very thin, ¼ inch or roll between sheets of waxed paper. Salt each piece lightly. Lay 1 slice ham, 1 slice cheese on each slice of veal. Fold over and skewer with toothpick. Dip in flour, then into beaten egg, then into bread crumbs. Fry until lightly brown on both sides in heavy skillet with oil heated until it smokes. Drain excess grease on paper towels and serve while hot, garnished with slice of fresh lemon. Veal, cheese and ham may be put together ahead of time and frozen. Serves 4.

Mrs. Paul Zehnder, Jr.

VEAL SPAGHETTI

2-3 green peppers, cut into strips
¼ cup salad oil
2 pounds cubed veal, as for stew
salt and pepper to taste
1 (28 ounce) can whole tomatoes,
    cut up

1 (4 ounce) can mushrooms, undrained
½ cup dry red wine
1 clove garlic, minced
1 (12 ounce) package spaghetti

Sauté green peppers in hot salad oil until tender. Remove from skillet and set aside. Season veal with salt and pepper. Brown in the hot salad oil. Add to-matoes, mushrooms with juice, wine, garlic and green peppers. Simmer uncov-ered for 1 hour or until meat is tender. Season to taste with salt and pepper. Serve over cooked spaghetti. Serves 4-6.

Pete Saporito
New Orleans, LA

VITELLO TONNATO

2 pounds leg or loin of veal, boned,
    rolled and tied
3 stalks celery
1 medium onion

1 carrot
4 peppercorns
3 cloves
3 quarts rich chicken stock

Simmer all ingredients in pot for 1½ hours, keeping pot covered. Remove veal from pot, cool and refrigerate until firm. Reserve stock. Serve with sauce.

Sauce:
1 (3½ ounce) can tuna, drained
4 anchovy fillets
1 inch piece dill pickle half
½ stalk celery, chopped
1 tablespoon chopped green onion
2 egg yolks

½ cup olive oil
black pepper
2 tablespoons lemon juice
Garnishes: lemon slices, capers, fresh
    parsley or tarragon

To prepare sauce place first 5 ingredients and 1 tablespoon oil in food processor with steel blade and mix thoroughly. Add egg yolks and process for a few seconds. Pour in through feeding tube 1 tablespoon lemon juice and oil slowly, continually processing, until thick and shiny. Add more lemon juice to taste and enough veal broth to give sauce consistency of cream. To serve slice veal thinly and cover with sauce. Refrigerate overnight to marinate. Garnish and serve with cold rice sea-soned with vinaigrette and peas. Wonderful as appetizer before an Italian dinner. Serves 6 as main course, 10-12 as appetizer.

Carola Bacqué

MARINATED LEG OF LAMB

1 (6 pound) leg of lamb, boned and butterflied
1 teaspoon coarsely cracked pepper
4 cloves garlic, sliced
2 tablespoons vinegar
½ cup red wine
½ cup olive oil
2 bay leaves
½ teaspoon dried tarragon
2 tablespoons salt

Spread the lamb flat in an oblong pyrex container. Sprinkle with pepper and garlic. Mix the remaining ingredients, add to the lamb and marinate in the refrigerator for 24 hours before cooking. Turn occasionally.

Remove the lamb from the marinade and cook over very hot coals for 6 minutes each side. Meat should be well browned and crusty. Spread out coals to reduce intensity of heat, and continue cooking 6-7 minutes each side or a total of 25 minutes. Lamb may also be cooked in a very hot oven. Should register 120° on meat thermometer for pink center. Slice as you would a steak. Serves 8.

Judy Fuller

BRAISED LAMB SHANKS BURGUNDY

1 tablespoon oil
4 pounds meaty lamb shanks
1 onion, chopped
1 large carrot, sliced
1 celery stalk, sliced
12 cherry tomatoes, peeled
2 garlic cloves, minced
1 cup red burgundy
½ cup beef broth
1 teaspoon thyme
1 bay leaf
salt and pepper to taste

Preheat oven to 325°. Heat oil in large oven proof casserole over medium high heat. Add lamb and brown well. Drain off fat. Place vegetables in casserole. Stir for a few minutes. Add remaining ingredients and blend with meat and vegetables. Cover and bake 2-2½ hours, or until lamb is tender. Serve over rice or noodles. Serves 6.

Carola Bacqué

SHEPHERD'S PIE

4 cups cold roast lamb that has been
   put through meat grinder
½ cup clear leftover lamb drippings
   or gravy
¾ cup canned beef consomme
2 tablespoons butter
1-2 tablespoons flour

1 teaspoon Worcestershire
1 teaspoon A-1 sauce
½ teaspoon salt
½ teaspoon pepper
1 cup finely diced, boiled carrots
4 servings instant mashed potatoes, to
   use as topping

Heat the clear lamb gravy and beef broth together in saucepan. In frying pan, melt butter, slowly stir in flour with wooden spoon. Gradually add hot broth and gravy, making a smooth consistency. Cook until thickened into a sauce. Add seasonings. Pour this sauce over cooked roast lamb that has been put through meat grinder. Stir in drained, cooked carrots. Place in 1½ quart buttered baking dish. Prepare 4 servings instant mashed potatoes. Place mashed potatoes on top of meat mixture. Place in hot oven and cook until potatoes are a golden brown. Serve immediately. Serves 4-6.

Sue Alves

CHOW MEIN

1 pound pork, diced
1 pound beef, diced
1 pound veal, diced
6 tablespoons oil
2 cups water
2 cups onions, sliced
6 cups celery, sliced
1 teaspoon salt

¼ teaspoon pepper
¼ cup cornstarch
1 cup water
½ cup soy sauce
2 (20 ounce) cans bean sprouts
1 cup mushrooms
2 (10 ounce) cans water chestnuts, sliced

Brown meat, thoroughly in hot oil in pressure cooker. Add water, onions, celery, salt and pepper. Cover, set control and cook for 8 minutes after control jiggles. Cool cooker normally for 5 minutes, then place under faucet. Add cornstarch mixed with water. Add soy sauce, bean sprouts, mushrooms and chestnuts. Cook and stir until thickened. Serve on hot rice or chow mein noodles. Serves 6-8.

Mrs. Carroll Reeves

LIVER JARDINIERE

2 pounds calves liver
milk
2 tablespoons regular flour
½ pound bacon
3 medium onions, thinly sliced

3 large green peppers, thinly sliced
2 teaspoons salt
¼ teaspoon pepper
1 (16 ounce) can whole tomatoes

Soak liver in milk for about 30 minutes. About 1 hour and 15 minutes before serving, coat liver with flour. Fry bacon and drain. Brown liver in bacon grease and drain. In small amount of bacon grease sauté onions and peppers. Place onions and peppers in baking dish, 9x9 inch pyrex, salt and pepper, place liver over this, place tomato on each piece of liver, no juice. Cover tightly and bake for 30 minutes at 325°. Before serving add bacon and reheat. Serves 4-6.

Mrs. Dick Crandall
Kansas City, Kansas

QUICK BARBECUE SAUCE

⅓ cup cooking oil
1 large onion, chopped
¾ cup tomato catsup
¾ cup water
⅓ cup lemon juice

3 tablespoons sugar
3 tablespoons Worcestershire
2 tablespoons prepared mustard
2 teaspoons salt
½ teaspoon pepper

Cook onion in hot oil until soft. While this is cooking, combine all other ingredients in a bowl and mix well. Add to onion when cooked. Simmer 15 minutes. Stir often while cooking to keep the oil mixed. Makes enough sauce to baste and serve 2 chickens. Yields about a pint of sauce. Can be refrigerated for several weeks in tight container. Good on hamburgers,. hot dogs and any ribs of pork if desired.

Marilyn T. Taylor

CURRY SAUCE FOR FONDUE

3 tablespoons butter
1 teaspoon curry powder
2 tablespoons flour

½ teaspoon salt
dash pepper
1 cup milk

Melt butter in saucepan. Stir in curry. Blend in flour, salt and pepper. Add milk all at once. Cook until boiling. Serve as accompanying sauce for beef pieces cooked in fondue pot in peanut oil. Yield: 1 cup.

Charlotte K. O'Flarity

MUSHROOM FONDUE SAUCE

2 tablespoons butter
2 tablespoons flour
1 beef bouillon cube dissolved in ⅔
   cup boiling water

½ cup sour cream
1 (3 ounce) can chopped, drained
   mushrooms
2 teaspoons Worcestershire

In small saucepan melt 2 tablespoons butter over low heat. Blend in flour. Add bouillon all at once, mixing well. Cook quickly until thick and bubbly. Stir in sour cream, mushrooms and Worcestershire. Heat thoroughly, serve hot as a sauce for bite-size pieces of beef cooked in peanut oil in fondue pot. Yield: 1⅓ cups.

Charlotte K. O'Flarity

BARBECUE SAUCE I

1 stick margarine
1 large onion, chopped
2 pods garlic, pressed

¾ bottle catsup (small size)
1 tablespoon Worcestershire

Melt margarine in saucepan. Add onion and garlic and simmer until onion is clear. Add catsup and Worcestershire sauce stirring to blend. Let sauce simmer low for 15-30 minutes. This sauce is good on top of potato salad, French bread or meat. It is not a sauce to use on meat while cooking on grill as it will burn. Yield: 1½ cups.

Mrs. John Tolson, III

BARBEQUE SAUCE II

2 sticks margarine
3 cloves garlic
¼ cup catsup
¼ cup mayonnaise
2 tablespoons mustard

juice of ½ lemon
salt
red pepper
paprika

Melt margarine in saucepan. Add garlic that has been put through a garlic press. In a separate bowl mix: catsup, mayonnaise, mustard, lemon juice and seasonings to taste. Beat this with a rotary beater for about 2 minutes. Add this mixture to the melted margarine and beat 1 minute longer. Stir often while heating the sauce. This sauce is good for basting chicken, ham or beef. French bread is also good dipped in this sauce. Yield: 1 pint.

Charlie Osborn McBride

BASIC RED SAUCE

2 ounces olive oil
4 medium garlic toes
1 (12 ounce) can tomato paste

½ gallon water
1 heaping tablespoon sugar
seasonings to taste

Heat olive oil in heavy black iron pot. Add minced garlic and carefully brown. When garlic is golden brown, add tomato paste and fry for about 5 minutes. Add water and stir well. Add sugar. Cook slowly, 2 hours, stirring to keep from sticking. This is a basic red sauce that can be used as is for spaghetti or many delicious additions can be added. Try adding a can of sliced mushrooms or sliced fresh mushrooms. Raw seasoned meatballs can be added 1½ hours before you are ready to serve. The longer it cooks, the better the flavor. Serves 6.

Suzanne Bernard

BEARNAISE SAUCE

¼ cup wine vinegar
¼ cup dry white wine
1 tablespoon finely chopped
  green onions
1 tablespoon tarragon
½ teaspoon salt

⅛ teaspoon white pepper
3 egg yolks
2 tablespoons butter
½ cup melted butter
2 tablespoons chopped parsley

Boil first six ingredients over medium heat until reduced to 2 tablespoons. Cool mixture. Beat egg yolks well. Strain vinegar mixture into egg yolks and blend well. Return to heat and add 1 tablespoon cold butter. Cook until thickened. Add the other tablespoon butter, then slowly beat in warm melted butter. Adjust seasonings and beat in parsley. Serve immediately.

OPENING OYSTERS ON BAYOU PETTITANCE

People have enjoyed eating raw oysters in South Louisiana for hundreds of years. Legend has it that the pirates who hid out in the bayous of South Louisiana ate nothing but raw oysters. Today, oyster bars are found in small and large restaurants throughout the area. Oysters are considered quite a delicacy.

Anyone who has ever opened an oyster understands that it is much easier to eat one than to open one. My research for this painting was easily done, I simply painted a Saturday afternoon gathering at a friend's house, where he opened the oysters and I watched and enjoyed eating them.

POULTRY AND GAME

CHICKEN CAWTHORN

6-8 chicken breasts or thighs

½ stick butter

1 can cream of mushroom soup

1 can cream of chicken soup

1 can chicken broth

minced garlic, to taste

1 onion, chopped

2 fresh tomatoes, quartered

Salt chicken lightly. Melt butter in skillet and brown chicken. Mix well all canned soups with garlic and onion. Add soup mixture to the drippings once the chicken has been removed. Sauté 5 minutes and add the chicken. Cover and cook slowly until almost done. Add the tomatoes and finish cooking. Serve over rice. Delicious with a fruit salad. Serves 4-6.

Mrs. Gary L. Ruffin

TARRAGON CHICKEN

4 whole chicken breasts, halved

salt and pepper

2 tablespoons tarragon vinegar

2 tablespoons olive oil

1 clove garlic, minced

2 tablespoons minced parsley

2 tablespoons butter

1 medium can sliced mushrooms

¼ cup dry sherry

Wash and dry breasts and season with salt and pepper. Sauté in mixture of vinegar, olive oil, garlic and parsley until a light brown, turning frequently. Add mushrooms and butter, place in oven at 350° and bake until tender. Remove, add sherry and sauté until thoroughly blended. Serve with the sauce. Chicken legs prepared this way are nice for cocktail parties. Serves 6-8.

Frances Wallace

GARLIC SOUR CREAM CHICKEN

Disjoint 1 (3 pound) fryer or use 6 boned breasts and/or thighs; pat dry. Mix first eight ingredients and coat chicken.

½-¾ cup sour cream

1-2 cloves crushed garlic

1 teaspoon celery salt

2 teaspoons Worcestershire sauce

1 teaspoon salt

½ teaspoon paprika

pepper to taste

1 tablespoon lemon juice

½ cup margarine

¾ cup bread crumbs

Preheat oven to 350°. After chicken is coated, arrange skin side up in a large, shallow, greased baking dish. Top with mixed margarine and bread crumbs. Bake for 1 and ¼ hours uncovered. Author's note: for dieters cottage cheese may be substituted for sour cream. Whip or blend it until it is the consistency of sour cream. Omit margarine but add dry bread crumbs to the top. Serves 4.

Kathleen R. Short

CHICKEN IN ARTICHOKE CASSEROLE

3 pound fryer, cut up
1½ teaspoons salt
¼ teaspoon pepper
½ teaspoon paprika
flour, enough to coat chicken
6 tablespoons butter

¼ pound mushrooms, cut in pieces
2 tablespoons flour
⅔ cup chicken consomme or bouillon
3 tablespoons sherry
1 (12-15 ounce) can artichoke hearts,
   drained

Preheat oven to 375°. Salt, pepper and paprika the chicken pieces. Coat them lightly with flour. Brown chicken pieces in 4 tablespoons of the butter and put them in a large casserole dish. Set aside. Melt the other 2 tablespoons of butter in frying pan and sauté the mushrooms in it for 5 minutes. Then sprinkle the 2 tablespoons of flour over the mushrooms. Stir in the chicken consomme and the sherry. While this cooks for 5 minutes, open a can of artichokes and arrange them between the chicken pieces. Pour the mushroom sherry sauce over them. Cover and bake for 40 minutes. Serves 6.

Susan Lentjes

PARISIENNE CHICKEN

4 chicken breasts, deboned
salt and pepper
3 tablespoons butter
3 shallots, chopped
2 ounces cognac, warmed

¼ cup dry vermouth
¾ cup heavy cream
4 large mushroom caps scored and
   sautéed lightly in butter

Season the chicken breasts and brown them well in hot butter. Arrange in a rather shallow casserole. In the fat remaining in the skillet sauté the shallots a moment and add to the breasts. Light the warmed cognac and pour flaming over the chicken. When the flames die down add the vermouth and cream mixed. Cover and bake 30-40 minutes at 300° until tender. To serve, remove and place on a small platter filled with wild rice and edged with ruffled parsley. Broccoli Hollandaise is a good side dish with this menu. Serves 4.

Sandy Hamilton
London, England

ITALIAN HUNTER'S CHICKEN

1 cup minced onion
½ cup butter
½ cup chopped parsley
1 (2-3 pound) fryer, cut up
1 cup water
1 cup sliced mushrooms

¼ cup minced fresh basil or 1 tablespoon
   dried basil
1 teaspoon dried rosemary
1 bay leaf
salt and pepper
½ cup dry white wine

In a large skillet, sauté onion in hot butter for 5 minutes or until soft. Add parsley and cook for 1 minute. Add chicken pieces and cook until brown. Add water, mushrooms, basil, rosemary, bay leaf and salt and pepper to taste. Cover and simmer 15-20 minutes. Add wine and cook 15-20 minutes more or until chicken is tender. Serve with buttered noodles. Serves 4.

Annette Myers

CHICKEN ITALIAN

6-8 pieces chicken
¼ cup Wishbone Italian salad
　dressing
¼ cup Worcestershire
1 tablespoon liquid smoke

¼ teaspoon onion puree
¼ teaspoon garlic puree
lemon juice or ¼ to ½ cup water (enough
　to make ¾ cup sauce)

Salt chicken and place in uncovered Dutch oven. Mix other ingredients in bowl to make sauce. Pour sauce over chicken. Bake in oven at 350 degrees for 1 hour. Continue basting chicken with sauce while baking. Serves 4.

Pamela Ann DeHart

SAUTEED CHICKEN MEDALLIONS

6 small chicken breasts
2 sticks butter
bread crumbs

salt and pepper to taste
lemon juice

Skin, bone and halve the breasts. Trim the pieces into rounds and flatten. Season to taste. Dip the medallions into half of the melted butter and roll in the bread crumbs. In the skillet fry the medallions with the other stick of butter. Sprinkle with lemon juice. Serves 6.

Mary T. Miller

CHEESE GLAZED CHICKEN

6 whole chicken breasts, skinned
　and boned
½ cup flour
1 teaspoon paprika
1½ teaspoons salt
2 tablespoons butter
1 tablespoon oil

¼ cup dry sherry
1 teaspoon corn starch
¾ cup light cream
⅓ cup dry white wine
1 tablespoon lemon juice
½ cup grated Swiss cheese

Dredge chicken breasts in mixture of flour, paprika and salt. Brown chicken in heated butter and oil over moderate heat. Add sherry. Cover and simmer until tender, about 25 minutes. Blend corn starch with cream and stir into pan drippings. Continue cooking until sauce thickens. Add wine and lemon juice. Sprinkle cheese over chicken breasts. Cover and let stand 5 minutes to brown or glaze the top. Delicious on a bed of wild rice. Serves 6.

Mrs. Stephen Goldware

GREEK CHICKEN OREGANO

2½ pound fryer, cut up
½ teaspoon Lawry's seasoned salt
½ teaspoon salt
½ teaspoon pepper
½ teaspoon garlic salt
¼ teaspoon oregano
1 large onion, chopped

Sauce:
3 tablespoons oil
3 tablespoons margarine
3 tablespoons sherry
2 tablespoons Worcestershire
juice of 1 lemon
small sprigs of parsley

Preheat oven to 400°. Season fryer with Lawry's seasoned salt, salt, pepper, garlic salt and oregano. Place fryer in foil lined baking pan. Spread chopped onion over chicken. Heat the oil, margarine, sherry, Worcestershire, lemon juice and parsley sprigs in a saucepan. Pour sauce over chicken, Cover tightly with foil. Bake for 45 minutes then uncover and brown. Serve 4-6.

Elsie Henderson

CHICKEN AND SHRIMP IN WINE SAUCE

1 hen or fryer, cut up
2 tablespoons oil
1 onion, chopped
garlic, minced (to taste)
2 cans tomato sauce

1 teaspoon basil
salt and pepper to taste
2 tablespoons roux
1 pound peeled shrimp
½ cup white wine

Brown chicken in oil and remove. Sauté onion and garlic. Add tomato sauce, basil and salt and pepper. Add roux and about 2 cups of water. If using hen, add at this time and simmer for 2 hours. If using fryer, add after simmering. Cook for 30 minutes and add shrimp and white wine. Cook another 20 minutes. Serve over rice. Serves 6.

Mrs. Paul Broussard

CHICKEN CORDON BLEU

2 whole chicken breasts
4 slices thin ham, about 3 inches
    square
2 triangles Gruyere or Gouda cheese,
    halved

1 stick butter
½ cup seasoned bread crumbs

Remove skin from breasts, split and debone. Cut pockets in each breast half. Wrap each piece of cheese with ham slice and tuck into each pocket. Roll stuffed breast first in melted butter then in crumbs, coating well. Place in buttered baking dish. Bake 40 minutes in 400° oven. Serves 4.

Suzanne A. Dupuis

CHICKEN CHAMPIGNON

6 chicken breasts, salted and
 peppered
¼ cup butter or margarine
1 box of fresh mushrooms, sliced
4 stalks shallots, chopped (green
 and white parts)

¼ cup oil
¼ cup flour
2 tablespoons tomato paste
1 can beef bouillon
½ cup sherry
½ cup Hollandaise sauce

In one skillet brown and cook the chicken breasts in the butter. Remove the skin and bones and set aside in a nice serving dish to keep warm. In the same skillet cook the mushrooms and the shallots until tender adding more butter if necessary. Set aside and keep warm. In another skillet make a dark brown roux with the oil and flour. Add the tomato paste and heat 5 minutes stirring constantly. Add the bouillon and the sherry. When well heated add the Hollandaise sauce. Combine with the mushrooms and the shallots. Season if necessary and pour over the chicken. This can be made the day before and heated in a moderate oven until heated through. Serves 6.

Malise L. Foster

CHICKEN SPAGHETTI

2 packages chicken breasts and
 2 packages chicken thighs or
 large hen
salt and pepper to taste
2 tablespoons bacon drippings
2 large onions, chopped
4 ribs celery, chopped
1 bell pepper, chopped
3 cloves garlic, chopped

5 green onions, chopped
1 (6 ounce) can sliced mushrooms,
 drained
3 tablespoons chopped parsley
1 cup tomato soup
1 pound spaghetti
1 can green peas
1 (8 ounce) package sharp cheddar
 cheese, grated

Boil chicken in 2 quarts seasoned water with salt, pepper and one of the onions. Reserve stock. When tender remove and debone. Sauté the chopped vegetables and mushrooms, except peas in the bacon drippings in large Dutch oven. When limp add soup and season. Boil spaghetti in reserved stock. Cook according to directions. Add spaghetti to chicken mixture. Fold in peas and grated cheese. Serve when cheese melts. Good made the day before and reheated. Serves 6-8.

Dorothy Green
Beaumount, TX

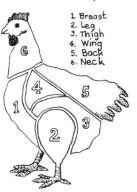

1. Breast
2. Leg
3. Thigh
4. Wing
5. Back
6. Neck

COQ AU VIN

1 pound chunk lean bacon	2 tablespoons butter

Remove rind, slice into ¼ inch pieces. Simmer for 10 minutes in 2 quarts of water. Rinse in cold water, dry. Freeze all but 3 ounces for future use. Sauté bacon slowly in hot butter until lightly browned. Remove to a side dish.

**3 pounds assorted pieces frying chicken,
    legs, thighs and breasts**

Dry chicken thoroughly. Brown in hot fat, using an electric skillet at 360°.

½ teaspoon salt	¼ cup cognac
⅛ teaspoon pepper	

Season chicken. Place bacon and chicken in a large casserole plus fat from above, you may have to add a little more butter. Cover and simmer 10 minutes. Uncover and pour in cognac. Averting your face, ignite the cognac. Shake casserole for several seconds.

3 cups burgundy	2 cloves mashed garlic
1 can beef broth	½ teaspoon thyme
½ tablespoon tomato paste	1 bay leaf

Pour wine into casserole. Add just enough broth to cover the chicken. Stir in tomato paste, garlic and herbs. Bring to simmer. Cover and simmer for 30 minutes, or until the chicken is tender and its juices run a clear yellow when the meat is pricked with a fork.

1 jar small white onions	2 tablespoons butter
½ pound sliced fresh mushrooms	1 tablespoon lemon juice

Sauté the onions and mushrooms in butter after sprinkling them with the lemon juice.

salt	pepper

Simmer the chicken cooking liquid in the casserole for a minute or two, skimming off fat. Then raise heat and boil rapidly, reducing liquid to about 2¼ cups. Correct seasoning. Remove from heat and discard bay leaf.

3 tablespoons flour	half whisk
2 tablespoons softened butter	

Blend the butter and flour together into a smooth paste. Beat the paste into the hot liquid. Bring to simmer, stirring and simmer for 1-2 minutes. Arrange the chicken in the casserole, place onions and mushrooms around it and baste with the sauce. If the dish is not to be served immediately, film the top of the sauce with broth or dot with small pieces of butter. Set aside uncovered. It can now wait indefinitely.

This recipe takes time and trouble, it is well worth all the trouble. I like to freeze it in oval, enameled roasting pans. That way, I can quadruple this batch and it doesn't take any more time. It keeps easily for 6 months frozen. Serves 4.

Frances Wallace

CHICKEN ROCHAMBEAU

Mushroom Sauce:

2 tablespoons butter	½ cup chopped mushrooms
1 cup finely chopped scallions	½ cup dry red wine
1 teaspoon finely chopped garlic	1 tablespoon Worcestershire
2 tablespoons flour	½ teaspoon salt
2 cups chicken stock	dash cayenne

Melt butter; add scallions and garlic. Stir about 5 minutes or until soft. Add flour and mix well. Pour in chicken stock in a slow stream stirring constantly. Cook until sauce comes to a boil. Stir in mushrooms. Simmer partially covered for 15 minutes. Add wine, Worcestershire, salt and cayenne pepper. Stir over low heat heat for 2-3 minutes. Remove from heat and cover tightly. The mushroom sauce can be made one day ahead and refrigerated.

Chicken:

4 chicken breasts, deboned	½ cup all purpose flour
1 teaspoon salt	12 tablespoons butter
1 tablespoon Tony's creole dressing	

Buy or debone chicken breasts. Sprinkle with salt and Tony's creole seasoning. Roll chicken breasts into flour and coat well. Melt butter in a large skillet. Pan fry chicken breasts until tender and golden brown. Drain on paper towels and set aside.

Ham:
1 teaspoon butter
4 (½ inch thick) Canadian bacon slices
4 Holland Rusks
Sauté Canadian bacon in butter until brown but not crisp. Keep warm.

Bearnaise Sauce:

⅔ cup tarragon vinegar	½ cup butter
¼ cup finely chopped scallions	3 egg yolks
1 teaspoon crumbled dried tarragon	2 tablespoons lemon juice
4 sprigs fresh parsley	¼ teaspoon salt
¼ teaspoon whole peppercorns	½ teaspoon prepared mustard
	dash of white pepper

Combine vinegar, scallions, tarragon, parsley and peppercorns in saucepan. Bring to a boil over high heat until reduced to about 2 tablespoons. Strain liquid through sieve and set aside. Heat butter in a small saucepan until bubbly but not brown. In an electric blender jar, put egg yolks, lemon juice, seasonings and mustard. Cover and blend on speed 2 for 5 seconds. Add tarragon mixture and blend for 5 seconds. Add the ½ cup butter very slowly blending on speed 2 then switching to speed 6. Blend for 30 seconds. Now you are ready to assemble this delicious dish.

Place Holland Rusks on serving platter. Place one slice of Canadian bacon on top of each Rusk. Add a generous serving of mushroom sauce over each. Top with chicken breasts and cover chicken with Bearnaise sauce. Serve with a vegetable and tossed salad. Serves 4.

Ramona Mouton

CHICKEN AND DUMPLINGS

2 tablespoons roux (page 125)
1 hen, cut up
salt
red pepper
garlic powder
¼ cup cooking oil

2 chopped onions
2 ribs celery, chopped
1 bell pepper, chopped
water
dumplings
onion tops, finely chopped

Season hen with salt, red pepper and garlic powder. Fry in oil until very brown. Remove chicken from oil. If chicken is very fat, remove excess oil before sauteing onions. Add celery and bell pepper. Place chicken back in pot. Add water to cover chicken. Bring to a boil. Add 2 tablespoons of roux. Simmer until meat is tender adding water if necessary. Drop dumplings in gravy. Cover tightly and cook about 15 minutes more. Add onion tops before serving. Serves 8-10.

Dumplings:
2 cups sifted flour
1 teaspoon salt
3 teaspoons baking powder
¼ teaspoon baking soda

¼ teaspoon red pepper
1 egg, beaten
3 tablespoons melted butter
milk (about ⅔ cup)

Sift together dry ingredients. Add egg, melted butter and enough milk to make a *stiff* batter. Drop by teaspoonfuls into boiling liquid gravy. Cover and cook for 15 minutes. Makes about 2 dozen dumplings.

Hugh P. Langlinais

CHICKEN A LA KING

1 stick butter
½ green pepper, chopped very fine
½ cup celery, chopped fine
1 small can mushrooms, sliced
1 medium onion, minced
3 tablespoons flour
2 egg yolks, beaten
2 cups milk or (1 cup milk, 1 cup Carnation)

2 cups cold chicken, cooked and diced
lemon juice
salt
red and black pepper
1 small can petite pois
1 small jar pimento, chopped

Melt butter in a pan and add green pepper, celery and mushrooms. Saute about 5 minutes. Add onions and flour mixed with part of milk. Beat egg yolks and add remaining milk. Stir until thickened. Add the chicken and cook a few minutes longer stirring constantly. Add lemon juice to taste and seasonings. Stir in peas and pimento. Serve in bite size patty shells. For variety add a dash of curry powder. Serves 8 in regular patty shells.

CHICKEN KIEV

12 chicken breasts, deboned
2 sticks butter, soft
2 teaspoons lemon juice
1 teaspoon finely minced garlic
1 tablespoon finely chopped parsley
2 teaspoons salt

8 egg yolks
4 tablespoons vegetable oil
¾ cup flour
2 cups Italian bread crumbs
1½ quarts oil for deep frying

To debone breasts: Peel off the skin using your fingers, next, using a sharp knife lay the breast bone side up, slip the knife under the rib bone and pull the knife away from you cutting meat from the bone. Grab the meat with free hand and gently pull while cutting with the knife.

To prepare Kiev: Lay breast smooth side down between 2 sheets of wax paper. With meat mallet pound meat flat. Keep meat in paper and refrigerate for 30 minutes. In that time make the seasoned butter. Cream butter with mixer, when smooth beat lemon juice in a little at a time until blended, then add garlic and parsley and stir into a ball. Wrap and freeze until firm.

Assemble the cutlets by peeling the top layer of wax paper and sprinkle with salt. Turn the breast so the wide end is toward you. On this side put one tablespoon butter. Roll up the breast, freeing meat from the paper. Line on a tray of wax paper and refrigerate 15 minutes.

One hour before cooking give the meat its covering. In a small bowl, beat egg yolks with fork and slowly add oil. Arrange separate mounds of flour and bread crumbs along a strip of waxed paper. Dip meat into flour, cover thoroughly and shape into a cylinder. Press together any cracks that appear, making sure meat is sealed with flour. Now using a pastry brush paint the floured meat with the egg mixture. Finally roll the meat in the bread crumbs making sure that all is covered. Refrigerate until ready to cook.

Deep fry at 375° for 5-8 minutes, only 3-4 at a time. Place cooked meat on platter in a heated oven. Pour any seasoned butter left over the rolls and serve. Serves 6.

Mrs. Carroll Pooler, Jr.

EASY, DELICIOUS BAKED CHICKEN

1 large split broiler
poultry seasoning to taste

garlic powder to taste
½ cup soy sauce

Wash chicken and place in small roaster. Sprinkle with poultry seasoning and garlic powder to taste. Pour soy sauce all over. Cover and bake at 325° for 2 hours. Delicious. Serves 4.

Ibby Eggart

CHICKEN PIE

Pastry:

2½ cups flour
½ teaspoon salt
4 tablespoons shortening

8 tablespoons butter
ice water to moisten

Filling:

6 tablespoons butter
3 tablespoons chopped onion
1 tablespoon chopped bell pepper
2 tablespoons chopped celery
6 tablespoons flour

1¾ cups rich chicken broth
⅔ cup milk
3 cups cooked chicken
salt and pepper

Make pastry by combining flour, salt, shortening and butter. Cut with blender until mixture resembles coarse meal. Add ice water until dough can be gathered together with a fork. Wrap in wax paper and chill while making filling.

For filling melt butter in sauce pan and sauté vegetables until limp. Add flour stirring to make a smooth paste, off the heat. Add liquids and stir until smooth. Cook over medium heat stirring constantly until thickened. Add chicken and salt and pepper to taste.

Using half of pastry roll and place in 9 inch pie pan. Trim edges. Roll out other half of pastry for top crust. Make a small hole in center for steam vent. Fill pastry shell with filling and top with crust. Crimp edges. Bake at 425° for 35 minutes. Cool 15-20 minutes before serving. Serves 4-6.

Jane L. Hutchinson

CHICKEN MOMI

1½ slices white bread
¼ cup light cream
1 onion, chopped
6 water chestnuts
¼ pound ground veal
½ pound ground pork
¼ pound ground beef
1 egg
2 teaspoons soy sauce

¼ teaspoon ginger
dash red pepper
dash Monosodium Glutamate
2 teaspoons salad oil
salt and pepper
6 chicken breasts, deboned
butter or oil
6 teaspoons honey
sesame seeds

Preheat oven to 325°. To make stuffing soak bread in cream. Mash bread with fork and add to chopped onions and chestnuts. Then add the next 9 ingredients. Sprinkle salt and pepper on each chicken breast. Put ⅓ cup stuffing in the flattened breasts and secure with toothpicks. Arrange in a baking dish and brush with oil or butter. Bake at 325° for 35-40 minutes. Brush chicken with honey and pan drippings. Sprinkle with sesame seeds and bake at 450° for 10 minutes. Serves 6.

Tip: This may be served on fresh pineapple halves that were cooked under the chicken breasts in the last 10 minutes of baking.

Lucille Roy Copeland

CHICKEN CHOW MEIN AND CHOP SUEY

12 pounds large fryers
2 (5-ounce) bottles soy sauce
14 pounds onions, cut in quarters
4 bunches green celery (cut cross
    ways, no leaves)
40 ounces sliced mushrooms (5 cans)
24 ounces water chestnuts (3 cans,
    sliced and drained)

16 ounces bamboo shoots (2 cans)
7 cans bean sprouts (1 pound 3 ounce
    can)
⅓ box curry powder
1 teaspoon blackstrap molasses
½ box corn starch

Parboil salted chickens in large pot of water. Remove chicken. Add soy sauce and onions to water. Boil until clear. Then add celery and boil until clear. Add mushrooms, water chestnuts, bamboo shoots and bean sprouts. Add curry powder and molasses and simmer. While this is simmering, debone chicken. Add diluted corn starch to pot. Chop chicken skin fine. Add chicken and skin to pot. Stir and cook until chicken breaks. Serves 40-50.

Serve with noodles for Chow Mein.

Serve with rice for Chop Suey.

Mrs. J. C. Chargois

SWEET 'N SOUR CHICKEN

1 fryer, cut up
½ cup flour
1 teaspoon salt
¼ teaspoon pepper
⅓ cup oil

½ cup cider vinegar
3 tablespoons brown sugar
⅓ cup chopped sweet pickles
1 tablespoon Worcestershire
1 tablespoon catsup

Preheat oven to 350°. Wash and dry chicken. Combine flour, salt and pepper. Coat chicken with this flour mixture. Heat oil and brown chicken a few pieces at a time. Combine vinegar and brown sugar with other ingredients. Brush well then pour the rest over the chicken which has been placed skin side up in a 9 by 13 inch baking dish. Bake covered for 30 minutes then baste. Uncover and bake for 15 minutes longer. Serves 4.

Toni B. Daigre

CHICKEN BREASTS TAIWANESE

4 large chicken breasts, deboned
1 tablespoon white wine
1 teaspoon sesame oil
salt and pepper
½ can bamboo shoots
4 green fresh onions

2 small carrots
1 can water chestnuts
2 dried Chinese mushrooms, soaked
1 egg white
small amount of corn starch

Marinate breasts in wine, oil, salt and pepper. Chop finely bamboo shoots, onions, carrots, water chestnuts and mushrooms. Beat egg white and add enough corn starch to make a weak paste. Remove chicken from marinade. Pour marinade over bamboo shoots mixture and mix well. Dip chicken in egg white mixture and place on a platter. Place the vegetable mixture firmly on chicken breasts, individually. Fry in deep fat. Reduce heat so that chicken will cook. Serves 4.

Grace Cox Black
Quitman, TX

FRIED CHICKEN WITH CASHEW NUTS

1 pound chicken filet, cut into ½ inch
    cubes (or use chicken leg meat)
Marinade:
1 teaspoon salt
1 tablespoon wine
1 teaspoon ginger juice
1 tablespoon corn starch
1 egg white
oil for deep frying

2 cups cashew nuts
8 green onions
8 green peppers, cut into ½ inch squares
1 teaspoon salt
2 tablespoons soy sauce
1 tablespoon sugar
1 tablespoon wine
1 teaspoon corn starch diluted with ¼
    cup water

Mix chicken cubes in marinade. Soak for 15 minutes. Heat the oil and deep fry the cashew nuts to a golden brown. If nuts are salted, wipe off the salt with a damp cloth so they do not burn while frying. You may substitute walnuts for the cashews but you must remove the skins. Remove the cashew nuts from the oil immediately after frying. Add the chicken cubes to the oil and fry for a few minutes. When chicken changes its color, remove it to a plate. In 3 tablespoons of the oil, sauté green onions and green peppers. Add salt, soy sauce, sugar, wine, chicken and cashew nuts. Then add the diluted corn starch. Mix well and serve hot. Serves 10.

Tip: celery and asparagus can be added.

Dr. Thomas C. Naugle

CHICKEN SCALLOPINI WITH ZUCCHINI

1 envelope Adolph's Chicken
  Marinade
¾ cup dry sherry
8 chicken breasts (halves)
1 cup all purpose flour
2 teaspoons salt
½ teaspoon freshly ground pepper
½ cup butter

½ cup walnut or pecan halves
8 small zucchini, sliced thin
garlic salt to taste
freshly ground pepper to taste
2 cups half and half
1 teaspoon Italian seasoning
½ cup grated Parmesan cheese
chopped parsley

Preheat oven to 200 degrees. De-bone chicken breasts and pound so they attain an even thickness of approximately ⅓ inch all over, resembling veal cutlets. Dissolve the Chicken Marinade in the sherry and pour over skinned breasts. Refrigerate overnight. Dip "cutlets" in mixture of flour, salt and ground pepper. Coat firmly on both sides. Shake off excess flour. Reserve 2 tablespoons of remaining flour mixture. Chill floured cutlets thoroughly. In 4 quart Dutch oven, heat butter until it sizzles. Sauté cutlets in butter until nicely browned and cooked about 4 minutes on each side. As they cook, transfer to an ovenproof dish and keep warm in 200 degree oven. Add nuts to your drippings and sauté 3 or 4 minutes while stirring. Remove nuts from pan and keep warm in the oven along with the chicken.

If necessary add 2 tablespoons butter to the pan and sauté the zucchini slices stirring until almost fork tender. Season to taste with garlic salt and ground pepper. Toss nuts and zucchini together and arrange on a large serving platter with the chicken cutlets in the center. Return to warm oven while preparing sauce. In the same pan used to prepare the above, heat the half and half over a low fire. Make a paste by adding a little water to the reserved 2 tablespoons of flour mixture. Add this mixture stirring constantly to the hot cream and bring to a gentle boil. Cook until slightly thickened—about 5 minutes. Add the Italian seasoning, grated cheese, and season to taste with additional salt and pepper if necessary. Pour sauce over cutlets serving extra sauce alongside. Sprinkle chopped parsley over before serving. Serves 8.

Lydia Bacqué

CHICKEN CASSEROLE

1 large fryer, boiled in salted water
  and deboned
1 box long grain and wild rice, cooked
  as directed on box
2 (5 ounce) cans water chestnuts,
  thinly sliced

1 can cream of celery soup
3 tablespoons chopped onion
½ cup mayonnaise
1 small jar pimento, finely chopped
1 can French cut green beans, drained

Combine the above ingredients, leaving the French cut green beans until last. Put into ungreased 2 quart casserole dish. Bake in moderate oven, 350°, until heated through. This dish freezes quite well. It can also be made 2 days in advance of serving and kept in the refrigerator. Serves 8-10.

Mrs. Florence Mercer

CHICKEN AND CRAB CASSEROLE

5 tablespoons butter or chicken fat
½ cup finely chopped onion
¼ cup flour
1 cup chicken stock
1 cup light cream
½ teaspoon salt
¼ teaspoon freshly ground black
   pepper

2 cups cooked chicken, cut in large
   pieces
1 cup cooked peas
1 cup fresh or canned crabmeat, picked
   over
1 cup soft bread crumbs, buttered

Preheat oven to 325°. Melt the butter in a saucepan. Add the onion and sauté about 10 minutes or until soft. Stir in the flour. Add the stock and the cream slowly, stirring. Add the salt and pepper. Bring to a boil and cook one to two minutes stirring. Arrange the chicken, peas and crabmeat in layers in a buttered 1½ quart casserole. Cover with the sauce and top with the bread crumbs. Bake about 25 minutes or until casserole is browned on top and bubbly hot. Serves 6-8.

Wendy Edmundson

CAJUN CHICKEN CROQUETTES

1 large fryer, boiled in onion, celery,
   and bell pepper, deboned—
   reserve broth
6 tablespoons butter
⅔ cup flour
2 cups broth
2 ¼ teaspoons Tony's Creole
   Seasoning

1¼ teaspoons pepper
2 teaspoons chopped parsley
4 eggs
4 tablespoons milk
3 cups seasoned bread crumbs
oil for frying

Melt butter in saucepan over low heat. Stir in flour. Gradually add chicken stock. Add Tony's seasoning and pepper. Cook and stir over low heat until thick. Add chicken and parsley. Blend and remove from heat. Beat 2 eggs and add to mixture; cook 1 minute longer. Cool. Shape into croquettes.

Combine 2 eggs with milk. Beat well. Add ½ teaspoon Tony's Seasoning and pepper to taste. Roll croquettes in the crumbs then dip in egg mixture. Roll again in crumbs. Allow to stand in refrigerator for 1 hour so crumbs adhere. Heat oil in deep skillet to 375° F. Oil should be 1 inch deep. Add croquettes and fry 1½ to 2 minutes on each side. Drain on paper towel. Serves 8-10.

Mrs. Carl Vincent

CHICKEN SOUFFLE

9 slices white bread (crust removed) and buttered
4 chicken breasts, cooked and cut up
½ pound fresh mushrooms
butter for sauteing
1 can sliced water chestnuts, drained
½ cup mayonnaise
9 slices Old English process cheese
4 eggs well beaten
2 cups milk
1 teaspoon salt
1 can cream of mushroom soup
1 can cream of celery soup
1 (2-ounce) jar pimento

Preheat oven to 350°. Line a 2 quart buttered pyrex casserole with bread. Top with chicken. Sauté mushrooms in butter for 5 minutes. Spoon over chicken. Add water chestnuts. Dot with mayonnaise. Top with cheese. Combine eggs, milk, salt, soups and pimento. Pour over casserole. Cover with foil. Store in refrigerator overnight. Bake in preheated oven until bubbly. Leave covered with foil until the last 30 minutes of baking. Serves 8.

Jimmie Ruth Procter

PAELLA

½ cup olive oil
12 small chicken pieces, seasoned
¼ pound lean pork, chopped finely
1 bell pepper, sliced thinly
1 large garlic clove, chopped finely
1 (14 ounce) can tomatoes, drained and chopped
1 large onion chopped finely
1 pound smoked sausage
3 cups raw rice
6 cups chicken broth
½ teaspoon crushed saffron
½ pound crawfish tails
½ pound large shrimp, peeled and deveined
1 (10 ounce) jar oysters, drained
2 lobsters tails, cut into sections leaving shell intact
½ cup frozen peas
6-7 asparagus spears

Brown chicken pieces in ¼ cup oil. Set aside. In ¼ cup fresh oil, brown pork pieces. Add garlic, bell pepper, onion and tomatoes which have been chopped. Cook over low heat until mixture is thick. Set aside. Prick sausage and place in skillet in water. Bring to boil, turn down heat and cook for 5 minutes. Let sausage cook and slice into ½ inch rounds. When you are ready to assemble paella, boil 6 cups chicken broth. Combine pork chop mixture and rice in paella pan. Place on large burner over high heat. Pour in broth and bring all to boil. Add saffron and turn off heat. Taste for seasoning. Arrange all other meats and seafood over rice mixture. Sprinkle peas on top. Bake covered for approximately 1 hour in 350° oven. Test rice for doneness. When ready to serve, arrange asparagus in center of paella, tips pointing outward. Other possible garnishes: mussels, clams, veal, ham, artichokes, pimentos. Serves 12-14.

Mrs. Odon Bacqué, Sr. taught me how to prepare paella. This recipe includes my favorite ingredients and variations. Browning steps may be done ahead. Paella may be frozen.

Carola Bacqué

ENCHILADAS MONTEREY

Sauce:

¾ cup butter
¾ cup flour
1 quart very rich chicken stock
¾ cup cream, half and half
1 tablespoon chopped pimientoes

1 tablespoon green chilies
1 tablespoon chopped fresh cilantro
2 teaspoons salt
¼ teaspoon white pepper

Over low fire melt butter, mix in flour very slowly mixing until flour and butter are blended well. Do not let this mixture brown. Remove from fire and add warm, not boiling, chicken stock. Stir over low heat until sauce is smooth and thickened. Stir in warm cream. Do not allow to boil. Add pimientos, green chilies, fresh cilantro and salt & pepper. Stir and keep warm.

Filling:

1 tablespoon chopped onion
3 ounces cooking oil
1 pound cooked chopped chicken
salt and pepper to taste
4 ounces cream cheese
4-6 ounces sour cream

1 tablespoon chopped jalapeno or
    canned green chilies
1 dozen soft corn tortillas
8 ounces shredded Monterey Jack
    cheese

Cook chopped onions in oil until soft, add chopped chicken, add salt and pepper and stir until ingredients are mixed well. Remove from fire. In a mixing bowl cream 4 ounces of cream cheese with enough sour cream to make a nice creamy base. Add chicken mixture, chopped peppers, salt and pepper to taste. Stir and mix ingredients. Roll filling into soft tortillas. Tortillas can be dipped in hot oil to make them more pliable. Cover enchiladas with hot Monterey sauce, top with a generous amount of shredded Monterey cheese. These enchiladas can be portioned into individual servings or placed into a flat casserole dish. Either way heat to serve by placing in a 350° oven or run under a broiler until sauce and cheese begin to bubble. Serves 6.

LaFonda's of Lafayette

MEXICAN CHICKEN

1 fryer-seasoned, boiled and deboned
1 large onion, chopped
3 cans cream of chicken soup
2 (4 ounce cans) green chilies, drained
    reserving ¼ can of juice

1½ teaspoons camino
Dorito chips
grated cheddar cheese

Preheat oven to 350 degrees. Sauté onion in a small amount of leftover chicken broth. Add soup, chilies and ¼ can of juice. Stir in camino and add chicken. Line a long pyrex dish with Doritos and add mixture. Top with more chips and grated cheese. Bake for 30 minutes. Serves 8.

Mrs. Gary Ruffin

ARROZ CON POLLO
(YELLOW RICE AND CHICKEN)

1 chicken, cut in pieces	3 stalks celery
salt	cooking oil
pepper	1 cup long grain rice
parsley flakes	2 chicken bouillon cubes
margarine	⅓ package Spanish Saffron
1 medium onion	1 small bottle stuffed olives (drained)
½ bell pepper	

Place pieces of chicken in a baking pan. Salt and pepper to taste; sprinkle with parsley flakes and dot each piece with margarine. Bake uncovered in 350 degree oven for 1 hour.

While chicken is baking, sauté in heavy 2½ quart saucepan chopped onion, bell pepper and celery in a little cooking oil. Sauté until onion becomes clear. Add rice, bouillon cubes, Saffron and 1½ cups water. Salt and pepper to taste; sprinkle with parsley flakes. Bring to a boil, cover and cook 25 minutes on simmer setting. When rice is cooked, add olives and serve with the baked chicken. Serves 4.

Dorothy Cabe-Maury

AZALIE'S MEXICAN CHICKEN

1 large hen, boiled (reserve 3 cups stock)	2 teaspoons Worcestershire sauce
2 cups diced celery	1 teaspoon chili powder
2 cups diced onion	salt, red and black pepper to taste
small jar pimentos, chopped	2 (5-ounce) packages wide noodles
1 large bell pepper, chopped	1 can mushroom pieces
2 cans tomato soup	1 can ripe olives

Cook hen until tender and debone. Add 3 cups of chicken stock to the celery. onions, pimentos, bell pepper, tomato soup, Worcestershire sauce and chili powder. Season highly with salt and red and black pepper. Cook until vegetables are tender. Add the chicken and wide noodles. Cook covered on low heat 20 minutes and add mushrooms and olives. Serves 10-12.

Azalie Webb Crain

STUFFED CORNISH HENS

4 cornish hens	½ bell pepper, chopped
salt and pepper to taste	giblets from hens
2 stalks celery, chopped	1 box wild and long grain rice

Salt and pepper hens. Cook covered in 325° oven for 45 minutes. Check occasionally and add water if necessary. Cook onion, celery and green peppers and giblets in seasoned water until done. Remove giblets and chop and return to broth. Cook rice according to directions in this broth. Stuff hens and cook covered 45 minutes. Brown hens under broiler at last minute. Serves 4.

Phern Stelly Stagg

ROCK CORNISH HENS IN WALNUT SAUCE

4 Rock Cornish hens cut in half
1 teaspoon salt
¼ teaspoon cayenne
½ cup flour
2 tablespoons butter
¼ cup vegetable oil
1 cup dry white wine

2 tablespoons cornstarch
½ cup Curacoa or orange brandy
½ (6 ounce) can orange juice
    concentrate
1 small can mandarin orange slices
½ cup finely chopped walnuts or pecans

Season hens thoroughly, dredge in flour and brown in butter and oil using large skillet. When thoroughly browned remove hens from skillet and set aside. Add wine to skillet and scrape pan carefully while wine comes to a boil. Return hens to skillet, baste well, cover and simmer for 30 minutes. Again remove hens to a warm platter and set aside. Mix corn starch with liquor and whisk this into liquid in skillet. Add frozen concentrate and cook until sauce thickens. Add mandarin oranges an nuts. Adjust seasoning. Serve hen on bed of rice with sauce ladled over it. Serves 8.

Kathy Leonard

TURKEY ACAPULCO

3 cups minced turkey or chicken
½ teaspoon oregano
⅛ teaspoon black pepper
¼ teaspoon salt
2 cups sour cream
1 cup sliced mushrooms
1 (4-ounce) can chopped green chilies

1 large onion, minced
½ cup toasted sliced almonds
14 soft tortillas
1 can cream of chicken soup
1 cup grated sharp cheese
⅓ cup light cream

Preheat oven to 350°. Mix above ingredients well except for tortillas, soup, cream and cheese. Place portion of mixture in center of each tortilla. Roll up and place seam down in 13 by 9 by 2 inch baking pan. Combine the soup, cheese and cream. Pour over tortilla rolls. Bake in preheated oven for 35 minutes. Serves 2 or 3 per serving.

Kathe Haxthausen

Ms.   Mr.

CAMILLE'S CHAMPAGNE TURKEY

1 12-pound turkey, thawed	1 small can Parmesan cheese
1 (1½-ounce) bottle garlic salt	3 tablespoons parsley flakes
1 tablespoon garlic powder	½ to 1 small can poultry seasoning
1 tablespoon onion salt	1 to 2 bottles domestic champagne
1 teaspoon salt	1 small bottle Worcestershire sauce

Mix all dry ingredients with hands. Coat inside and outside of turkey and refrigerate overnight (12 to 24 hours). Smoke turkey on slow fire on BBQ pit for 6 to 8 hours. When approximately half done, begin basting with Worcestershire sauce and champagne. Use enough liquid to keep moist. Makes juicy turkey and additional liquid makes good gravy.

Katherine David Gravel

TURKEY LASAGNA

½ package (12-ounce) lasagna noodles	1 cup creamed cottage cheese
1 can cream of chicken soup	⅓ cup chopped green onions
⅔ cup cream	¼ cup finely minced parsley
½ teaspoon seasoned salt	2 cups diced leftover turkey
½ teaspoon poultry seasoning	1 cup soft bread crumbs
2 (3-ounce) packages cream cheese	2 tablespoons margarine

Preheat oven to 325°. Cook noodles as directed on package. Mix soup, cream and seasonings together. Beat cheese together until smooth. Add onions, parsley and turkey to cheese. Add to soup mixture. Place half the cooked drained noodles in buttered baking dish. Cover with half of the cheese and turkey mixture. Repeat layers. Toss bread crumbs with soft margarine and sprinkle over casserole. Bake for 30-40 minutes or until it bubbles in the center. Let stand for 10-15 minutes before serving. Serves 4-6.

Mrs. J. R. Romero, Jr.
Lake Charles, LA.

DUCKLINGS IN ORANGE SAUCE

2 (5-pound) ducklings	1½ cups orange juice
1 tablespoon salt	1 cup dry sherry
½ teaspoon pepper	2 tablespoons corn starch
1½ cups sugar	1 cup water
2 cups currant jelly	orange strips

Preheat oven to 400°. Wash ducks and remove as much fat as possible. Season with salt and pepper. Place on rack in a large roasting pan. Roast in a 400 degree oven for 1¼ hours basting frequently. Reduce heat to 350° and roast 1 hour longer or until ducks are tender, crisp and brown. For the orange sauce, combine the sugar, currant jelly and orange juice in a saucepan. Bring to a boil and cook over low heat for 15 minutes. Stir in sherry and cook 5 minutes longer. Mix the corn starch with the water and add to the orange sauce stirring constantly until thickened. Add orange strips. Carve ducks in one fourths and pour sauce over them. Garnish with a slice of orange and a cherry. Serves 8.

Brenda B. Hawes

BAKED DUCKS

olive oil
2-3 medium onions
4-5 celery stalks
4-5 large ducks
2 tablespoons chopped green onions
2 (4 ounce) cans mushrooms

1½-2 cups wine
1 cup water
Choice of cooking wines:
   1) Marsala
   2) Almond Creme
   3) Creme Sherry

Rub ducks thoroughly all over with olive oil. Salt and pepper thoroughly. Put ¼ to ½ onion and a piece of celery in the cavity of each duck. Cover the bottom of a large iron pot or magnalite roaster with olive oil. Heat oven to 400°. Cook uncovered for 1 hour or until brown, occasionally basting and turning. When ducks are brown add chopped green onions, mushrooms, wine and water. Reduce heat to 325°. Cook covered about 2½ hours. Brit brought this recipe from a duck hunting camp. It is easy and good. Serves 8.

Mrs. Brit Busch

BARBEQUED DUCK

2 whole ducks, split in half
   and flattened

Sauce:
½ pound butter or margarine
½ cup catsup
1 tablespoon sugar
1½ tablespoons lemon juice
1 tablespoon Worcestershire

1 teaspoon salt
1 clove garlic, chopped
1 small onion, chopped
½ teaspoon Tabasco
ground pepper to taste

Simmer all sauce ingredients for 5 minutes in saucepan. Place duck halves in shallow baking pan with rack at 375° for 1 hour. Baste every 10 minutes with sauce. Turn and cook other sides 1 hour, continue basting. Serves 4, sauce for 4 halves.

Mrs. Paul Short, Jr.

BROWNING BAG WILD DUCK

3 ducks
8 onions
8 potatoes
15 strips of bacon

garlic salt
pepper, red and black
Tony's Creole Seasoning, to taste
1 large browning bag

Season ducks inside and out with salt and pepper and seasoning. Slit the breast on each side and stuff with a slice of bacon. Place an onion inside each duck. Put 3 strips of bacon on top of each duck and place in browning bag. Puncture bag according to directions. Peel the remaining onions and potatoes and place whole around the ducks. Salt and pepper them lightly. Bake for 2-2½ hours at 350°. Serves 4-6.

Mrs. J. Oran Richard

BYRON'S WILD DUCK

½ cup vinegar
salt, red and black pepper
3 large onions, chopped
1 bell pepper, chopped
4 large ducks, mallards
cooking oil to cover bottom of pot

1 cup water
1 pound smoked sausage
1 small jar pimentoes, optional
1 small can chopped mushrooms,
    optional

Early in the day, or preferably 1-2 days before cooking, sprinkle vinegar on ducks and season liberally with salt, and red and black pepper. Place chopped onion and bell pepper in bottom of shallow pan or pyrex dish large enough to hold 4 ducks. Place ducks, breast down, on onions and bell pepper, cover and refrigerate until ready to cook.

Cover bottom of roasting pan with oil and brown ducks on all sides. Remove ducks and sauté vegetables which ducks have been sitting in, juice and all. Return ducks to pot, breast down, add 1 cup water, cover and put in 275°-300° oven. One hour later, slice sausage thinly and add to pot and continue cooking, adding water if necessary, until ducks are tender. (Usually 3-4 hours.) When ducks are done, I remove them from the pot and skim excess grease from the gravy and if necessary, add a little flour mixed with water to thicken gravy. At this point you may add the pimentoes and mushrooms to the gravy and return ducks, breast down, to the gravy to keep warm until ready to serve. You may either serve the gravy over rice or mix the rice with gravy and sausage to make a type of jambalaya. Serves 8-10.

Tessie Schoeffler

SMOTHERED DUCKS WITH MUSHROOMS

2 ducks, cleaned and parboiled 20
    minutes
2 large onions, cut into ¼ inch rings
½ pound small fresh mushrooms,
    halved

6 tablespoons butter
½ cup dry sherry
2 cans onion soup
paprika

In a large roaster sauté the onions and mushrooms in the butter. Pour in ¼ cup of the sherry. Cover and simmer 10 minutes. Split the ducks lengthwise, after parboiling. Salt and pepper the birds and add them to the vegetables. Sprinkle generously with paprika. Pour in the onion soup and remaining sherry. Cover and cook over medium heat for 2 hours or until tender. I always add some water along with the soup to cover ducks. Serves 2-3.

Candice S. Robinson

ROY'S POT ROASTED WILD DUCK

4 mallards or 8 teal	1 can whole mushrooms
cooking oil or bacon drippings	1 can brown gravy
6 large onions	1 cup burgundy wine
2 bell peppers	8 teaspoons salt
garlic	8 teaspoons red pepper
1 stick butter	6 chicken bouillon cubes
1 teaspoon sugar	instant flour, optional

Stuff duck breasts with slivers of garlic. Cut 2 large onions in quarters and stuff into duck cavity, with a large slice of bell pepper. Mix 8 teaspoons of red pepper with 8 teaspoons of salt and then rub this seasoning inside and outside of the duck. In a large magnalite pot or black iron pot, wet the bottom of the pot with bacon drippings or cooking oil. Heat oil until hot, then place seasoned ducks, breast down and brown ducks in oil. After 20 minutes of browning, reduce heat to medium heat and continue to brown 1 hour. After browning, remove ducks and drippings from pot. Place in the pot four medium sized onions, chopped finely, with the stick of butter and 1 teaspoon of sugar. Sauté the onions on medium heat until thoroughly wilted. Replace ducks into pot with onion mixture, together with four cooking spoons of duck drippings. Add water to ducks (just enough to cover the ducks) and bring fire to high heat and water to boiling. Then put in the chicken bouillon cubes. Reduce heat to medium and cover pot almost completely, leaving enough opening for steam to escape. Continue cooking for ½ hour, then remove cover and put in the contents of can of brown gravy and mushrooms. Recover and continue cooking, partially uncovered over low heat for 1 more hour. Now remove cover and put in 1 cup of burgundy wine. Recover partially, and continue simmering gravy, uncovered, until thickened. You may wish to use 3-4 teaspoons of instant flour to thicken the gravy at this time. Add any additional salt and pepper to gravy to suit taste. Serves 8.

Harmon F. Roy

WILD DUCK

salt, red pepper, flour	2 stalks celery
4 mallards, pintails	1 cup orange juice
1 onion	1 cup sherry
1 large clove garlic	1 small jar mushrooms
½ bell pepper	1 tablespoon bacon grease

Generously salt, pepper and dust with flour ducks to be cooked. Melt bacon grease in pot. Put ducks in pot, breast side down, do not stack ducks. Chop vegetables or chop in a food processor. Throw all vegetables on top of ducks. Cover and cook in 500° oven for 30 minutes. Push vegetables around ducks, pour orange juice and sherry over all. Cover and cook in 300° oven until tender. This makes a marvelous brown gravy. Put mushrooms in gravy and serve over rice. Serves 4.

Blair Bowden Cabes

CHATEAU TEAL

4 teal ducks
1 lemon
2 teaspoons salt
1 teaspoon black pepper
1 teaspoon paprika
1 teaspoon garlic salt
2 teaspoons herb seasoning
1 apple, quartered
flour
½ stick butter plus 1 teaspoon oil

2 large onions, chopped
1 green pepper, chopped
2 pods garlic, chopped
1 package onion soup mix
2 cups water
⅓ cup orange juice
1 (4 ounce) can mushrooms stems & pieces
3 tablespoons orange marmalade
⅓ cup red wine

Clean inside of ducks with cool running water, removing lungs and bits of inside membrane and tissue. Pat dry and rub outside with lemon slices. Season well inside and out. Stuff each teal with a quarter of an apple. Dust lightly with flour. Brown birds in butter and oil on both sides, starting with the breast, then turn over to back and brown. After browning, add chopped onion, green pepper and garlic to the pot to wilt, approximately 5-10 minutes. When vegetables are wilted, add 1 package onion soup mix and 2 cups water and turn teal over with the breasts down. Cover pot and turn fire to lowest simmer. Cook approximately 2 hours. Halfway through cooking time, add ⅓ cup orange juice. Thirty minutes before end of cooking time, add can of mushrooms and marmalade and squeeze juice of ½ lemon into pot. Adjust seasonings. Last 15 minutes add ⅓ cup red wine. Ducks are done when meat at breastbone begins to separate slightly. Serves 4.

Ann LeJeune

MARINADE FOR DUCK OR VENISON

1 medium onion, sliced
1 carrot, sliced
2 cloves garlic
2 tablespoons vinegar

½ cup olive oil
1 teaspoon black pepper
1 bottle (fifth) red burgundy wine or hearty burgundy

This is enough marinade for approximately 6 pounds of game. Mix all ingredients and marinate meat overnight or even for 2-3 days in a covered container in the refrigerator. These ingredients may be doubled or tripled if more game needs to be marinated.

Hazel Burdin Francisco

BAKED DOVES

8-12 whole doves
8-12 thick slices bacon
1 cup melted butter or margarine
1 teaspoon onion juice concentrate

⅛ cup chopped parsley
onion salt
pepper
½ onion, chopped

Wash and dry doves. Melt butter and add onion juice. Drop each dove in butter. Remove and season well with onion salt and pepper. Wrap each dove with slice of bacon. Place all doves in single layer in baking dish. Cover and cook 1½ hours at 350° or until tender, basting every ½ hour with sauce listed below. After 1½ hours remove cover, baste, turn oven to 375° and cook another ½ hour. Baste again before serving.

Basting Sauce:
Using same melted butter, make sauce by adding parsley, seasoning and chopped onion. Cook on top of stove until onions are tender, or for 2 minutes in microwave. Serves 4-5.

Connie Gauthier

BARBEQUED DOVE BREASTS

30 dove breasts
1 small bottle soy sauce
1 small bottle olive oil
1 medium onion, sliced

garlic, according to taste
salt
red and black pepper
30 slices bacon

Doves must be skinned. Season highly with salt and pepper. Marinate doves for 4 hours. To make marinade sauce add soy sauce, oil, garlic and onions. Season well. You may add any other ingredients you prefer. After 4 hours remove from marinade sauce and wrap each dove in bacon strips. Put doves on barbeque pit over hot coals with cavity down. Close cover and cook for about 7½-9 minutes. Remove from grill. Serves 6. This can be used as a finger food.

Jimmie Stagg

RUBY PORT DOVES

12-15 doves
1 stick butter
½ bottle Ruby Port wine

salt
pepper
1 cup flour

Wash doves, pat dry, season with salt and pepper. Shake birds in flour and brown in a large cast iron skillet in which a stick of butter has been melted. After doves are browned, add wine with a little water if necessary so that doves are ¾ covered. Cover skillet tightly. Simmer 1½ hours. Add a small amount of water if necessary. Serves 3 doves per person.

Mrs. Robert F. Tarpy

DOVE AND OYSTER PATTIES

8 doves
1 onion, quartered
1 stalk celery, quartered
2 teaspoons salt

½ teaspoon red pepper
½ teaspoon black pepper
2 cups water

Early in the day or the day before, wash doves well, inside and out. Place in large heavy saucepan with vegetables and seasonings and water. Bring to a boil, lower temperature to medium-low, cover and simmer approximately 45 minutes to 1 hour or until fork tender. Set aside doves to cool. Strain and reserve broth. When doves are cool, discard skin and bones and cut meat into bite sized pieces.

1½ pints or 2 (10 ounce) jars oysters
½ stick butter
½ cup onion chopped finely
4 tablespoons flour
salt and red pepper

3 tablespoons chopped parsley
3 tablespoons chopped onion tops
8 patty shells from the bakery or frozen
    Pepperidge Farm Puff Patty shells
    baked according to directions

Strain oyster liquor (or juice) into bowl and pick over oysters for shell or grit. If oysters are very large, cut each in half with kitchen scissors. Place oysters and strained liquor in pan on top of stove on medium-high. Bring to boil and cook just until edge of oysters begin to curl. Remove from heat and drain oysters reserving liquor. In medium sized heavy sauce pan, melt butter and sauté onions until transparent. Add flour and cook until bubbling, but not brown. Pour in 1 cup reserved oyster liquor and 1 cup reserved broth. Cook, stirring constantly, until thick. Stir in oysters and doves. Adjust seasoning to taste. Add parsley and onion tops. Fill patty shells with oyster and dove filling. Heat in 350° oven approximately 15 minutes and serve hot. This is very good for a brunch with scrambled eggs or as a luncheon or late night supper dish. A sweet salad or side dish is especially good, such as cranberry salad mold or fresh fruit with poppy seed dressing. Serves 8.

Mrs. Carroll Fleniken

le lapin

ROAST GOOSE BENNETT

2 speckled-belly geese
4 cups sauerkraut
1½ cups coarsely chopped onion
2 tablespoons salt
1 teaspoon red pepper
1 teaspoon black pepper

½ teaspoon garlic powder
3 cups honey
1 tablespoon oil
1 cup water
2 tablespoons cornstarch
1 cup water

Mix salt, red and black pepper and garlic powder in a small bowl. Wash geese with cold water, carefully cleaning cavity. Pat dry, inside and out, and season cavity with ½ seasoning mixture. Stuff geese with a mixture of sauerkraut and chopped onion. Season outside of geese with remaining seasonings. Oil the bottom of a heavy 14 inch roaster. Place stuffed geese with the breast up in the uncovered roaster. Put into hot oven, 450° for approximately 30 minutes, or until is brown. Remove roaster from oven and pour honey over geese, cover roaster tightly with lid. Remove cover and add 1 cup water to drippings in bottom of roaster. Replace cover and continue to bake at 325° approximately 2½-3 hours, or until geese are tender when stuck with a kitchen fork. Remove geese to a platter and cover loosely with foil to keep warm. Thicken pan juices with a mixture of cornstarch and water. Taste and adjust seasonings in gravy. Carve geese as you would a roasted chicken and serve thickened gravy and sauerkraut from the cavity. The sauerkraut will not have a strong taste and is usually enjoyed by everyone. This is nice served with candied sweet potatoes and rice dressing. Serves 6-8.

Bettye Walker

BAKED QUAIL

12 quail
salt and pepper
Kitchen Bouquet
¼ cup oil

2 tablespoons dry onion soup mix
1 cup water
1 tablespoon chopped parsley
1 tablespoon chopped onion tops

Clean quail and pat dry. Season with salt and pepper to taste. Rub each quail with Kitchen Bouquet. Put oil in large magnalite pot. When oil is hot, brown quail for about 15 minutes. Add 1 cup water and 2 tablespoons dry onion soup mix. Stir and cover. Bake in oven for about 2 hours at 300° stirring 2-3 times. When tender, stir in parsley and onion tops. Serve with gravy over steamed rice. Serves 6.

Mrs. Matt Guidry

DWIGHT'S QUAIL OR DOVE ROASTED IN OVEN

12-16 quail or dove
3-4 pods garlic
1 bell pepper
salt, red and black pepper

dry sherry or white wine
flour
oil to cover bottom of roaster
approximately 1 cup water

Quail is very good potted or roasted in the oven in a heavy roaster or on top of the stove in a Dutch oven. I roast mine in a magnalite roasting pan. Do not crowd the birds when cooking.

Season the birds early in the day, or even the night before, if they are to be cooked for night dinner. Slit the breast of each bird and stuff with a sliver of garlic and small piece of bell pepper. Season well with salt and red and black pepper. You can also sprinkle with a little dry sherry or white wine and put into the refrigerator to chill.* When ready to cook, remove from the refrigerator and lightly sprinkle each bird with flour. (Be careful to sprinkle lightly.) Have the oven set at 300°-350°. Heat oil in roasting pan over medium heat and put birds in to brown. Turning frequently, cook about 30 minutes, then add ½ cup dry sherry or white wine. I prefer the sherry, but the white wine is very good. When birds are browned evenly, add small amount, about 1 cup, of water to make the gravy and cover. Baste frequently and cook the birds until all are tender and the gravy is brown. There will be enough gravy to serve with white rice. For a special treat, use wild rice which has been cooked and drained according to directions. After draining, sauté in butter, then add small amount of chicken broth, chopped mushrooms, onion tops and parsley. To make an even prettier dish, add some chopped black olives, a little pimento and bell pepper. Serve with gravy from quail.

You may have to raise the oven temperature as you cook them. Judge for yourself.

*Be sure to chill birds well, at least 1 hour, before browning. Any meat which has been well chilled will brown better and more evenly. Serves 6-8.

Dwight Andrus, Sr.

QUAIL AND GRAPES

12 quail
12 seedless green grapes cut in half
12 grape leaves
bacon

½ cup chicken broth
½ cup dry white wine
½ pint sour cream

Season quail inside and out with salt, red pepper and black pepper. Stuff the cavities with the grapes. Wrap each quail with 1 slice bacon and then 1 grape leaf and secure with toothpicks. Place birds in a casserole or baking dish, put in wine and chicken broth, cover with tin foil and bake in oven at 350° for 1½ hours. Occasionally add more chicken broth if liquid evaporates. After baking for 1½ hours, remove tin foil and grape leaves from the quail. Pour liquid in sauce pan and allow to cool for a few minutes. Turn oven to high and brown the quail. Add the sour cream to the cooled liquid and reheat but do not bring to a boil. Pour the sour cream gravy over the birds and serve. Serves 6.

Henry L. Mayer, Jr.

FRIED QUAIL SUPREME

Marinade:
1 quart buttermilk
2 teaspoons Tabasco

4 tablespoons Worcestershire

12 quail
3 eggs, whipped
½ milk
1 cup Italian bread crumbs
salt
black pepper

flour
garlic salt
paprika
margarine
butter
lemon

Marinate quail overnight in buttermilk, Tabasco and Worcestershire. Remove from marinade and pat quail dry. Roll them in whipped eggs and ½ cup milk. Then roll in Italian bread crumbs and then in flour that has had salt, black pepper, garlic salt and paprika added to it. Fry in ½ margarine and ½ butter in large skillet. The grease should cover about half the bird at the time. Fry for approximately 15 minutes or until brown. Do not fry too long as they will get tough. Serve with tart lemon butter poured over them. Serves 4-6.

Womack LeJeune

RABBIT CASSEROLE

1 rabbit, cut into serving pieces
salt water—1 teaspoon salt to 1 quart
    water
butter
½ teaspoon salt
fresh ground pepper to taste

¼ teaspoon thyme
3 bay leaves
5 slices cut bacon
1 cup water
1 cup seasoned bread crumbs

Cut rabbit into serving pieces. Soak 1-2 hours in salt water, 12-18 hours for older rabbits. After soaking wrap in damp cloth and store overnight in a cold place. Butter a casserole dish and add a layer of rabbit pieces, sprinkle with ½ teaspoon salt, fresh ground pepper to taste, ½ teaspoon thyme and 3 bay leaves. Add 5 slices cut bacon; repeat layering until ingredients are used up. Pour 1 cup water over casserole, cover and bake at 350° until tender, 1-2 hours, depending on age. Remove cover and sprinkle 1 cup seasoned bread crumbs over casserole; bake 30 minutes and serve. Serves 4.

Pat Lindsey

ROASTED VENISON

Marinade:

1 cup vinegar

enough water to cover roast

venison roast
salt and pepper
½ chopped bell pepper
4-5 pods garlic

approximately ½ cup flour
oil
1 envelope dry onion soup mix
1½ cups water

Place roast in large container with marinade and place in refrigerator overnight. Wash meat under cold water to draw all of the blood out of meat. Pat dry and stuff with garlic and bell pepper. Salt and pepper roast and roll in flour. On top of stove, heat enough oil to cover the bottom of heavy roasting pan and brown roast on all sides. Sprinkle dry onion soup mix over roast and add approximately 1½ cups water to make gravy. Bake covered at 350° for about 3½-4 hours or until fork tender. Baste roast with gravy while cooking. Serves 8-10.

Nell Tolson

VENISON N' BAG

1 (8 pound) venison ham
⅓ cup salt
¼ cup black pepper
2 tablespoons red pepper
4-6 pickled Tabasco peppers*

¼ cup vinegar
4 slices bacon
1 onion, thinly sliced
2 tablespoons flour
1 browning bag (turkey size)

Wash venison and trim any fat. Pat dry. Make small slits with sharp knife over entire roast. Make paste of vinegar, peppers and salt. Put ½ teaspoon paste into each slit ,½ Tabasco pepper and ⅓ slice bacon. After all slits are filled, rub any remaining paste on outside of roast. Marinate in refrigerator one to three days. When ready to cook, sprinkle flour inside bag to coat. Place roast in, lay sliced onion on top of roast. Make slits in bag according to directions and bake at 325° approximately 3½-4 hours. Roast will begin to pull away from bone when tender.

Note*–This will be rather hot with pepper. Adjust red pepper and pickled Tabasco peppers to your taste. Serves 10-12.

Bill Davis

VENISON POT ROAST

roast	½ gallon buttermilk
2 large onions	2 cans onion soup
6-8 toes garlic	1 cup water
3 tablespoons salt	2 large cans mushrooms
4 tablespoons red pepper	6 ounces sherry
1 stick margarine, melted	oil

Chop onions and garlic in blender. Add salt, pepper and melted margarine and mix well. With a syringe, inject this seasoning into the roast. Rub the remains on the outside of roast. Now, marinate the meat in buttermilk for 4-6 hours in the refrigerator. Remove meat from milk and wipe with a paper towel. Place in a slightly oiled pot and brown well. Add onion soup and water and continue to cook on top of the stove until fork tender, (lowering the heat and being careful not to burn meat). The size of the roast will determine the cooking time, probably 2½-3 hours. Thirty minutes before serving, add mushrooms and sherry to the gravy. If a syringe is not available, omit the margarine in the seasoning mixture and "stuff" the seasoning in small slits made in the roast with a knife. Serves 8-10.

Mrs. Larry Smith

VENISON ROAST

1 (4-5 pound) venison round roast	¼ cup apple cider vinegar
1 large onion, chopped	2 tablespoons red pepper or to taste
1 bell pepper, chopped	2 tablespoons salt
3 toes garlic, chopped	1 teaspoon garlic powder
½ cup cooking oil	

Place roast in colander and let cold water run over meat until it is pink. Pat dry and season in following manner: Mix salt, pepper and garlic powder in small bowl. Make small holes in roast and put small amount of seasoning in each. Rub remaining seasoning over roast and put in large bowl. Add vinegar, oil, onions, garlic and peppers. Marinate overnight in this liquid. Cook in same liquid for 2 hours at 350° in covered roaster. A small amount of water may be added to increase gravy.

Note—This will be very hot. Adjust red pepper according to taste.

My mother-in-law, many years ago, taught me how to prepare a venison roast. The washing of the meat is most important. Serves 8-10.

Mrs. Frederick Schoeffler

VENISON ROAST WITH CLARET MARINADE

venison roast	2 large cloves garlic
1 cup olive oil	1 onion
2 cups claret	1 teaspoon salt
1 jigger gin	6 crushed peppercorns

Place roast in large container, bowl or crock. Blend remaining ingredients and pour marinade over roast. Put bowl in a cool place to stand for 2-4 days. Turn meat twice a day. When ready to cook drain meat, save and and strain liquid. Dry and season with salt and pepper. Put roast in oven at 450° for 15 minutes. Lower heat to 325°. Cover pan, baste with liquid marinade every 20 minutes. Remove roast when cooked to your liking. You may add flour in pan for gravy. For well done roast cook 25-30 minutes per pound or until fork tender. Serves 8-10.

Mrs. J. L. Beyt, Jr.

FRIED VENISON

Batter:

2 cups flour	¼ teaspoon red pepper
1¾ cups milk	½ teaspoon black pepper
3 teaspoons salt	¼ teaspoon garlic powder

In a medium sized bowl, mix flour and milk with a whisk until all lumps are out. Add salt, red and black pepper and garlic powder. Mix well.

Shaking Flour:

| 4 cups flour | 2 teaspoons paprika |

Place flour and paprika in a plastic bag and mix well for shaking.

| oil—1-2 inches deep in pot | 1-1¼ pounds venison backstrap |

Slice backstrap in ¼ inch slices. Pound each slice with a meat tenderizing mallet. Dip venison in batter with a fork until completly covered. Drop into bag with flour and shake well. Preheat oil in a skillet on medium-high setting. Drop the floured venison into the hot oil and fry until golden brown. Drain meat on paper towel and serve hot. When cooking a lot of venison, the "shaking flour" will become very lumpy. Sift to remove lumps and add more flour as needed. This is delicious with a cream gravy made with the browned particles left in the skillet after frying.

Gravy

4 rounded tablespoons flour	1 teaspoon salt
¾ cup water	½ teaspoon black pepper
2 cups milk	

Using the same skillet, pour off excess oil, leaving browned particles and approximately 3 tablespoons oil. Turn burner to medium-high and add flour, stirring constantly, until medium brown. Add water and milk and continue stirring with a whisk. Turn heat to low and cook until thick. Add salt and pepper to taste and serve immediately. Serves 8.

Mike Walker

VENISON CHILI

5 tablespoons salt
4 pounds ground venison
4 pounds lean ground beef
5 large onions, chopped
3 pods garlic, chopped
1 large bell pepper, chopped
2 fresh jalapeno peppers, seeded and
   chopped

4 tablespoons flour
1 teaspoon red pepper
1 (1 ounce) can ground cumin
1-1½ (3 ounce) bottles chili powder
5-6 cups boiling water

Sprinkle 1 tablespoon salt into bottom of largest magnalite roaster and place over medium heat on top of stove approximately 10 minutes or until bottom begins to heat. Place all 4 pounds ground beef into roaster and spread evenly over bottom of pan. When meat begins to "fry" and begins browning, stir and break up with large spoon or fork. Continue to stir and as beef looses red color and juice accumulates in bottom of pan, add half of the venison and stir until well mixed with the beef. Add remaining venison and repeat process. Cook all meat over medium to medium-high heat until all pink color is gone. Pick out any gristle from venison as you stir meat. Add chopped onions, garlic and peppers to meat mixture and continue to stir until all vegetables are wilted and onions are transparent. Sprinkle flour over meat mixture and stir well. Add remaining 4 tablespoons salt and all ground cumin. Stir to mix thoroughly. In a large bowl, mix chili powder to 3 cups boiling water and pour into meat and vegetable mixture in roaster. Stir well and add enough remaining boiling water to bring mixture to a medium thin consistency. Turn heat on burner to medium-low and cook uncovered for several hours. Stir occasionally to prevent sticking and skim off excess oil from top as you stir. Be careful to skim only the fat and not any of the gravy. It has been my experience that the longer the chili cooks, the better the flavor. I usually cook my chili about 3-4 hours. The flavor is even better after being frozen and then thawed and reheated. Therefore, I always make at least this quantity or more, and freeze part of it. You may adjust this recipe to your needs by increasing or decreasing all ingredients proportionately. Be sure to maintain half and half balance of ground venison and ground beef.

Note: I have used other pots for this recipe, but have found that when cooked in a 16 inch magnalite roaster, the browning and cooking process is much simpler and the taste is far superior.

If you wish to use this as a dip in a chafing dish with Fritos or Doritos, cook down to a thicker consistency, or if necessary, thicken with a little cornstarch and water. Serves approximately 30.

Mrs. Haskell Walker

SQUIRREL WITH WINE AND MUSHROOMS

Cut 3-4 squirrels in six pieces, forelegs, hindlegs, and across back. Marinate overnight, turning occasionally, using:

1 teaspoon salt	1 cup dry white wine
Tabasco to taste	1 onion, sliced
1 tablespoon Worcestershire	½ lemon, sliced
1 tablespoon Italian dressing	2 buds garlic, sliced
1 tablespoon vinegar	

Ingredients for cooking squirrel:

¼ cup butter	1 cup chicken broth
¼ cup olive oil	1 cup dry white wine
1 bell pepper, chopped	1 (8 ounce) can sliced mushrooms
1 onion, chopped	1 cup chopped onion tops and parsley
2 ribs celery, chopped	salt and pepper
2 buds garlic, mashed	

Wipe squirrel dry; add salt and pepper to taste. Sauté cut up squirrel in butter and olive oil. Remove, add onions, bell pepper, celery and garlic and fry until wilted and lightly browned. Remove excess oil from pot and return squirrel. Add chicken broth, cover and cook for approximately 45 minutes in 350° oven. (Check during cooking to see that all liquid has not cooked out; add broth or wine if necessary.) Add wine and cook 30 minutes longer. Add mushrooms, onion tops, and parsley and cook 30 minutes longer. When squirrel is tender and gravy has reached desired consistency, remove cover and cook for about 10 minutes at 450°. Serve with rice.

Note: The cooking time is approximate. It is hard to say exactly how long this small game should be cooked because of its size. It should not be overcooked because it will fall apart, therefore, it should be checked carefully. Serves 6.

Tuttie and Bob Billeaud

SQUIRREL OR RABBIT ROTI
(Roasted)

6 squirrels or rabbits, quartered
3 cloves garlic, chopped
5 Tabasco peppers, chopped

Tony's Creole Seasoning, to taste
bacon grease
½-1 cup beef broth*
onion tops

Make 1 or 2 slits in each piece of game, stuffing with mixture of chopped garlic, chopped peppers and Tony's Creole Seasoning. After stuffing slits, season generously all over with Tony's Creole Seasoning. Heat large pot on high (preferable large black iron pot) covering bottom with bacon grease. Brown pieces gradually, heat may be lowered slightly to keep from burning. Continue adding bacon grease as it is absorbed. (This is important to keep gravy from burning.) After pieces have been well browned, lower heat, add ¼ cup beef broth and cover pot. Occasionally add more broth as this cooked down. Remove tender pieces as you cook to prevent them from falling apart. When all pieces are cooked, add remaining broth and raise heat to make gravy. Garnish with onion tops.

Note* I use homemade beef broth which is unsalted. You may substitute canned beef or chicken broth, however, this is salted, so you must reduce your seasoning accordingly. I find the canned chicken broth is less salty than the canned beef broth. Serves 12.

Mrs. Paul Blanchet

WILD RABBIT

4 rabbits cut in frying pieces,
   season to taste
3 tablespoons flour
1½ cups minced onion
½ cup minced bell pepper
½ cup minced celery

3 pods garlic, chopped finely
½ cup minced green onions and parsley
3 cups rich brown stock
½ cup red wine
¼ cup currant jelly

Cut rabbit into frying pieces, season well and marinate overnight if possible. Drain and fry brown, remove meat from pot. Add the following: flour, cook several minutes then add onions, bell peppers, celery, garlic, green onions and parsley, cook several more minutes, add rabbit pieces, 2 cups of water and cook until rabbit becomes slightly tender. Add rich brown stock, wine and simmer to reduce until almost ½. Add currant jelly, stir in until well blended. Serve with hot garlic bread and a green salad. Serves 6-10 depending on size of rabbits.

Helen Gankendorff

BAKED WILD TURKEY

1 (12-16 pound) wild turkey	2 bell peppers, quartered
salt	2-4 ribs celery
garlic salt	12 garlic slivers
red and black pepper	margarine, softened
2 medium onions, quartered	2 hot peppers, optional

Day before baking: Wash bird thoroughly and wipe dry. Season cavity with salt and pepper and stuff with onions, bell peppers, celery, garlic and hot peppers. Season outside of bird with salt, pepper and garlic salt rubbing the skin well as you season. Cover the entire bird with a liberal coating of margarine and then re-season if necessary. Wrap in heavy-duty aluminum foil, folding together loosely at breast of bird. Refrigerate until ready to bake.

With turkey still wrapped in foil, place in shallow baking pan, breast up, in preheated 450° oven. Bake for 1 hour. Unfold the foil opening and check to see if bird is browning. (If not, continue baking at same temperature for ½ hour more or until bird is brown.) Reduce oven temperature to 300° and continue baking with foil closed for approximately 1-2 hours more depending on size of bird. When turkey leg starts to separate from body, turkey is done and should be removed from foil wrapping. Reserve the gravy and place turkey on serving tray to cool. Cover loosely with foil. Use reserved gravy to mix with dressing and to spoon over carved turkey. Serves 10-12.

Nedra R. Andrus

WOODCOCK FOR COMPANY

24 woodcocks (doves may be used)	garlic powder
salt	red wine vinegar and olive oil in equal
red and black pepper	amounts

Make a paste of all ingredients and coat woodcocks inside and out. Marinate in refrigerator overnight.

flour	1 bunch green onions
¼ cup olive oil	½ cup chopped parsley
2 large onions	3 cups chicken broth
1 medium bell pepper	1 pound smoked sausage, browned
3 cloves garlic	½-1 cup red wine
3 ribs celery	2 cups thinly sliced mushrooms

Remove woodcock from marinade and pat dry. Flour lightly and brown well in olive oil. While birds are browning, chop finely all the vegetables. Remove birds and sauté vegetables over medium-low heat for approximately 10-15 minutes. To vegetables, add broth and wine. Replace birds in Dutch oven, breast down and simmer slowly approximately 2 hours or until done. About 30 minutes before birds are done, add mushrooms and sliced smoked sausage which has been browned. (These additions make a delicious gravy.) Correct seasoning to taste. Serves 8-10.

Carola Bacqué

SELLING CRAWFISH AT BUTTE LA ROSE

Today, as everyone knows, crawfish has become a delicacy which is being sold around the world. This was not always the case. There was a time when farmers complained about all the crawfish holes appearing among their crops. They came to realize, however, that crawfish were not a menace, but a kind of food that could be cooked many different ways. Today the modern Cajun has dishes such as crawfish stew, crawfish pie, etouffee, gumbo, bisque, fried crawfish, boiled . . . , just to mention a few.

This painting shows the early days when it was far easier to give the crawfish away than to try to sell them. Here I show the early Louisiana scene. The landscape was primitive, and I paint the people in a primitive or naive way, showing the effect of the land on the people.

SEAFOODS

BROILED SOFT SHELL CRABS

soft shell crabs, 1-2 per person
salt and pepper

flour, for dredging
butter or margarine

Clean crabs, Stick a knife point into the body between the eyes. Lift the pointed end of the top shell and scrape off the spongy white substance, between the shell and body on each side. Place the crab on its back and with a small sharp knife remove the "apron" or small loose shell which comes to a point about the middle of the undershell. Wash the crabs. Sprinkle lightly with salt and pepper and dredge in flour. Preheat oven broiler until pan is quite hot. Melt sufficient butter or margarine to allow dipping of crabs until thoroughly drenched. Wipe pan with butter and place crabs, shell side down. Return pan to oven right under broiler flame. Baste crabs frequently so they will not lose moisture. After about 15 minutes turn crabs over. Pour meuniere sauce or butter garlic sauce over crabs and serve on toast. Garnish with lemon quarters and parsley.

Mayers Caterers

FRIED SOFT SHELL CRABS

soft shell crabs—1-2 per person
salt and pepper
eggs

milk
flour
oil for frying

Clean crabs. Season with salt and pepper. Make a light batter by mixing beaten eggs with milk and dip crabs in batter. Dip in flour. Fry in deep fat shell side down. Turn over and brown on other side. Stick crabs with an icepick while cooking.

Mayers Catering

SAUCE FOR SHRIMP OR CRABMEAT COCKTAILS

1½ cups chili sauce
1 cup tomato catsup
6 drops Tabasco
1 teaspoon Worcestershire

1 teaspoon horseradish
3 green onions and tops chopped very
   thin

Add ingredients in order into a bowl, stir until well blended and pour into a jar or container with a tight lid. This should be made the day before using and can be refrigerated for a few weeks. Yield: 1 quart.

Marilyn Tankersley Taylor

HENRY'S BARBECUED CRABS

2 dozen crabs, live
red pepper
salt
2 sticks butter
¼-½ small bottle liquid crab boil

1 tablespoon lemon pepper, optional
1 teaspoon garlic powder
2 pounds butter
6 lemons quartered
1 tablespoon Worcestershire

Run hot tap water over live crabs. This will stun the crabs so they can't pinch. Pull back off the crabs, clean out the dead man fingers, lungs, and clean out center of crab. Crack the claws but do not remove. Sprinkle red pepper and salt over crabs. Mix remaining ingredients in a saucepan and melt over low heat for approximately 20 minutes. Brush the sauce over the crabs thoroughly. On a barbecue pit put the grill as far away from a medium to low fire as possible. Place the crabs, cavity side down, on the grill. Cook with lid of pit down for about 10 minutes, checking the crabs now and then to be sure they don't burn. Brush on more sauce and turn. Fill cavity with sauce, put down cover and cook for another 10-15 minutes or until done. Eat just like you would eat boiled crabs. Cooking time on the crabs may vary 10-15 minutes depending on how hot the fire is. Serves 4-6.

Henry Mayer

BAKED AVOCADO WITH CRAB

6 avocados
1 lemon
2 cans crabmeat
2 cups cream sauce*
1 teaspoon onion juice

⅛ teaspoon cayenne
1 teaspoon salt
1 cup grated sharp cheddar cheese
2 cups bread crumbs
1 tablespoon melted butter

Preheat oven to 400°. Don't peel avocados. Cut in halves. Sprinkle with lemon juice. Pick crabmeat taking out tendons, leaving it in as large pieces as possible. Make cream sauce. Season with onion juice, cayenne, salt and a little melted butter. Mix with crabmeat and spoon into avocado halves. Cover tops with mixture of bread crumbs and cheese. Set in oven for 15 minutes or until nicely brown and hot. Serve as a luncheon meat, or as entree for a formal dinner. Serves 12.

*Cream Sauce: To make a perfect cream sauce, always put butter in a skillet set over medium heat and stir until melted. Add flour and cook gently for 3-4 minutes. Then add milk slowly, stirring constantly until all the milk is used. Cook to the required thickness. The secret of cream sauce lies in the proper blending of butter and flour before the addition of milk or cream. Use 2 tablespoons butter, 2 tablespoons flour, 1 cup milk and season as desired, ¼ teaspoon salt is sufficient for 1 cup milk.

Wendy Beneke Edmundson

CRAB STEW

4 dozen cleaned crabs
⅔ cup shortening
⅔ cup flour
2 onions, chopped finely
1 bell pepper, chopped finely
3 garlic cloves, optional
2 cans whole tomatoes
1 can tomato sauce

1 cup chopped celery
½ lemon, chopped
⅓ cup parsley, dehydrated
⅔ cup chopped onion tops
⅓ cup red wine
2 tablespoons fresh lemon juice
2 tablespoons Worcestershire
salt, black and red pepper, to taste
Tabasco, to taste

Wash crabs. Boil claws. Remove and store meat. Reserve water. Make a dark roux with fat and flour. Add onions, bell pepper, garlic and cook 10 minutes. Add 2 quarts hot water, (include broth from boiled claws), tomatoes, tomato sauce, diced lemon, celery, parsley flakes. Stir well, season with salt, black pepper, red pepper and Tabasco. Cover and simmer 45 minutes. Put crab bodies in a large pot and pour roux over them. Add enough hot water so that crabs are almost covered. Add onion tops, wine and cook for 20 minutes. Stir every 5 minutes. Turn off fire, add lemon juice, and Worcestershire. Strain out crab bodies and add crab claw meat to stew and reheat. Serve over rice. Serves 8-10.

Matt Gordy

CRAB DIP

2 sticks margarine
2 large chopped onions
2 cups chopped celery
2 large bell peppers
6 large garlic pods
6 green hot peppers
1 cup parsley and shallots

4 ounces Velveeta cheese
2 pounds crabmeat
4 cans mushroom soup
2 small jars pimento
1 (4 ounce) can mushrooms
1 stick margarine, melted
8 tablespoons flour

Sauté first 6 ingredients for 45 minutes. Add next 6 ingredients and cook for 30 minutes. Mix 1 stick margarine and flour in small pot and cook until thickened. Then add it to crab mixture and cook an additional 15 minutes. Serve with chips for dipping. For a luncheon, serve over toasted English muffins. Serves 8.

Mrs. Bradley Hanks

CRAB CHARLENE

1 stick butter or margarine
1 tablespoon chopped onion
1 teaspoon garlic salt or minced garlic
½ cup chopped green onion
1 cup chopped fresh parsley
2 tablespoons corn starch
1 pint half and half
10 ounces jack cheese, cut up

3 egg yolks, well beaten
garlic and salt to taste
Tabasco to taste
½ cup sliced black olives, optional
1 small jar pimento, optional
2 pounds crabmeat, picked
French bread crumbs

Preheat oven to 350°. Melt butter in skillet. Sauté onions and minced garlic if used. Add green onion, parsley and turn off heat. Soften corn starch in a little water. Add this to half and half and stir constantly with wire whisk until slightly thick. Add cheese and melt. Stir in 3 well beaten egg yolks, continuing to stir constantly. Cook until thick. Add garlic salt and Tabasco to taste. Add olive and pimento if desired. Add crabmeat. Place in buttered casserole. Cover with French bread crumbs. Bake at 350° until brown and bubbling. Serves 8.

Charlene C. Baker
New Orleans, LA

CRAWFISH ELEGANTE

1 stick butter
¼ large onion, chopped
⅓ cup green onion tops, chopped
3 tender stalks celery, chopped
2 tablespoons flour

1 large can evaporated milk
1 egg yolk
1 pound freshly peeled crawfish tails
salt and pepper
⅓ pound Velveeta cheese, shredded

Preheat oven to 350°. Melt butter in saucepan. Sauté onions, onion tops and celery. Sprinkle flour over mixture in pot, blending well. Add milk slowly blending well. Remove pot from heat. Add egg yolk, crawfish, salt, pepper and cheese. Return to low heat until cheese is melted. Put in individual casserole dishes or one large dish. Bake until bubbly. Serves 4-6.

Mrs. Richard R. Kennedy

CRAWFISH AND OKRA CASSEROLE

oil to cover bottom of skillet
1 medium onion, chopped fine
1 bell pepper, chopped fine
1 (1½ pound) bag, frozen cut okra
2 pounds peeled crawfish tails,
   crawfish fat, optional

1 large can mushroom steak sauce
1 can Rotel tomatoes
¼ cup cooking oil
1 can cream of mushroom soup
1 cup raw rice
salt and red pepper to taste

Sauté onions and bell pepper 15 minutes. add okra for 5 more minutes. Remove from stove. Mix rest of the ingredients together well, then add onions and okra mixture. Place in a 4 quart casserole dish, cover and bake for 1 hour and 15 minutes at 375°. Serves 8.

If you wish to freeze it, cook for 30 minutes. Also it would be a good idea to divide it into 2 2-quart casseroles for easier thawing.

Gloria Tullier

CRAWFISH A LA JUDY

1 pound peeled crawfish tails
½ stick butter
lemon juice
Blender Bearnaise Sauce:

¼-½ teaspoon dill weed
green onions and parsley
seasonings to taste
bread crumbs

Preheat oven to 350°. Sauté crawfish tails in butter and lemon juice until barely tender. Drain. Add to Bearnaise sauce to which dill weed, green onion tops and parsley have been added. Correct seasonings. Spoon into ramekins, sprinkle bread crumbs over top. Heat at 350° until thoroughly warmed. Be careful not to overheat as sauce may curdle. Serves 4-6.

Blender Bearnaise Sauce:
3 egg yolks
2 tablespoons lemon juice
¼-½ teaspoon salt
dash red pepper
1 stick butter, melted

2 tablespoons white wine
1 tablespoon tarragon vinegar
2 teaspoons minced green onion tops
1 teaspoon dried tarragon, pulverized
½ teaspoon white pepper

With blender on highest setting, mix egg yolks with lemon juice, and salt and red pepper. Pour melted butter into blender in steady stream. Set aside. Reduce wine vinegar, onion tops and dried tarragon over high heat until liquid is almost absorbed. Blend with egg yolk mixture and white pepper. Note: Lump crabmeat, lightly sauteed may be substituted.

Judy Griffin

GRAND ISLE SPECKLED TROUT

4 specks filleted	flour
salt and cayenne	1 stick butter

Make certain all skin is removed from fillets. Wash fillets and dry on paper towels. Season generously with salt and cayenne. Preheat skillet to 400°. Coat fillets in flour and shake off excess. Put ½ stick of butter in skillet and when bubbly add fillets and pan broil until brown and crisp. Turn and do the same for the other side, adding the rest of the butter as needed. When cooked drain on towels and serve immediately. You may serve with lemon juice and homemade mayonnaise or any of various fish sauces are delicious on top. This can be a very simple meal or may be used for a formal occasion if topped with an appropriate sauce. Serves 4.

Mrs. J. J. Burdin, Sr.

BAKED SPECKLED TROUT

milk	Progresso bread crumbs
8 fillets speckled trout	1½ sticks butter
salt and pepper	slivered almonds, optional

Preheat oven to 350°. Soak fillets in milk for 2-3 hours, the longer the better. Drain fish, season with salt and pepper. Roll in bread crumbs. Melt ½ stick of butter and pour in bottom of oblong pan. Place trout side by side in dish. Add slivered almonds if desired. Pour remaining butter over trout. Bake for 20 minutes. Serves 6.

Mrs. Henry·W. Busch, Jr.

TROUT MEUNIERE

6 (¾ pound) fillets of speckled trout	1 cup flour
salt and pepper to taste	1 tablespoon baking powder
1 egg	1 stick margarine
1 cup water	

Season trout with salt and red pepper. Make batter with egg and water. Sift flour and baking powder together. Dip fish in egg batter, coat with flour mixture. Melt margarine in heavy pan on low heat. Broil fish in margarine very slowly until flour coating is golden brown. Remove to serving tray. Serve with sauce. Serves 6.

Sauce:

1 stick butter	1 tablespoon Worcestershire
1 tablespoon lemon juice	1 teaspoon vinegar, white

Melt butter. Add lemon juice, Worcestershire and vinegar. Blend well. Serve over fish.

Hugh P. Langlinais

TROUT WITH SAUCE DE MER

½ cup melted butter
¾ cup flour
3 cups Half and Half, more or less
  depending upon thickness desired
¾ coarsely chopped shrimp
½ cup chopped mushrooms
⅔ teaspoon salt

½ teaspoon paprika
¼ teaspoon celery seed
½ cup grated Hoop cheese
½ cup dry sherry more or less
  depending upon taste
6 (8 ounce) filet of trout
small amount of water

Melt butter in heavy saucepan, stir in flour and mix well. Add Half and Half slowly until thoroughly blended. Add shrimp, mushrooms and seasonings. Cook over medium heat until thick and creamy. Remove from heat and stir in cheese and sherry. Place trout filets in small amount of water in ovenproof dish. Poach in 350° oven until about half cooked. Remove from oven and with a slotted spoon remove trout from water and place in a clean, shallow ovenproof dish. Cover trout with the prepared sauce and return to 350° oven until cooked through, approximately 15 minutes, depending upon thickness of trout. Serves 6-8.

This special trout dish was first prepared by Mrs. James Blair's mother-in-law, Mrs. Barbara Thorn, a gourmet cook par excellence. Mrs. Thorn's love of travel eventually took her to Alaska where she worked for a season as cook to guests at a private hunting lodge. Due to the availability of fresh fish and wild game, Mrs. Thorn invented several excellent recipes, but a favorite with the guests at the lodge was her "Trout with Sauce de Mer." Upon Mrs. Thorn's return to Louisiana, she prepared her special trout for her family. It was enjoyed so much that Mr. Blair persuaded her to allow him to include this delicious trout on his menu of specialty dishes.

Barbara L. Thorn
Blair House Restaurant

FILET OF SOLE WITH GRAPES

2 cups milk
2½ pounds filet of sole or flounder
½ pound fresh mushrooms, sliced
¼ cup butter
2 cups white seedless grapes
3 tablespoons butter

4 tablespoons flour
salt and pepper
½ cup buttered bread or corn flake
  crumbs
2 tablespooons grated Parmesan cheese

Preheat oven to 400°. Put milk in a heavy skillet, heat to just below boiling and poach the filets in it 5 minutes, reducing the heat immediately so the milk just simmers. Sauté the mushrooms in ¼ cup butter about 3 minutes. Combine mushrooms with grapes and spread in large shallow casserole. With a slotted spatula lift the fish filets very carefully from the milk and lay them on top of the grape and mushroom mixture. Make a cream sauce with the 3 tablespoons butter, flour and milk in which the filets were cooked. Season to taste and spread over the fish. Top with crumbs and cheese mixed together. Bake in hot oven about 25 minutes, or until golden brown. Serves 6.

Sandy Hamilton
London, England

CHABLIS SAUCE

2 teaspoons cornstarch
dash salt
½ cup light cream
½ cup chicken broth

¼ cup chablis
1 beaten egg yolk
½ cup halved seedless green grapes

Delicate flavor goes well with all varieties of fish.

In a small saucepan, blend together cornstarch and salt; stir in cream, chicken broth and chablis. Cook, stirring constantly until mixture thickens and bubbles. Stir some of the sauce into the egg yolk; return to mixture in saucepan. Cook and stir until mixture is thickened and bubbly. Add grapes; heat through. Ladle sauce over poached or baked fish. Yield: 1½ cups.

Sandy Hamilton
London, England

BAKED RED SNAPPER FILETS

1 quart fresh red snapper filets
seasoned salt
1 chopped onion

1 stick butter, melted
1 bunch diced green onions

Preheat oven to 350°. Season filets with seasoned salt. Sauté onion in butter in saucepan on top of stove. Place seasoned filets in pyrex and pour butter-onion mixture on top. Cook for 30 minutes at 350°, occasionally spooning butter over filets. When fish are tender, remove from oven and sprinkle green onions on top. Serves a family of 5.

Raymonde Ballbach

JUDY'S BAKED RED SNAPPER

2 large onions
5 stalks celery
1 large bell pepper
5 toes garlic
½ cup cooking oil
2 cans Rotel tomatoes

1 can tomato sauce
salt to taste
red pepper to taste
1 can mushrooms
1 (5-8 pound) red snapper
¾ pound raw shrimp, peeled

Preheat oven to 350°. Sauté onions, celery, bell pepper and garlic in cooking oil. Add tomatoes, sauce, salt and red pepper. Add mushrooms and cook, covered for 2 hours. Tomatoes are very acid and must be cooked this long for a good gravy. Wash and dry fish. Season to taste and fill stomach cavity with shrimp. Pour cooked gravy over fish and bake uncovered in large roaster until fish is done. Fish is cooked when there is an absence of milky liquid coming from same. Remove to large platter. Slice fish and serve over cooked rice. Serves 6-8.

Mrs. Frederick Schoeffler

RED SNAPPER WITH POTATOES AND ONIONS

1 tablespoon olive oil
1 (5 pound) red snapper
salt, red and black pepper
3-4 garlic cloves
5 medium red potatoes, peeled and
    cut in chunks
2 medium onions, sliced thinly in
    rings

1 small lemon, sliced
3 tablespoons celery, chopped
¼ cup parsley, chopped
¼ cup green onions, chopped
1 can peeled tomatoes
2 tablespoons tomato paste dissolved in 2
    cups water

Preheat oven to 375°. Put 1 tablespoon olive oil in bottom of large baking dish, 9x13 inches. Make 3-4 deep slits in each side of fish. Season with salt and pepper and insert garlic slivers in slits. Put in baking dish, then arrange remaining ingredients over top of fish. Bake for about 2 hours. Serves 6.

Mrs. Paul J. Azar, Sr.

POACHED FISH FOR WEIGHTWATCHERS

3 pounds fish fillets
2 bay leaves
1 tablespoon salt
1 small onion, sliced
¼ cup celery leaves
½ teaspoon pepper

dash of Tabasco
1 small lemon sliced
4 tablespoons butter
3 tablespoons flour
1 egg, beaten
¼ cup evaporated milk

Use any fish with a white, flaky texture such as speckled trout, red fish, bass. Fill large skillet half full of water; add bay leaves, salt, onion, celery, pepper, Tabasco and lemon slices. Boil 5 minutes. Add fish, simmer 10 minutes. Remove fish to warm platter. Reserve the liquid left. It is the stock. Melt butter, blend in flour until it makes soft paste. Add 2 cups fish stock. Stir constantly over low heat until mixture thickens. Mix together egg and milk; add to stock mixture stirring constantly until sauce thickens. Pour over fish. Garnish with freshly chopped green onions and parsley or paprika if desired. For variety make sauce as above and add ½ cup grated cheese before egg and milk is mixed into stock. Serves 4-6.

C. Earl Weber, Sr.
New Orleans, LA

FRIED FROG LEGS

6-8 small frog legs per serving
milk to cover legs while soaking in
 refrigerator
salt and red pepper to taste

cooking oil 3 inches deep in heavy fry pot
self-rising flour to coat legs when shaken
 in brown bag
onions, thinly sliced

Batter:
2 whole eggs
1 cup flour
1 teaspoon salt

juice of 2 lemons
2 cups milk
½ teaspoon red pepper

Soak legs in milk at least ½ day before frying, (helps to tenderize).

Prepare batter: Beat eggs; add lemon juice, milk, salt and pepper. Blend in flour until mixture is smooth Should not be prepared more than 30 minutes before intended use, as batter will get too thick.

Heat oil. Oil should not be hot enough to smoke, but it should bubble briskly when legs are dropped in. Remove legs from milk, drain slightly, season with salt and red pepper generously and drop into batter. Coat legs with batter carefully, retaining as much of the seasonings as possible. Drop separately into bag of flour (self-rising flour makes lighter, thicker crust). Shake to coat well. Prepare platter lined with several thicknesses or paper toweling and thinly, sliced raw onion rings to toss with fried legs, while draining, for extra flavor. Now, that you (up to both elbows) and the frog legs are battered and floured, you are ready to fry. Fry only enough legs at one time to make a single layer in fry pot. Over-crowding, while frying, will loosen batter as you turn the legs. Be careful not to over fry the frog legs, as they will get tough, if fried too long. When they "float" in oil and batter seems crisp, take one out for a quick test for doneness. To test, cut into center. Remove immediately onto paper towel and toss with raw onion rings. While next batch is frying, prepare new towel and onion tray. If I have more than two batches to fry, I transfer drained legs and the onion, in that batch, into a clean, paper towel-lined brown, grocery bag and keep warm in low oven or warmer, while other batches fry. One large brown bag holds several batches of well-drained, fried legs and helps keep them crisp as well as warm. Frying frog legs is a messy, last minute job but the results always justify the wreck it makes of the kitchen and cook.

Janet Begneaud

SCALLOPED OYSTERS

½ cup butter
1 medium onion, finely chopped
7 tablespoons flour
milk plus juices to equal 3 cups
2 tablespoons chopped onion tops
3 tablespoons parsley
¼ pound ham or Canadian bacon,
    chopped

4 dozen oysters, drained, save juice
2 small cans mushroom buttons,
    drained, save juice
2 cups finely crushed cracker crumbs
butter

Preheat oven to 375°. Melt butter, add onion, cook until clear. Blend in flour, add 3 cups of liquid. Stir constantly until thick and boiling. Remove from heat and add onion tops and parsley. Add to white sauce ham or chopped bacon. Season to taste. Place oysters and mushrooms in casserole and pour white sauce on top. Sprinkle with cracker crumbs. Dot with butter. Bake for about 20 minutes or until golden brown. Serves 6-8.

Mrs. J. L. Beyt, Jr.
New Iberia, LA

OYSTERS BECKY

oysters
onions
butter

salt and pepper
Worcestershire
Waverly wafers, crumbled

Drain oysters and lay on bottom of rectangular pyrex baking dish. Sauté enough onions in butter to cover oysters, but not be too soupy. Salt and pepper each oyster, dot each with Worcestershire. Cover with Waverly wafer cracker crumbs and bake 30-35 minutes at 350°.

Rebecca C. Marvin
Minden, LA

OYSTERS LOUISIANA

1 dozen oysters	3 tablespoons flour
3 tablespoons butter	few grains cayenne
2 teaspoons chopped onion	½ cup grated Parmesan cheese
2 teaspoons chopped red peppers	salt and pepper to taste

Preheat oven to 350°. Parboil the oysters, remove from pan, saving the liquid and add enough water to make 1½ cups. Melt the butter and fry the onion and red pepper in it. Add the flour to the onion and red pepper and blend; then gradually pour on the liquid and stir constantly. Bring to a boil and season. Arrange the oysters in a casserole. Pour the liquid over them, add the grated cheese and bake until thoroughly heated. Serves 2.

Mary Lenny Perrin

OYSTER DRESSING

1 bunch celery	1 gallon oysters
2 large onions	1 large can Italian bread crumbs
2 sticks butter	1 cup parsley
1 loaf French bread	

Drain oysters and let oyster water collect in a bowl. Break French bread into small pieces and place bread in oyster water to soak.

Melt butter in large pot. Sauté celery and onions in butter until soft. Squeeze oyster water from French bread and place bread in the celery and onion mixture. Cook for about 5 minutes. Add drained oysters to the bread, celery and onion mixture, and cook and stir for a few minutes. The dressing will become quite soupy after a while, so after stirring, start adding bread crumbs. Add parsley. Serves 20.

Mrs. George Rees

OYSTER SPAGHETTI

6 dozen oysters	1 cup sliced mushrooms, optional
1 clove garlic	½ teaspoon basil
1 bunch green onions	1 pound spaghetti
1 cup chopped parsley	½ cup Parmesan cheese
¼ cup olive oil	salt and pepper to taste

Drain oysters well. Reserve liquid. You may need it if spaghetti is too dry. Sauté garlic, onions, parsley in olive oil. Add mushrooms and oysters. Cook over low heat until oysters curl. Add basil. Toss oyster mixture with cooked spaghetti and Parmesan cheese. If spaghetti is too dry you may add olive oil or oyster liquid. If spaghetti has too much liquid you could add Italian bread crumbs and/or more Parmesan cheese. Serves 6 generously.

Carola Lipsey Bacqué

HERBED SHRIMP

3 pounds large shrimp
1 stick butter
⅓ cup worcestershire
1 teaspoon each salt, pepper and
  cayenne

1 teaspoon thyme
2 teaspoons rosemary
½ teaspoon celery salt
1 teaspoon olive oil

Mix all ingredients together. Marinate shrimp with shells in refrigerator for 2-3 hours. Preheat oven to 400°. Take out and bake in marinade uncovered for 20-25 minutes. This recipe has placed in several contests. Serves 4-6.

Mardel Williams Martinez

SHRIMP MEUNIERE

1½-2 pounds fairly large shrimp
¼ cup flour
4 tablespoons butter
2 green onions, finely chopped

4 tablespoons chopped parsley
1 clove garlic, minced
salt and pepper
½ cup dry white wine

Peel and devein shrimp, place on paper towels to dry them. Put the flour in a paper bag and add the shrimp a few at a time, and shake to coat lightly with flour. They should have the thinnest possible coating of flour. Heat the butter in large skillet. As soon as it stops sizzling add the shrimp. Sprinkle with the chopped onions, parsley and garlic and keep tossing them over high heat until the shrimp have turned on all sides. Season with plenty of pepper and not too much salt. Turn the heat to low, add the wine and stir and scrape until the wine has dissolved any brown bits at the bottom of the pan. Simmer a few minutes to finish cooking the shrimp. Delicious simply as is with French bread or with rice. Serves 4.

Sue Billet Dinkins

STUFFED SHRIMP

½ cup margarine
½ cup onion, chopped
½ cup celery, chopped
½ cup bell pepper, chopped
2 tablespoons flour
½ cup milk
¼ cup bread crumbs
1 cup crabmeat

2 teaspoons worcestershire
¼ teaspoon salt
¼ teaspoon pepper
3 dozen large shrimp
3 eggs, beaten
bread crumbs
oil

Melt margarine in skillet. Sauté onion, celery and bell pepper. Mix in flour and milk, stirring constantly until thick. Add bread crumbs, crabmeat, worcestershire, salt and pepper. Mix well. Remove shell and vein from shrimp. If shrimp are large cut in butterfly fashion. Mold stuffing around each shrimp then dip in beaten eggs and roll in bread crumbs seasoned with salt and pepper. Fry in hot oil until golden brown. Serves 6.

Mrs. John Tolson, III

BUTTERFLY SHRIMP

4-5 pounds shrimp	ground black pepper
1 large onion	1½ teaspoons salt
1-1½ pints evaporated milk	flour or Fish-Fri
4 large cloves garlic, cubed	¾ teaspoon baking powder
dash Tabasco	shortening for frying
1 teaspoon sugar	

Clean shrimp and remove all of the shell except the last segment and the tail. Slit each shrimp lengthwise through the body down to the last segment of shell, leaving two long strips of flesh hanging loose. These curl back when shrimp is placed in the hot deep fat. Marinate shrimp in a liquid made by scraping onion into the evaporated milk and adding cubed garlic, Tabasco, sugar, pepper and salt. When shrimp have marinated for at least an hour, preferably longer, drop a few at a time into a paper bag into which you have placed the flour or Fish-Fri and a couple of pinches of baking powder added. Change the flour and baking powder mixture for a fresh mixture when it becomes damp to keep the coating light and crisp. Fry shrimp in deep, hot fat. Serve hot with tartar sauce. Serves 6.

Marianne Schneider

SHRIMP CREOLE

⅔ cup oil	2 bay leaves
¾ cup flour	1 lemon, squeeze juice and pulp
2 cups finely chopped onions,	⅔ can tomato paste or sauce
about 3 medium size	2½ or 3 pounds peeled shrimp
6 cloves garlic	salt, pepper, Worcestershire, chili
1 cup finely chopped celery	powder and red hot sauce to taste
1 cup finely chopped bell pepper	

Make a roux with oil and flour. Add onions and sauté slightly. Add all other ingredients and enough water to cover them. Cook slowly until shrimp are done and tender. This is better if it simmers over a low fire. Stir occasionally and season to taste. Serve over rice. Serves 6-8.

Mrs. Gladys Legendre Martin

PRAWNS WITH CHILI SAUCE

Ingredients A:
10 prawns, shelled, 2 pounds
2 tablespoons wine
1 teaspoon salt

2 tablespoons cornstarch
oil, enough to deep fry prawns

Ingredients B:
5 tablespoons chopped green onion
2 teaspoons minced ginger
2 teaspoons minced garlic

1 teaspoon chili pepper, crushed
4 tablespoons oil

Ingredients C:
2 tablespoons soy sauce
5 tablespoons catsup
1½ tablespoons sugar

1 tablespoon wine
dash of Accent

Remove black veins and cut each prawn into 3 pieces. Dredge with wine, salt and cornstarch. Heat oil, deep frying prawns until color changes; remove to a plate. Mix Ingredients C in a bowl. Heat 4 tablespoons oil, fry Ingredients B, add seasoning mixture and bring to a boil. Add fried prawns and mix well. Cook for a few minutes. Serve hot. Serves 2-4.

Thomas C. Naugle, Jr. M.D.
New Orleans, LA

CHINESE MANDARIN SHRIMP

2 pounds chopped bacon
½ can curry powder
1 large head garlic, chopped fine
½ cup turmeric
1 teaspoon black pepper
2 teaspoons thyme
2 teaspoons poultry seasoning
1 pinch tarragon
2 dashes onion and celery salt
15 bay leaves
10 pounds jumbo shrimp, cleaned
1 pound butter

salt to taste
4 bell peppers, chopped
30 medium onions, chopped large
4 bunches celery, chopped
5 cans mushrooms (40 ounces), chopped
1 can bamboo shoots
3 cans water chestnuts
½ bottle Worcestershire
½ bottle Heinz 57 sauce
½ teaspoon molasses
3 medium jars chopped pimentos

Fry bacon slowly in a large frying pan, and add seasoning. Boil bay leaves in separate pot in small amount of water for 15 minutes. Add shrimp to bacon and simmer. Remove to large pot. Add butter and simmer, salt to taste. Add chopped pepper and onions. Add celery. Simmer 25 minutes. Add mushrooms, simmer, add bamboo shoots and sliced chestnuts. Add Worcestershire and Heinz 57 sauce. Add molasses and stop cooking. After dish is cool, add 3 medium jars of chopped pimentos. Serve with rice. Serves 30 or more.

Mrs. J. C. Chargois, Sr.

SHRIMP CANTONESE WITH RICE

3 cups hot cooked rice
12 ounces peeled, deveined, raw
   shrimp, halved lengthwise
2 tablespoons butter, margarine or
   vegetable oil
2 cups diagonally sliced celery
2 cups sliced onions
1 quart (8 ounces) fresh spinach
   leaves

1 can (16 ounces) fancy mixed Chinese
   vegetables
red pepper to taste
¼ cup soy sauce
1¼ cups chicken broth
2 tablespoons cornstarch

While rice is cooking, sauté shrimp in butter 1 minute or until shrimp turn pink, using a large skillet. Add celery and onions. Cook, stirring 2 minutes. Add spinach and Chinese vegetables which have been rinsed and drained. Cover and cook 1 minute. Blend pepper, soy sauce, chicken broth and cornstarch. Stir into shrimp-vegetable mixture. Cook, stirring until sauce is clear and thickened, about 2 minutes. Serve over rice. Serves 6.

Marlene John Barry

SHRIMP NEWBURG

5 stalks celery, chopped fine
4 bell peppers, chopped fine
2½ quarts milk
1 quart coffee cream
7 pounds cleaned shrimp
6 sticks butter
salt
1 dozen egg yolks

1 pound American cheese, rat
1 (16 ounce) can button mushrooms or
   sliced
3 medium jars chopped pimentos
1 tablespoon paprika
4 cooking spoons flour
1 can water chestnuts, sliced
1 can bamboo shoots

Steam celery and bell pepper in small amount of water. Scald milk and cream and add celery and peppers. Fry shrimp in a separate pot with 1½ pounds of butter and salt to taste. Beat egg yolks and add to milk mixture. Grate cheese in milk, add paprika. Pour milk mixture over cooked, drained shrimp. Add mushrooms, add pimentos, mix flour to paste with water and strain slowly into sauce and cook slowly until thickened. Add water chestnuts and bamboo shoots and cook for a short time longer. Serve while hot. Serve with rice. One of the original recipes at Chag's Club. Serves 25-30, easily cut down in proportions.

Mrs. J. C. Chargois, Sr.

BETH'S LOUISIANA LOBSTER OR SHRIMP

2 red onions, chopped
1 stick butter
1 cup lobster meat or peeled shrimp
flour

1 cup sour cream
1 cup sliced mushrooms
salt and pepper to taste

Sauté onions in butter. Flour lobster pieces liberally, add to onions. Add sour cream, mushrooms and salt and pepper. Simmer until thickened and serve over rice or in patty shells. A very rich, easy dish for company. Serves 4-6.

Beth Mouton

SHRIMP JAMBALAYA

2 pounds fresh shrimp
salt and pepper
3 tablespoons fat
1 tablespoon flour
3-4 cups stock (shrimp, ham, chicken)
1 green pepper, finely chopped
6 scallions, finely chopped
4 stalks celery, finely chopped

2 dozen oysters
1½ cups cooked ham, diced
1 cup cooked chicken, diced
4-6 cups cooked rice
parsley
hearts of celery
radishes
scallions

Shell and clean shrimp. Cover with cold water; season with salt and pepper. Cook until shrimp are tender; about 5 minutes; drain, saving stock. Melt fat in pan, stir in flour, blend in hot stock, vegetables and oysters and simmer a few minutes until tender. Add shrimp, ham, chicken and rice. Stir until piping hot. Turn onto a hot platter and decorate with parsley, hearts of celery, radishes and scallions. Brandied peaches are good with this. Jambalaya is complimented with an aspic salad. Serves 12-15.

Mrs. Richard D. Chappuis, Sr.

SHRIMP SPAGHETTI

3 tablespoons butter
1 large onion, minced
½ cup chopped green pepper
2 teaspoons salt
1 can Rotel tomatoes and 2
    tablespoons tomato paste, or just
    2½ cups canned tomatoes

1 teaspoon Worcestershire
2 tablespoons sugar
1 (8 ounce) package spaghetti, cooked
1 cup grated cheddar cheese
2 cups fresh shrimp

Preheat oven to 350°. Cook the first seven ingredients about 10 minutes and add shrimp. Then add alternately, in layers, spaghetti and the sauce in a 2 quart casserole. Add the grated cheese on top and bake about 30-35 minutes. A quick casserole for unexpected company. Serves 4-6.

Mrs. L. A. Shelton

EASY SHRIMP STUFFED PEPPERS

1 tablespoon flour
1 tablespoon shortening or fat
½ cup celery
½ cup onion
2 cloves garlic

1 pound shrimp, peeled and deveined
crackers or breadcrumbs
pepper—red and black to taste
6 green peppers—parboiled

Preheat oven to 350°. Make a roux with flour and fat. Sauté celery, onion and garlic in the roux. After the onions have wilted, add shrimp. Cook about 15 minutes. Add enough cracker or crumbs to get a good consistency. (you just have to eye this.) Season all and stuff green peppers which you have boiled separately. Place peppers in a buttered baking dish and bake 20 minutes. Serves 6.

Jean Hurley

STUFFED SQUASH CASSEROLE

12-15 yellow squash
bacon drippings
2 onions
½ small green pepper, chopped
¾ stick butter or margarine

2 cans medium shrimp or 1½ pounds
  boiled shrimp
4-6 slices bread
salt, pepper, garlic powder to taste
2 eggs

Preheat oven to 325°. Slice squash in ½ inch round slices and smother in bacon drippings. Add chopped onions and bell pepper to squash while it is cooking down. You may have to add a little hot water to prevent sticking. Add butter and shrimp after squash mixture is "mushy" consistency and water has cooked out. Toast bread, wet it with water and break it up in mixture. Add seasonings and then beat eggs and add. Grease casserole, pour in mixture, sprinkle with bread crumbs and dot with butter. Bake for approximately 45 minutes. Serves 8.

Lynn Wilson Blevins

CRAB-SHRIMP BAKE

1 cup cleaned, cooked shrimp or
  canned shrimp
½ cup chopped green peppers
2 tablespoons finely chopped onions
1 cup diced celery
1 (7½ ounce) can crabmeat, flaked

½ teaspoon salt
dash of pepper
1 teaspoon Worcestershire
¾ cup mayonnaise
1 cup soft bread crumbs
1 tablespoon butter, melted

Preheat oven to 350°. Cut any large shrimp in half lengthwise. Combine all the ingredients except the butter and bread crumbs. Place this mixture in casserole or baking shells. Combine bread crumbs and melted butter. Sprinkle over the seafood mixture. Bake at 350° for 30-35 minutes for the casserole or 20-25 minutes for the baking shells. Serves 6.

Janet Scanlan McIntyre

SEAFOOD SQUASH CASSEROLE

6 summer squash
¼ cup butter or bacon drippings
1½ cups chopped onions
3 pods garlic, minced
1 can mushrooms
2 cups peeled shrimp (2-3 pounds)
   crabmeat or cubed ham
1 teaspoon salt
¼ teaspoon cayenne

2 teaspoons McCormick seafood
   seasonings
3 slices squeezed wet bread
2 cups seasoned bread crumbs
½ teaspoon sage
½ cup shallots or 2 teaspoons
   freeze-dried chives
2 beaten eggs

Parboil and peel squash. Sauté onions, garlic and mushrooms in fat. Add squash-mushroom liquid and mash. Add shrimp, salt, pepper, seafood seasoning and cook over medium-high heat until shrimp are done, approximately 10 minutes. Reduce heat and add bread and bread crumbs, sage, and shallots. Stir in beaten eggs. Depending on amount of liquid in squash, you may need to add more crumbs. (Should be consistency of dressing.) Place in 3 quart casserole dish and top with bread crumbs. Bake at 350° for 20-30 minutes. Serves 10-12

Marilyn B. Hoffpauir

SEAFOOD EGGPLANT CASSEROLE

2 large eggplants
⅓ cup finely chopped onions
⅓ cup finely chopped celery
⅓ cup finely chopped bell pepper
1 pound raw, peeled, medium shrimp

½ pound claw crabmeat
½ pound butter
½ cup bread crumbs
salt and pepper to taste

Peel and finely chop eggplants, add onions, celery, bell pepper and butter and cook in a saucepan on very low fire for about 1-1½ hours. Do not brown. Add shrimp and crabmeat. Continue to cook on low fire until shrimp are cooked, about 10 minutes. Remove from fire, season to taste and add bread crumbs. Mix well. Dish into individual casseroles or one large casserole. Bake in 350° oven until bread crumbs are browned. This casserole may be served immediately or frozen for later use. Serves 6.

This casserole dish was originally prepared by Mrs. Roy Blair's mother, Magda DuBernard who invented the recipe because of the abundance and availability of the ingredients. Mrs. Roy Blair (Malou) included the casserole on her menu but thought it could be improved upon as the original recipe called for boiled shrimp and bread soaked in milk. Through the skill of Mrs. Ritel Broussard, chief day cook at Blair House for 26 years, the recipe was changed to include fresh shrimp, crabmeat and bread crumbs. So you may say that this particular recipe is the end result of the skills of three excellent cooks.

Blair House Restaurant

CRABMEAT AND SHRIMP CASSEROLE

1 large onion, diced
2 sticks margarine
salt and Tabasco to taste
garlic powder
red and black pepper
1 cup flour
7 cups liquid, use the evaporated
   milk, liquid from the mushrooms
   and then finish with tap water to
   total 7 cups

1 tall can evaporated milk
1 (8 ounce) can mushrooms, sliced
2 pounds crabmeat or cooked shrimp or
   1 pound of each

Preheat oven to 325°. Cook onions in margarine with the salt, pepper and season-ing until onion is soft. Add flour and cook until bubbly. Add 7 cups liquid slowly and cook until thick. Add mushrooms, stir well and then fold in the crabmeat or shrimp. Pour in 3 quart casserole and bake until bubbly. Serve on toast, patty shells or use as a dip with Melba rounds. This freezes very well. You can use 2 pounds of crabmeat or 2 pounds of shrimp or 1 pound of each. Best when you use both. My favorite is as a dip. Serves 6-8.

Marlene Dauterive

SEAFOOD CASSEROLE

4 tablespoons butter
4 tablespoons flour
1 teaspoon salt
⅛ teaspoon pepper
1 cup thin cream or milk
1 cup bouillon
½ cup mushrooms

1 cup shrimp, cooked
1 cup crabmeat
¼ teaspoon prepared mustard
1 egg beaten
breadcrumbs
2 tablespoons sherry

Preheat oven to 425°. Melt butter in saucepan. Add flour, salt and pepper. Blend, then add cream and bouillon. Stir constantly. When it thickens, add sliced mush-rooms, seafood and mustard. Add a little of this mixture to well beaten egg, gradually add all mixture to egg. Put in casserole or shells. Top with buttered bread crumbs. Place in oven for about 20 minutes. I add a little sherry when mixing ingredients. Serves 6.

Mrs. David S. Foster

SEAFOOD TARTS

2 cans tuna, drained or crabmeat,
  shrimp or lobster
2 tablespoons oil from seafood
½ cup grated onion
¼ cup chopped parsley
½ teaspoon garlic salt
½ teaspoon celery salt
¼ teaspoon pepper
½ teaspoon Worcestershire
1 egg, well beaten
1 cup grated cheddar cheese
2 cans refrigerated crescent rolls
paprika

Preheat oven to 350°. Mix all ingredients except rolls, paprika and ½ cup cheese. On ungreased cookie sheet unroll crescent dough and separate into 4 rectangles. Fill the center of each with filling. Place the other 4 rectangles on top of the filling. Seal with fork. Slit tops with fork in two places. Sprinkle with paprika and cheese. Bake for 15-20 minutes. Remove tarts and serve. Very good for a luncheon. Serves 8.

Mrs. Thomas J. R. Low

MÉLANGE DE LA MER

3 sticks margarine
2 cups chopped onion
1 cup chopped celery
6 tablespoons flour
2½ pounds peeled shrimp or any
  combination of crabmeat, crawfish
  oysters
1 teaspoon Worcestershire
1 teaspoon garlic powder
4 ounces tomato sauce
½ cup water
¼ cup chopped parsley
¼ cup green onions, chopped
salt, black pepper and cayenne to taste

Melt margarine, sauté onions and celery. Blend in flour. Add seafood, seasonings and tomato sauce and simmer approximately 10 minutes. Add water, parsley and onion tops and heat through. Adjust seasonings. Serve over rice or patty shells. Serves 6.

Helen Nugier Sobiesk

COQUILLE ST. JACQUES

1 cup mushrooms
1 stick butter
2 tablespoons olive oil
1 cup chopped parsley
1 cup green onion tops
2 tablespoons oil
2 tablespoons flour
4 ounces Sauterne
3 pounds shrimp
1 cup lobster
2 cups crabmeat

Sauté mushrooms in butter. Add olive oil and parsley and green onion tops. Simmer. In another skillet put 2 tablespoons oil and flour. Add mixture to flour and oil. Add Sauterne and maybe a little water. Add shrimp, lobster and crabmeat. Simmer. Season to taste. Serve in ramekins or over toast points. Serves 8-10.

Rebecca Campbell Marvin
Minden, LA

COQUILLES ST. JACQUES—SCALLOPS

1 cup dry white vermouth	1 bay leaf
½ teaspoon salt	1 pound washed scallops
¼ teaspoon pepper	½ pound sliced fresh mushrooms

Simmer the wine and flavorings for 5 minutes. Add scallops and mushrooms and pour in enough water barely to cover ingredients. Bring to simmer, cover and simmer slowly for 5 minutes. Remove scallops and mushrooms with a slotted spoon and set aside in a bowl.

Sauce:

3 tablespoons butter	2 egg yolks
4 tablespoons flour	½ cup whipping cream
scallop liquid	salt and pepper
¾ cup milk	drops of lemon juice

Cook butter and flour slowly for 2 minutes. Off heat, blend in the boiling scallop liquid, then the milk. Boil 1 minute. Blend the egg yolks and cream in a bowl, then beat the hot sauce into them by driblets. Return sauce to pan and boil, stirring for 1 minute. Season to taste with salt, pepper and lemon juice. Strain. The egg yolks and whipping cream may be omitted if you don't want it so rich.

Final Assembly:

6 ramekins or scallop shells	6 tablespoons grated Swiss cheese
1½ tablespoons butter	

Slice the scallops. Blend ⅔ of the sauce with the scallops and mushrooms. Butter the ramekins or shells. Spoon the scallops and mushrooms into them and cover with the rest of the sauce. At this point, you can dot with butter and refrigerate until ready to serve. Fifteen minutes before serving, sprinkle with cheese and set shells 8-9 inches under a moderately hot broiler. Serve as soon as possible. Serves 6. Do not freeze.

Frances Wallace

SEA JEWELS CREOLE

1 tablespoon butter	1 cup crabmeat
1 tablespoon vegetable oil	3 tablespoons parsley
1 tablespoon olive oil	2 teaspoons Accent
½ cup chopped bell pepper	1 teaspoon Worcestershire
½ cup chopped shallots	½ teaspoon garlic salt
1 can tomato soup plus ½ can water	dash of oregano
1 (4 ounce) can sliced mushrooms with juice	1 tablespoon sherry
2 pounds raw shrimp, peeled	salt and cayenne pepper to taste

Sauté bell pepper and onions in butter and oils. Add tomato soup and water, mushrooms and their juice, shrimp, parsley, crabmeat and seasonings. Simmer 20 minutes. Serve over rice. Serves 4-6.

Mrs. Edwin S. Richardson

SHRIMP AND CRAB SUPREME

1 onion, sliced	8 tablespoons butter
1 tablespoon dill seed	¼ cup flour
2 bay leaves	2 cups half and half
6 peppercorns	1 teaspoon garlic juice
2 cans beer or 6 cups water	2 teaspoons Worcestershire
2 pounds raw shrimp in shells	¼ teaspoon hot sauce
3 packages frozen chopped spinach	¼ teaspoon paprika
3 tablespoons grated onion	8 tablespoons sherry
2 tablespoons lemon juice	12 ounces frozen crabmeat, thawed
salt, pepper and cayenne to taste	grated Parmesan cheese

Preheat oven to 325°. Combine onion, dill seed, bay leaves, peppercorns, and beer in a deep pot and bring to a boil. Add shrimp and boil 5 minutes. Drain, let cool, and shell. Set aside. Cook spinach, drain and mash as dry as possible. Season with grated onion, lemon juice, salt, pepper and cayenne. Make a cream sauce of butter, flour and cream. Add garlic juice, Worcestershire, hot sauce, paprika and sherry. In a shallow casserole, alternately layer the shrimp, crabmeat, spinach and cream sauce. Generously sprinkle grated Parmesan cheese over top and heat for about 30 minutes. Serves 6.

Mrs. Gilbert T. Wingate
Beaumont, TX

TURTLE SAUCE PIQUANTE

2 pounds turtle meat, seasoned	1 can golden mushroom soup
oil to cover bottom of pot	4 cloves garlic, pressed
1½ onions, chopped	1 soup can dry vermouth
3 stalks celery, chopped	few dashes Worcestershire
1 bell pepper, chopped	few dashes bitters
1 can Rotel tomatoes	1 teaspoon rosemary
1 (16 ounce) can whole tomatoes	1 teaspoon thyme

Brown turtle meat well, discard excess oil. In same pot sauté chopped vegetables. Add rest of ingredients. Bring to boil and turn heat down to simmer. Cook for 1½-2 hours or until meat is tender. Serves 6-8.

Odon Bacque, Sr.

WINNING CAKES

I chose to paint the Cajun people in a timeless setting caught among the large oaks, ghost-like, and suspended in their own unique landscape. All of these qualities come through strongly in this particular painting. I have grouped all of these women symbolically suspended between the ground and the sky, showing that the Acadian culture has remained largely unaffected by other cultures and influences.

The spirit of competition is Cajun, just as much as it is American. The Cajuns compete in everything from cake making, to crawfish eating, and pirogue racing. Home baked cakes are still an important part of every festival and fair and church bazaar in South Louisiana.

SWEETS

BUCKEYES

1 stick softened butter	3 cups Rice Krispies
1 box powdered sugar	1 (12 ounce) package chocolate chips
2 cups crunchy peanut butter	½ stick paraffin wax

Mix all together and form into size of golf balls. Melt one (12 ounce) package of chocolate chips and ½ stick paraffin wax over low heat. Drop balls into chocolate mixture and place on wax paper. Freezes well. Tip: Keep chocolate mixture on low heat while dipping balls into it. Use large mixing bowl. Mixture will be crumbly. Yield: 6 dozen.

Pamela DeHart

PEANUT BUTTER BARS

2 sticks margarine
2⅓ cups powdered sugar
1 cup peanut butter

1¾ cups crushed graham crackers
1 large package milk chocolate chips

Melt margarine in saucepan; remove from heat and add powdered sugar, peanut butter and crushed graham crackers. Spread in 9x13 inch buttered pan. Melt chocolate chips, spread over peanut butter mixture and chill.

Judy Roberts

ROCKY ROAD CANDY

1 small package semi-sweet
  chocolate chips
1 small package milk chocolate chips
4 ounces chocolate Hershey bar
1 can Eagle brand milk

pinch salt
1 teaspoon vanilla
1 cup nuts
½ large package of large marshmallows

Melt all chocolate in double boiler over boiling water. Add milk, salt and vanilla. Stir in nuts and marshmallows. Pour into buttered pan and cut into squares when cool.

Elsie Henderson

GOLD BRICKS

1 (12 ounce) package semi-sweet
  chocolate chips
4 cups pecans
1 (7 ounce) jar marshmallow creme

1 (13 ounce) can evaporated milk
3½ cups sugar
2 sticks butter

Place semi-sweet chips, pecans and marshmallow creme in a large bowl. Butter the sides and bottom of a large pan. Place milk, sugar and butter in a pot over medium heat and let come to a boil. When this mixture begins to boil, time for 10 minutes. Remove from heat and pour over mixture in bowl. Stir vigorously until well blended, then place in buttered pan. Put pan in refrigerator until completely cooled. Yield: 5 pounds.

Mrs. George Rees

MILLIONAIRES

1 (14 ounce) package caramels
3-4 tablespoons milk
2 cups pecan pieces
butter or margarine

¼ bar paraffin
1 (12 ounce) package milk chocolate
  morsels

Melt caramels in milk over low heat; add pecans. Drop by teaspoons onto buttered wax paper. Chill. Melt paraffin and chocolate morsels in a heavy saucepan over low heat. Dip candy into chocolate and return to waxed paper. Chill. Yield: 3-4 dozen.

Mrs. Brad Hamilton

MINT PATTIES

¼ pound margarine
1 box powdered sugar
dash salt
¼ cup crushed pecans

¼ cup creme de Menthe
1 large package semi-sweet
   chocolate chips
2 ounces paraffin

Cream margarine well. Add sugar, salt, pecans and creme de Menthe. Use powdered sugar on hands and roll mixture into small balls or mint shapes. Place on cookie sheet and freeze until firm. Melt chocolate chips and paraffin in top of double boiler. Dip frozen candy in chocolate and then place on waxed paper.

Elsie Henderson

ENGLISH TOFFEE

2 cups almonds
1 cup sugar
1 cup butter

5 tablespoons water
¼ teaspoon salt
sweet chocolate (large chocolate bar)

Blanch almonds and toast to a golden brown. Put half through food chopper and cut remainder in pieces. Combine sugar, butter, salt and water and boil to 300° stirring constantly. Remove from fire; add broken nut meats and pour in buttered 8x8 inch pan. Grate ½ of sweet chocolate over top and sprinkle generously with ½ of chopped nut meats. Turn upside down and sprinkle with remaining grated chocolate and nut meats. When cold break in pieces.

Azalie Webb Crain

PRALINES

2 cups white sugar
1 cup light brown sugar
1 stick butter
1 cup milk

2 tablespoons white syrup
4 cups pecan halves
2 teaspoons vanilla extract

Combine first 6 ingredients in saucepan. Cook about 20 minutes on a medium fire until it comes to a boil. Stir occasionally and continue cooking until mixture forms a small ball in cold water. Remove from heat; add vanilla and stir until mixture begins to lose its gloss. Then drop small portions onto waxed paper (put foil under waxed paper to keep it from sticking to your counter top). Work FAST, keeping saucepan over a warm surface if it seems to harden too fast. Let pralines cool before removing from wax paper.

Mrs. L. A. Shelton

RUTH'S CHERRY BON-BONS

1 can cherry pie filling
1 large can crushed pineapple,
　drained
1 can condensed milk
1 medium size carton Cool Whip

¼ teaspoon salt
1 teaspoon vanilla
1 teaspoon almond extract
pecans, finely chopped
maraschino cherries

Mix all ingredients except pecans and cherries in a large mixing bowl. Spoon into individual paper baking cups and place in muffin tins. Sprinkle finely chopped pecans on top of each and center with a cherry and freeze. Remove paper cup and put in dessert dish when serving. Makes 24-30.

Mrs. Ruth Stuart
Beaumont, TX

ORANGE BALLS

1 (12 ounce) package vanilla wafers
1 pound powdered sugar
1 (6 ounce) can frozen orange juice,
　thawed

1 stick margarine, softened
1 cup chopped pecans, optional
1 small can angel flake coconut

Crush wafers until real fine (may use blender). Mix with sugar, orange juice, softened margarine and chopped nuts. Roll into small balls and roll in coconut. Refrigerate. Yield: 4 dozen.

Ruby Lewis

STRAWBERRY APPLE TARTS

Crust:
1 cup butter
6 ounces cream cheese

2 cups flour

Filling:
18 ounces strawberry
　preserves
7 ounces chopped walnuts

1 cup chopped, dried apple, gently
　packed
¼ cup sugar

Preheat oven to 350°. Cream butter and cream cheese. Work in flour. Chill 1 hour. Spray tart pans with Pam. Press dough, about the size of a walnut into miniature tart pans. Mix filling and place 1 teaspoon of filling in each tart. Bake for 15 minutes until light brown. Yield: 6 dozen. Optional topping: Cool Whip.

Genevieve Meche Verrett

REFRIGERATOR COOKIES

1 cup shortening
1 cup brown sugar
1 cup white sugar
3 eggs
3½ cups flour

1 teaspoon soda
2 teaspoons cinnamon
½ teaspoon salt
1½ cups pecans

Cream shortening and sugar, add eggs and beat thoroughly. Sift dry ingredients together, mix with first mixture and add pecans. Roll in long roll about 2 inches in diameter. Wrap in wax paper. Place in refrigerator and let chill. Slice ¼ inch thick as needed for "delish" cooked fresh. Will last in refrigerator until too crumbly to slice. Bake in moderate oven, 375°, for 8-10 minutes.

Mrs. W. T. Black, Jr.
Quitman, TX

SWEDISH SPRITZ

1½ cups butter
1 cup sugar
1 egg
1 teaspoon vanilla

½ teaspooon salt
4 cups flour
1 teaspoon baking powder

Preheat oven to 400°. Cream butter and sugar thoroughly. Add egg, vanilla, and salt. Beat well. Sift flour and baking powder and add to mixture. Mix until smooth. DO NOT CHILL. Force through cookie press forming various shapes. Place on ungreased chilled cookie sheet. Bake in 400° oven for 8-10 minutes. Cool, decorate. Yield: 4 dozen.

Mrs. Micki Miller
Midland, TX

ROSIE LEE COOKIES

1 pound margarine
1¹/₅ cups sugar
1 teaspoon vanilla

pinch salt
4 cups sifted flour
pecan halves

Preheat oven to 350°. Mix above ingredients, except pecan halves, after letting oleo get soft. Roll into small balls and place on cookie sheet. Press each ball with a pecan half to make almost flat. Bake at 350° until golden brown. Remove from baking sheet and place on wax paper until cool.

Pat McBride Naumann

DOUBLE FROSTED BOURBON BROWNIES

¾ cup sifted all-purpose flour
¼ teaspoon baking soda
¼ teaspoon salt
½ cup sugar
⅓ cup butter
2 tablespoons water

1 (6 ounce) package semi-sweet
  chocolate chips
1 teaspoon vanilla
2 eggs
1½ cups coarsely chopped walnuts
4 tablespoons bourbon

Preheat oven to 325°. Sift flour, baking soda and salt together. Combine sugar, butter and water in a medium size saucepan. Heat, stirring constantly until sugar melts and mixture comes to a boil. Remove from heat and stir in chocolate chips, vanilla and blend until smooth. Beat in eggs, one at a time. Stir in flour mixture and walnuts. Spread evenly in a 9x9x2 inch greased pan. Bake for 25-30 minutes or until shiny and firm on top. Remove from oven, sprinkle bourbon over top and cool completely. Spread white frosting evenly over top; chill until firm. Spread chocolate glaze over frosting; chill. Cut into squares. Keep refrigerated and covered until ready to use.

White Frosting:
½ cup butter or margarine
1 teaspoon vanilla or rum extract

2 cups confectioners sugar

Beat butter and vanilla in a medium size bowl until creamy, gradually beat in sugar until mixture has become smooth and spreadable.

Chocolate Glaze:
1 (6 ounce) package semi-sweet
  chocolate chips

1 tablespoon margarine

Combine chocolate chips and margarine in double boiler. Set over hot, not boiling water until melted.

Doris Y. Ottinger

BLONDE BROWNIES

2 cups flour
1 teaspoon baking powder
1 teaspoon baking soda
1 teaspoon salt
2 eggs slightly beaten

2 cups granulated brown sugar
⅔ cup melted shortening
1 teaspoon vanilla
1 cup chopped nuts
1 (12 ounce) bag chocolate chips

Preheat oven to 350°. Sift dry ingredients in a large bowl. In another bowl, combine eggs and brown sugar, add shortening and vanilla. Pour this mixture into flour mixture. Mix by hand until well blended. (Batter will be thick.) Add nuts and pour into a greased 13x9x2 inch baking.dish. Sprinkle with chocolate chips. Bake for 20-25 minutes.

Mary K. Hamilton

ROCKY ROAD FUDGE BARS

Bar:

½ cup butter
1 (1 ounce) square unsweetened
  chocolate
1 cup sugar
1 cup flour

1 teaspoon baking powder
2 eggs, slightly beaten
1 teaspoon vanilla
1 cup pecans, broken

In sauce pan, over low heat, melt butter and chocolate. Stir in sugar, flour and baking powder, then eggs and vanilla. Stir in nuts. Spread in buttered baking pan. Prepare filling and spread on top of this.

Filling:

¾ of 1 (8 ounce) package cream
  cheese
½ cup sugar
¼ cup butter

2 tablespoons flour
1 egg
¼ cup pecans, broken
1 (6 ounce) package chocolate chips

Combine cream cheese with sugar, butter, flour, egg and nuts. Beat until fluffy. Spoon evenly over bar mixture. Sprinkle with chocolate chips. Bake at 350° for 25-30 minutes. Prepare frosting.

Frosting:

¼ cup butter
1 (1 ounce) square unsweetened
  chocolate
2 ounces cream cheese

¼ cup milk
1 (1 pound) box confectioners sugar
1 teaspoon vanilla
2 cups miniature marshmallows

In saucepan combine butter, chocolate, cream cheese and milk. Melt and stir in sugar and vanilla. When bar is baked, sprinkle with marshmallows, return to oven for 2-3 minutes until soft. Remove and pour frosting mixture over marshmallows, swirl together. Cool and store in refrigerator. Cut in small squares.

Diane Primeaux Brown

CINNAMON STICKS

1 cup margarine
1 cup sugar
1 beaten egg yolk
2 cups flour

3 teaspoons cinnamon
1 cup chopped pecans
1 egg white beaten stiff

Preheat oven to 300°. Cream margarine and sugar, add beaten egg yolk. Sift flour and cinnamon together and add to above mixture. Spread thinly on a large cookie sheet. Press chopped pecans into dough. Spread beaten egg white over the top. Bake for 1 hour. Do not cook until brown as they will taste scorched. Cut into 1x3 inch strips while hot. If you want squares, then cut accordingly. Yield 60 cookies.

Lyn Taylor Domingue

BLARNEY STONES

4 eggs
1 cup sugar
1 cup flour
1½ teaspoons baking powder

¼ teaspoon salt
½ cup boiling water
½ teaspoon vanilla

Separate eggs reserving 1 yolk for icing. Beat remaining yolks with rotary beater until thick and lemon colored. Add sugar gradually beating continuously. Add dry ingredients, sifted together, alternately with boiling water. Add vanilla and beat well. Fold in stiffly beaten egg whites. Bake 20 minutes at 350° in shallow sheet cake pan. When almost cool, ice with Blarney Stone Frosting. Cut in squares.

Frosting:
1 cup butter
1 egg yolk
2½ cups confectioners sugar

1 teaspoon vanilla
crushed salted peanuts

Cream butter and egg yolk. Gradually blend in sugar. Cream until soft and smooth. After spreading frosting on Blarney Stones, sprinkle crushed peanuts over frosting. Yield 3 dozen squares.

Lucille Smith

SOUTHERN PRALINE BARS

1½ cups flour, sifted
1 teaspoon salt
½ teaspoon baking powder
½ cup shortening

1½ cups brown sugar, packed
2 eggs, beaten
2 teaspoons vanilla
¾ cup chopped pecans

Sift together the flour, salt, and baking powder. Melt shortening in large sauce pan, then put remaining ingredients and stir well. Spread in 13x9 inch greased and floured pan. Bake at 350° for 30 minutes. Cool slightly in pan, then spread on Praline Frosting.

Praline Frosting:
2 tablespoons butter
¼ cup firmly packed brown sugar
2 tablespoons cream

1 cup confectioners sugar
chopped pecans

Melt butter, brown sugar and add cream. Stir in confectioners sugar and beat until smooth. Top with chopped pecans. Yield 4 dozen.

Mary Julia Hooten

FORGOTTEN COOKIES

2 egg whites, room temperature
⅔ cup sugar
¼ teaspoon cream of tartar
1 cup chopped pecans, optional

1 package chocolate chips, mini or
  regular
1 teaspoon vanilla

Preheat oven to 350°. Beat egg whites until stiff. Gradually add sugar, cream of tartar. Stir in pecans, chips and vanilla. Drop by spoonfuls on foiled cookie sheets. Turn preheated oven off when you place cookies in. Do not open until following morning or 8 hours later.

Myrtle Raymond

LACY OATMEAL COOKIES

1 cup brown sugar
½ cup shortening
4 tablespoons butter or margarine
½ teaspoon soda

1 teaspoon salt
2 cups quick cooking rolled oats
1 well beaten egg

Preheat oven to 375°. In saucepan, combine brown sugar, shortening, and butter or margarine. Stir over low heat until butter melts; remove from heat; stir in soda, salt and rolled oats. Add egg and mix well. Drop from teaspoon onto ungreased cookie sheet, about 3 inches apart. Bake in moderate oven 6-7 minutes. Cool 2 minutes on cookie sheet. Carefully transfer to cooling rack. (Baking and cooling time should be carefully observed.) Yield: 4 dozen. Use a Teflon coated cookie sheet.

Lynn McCarthy Ferguson

YO-YO COOKIES

¼ cup margarine
¼ cup shortening
½ cup peanut butter
½ cup sugar
½ cup brown sugar, firmly packed

1 egg
1¼ cups flour
¾ teaspoon soda
½ teaspoon baking powder
¼ teaspoon salt

Mix thoroughly margarine, shortening, peanut butter, both sugars and egg. Blend into this mixture all dry ingredients. Cover mixture and chill about ½ hour. Remove from refrigerator and shape into ¾ inch balls. Place on lightly greased cookie sheet 2 inches apart. Do not flatten. Bake 10 minutes at 350° or until done. When cookies are cool take two of them at a time and stick the bottom or flatten sides together with chocolate frosting, jelly or jam—hence Yo-Yo.

Anne Roberts Sonnier

PEANUT BUTTER COOKIES

2 sticks margarine
1 scant cup granulated sugar
1 scant cup brown sugar
2 eggs
1 full cup peanut butter

1 teaspoon vanilla
2 cups sifted all-purpose flour
½ teaspoon salt
1 teaspoon baking soda

Preheat oven to 325°. Cream margarine, sugars, until fluffy. Add eggs, peanut butter and vanilla. Sift flour, salt and soda. Add dry ingredients to creamed mixture and blend well. Form small balls and flatten with a fork—place on greased and floured cookie sheet. Bake 8-10 minutes. Makes 225 bite-size cookies. Freezes baked.

Kathleen R. Short

DATE SKILLET COOKIES

1 stick margarine
1 egg, well beaten
1 cup dates, cut fine
1 cup sugar

1½ teaspoons vanilla
3 cups chopped nuts
2¾ cup Rice Krispies
powdered sugar or coconut

Combine first 4 ingredients. Cook in skillet for 10 minutes or until bubbles form in soft ball. Add vanilla, nuts, cereal and form into balls. Roll in powdered sugar or coconut. Yield: 4 dozen.

Barbara Klees Golden

KIPFEL

Dough:
¾ cup shortening
8 ounces cream cheese, room
   temperature

1 teaspoon salt
2 cups flour

Filling:
½ cup chopped pecans or walnuts
3 tablespoons sugar

½ cup strawberry preserves
½ teaspoon cinnamon

Cream shortening and cream cheese. Sift salt and flour and work it into shortening mixture. Refrigerate dough over night. Divide dough into 3 equal parts. Roll out very thin on floured surface. Cut dough into 2 inch squares. Put about ¼ teaspoon filling into the center of each square. Starting from a corner, roll square to look like a crescent dinner roll. Bake on an ungreased cookie sheet at 400°-425° tional at Christmas time in our home. Yield: 10 dozen cookes. (More filling may be desired, according to your taste.)

Elsie Hruschka

LEMON ICING

1 bar butter, ½ cup
1 box powdered sugar, sifted
juice of 1 medium lemon

evaporated milk to add for
spreading consistency
drops of yellow food coloring

Cream together softened butter and powdered sugar. Mix in juice of 1 lemon. Gradually add evaporated milk to spreading consistency. Add drops of yellow food coloring.   Mrs. Ella Mae Arnaud Tally
Henderson, LA

LEMON FILLING

2 cups sugar
1 (4½-ounce) lemon flavor
   pudding and pie filling
2 heaping tablespoons cornstarch

juice of 2 lemons
2 or 3 egg yolks
2 cups hot water

Mix all the above ingredients in a heavy, large saucepan. Cook over a medium heat, stirring constantly. When it begins to boil, it should be thick enough. I let it cool about 5 minutes before filling the cake layers. There should be enough to fill 2 cakes, plus a little left over which I generally just place in a pyrex or corning ware dish and use as a pudding.   Mrs. Ella Mae Arnaud Tally
Henderson, LA

INSTANT FUDGE FROSTING

1 pound unsifted powdered sugar
½ cup dry cocoa
¼ teaspoon salt
1 teaspoon vanilla

4 tablespoons boiling water
3 tablespoons hot coffee
6 tablespoons soft butter or margarine

Mix dry ingredients so no lumps can be seen. Add vanilla and hot liquids, stir smooth. Add soft butter and stir or beat until smooth, just stiff enough to spread. The frosting thickens as it cools—if too thick add few drops hot water. Goes well with three layer cake recipe.   Rosemary Cherry Patterson
Amarillo, TX

FLUFFY WHITE FROSTING FOR THREE 8 INCH LAYERS

1 cup granulated sugar
½ cup boiling water
3 egg whites

1 cup confectioners sugar
1 teaspoon vanilla

Boil granulated sugar and water together rapidly until the syrup forms a soft ball (238°). Whip egg whites, adding gradually ⅓ cup of the confectioners sugar and beating until the consistency of a meringue. Add syrup gradually, beating constantly. Beat until mixture is thick and creamy. Add remaining ⅔ cup of confectioners sugar or until frosting will hold its shape when spread. Add vanilla.

This frosting can be kept in a covered container in the refrigerator for several days. Then, before using, add a small amount of hot water to make a smooth mixture.   Mary Blanchet Prejean

SOUR CREAM ORANGE PECAN POUND CAKE

3 cups sugar
1 cup shortening
6 eggs, separated
1 ounce pure orange extract
½ pint sour cream

3 cups flour
¼ teaspoon soda
½ teaspoon salt
2 cups chopped pecans

Cream the sugar and shortening, add egg yolks, well beaten, the ounce of orange extract and ½ pint of sour cream and mix well. To this, add the flour, soda, salt and mix well. Then fold in 6 egg whites which have been beaten stiff. Fold in chopped pecans. Bake in a greased and floured Bundt pan for 1½ hours at 325°. Remove while hot.

Billie M. White

NEW BACARDI CHOCOLATE RUM CAKE, DEVILISH

1 (18½ ounce) package chocolate cake
  mix
1 package (4 serving size)
  chocolate instant pudding
  and pie filling
4 eggs

½ cup Bacardi dark rum (80 proof)
½ cup cold water
½ cup oil
½ cup slivered almonds (optional)

Filling:
1½ cups cold milk
½ cup Barcardi dark rum (80 proof)
1 package (4 serving size)
  chocolate instant pudding
  and pie filling

1 envelope whipped topping mix

Preheat oven to 350°. Grease and flour two 9 inch layer cake pans. Combine all cake ingredients together in large bowl. Blend well, then beat at medium mixer speed 2 minutes. Turn into prepared pans. Bake 30 minutes or until cake tests done. DO NOT UNDERCOOK. Cool in pans 10 minutes. Remove from pans, finish cooling on racks. Split layers in half horizontally. Stack. Spread 1 cup filling between each layer and over top of cake. Keep cake chilled. Serve cold. OPTIONAL: Garnish with chocolate curls.

Filling: Combine milk, rum, pudding and topping mix in deep narrow-bottomed bowl. Blend well at high speed for 4 minutes, until light and fluffy. Makes 4 cups.

JoAnn Gankendorff

BLACK FOREST CAKE

Cake:

¾ cup butter
½ cup sifted unsweetened cocoa
9 eggs

1½ cups granulated sugar
¾ cup sifted cake flour
1½ teaspoons vanilla extract

Chocolate Filling:

2 egg whites
½ cup sugar
2 tablespoons cocoa

2 ounces German chocolate, melted
1 cup butter, slightly melted

Syrup:

½ cup granulated sugar
2 tablespoons water

¼ cup brandy

Frosting:

2 cups heavy cream
¼ cup unsifted confectioners sugar

2 tablespoons brandy or 2 teaspoons
   vanilla extract

Cake: Preheat oven to 350°. Lightly grease and flour and line with wax paper 3 9-inch layer cake pans. Melt butter over very low heat, add cocoa to butter, set aside. Warm large bowl of electric mixer over pan of boiling water. (Water should not touch bottom of bowl.) In warm bowl, beat eggs slightly with sugar. Let stand over water, stirring occasionally until eggs are lukewarm, 5-10 minutes. Meanwhile, sift flour, set aside. When eggs seem lukewarm to the touch remove bowl to mixer; beat at high speed 10-15 minutes, until mixture has tripled in bulk and is as thick as whipped cream. On low speed of mixer, gently fold flour into egg mixture until thoroughly combined. Fold in melted butter and cocoa and vanilla, mixing well. Turn batter into prepared pans, bake 25-30 minutes. Let cake layers cool in pans on wire racks several minutes, then loosen edges and turn out on wax paper.

Chocolate Filling: Whip egg whites over hot but not boiling water. Add sugar and whip in very well, until stiff. Add cocoa and whip in. Remove from heat. Add German chocolate then fold in butter. Set in refrigerator until cool enough to spread.

Syrup: In small saucepan, combine sugar with water. Bring to boiling, reduce heat. Simmer until mixture is thick and syrupy, about 5 minutes. Stir in ¼ cup brandy. Sprinkle syrup evenly over warm cake layers.

Frosting: In small bowl of electric mixer, combine cream with confectioners sugar, refrigerate, along with beater 1 hour. Beat just until stiff, gradually add brandy or vanilla.

Assemble: On cake platter, put cake together with chocolate filling between layers. Frost top and sides with whipped cream mixture. Sprinkle top with shaved chocolate; refrigerate several hours before serving. Serves 12.

Marianne Schneider

CHOCOLATE DOBERGE CAKE

2 cups sifted cake flour
1 teaspoon soda
1¼ teaspoons salt
1 stick plus 2 tablespoons margarine
1½ cups sugar
3 eggs separated

1 cup buttermilk
1½ squares melted unsweetened
   chocolate
1¼ teaspoons vanilla
1 teaspoon almond extract

Preheat oven to 300°. Grease and flour two 9 inch round cake pans. Sift 3 times flour, soda and salt into medium bowl. Cream margarine and sugar in large mixing bowl. Add 3 egg yolks, one at a time. Add gradually, alternating flour mixture and buttermilk. Add chocolate. Mix thoroughly beating about 3 minutes. Fold in 3 beaten egg whites, vanilla and almond. Bake for 45 minutes. Leave to cool. Cut each layer in half horizontally. Cake can be placed in freezer until next day before icing. This keeps cake from crumbling. Ice while cold.

Chocolate Doberge Filling:
2½ cups evaporated milk
2 squares chocolate (semi-sweet)
1¼ cups sugar
5 tablespoons flour

4 egg yolks
2 tablespoons butter
1¼ teaspoons vanilla
¼ teaspoon almond extract

Put milk and chocolate in saucepan and heat until chocolate is melted. In bowl, combine sugar and flour. Add by tablespoons and mix hot milk-chocolate to sugar and flour until sugar and flour are mixed and make a paste. Then add this back to saucepan. Cook on medium flame— stirring until mixture is very thick. Add 4 egg yolks and continue to cook 2 or 3 more minutes. Remove from heat and add butter, vanilla and almond extract. Cool. Spread between layers of cake.

Chocolate Doberge Icing:
3 cups sugar
⅔ cup cocoa
2 tablespoons Karo (white)

1½ cups Half and Half
1 teaspoon vanilla
4 tablespoons margarine

Combine sugar, cocoa, Karo, Half and Half in saucepan—boil until mixture reaches 232°. Remove from heat, add vanilla and margarine. Allow to cool. If mixture gets too hard, add Half and Half to get spreading consistency. Spread over cake.

Letha Doiron

CHOCOLATE SURPRISE

2 tablespoons butter
8 ounces cream cheese
¼ cup sugar
1 tablespoon cornstarch
1 egg
3 tablespoons milk
½ teaspoon vanilla extract
½ cup soft butter
2 cups sugar

2 eggs
1 teaspoon vanilla extract
2 cups flour
1 teaspoon salt, baking powder
½ teaspoon baking soda
1⅓ cups milk
4 envelopes (4 ounce) premelted
    unsweetened chocolate

Frosting:
¼ cup milk
¼ cup soft butter
2 envelopes (2 ounce) chocolate
    (unsweetened)

1 teaspoon vanilla extract
1½ cups confectioners sugar

In a small bowl combine butter, cream cheese, sugar, cornstarch, egg, milk and vanilla, (first seven ingredients). Beat at a high speed until smooth and creamy. Set aside. Cream together butter, sugar, eggs and vanilla, (next four ingredients). Mix well. Add sifted flour, salt, baking powder and baking soda alternately with milk. Finally add the melted chocolate. Mix well. Spread half of the chocolate mixture in a greased and floured 13x9 inch pan. Smooth cheese mixture over batter. Top with remaining batter. Bake for 50-60 minutes or until cake springs back at 350°. Cool and frost.

Frosting: Combine milk, soft butter, chocolate, vanilla extract and confectioners sugar. Beat until smooth.

Barbara Pooler

APPLE CAKE

2 cups sugar
1½ cups oil
3 eggs
3 cups sifted all-purpose flour
1½ teaspoons soda

1 teaspoon salt
½ teaspoon each cinnamon, cloves and
  nutmeg
3 cups unpeeled, finely chopped apples
1 teaspoon vanilla

Cream sugar and oil. Add eggs one at a time. Combine flour, soda, salt and spices. Add dry ingredients. Fold in apples and vanilla. Grease and flour tube pan. Bake at 325° for 1 hour and 15 minutes. After cooking, let stand in pan 10-15 minutes, then turn out.

Azalie Webb Crain

BLACKBERRY-APPLE CAKE

1½ cups sugar
½ cup margarine
3 eggs
2 cups flour
2 teaspoons baking powder

½ cup milk
1 teaspoon vanilla
2 cups blackberry preserves
1 apple—peeled and chopped very fine

Cream sugar and margarine. Add eggs; beat well. Sift flour and baking powder together and add alternately with milk mixing thoroughly. Add vanilla, then preserves and apples. Beat well. Bake in 350° oven in a 9 inch square cake pan for 45 minutes. Serves 8.

Mrs. Guy Wimberly
Ringgold, LA

BANANA CAKE

½ cup butter
1½ cups sugar
2 eggs
1 teaspoon vanilla
1½ cups flour
1 teaspoon baking powder

1 teaspoon soda
4 tablespoons buttermilk*
3 large or 4 small very ripe bananas,
  mashed
1 cup chopped pecans

Cream butter and sugar; add eggs one at a time; add vanilla. Sift flour and baking powder together. Add soda to buttermilk. Add flour and milk alternately to creamed mixture, beating well after each addition. Fold in mashed bananas and pecans. Pour into greased 9x13 inch pan and bake at 300° for 45 minutes. *You can sour regular milk by adding 1 teaspoon vinegar. Serves 12.

Doreen S. Duhe

MOUSSE AU CHOCOLAT A LA NORMANDIE

For mold:
oil   butter
2 dozen lady fingers

Mousse:
¾ pound dark semi-sweet chocolate   ½ cup confectioners sugar
   or 1½ packs Hershey bars   3 eggs separated
5 tablespoons light rum   ½ cup salted almonds, finely ground
2 tablespoons water   2 cups heavy cream
1½ sticks sweet butter, at room   ¼ cup confectioners sugar
   temperature   2 inches vanilla bean stix

Oil a one quart charlotte mold. Line the sides of the mold with lady fingers. (Put a speck of butter on the flat side of the lady fingers and stick them to the walls of the charlotte mold, standing upright. Be very careful not to leave gaps or spaces between them.)

Mousse: Cut chocolate into small pieces and put into medium-size heavy pan with rum and water. Stir with a wooden spoon over a very slow fire until the chocolate dissolves. Remove from fire to cool, but do not allow the chocolate to set. In a mixer bowl, cream the sweet butter until light and creamy, then add ½ cup confectioners sugar. Beat very well. Add one at a time, 3 egg yolks, then almonds, then the cool chocolate mixture.

In a metal bowl, over another bowl of ice, whip with a large metal whisk the heavy cream. Beat until cream begins to thicken, then add ¼ cup confectioners sugar, the vanilla bean (stix opened lengthwise, and its little seeds thoroughly scraped into the cream). Continue beating until the cream is stiff enough to hold its shape. Add to the chocolate mixture ½ of the whipped cream and 3 egg whites, beaten to soft peaks. Blend carefully with rubber scraper. Fill mixture into the lined mold. Cover top with transparent wrap and freeze for 2 hours. Run a knife carefully between mold and lady fingers, and turn out on a flat serving dish. Decorate with the rest of the whipped cream which has been filled into a pastry bag with a rose tube. Pipe rosettes of cream around the top. Tie a satin ribbon around the sides. (It will cover the spots of butter on the outside of the lady fingers. Besides, many French cakes are traditionally brought to the table decorated with a satin ribbon and bow, and it is a charming Gallic touch.) This mousse may be made ahead of time and freezes very well.

Anita Guilliot Saitta

SPANISH BUTTER CAKE

½ cup butter
2 cups brown sugar (packed)
4 eggs (save 2 egg whites for icing)
1 cup milk
3 teaspoons baking powder
2⅔ cups cake flour

½ teaspoon each of nutmeg, cloves and
    cinnamon
2 tablespoons water
1 cup chopped pecans (if pecans are
    used add ½ teaspoon salt)

Seven Minute Caramel Icing:
1¼ cups firmly packed brown sugar
1 cup white sugar
5 tablespoons water

2 egg whites (saved from cake)
1 teaspoon vanilla

Cream butter, add sugar, beat until smooth. Beat eggs in separate bowl and add
to mixture. Sift all dry ingredients together; flour, baking powder and spices.
Add them alternating with the milk. Stir in water. Fold the pecans into batter.
Pour into a greased and floured pan, (9x13 inch or 2 8-inch round pans). Bake at
350° for 25-30 minutes.

Icing: Place all ingredients in the top of a double boiler except the vanilla. Beat
until thoroughly blended. Place these ingredients over rapidly boiling water.
Beat them constantly with an electric beater or whisk for 7 minutes. Remove
from double boiler and continue to beat a minute and add vanilla. Continue
beating until icing is right consistency to spread. Serves 10-12.

Marilyn Tankersley Taylor

PUMPKIN CAKE ROLL

3 eggs
1 cup granulated sugar
⅔ cup pumpkin
1 teaspoon lemon juice
¾ cup flour
1 teaspoon baking powder

2 teaspoons cinnamon
1 teaspoon ginger
½ teaspoon nutmeg
½ teaspoon salt
1 cup chopped pecans
powdered sugar

Filling:
1 cup powdered sugar
2 (3-ounce) packages cream cheese

4 tablespoons margarine
½ teaspoon vanilla

Beat eggs on high speed of mixer for 5 minutes. Gradually beat in granulated
sugar. Stir in pumpkin and lemon juice. Stir together flour, baking powder, cinnamon, ginger, nutmeg and salt. Fold into pumpkin. Spread in greased and
floured 15x10x1 inch pan. Top with chopped pecans. Bake at 375° for 15 minutes.
Turn out on towel sprinkled with powdered sugar. Starting at narrow end, roll
towel and cake together; cool. Unroll. Combine ingredients for filling and spread
over cake; roll. Chill. Slice into 8 servings.

Mrs. Easton Hebert

A SPECIAL HOLIDAY CAKE

2 sticks butter
½ cup shortening
3 cups sugar
5 large eggs
2 teaspoons vanilla
1 teaspoon almond flavoring

1 teaspoon coconut flavoring
3 cups plus 4 tablespoons flour
½ teaspoon baking powder
1 teaspoon salt
1 cup milk

Sift dry ingredients well before you start. Cream butter, shortening and sugar well by hand. Using mixer, add eggs, unbeaten, one at a time, beating well after each egg. Now add flavorings and flour and milk alternately, beating well after each addition. Pour in well greased and floured angel food cake pan and cook in oven at 325° for about 1½ hours, or until straw comes out clean.

For special occasions take out ½ cup of batter and tint light pink and another ½ cup of batter and tint light green. Drop by teaspoonsful in middle of cake, that is, put half of batter in pan, drop colored batters by teaspoonsful all around, then put another half of batter in cake. When cut, it will look festive. Other tints can be used. Ice cake in one of these tints.

Icing:
1 (1 pound) box powdered sugar,
   sifted
¼ teaspoon salt

2 tablespoons butter
evaporated milk

Heat milk and butter until melts, add sugar, then add enough evaporated milk to make it consistency to spread. Add flavoring and some coloring. Serves 12.

Mrs. L. A. Shelton

SPRINGTIME POUND CAKE

3 cups sugar
1 cup shortening
6 eggs, separated
2 teaspoons lemon extract

3 cups sifted flour
½ teaspoon salt
¼ teaspoon soda
1 cup buttermilk

In large mixing bowl, blend sugar and shortening until light and fluffy. Add egg yolks one at a time, beating well after each. Add flavoring. Sift dry ingredients together; add to first mixture alternately with buttermilk. (Begin and end with dry ingredients.) Beat egg whites stiff; fold carefully into batter. Pour into 10 inch greased and floured tube pan. Bake at 350° for 1 hour and 10 minutes or until done. Serve with fresh or frozen berries and whipped cream. Or frost if desired. This cake will keep and is even better the next day.

Annette Myers

CARAMEL CAKE

Burnt Sugar Syrup:

⅔ cup sugar   ⅔ cup boiling water

Melt (caramelize) sugar in a large heavy skillet, stirring constantly—it's hot!!!
When a dark brown syrup, remove from heat, slowly add ⅔ cup boiling water.
Heat and stir until all dissolves. Boil to reduce syrup to ½ cup. This is enough for
both cake and frosting (cool).

Cake Ingredients:

1½ cups sugar	2 teaspoons baking powder
½ cup butter	½ teaspoon salt
1 teaspoon vanilla	¾ cup cold water
2 eggs	3 tablespoons burnt sugar syrup
2½ cups sifted cake flour	

Gradually add sugar to butter, cream thoroughly. Add vanilla, then eggs one at a
time, beating 1 minute after each. Add sifted dry ingredients to creamed mixture
alternately with water, a small amount at a time, beating smooth after each addition. Add 3 tablespoons burnt sugar syrup.

Now beat very well, 4 minutes at medium speed, this is an old-time secret for
fine, tender cakes with lots of sugar like this one. Bake in 2 paper lined 9 inch
round pans in moderate oven, 375°, about 20 minutes—cool 10 minutes in pans;
turn out.

Frost with burnt sugar frosting, put toasted pecan halves on top and chop some
and sprinkle between layers with frosting.

Burnt Sugar Frosting:

2 egg whites	⅓ cup cold water
1¼ cups sugar	dash salt
3-4 tablespoons burnt sugar syrup	1 teaspoon vanilla

Place all ingredients except vanilla in top of double boiler (not over heat) beat 1
minute with electric mixer. Place over boiling water and cook, beating constantly
until mixture forms peaks, about 7 minutes. Remove from heat and add vanilla
and beat until of spreading consistency, about 2 minutes. Serves 12-14.

Joyce Blanchet Guilliot

SOUR CREAM COFFEE CAKE

½ cup butter
1 cup sugar
2 large or 3 small eggs
1 teaspoon vanilla

2 cups flour
1 teaspoon baking soda
1½ teaspoons baking powder
1 cup sour cream

Filling:
½ cup chopped nuts
½ cup sugar

1 teaspoon cinnamon

Cream butter. Add sugar, eggs and vanilla. Mix dry ingredients together and add to egg mixture alternately with sour cream. Pour half the batter into a well-greased tube pan. Sprinkle with half the filling which has been mixed together. Place remaining batter over the filling and sprinkle top with rest of filling. Bake in 375° oven for 35 minutes or in 350° oven if baked in glass pan.

Becky Warner

LEMON CHEESE FILLED CAKE

Cake:
1 package yellow cake mix
    (approximately 18½ ounces)
¾ cup apricot nectar

¼ cup butter or margarine, softened
3 eggs
1 capful almond extract

Filling:
2 (8 ounce packages) cream cheese,
    softened
½ cup sugar

2 tablespoons lemon juice
1 cup flaked coconut

Glaze:
2 cups sifted confectioners sugar
2 tablespoons lemon juice

2 tablespoons apricot nectar

In large bowl, combine first 5 ingredients; beat as directed on cake package. Grease and lightly flour 12 cup Bundt pan. Spoon batter into pan. In small bowl, combine all filling ingredients. Beat until smooth. Spoon filling over batter in pan, being careful not to let it touch sides of pan. Bake at 350° for 50-55 minutes or 60 minutes until cake tests done. Cool in pan ½ hour. Turn out on wire rack or serving plate to complete cooling. Combine all glaze ingredients and stir until smooth. Drizzle over cake.

JoAnn Gankendorff

PINEAPPLE COCONUT CAKE

1 box yellow cake mix
4 eggs
1 cup oil

½ can (20 ounces) crushed pineapple
   with juice
1 teaspoon almond extract

Icing:
½ box powdered sugar (2 heaping
   cups)
½ stick butter

remainder of pineapple
1 (3½-ounce) can coconut

Cake: Mix all together; be sure to use pineapple juice. Beat for 3 minutes at medium speed. Preheat oven to 325°. Bake 35 minutes or until done in a 9x13 inch greased and floured pan. As soon as cake is done, pierce with fork, and spread icing on cake while cake is still warm. Cool 45-50 minutes.

Icing: Beat first 3 ingredients well. Spread on warm cake. Sprinkle entire cake with coconut. Gently press coconut into pineapple icing and cover cake well. Serves 10-12.

Karen Gankendorff Jones

RING OF COCONUT FUDGE CAKE

1 cup vegetable oil
2 cups sugar
1 teaspoon vanilla
2 eggs
3 cups all-purpose flour
¾ cup cocoa

2 teaspoons soda
2 teaspoons baking powder
1 teaspoon salt
1 cup buttermilk
1 cup hot coffee or hot water
½ cup chopped pecans

Beat the first 4 ingredients on high speed for one minute. Add all other ingredients and mix on medium speed for 3 minutes. Pour half of the cake batter into a greased and floured bundt pan. Top with filling.

Filling:
1 (8 ounce) package cream cheese
1 egg
1 teaspoon vanilla

½ cup coconut
1 cup mini-chocolate chips

Pour remainder of cake batter over this filling. Bake at 350° for about 70 minutes. Does not need icing.

JoAnn Gankendorff

DATE CAKE WITH CUSTARD TOPPING

Cake:

2 eggs
¾ cup sugar
2 tablespoons flour
1 teaspoon baking powder

1 cup chopped pecans
1 cup packed chopped dates
cinnamon

Beat eggs, add sugar. Sift flour and baking powder. Stir into egg mixture. Fold in nuts and dates, stirring until well blended. Pour into a greased and floured 8 inch square pan. Batter is stiff, so smooth until bottom of pan is covered. Sprinkle cinnamon on top. Bake at 325° for 30 minutes. Leave in pan, cut into pieces while warm. Serve from pan.

Custard Topping:

3 eggs
¼ cup sugar
2 cups milk

1 teaspoon vanilla
Cool Whip (optional)

Topping: Place first 3 ingredients into top of a double boiler. Stir until well blended. Place into double boiler and cook stirring often until custard coats the spoon. Cool and add vanilla. Chill before pouring over pieces of date cake. This may be topped with Cool Whip. Oh, if custard should curdle, use an egg beater and beat until smooth. Serves 9-12.

Marilyn Tankersley Taylor

FIG CAKE

½ cup butter or margarine, softened
1 cup sugar
3 eggs
½ teaspoon vanilla extract
2 cups all-purpose flour
1 teaspoon soda
1 teaspoon ground cinnamon
1 teaspoon ground nutmeg

1 teaspoon ground cloves or all-spice
1 cup buttermilk
1½ cups fig preserves with juice, chopped
½ cup chopped nuts
½ cup coconut (optional)
1 cup raisins (optional)

Cream butter and sugar until light and fluffy; add eggs, one at a time, beating well after each addition. Stir in vanilla. Combine flour, soda, and spices; add to creamed mixture alternately with buttermilk, mixing well after each addition. Stir in figs and nuts; add coconut and raisins, if desired. Spoon batter into a greased and floured 10 inch tube pan or Bundt pan. Bake at 350° for 50 minutes or until done. Serves 12-14.

Mrs. Pat Cashman

OLD TIME SUGARPLUM CAKE

4 cups all-purpose flour (measure after sifting)
1 (8-ounce) package dates, chopped
1 pound orange slices (candy), chopped
1½ cups shredded coconut
1 cup chopped walnuts
1 cup chopped pecans

2 cups sugar
4 eggs
1 cup butter
1 teaspoon soda
pinch of salt
½ cup buttermilk
1 tablespoon lemon juice
1 teaspoon orange extract

Glacé (Mix together)
2 cups powdered sugar
1 cup orange juice

2 teaspoons orange rind

Sift 1 cup of flour over finely cut dates, candy, coconut and nuts dredging well with flour. (Use scissors to cut fruit and dates.) Mix sugar, eggs, butter. Beat well after each one. Sift 3 cups flour with soda and salt and add alternately with buttermilk, beginning and ending with flour. Beat in lemon juice and orange extract. Then by hand, stir in fruit mixture. Batter will be stiff. Pour into 2 large greased and floured loaf pans. Bake at 250° for 2½ hours. Remove from oven and punch holes with ice pick in warm cake. Pour glacé over cake. Let cool completely and remove from pan. This recipe has placed in several contests. Serves 15 and freezes well.

From the files of
Mrs. Jean Williams

BLACK RASPBERRY JAM CAKE

1 cup butter
1 cup sugar
3 cups flour
1 teaspoon soda
⅛ teaspoon pumpkin pie spice

1 cup buttermilk
4 eggs
1 heaping cup of black seedless raspberry jam (or any dark jam)

Caramel Frosting:
1 cup sugar, previously caramelized
2 cups sugar
1 teaspoon flour

1 cup milk
1 teaspoon vanilla
2-3 tablespoons butter

Mix butter and sugar until creamy. Sift dry ingredients. Alternately add dry ingredients and buttermilk to butter and sugar mixture. Add 4 whole beaten eggs. Stir in jam. Bake in 3 (8-inch) round layer pans lined with oiled paper or brown paper at 350° for 25 minutes.

Frosting: Stir 2 cups sugar to which 1 teaspoon flour has been added and 1 cup milk. Add these at same time. Cook for 6-8 minutes. (When milk is added—the sugar mixture may get hard and crackle, but don't let it upset you for it will melt as you stir.) Add vanilla and butter. Pour into a bowl and beat while it cools until it is thick and creamy. Frost between layers, on top and sides of cake.

Mrs. W. T. Black, Jr.
Quitman, Texas

POPPY SEED CAKE

2 eggs
1½ cups sugar
2 cups flour
1 heaping teaspoon baking powder
1 teaspoon salt

3-4 teaspoons almond extract
¾ cup cooking oil (liquid)
1 cup milk
½ cup poppy seeds

Combine eggs and sugar well. Sift flour, baking powder and salt and add to above mixture. Add last four ingredients and mix well. Pour into 2 greased and floured loaf tins. It will make 2 small loaves. Bake at 350° for 45-60 minutes, testing frequently. This recipe freezes well. Better if refrigerated after cutting. Very moist. Good for holiday gifts. Serves 8-10 per loaf.

Ann F. Martin

VICTORIAN PINEAPPLE UPSIDE DOWN CAKE

Pineapple pan coat:
1 (20-ounce) can pineapple slices
⅓ cup butter, melted
½ cup brown sugar

7 maraschino cherries
6 pecan halves

Drain pineapple slices, reserving syrup. Pour melted butter in bottom of a round 9 inch cake pan or a 10 inch skillet. Stir in brown sugar. Arrange 7 pineapple slices in the pan; place a cherry in the center of each slice and a pecan half between each end. Cut remaining slices in half and arrange around sides of pan. Keep pan in a warm place while making batter.

1½ cups sifted cake flour
1 cup sugar
2 teaspoons baking powder
¾ teaspoon salt
⅓ cup butter, softened
⅓ cup syrup from pineapple

⅓ cup milk
1 teaspoon grated lemon peel
1 teaspoon vanilla
½ teaspoon almond extract
1 egg

Resift flour with sugar, baking powder, and salt into mixing bowl. Add butter, pineapple syrup, milk, lemon peel and flavorings. Beat 2 minutes medium speed on mixer, scraping bowl often. Add egg and beat 2 minutes more.

Carefully pour batter over fruit in pan. Bake in a moderate oven, 350°, about 50 minutes or until cake tests done. Remove from oven and let stand in pan about 5 minutes before turning out upside-down on serving plate.

Leave pan in place a few minutes before removing from cake. This allows the thickened syrup to loosen itself from the pan, and cover the cake. Serve warm or cold.

Mrs. Brad Hamilton

STRAWBERRY TRIFLE CAKE

3 pints fresh strawberries
1 cup orange or pineapple juice
½ cup sugar
1 package (18½ ounce) yellow cake
  mix

½ pint whipping cream
½ teaspoon vanilla
1 tablespoon sugar

Clean, slice and mash 2½ pints of strawberries. Add fruit juice and ½ cup sugar. Place in refrigerator. Prepare cake as directed, bake in 2-8 inch round pans. Cool, with fork or ice pick, make holes in bottom layer of cake, pour half of strawberry mixture on top allowing juice to seep into holes. Place second layer on top and repeat procedure. Whip cream, adding vanilla and sugar, to stiff peaks. Use cream to ice cake, top and sides. Use remaining whole berries to garnish top of cake. Refrigerate for several hours before serving. Serves 12.

Doreen S. Duhe

CELEBRATION BREAD

4 cups sifted flour
2 teaspoons baking powder
1 teaspoon soda
1 teaspoon salt
1¼ cups sugar
⅔ cup shortening

3 eggs
2 cups applesauce
1 cup chopped nuts
1 (16 ounce) can red sour (or sweet)
  pitted cherries, well drained
2 teaspoons almond extract

Cherry Glaze:
1 cup powdered sugar
2 tablespoons cherry juice

1 tablespoon butter or margarine
1 teaspoon almond extract

Sift flour, baking powder, soda and salt; set aside. Blend sugar and shortening until creamy. Add eggs and beat well. Add flour mixture alternately with applesauce. Stir in nuts, drained cherries and almond extract. Pour into two greased and floured 9x5x3 inch loaf pans. Bake at 350° 45-55 minutes or until tests done. Remove from pans while warm and when cool spread with Cherry Glaze.

Glaze: Blend all ingredients until smooth and spread on cooled Celebration Bread loaves.

Yolanda V. Trahan

STRAWBERRY BREAD

3 cups flour
1 teaspoon salt
1 teaspoon soda
½ teaspoon cinnamon
2 cups sugar

2 packages frozen strawberries (10 ounce packets), thawed
4 eggs
1½ cups oil
1 cup chopped nuts

In one bowl mix the first five ingredients. In a second bowl mix the remaining ingredients. Combine the two mixtures. Grease and flour 2 large loaf pans. Fill pans ⅔ full. Bake at 325° for 1 hour.

Teenie Gouaux Trappey

"TIPSY" CAKE

2 regular size Sara Lee
  Butter Cakes
3 packages vanilla pudding to cook
3-4 tablespoons sugar
1-2 teaspoons vanilla

¼ stick butter
2 cups Pale Dry Sherry
1 cup whipping cream, whipped
1 small bottle of maraschino cherries, cut in four

Slice the frozen butter cakes the long way, very thin. Add 3-4 tablespoons sugar to pudding and cook as instructed on box. Add vanilla and butter while pudding is still hot. Cool pudding. When pudding is cool, layer cake and pudding in 9x13 inch pan. Start with a layer of pudding then cake followed by 2-3 tablespoons of sherry. Repeat this until pan is filled. Chill. Top with whipped cream. Decorate with cherries. (Use green and red cherries for Christmas.) This recipe came from London, England. Serves 10-12. (To prevent film from forming, cover with wax paper while pudding is cooling.)

Hazel Burdin Francisco

GRAND MARNIER CAKE

1 package butter recipe golden
  cake mix
1 regular size instant vanilla
  pudding mix
1 stick butter

4 eggs
¾ cup milk
⅓ cup Grand Marnier liqueur
½ cup chopped pecans
confectioners sugar

Have butter at room temperature. Mix cake mix and pudding. Add other ingredients and beat four minutes until smooth. Bake in greased Bundt pan at 325° for 60 minutes or until done. When cake is cool sprinkle with confectioners sugar.

Mary Blanchet Prejean

BLITZ TORTE

½ cup butter	1 cup flour, sifted
½ cup sugar	1 teaspoon baking powder
4 egg yolks	1 teaspoon vanilla
4 tablespoons milk	pecans

Meringue:

4 egg whites	1 cup sugar

Pineapple Filling:

¼ cup sugar	2 egg yolks (slightly beaten)
1 tablespoon flour	1 tablespoon butter
dash salt	1 can crushed pineapple (large size
⅔ cup milk	and drain)

Cream together sugar and butter. Add beaten egg yolks, milk, flour sifted with baking powder and vanilla. Mix well. Spread the batter over 2 buttered and lightly floured 9 inch loose bottom cake pans. Make a meringue of the egg whites beaten stiff, with sugar added very gradually. Cover each unbaked layer with meringue reserving enough to decorate one layer with meringue peaks made by dropping off the end of a spoon. This will be the top layer and the frosting. Sprinkle both layers with pecans. Bake at 300° for 45 minutes. Cool.

Filling: Combine sugar, flour and salt in top of double boiler. Mix milk with egg yolks. Add to sugar mixture. Place over boiling water, cook and stir 15 minutes or until thickened. Remove from heat and add butter and fruit.

Assembling cake: To assemble the cake use the custard filling between the two layers. Place the layer with meringue peaks on top. The cake will have meringue and nuts on both the bottom and the top. You may use a vanilla pudding mix (be sure it is the one you cook) instead of the pineapple filling.

Jenny Klug Strohm

a welcome addition to the table

RUM PUDDING PASTRY CAKE

1 package vanilla pudding and pie
   filling
¼ cup granulated sugar
1½ cups milk
1 egg yolk, slightly beaten
1 tablespoon butter
½ teaspoon rum extract
1 package (4 ounce) sweet cooking
   chocolate
¼ cup granulated sugar

¼ cup water
dash of cinnamon
1 teaspoon vanilla
1 package (10 ounce) pie crust mix
2 envelopes whipped topping mix
1 cup milk
1 egg white
1 teaspoon vanilla
½ cup toasted, slivered, blanched
   almonds

Combine pudding mix and ¼ cup sugar in a saucepan. Blend in 1½ cups milk and the egg yolk. Cook over medium heat, stirring constantly, until mixture comes to a full boil. Remove from heat; stir in butter and rum extract. Pour into a bowl and cover surface with wax paper. Chill at least 2 hours.

Meanwhile, break chocolate into a small saucepan. Add ¼ cup sugar, the water and cinnamon. Cook and stir over low heat until sauce is smooth. Remove from heat. Add 1 teaspoon vanilla. Cool to room temperature. When it is cooled, blend the chocolate into the dry pie crust mix. Divide pastry into four parts. Using a spatula or hands, press or spread each part over bottom of inverted 8 or 9 inch round cake pan to within ¼ inch of edge. Bake at 425° for about 6 minutes or until pastry is almost firm. Cook until firm about 5 additional minutes. Run tip of knife around edges to loosen from pans. Lift carefully; these layers are fragile. Cool. Remove cooled pudding from refrigerator and beat with a rotary beater until smooth. Combine whipped topping mix with milk, the egg white and vanilla in a small bowl with narrow bottom. Whip at high speed of electric mixer until peaks form. Continue beating until topping is soft and fluffy about 2 minutes longer. Blend this topping into the cooled pudding. Spread between pastry layers and over top. Sprinkle with toasted, slivered, blanched almonds. Chill at least 8 hours or over night. Buy slivered almonds. Toast in 400° oven until golden brown, stirring often. It won't take but a few minutes. Serves 12.

Sue VanNoy Willett
Independence, Kansas

DEEP DISH APPLE PIE

Pastry:

1¼ cups all-purpose flour
¼ teaspoon salt
2 tablespoons shortening

4 tablespoons cold butter or margarine
3-4 tablespoons cold water

Filling:

8 cooking apples, peeled and thinly
    sliced
1¼ cups sugar
3 tablespoons all-purpose flour

1½ teaspoons ground cinnamon
¼ teaspoon ground nutmeg
⅛ teaspoon salt
3 tablespoons butter or margarine

To make pastry, combine flour and salt and cut in shortening. Cut butter into small pieces and add to flour mixture; cut in until mixture resembles coarse cornmeal. Stir in only enough water to moisten flour. Form dough into a ball. Wrap in plastic wrap and chill 30 minutes. Roll dough to ¼ inch thickness on a lightly floured surface and cut into 1 inch wide strips. Arrange lattice fashion over filling. Yield: Pastry for one 9 inch pie.

For filling, arrange apple slices in a lightly greased 9x9x2 inch baking dish. Combine sugar, flour, cinnamon, nutmeg and salt; sprinkle over apples and dot with butter. Top with pastry and bake at 400 degrees for 40 minutes or until golden brown. Serves 6 to 8.

Elizabeth Preis

STREUSEL APPLE MINCE PIE

1 prepared pie crust
2 cups mincemeat
3 cups canned sliced apples,
    drained (1 (20 ounce) can
    sliced apples)

⅓ cup sugar
1 tablespoon lemon juice
½ cup sugar
½ cup flour
¼ cup butter

Turn mincemeat into unbaked shell. Combine apples, sugar and lemon juice. Arrange over mincemeat. Mix together sugar and flour. Cut in butter till crumbly. Sprinkle over apples. Bake at 450° for 10 minutes. Reduce heat to 325° for 45 minutes. Serve hot.

Tolley Odom

BRANDY ALEXANDER PIE

1 envelope plain gelatin
½ cup cold water
⅔ cup sugar
⅛ teaspoon salt
3 eggs, separated

¼ cup cognac
¼ cup creme de cocoa
2 cups whipping cream, whipped
1 graham cracker crust
    (9 or 10 inch)

Sprinkle gelatin over water in a heavy saucepan. Add ⅓ cup sugar, salt and egg yolks. Stir to blend. Cook over low heat, stirring until the gelatin dissolves and mixture thickens. Do not boil. Stir in cognac and creme de cocoa. Chill until mixture starts to mound slightly. Beat egg whites until foamy. Gradually beat in remaining ⅓ cup sugar, continuing to beat until stiff peaks form. Fold into thickened mixture. Fold in half the whipped cream. Turn into crust. Chill several hours or overnight. Decorate with remaining whipped cream and chocolate curls.

Mrs. James F. Pell

CAROLINA DREAM (BLUEBERRY PIE)

1 large can crushed pineapple
water
1 (6 ounce) package black cherry jello

1 cup cold water
1 can blueberry pie filling

Topping:
1 (8 ounce) cream cheese
½ pint sour cream

½ cup sugar
1 cup chopped nuts (optional)

Drain juice from pineapple and add enough water to make 2 cups. Bring juice to a boil and add gelatin. Stir until dissolved. Add cold water, pie filling, and pineapple. Pour into a large oblong pyrex dish. Chill until congealed. Mix topping ingredients together and spread over gelatin. Serves 10-12.

Usona Tomberlin

BUTTERMILK PIE

2 pie shells
3½ cups sugar
4 rounded tablespoons flour
2 sticks butter, melted
2 cups buttermilk

8 eggs, medium size
dash nutmeg
2½ teaspoons vanilla
2 tablespoons lemon juice
pinch of salt

Bake prepared pie shells for 5 minutes. Let cool. Combine above ingredients in order given. Mix well. Pour into shells. Bake at 350° for 50 minutes to 1 hour. Serves 16 to 18.

Eileen Knight

BLACKBERRY PIE

Filling:

5 cups blackberries
½ cup flour
1-1¼ cups sugar (depending on
    tartness of berries)
⅛ teaspoon salt

½ teaspoon vanilla
½ teaspoon almond extract
2 teaspoons lemon juice
1 tablespoon butter

Pastry:

2 cups sifted flour
½ teaspoon salt
1 tablespoon sugar

⅔ cup + 2 tablespoons shortening
about ⅓ cup cold milk
1 tablespoon melted butter

Toss all filling ingredients except butter together and set aside. Sift into a mixing bowl the flour, salt, and sugar. Add ½ of the shortening. Cut into the flour. Cut in remainder of shortening until the mixture is in even bits no larger than peas. Sprinkle milk, one tablespoon at a time, on a small area of the flour mixture. Toss the mixture lightly with a fork after each spoonful of milk is added. Continue this procedure, adding only enough milk to make the pastry mixture moist enough to form a ball when patted lightly together.

Roll out half of dough with quick light strokes. Fit into pie pan. Trim off surplus pastry. Brush this crust with melted butter. Roll out the other ball of dough for top of pie.

Fill the pie shell with blackberry mixture and dot with the tablespoon of butter. Place top pastry on pie. Trim and tuck in top edge. Flute edges if desired. If freezing, wrap, seal, label, and freeze.

If not freezing, preheat oven to 425°. Make a few slits in top crust. Brush with heavy cream, and bake 45 minutes, or until brown and berries are bubbling. Cool on cake rack and serve warm or cold.

To cook after freezing, slit top, brush with heavy cream and bake 55 minutes, or until brown.   Marianne Schneider

LEMON CHEESE CAKE PIE

8 ounce package cream cheese
2 tablespoons butter
½ cup sugar
1 whole egg
2 tablespoons flour
⅔ cup milk

¼ cup fresh lemon juice
2 tablespoons grated lemon peel
1 teaspoon vanilla
vanilla wafer crust, crushed vanilla
    wafers mixed with 2 tablespoons
    melted butter

Sour Cream Topping:

1 pint sour cream
3 tablespoons sugar

1 teaspoon vanilla

Cream cheese and butter; add sugar and egg. Mix well. Add flour, then milk. Stir in lemon juice and peel. Pour into unbaked vanilla wafer crumb shell. Bake 30 minutes at 350°. Raise heat to 425°. Spread sour cream mixture over the top of pie and bake 5 more minutes. Chill. Serves 8.   Marianne Schneider

CHERRY TART FILLING

2 (No. 303) cans tart pitted cherries
juice of 1 lemon
½ cup water or orange juice
1½ cups sugar
½ cup + 1 tablespoon flour
1 teaspoon red food coloring

1 tablespoon butter
½-1 teaspoon vanilla
⅛ teaspoon almond extract
whipping cream
8-10 tart shells

Drain the juice from cherries. Add juice of lemon and the water or orange juice to cherry juice. Dissolve the sugar and flour with some of the juice. Add food coloring. Then add the rest of juice and cook approximately 15 to 20 minutes or until thick. Add butter, vanilla and almond extract. Cool. Fold in the cherries. Put into tart shells when ready to serve. Add sweetened whipped cream to tops of tarts before serving.

Marianne Schneider

INDIVIDUAL CHOCOLATE MINT PIES

1 cup margarine
2 cups sifted powdered sugar
4 squares unsweetened chocolate,
   melted
4 eggs
1 teaspoon peppermint flavoring

2 teaspoons vanilla
18 vanilla wafer cookies
carton of Cool-Whip
chopped nuts
Maraschino cherries

Cream margarine and powdered sugar. Blend in melted chocolate. Add eggs, one at a time and beat well. Stir in flavorings. Place a vanilla wafer into the bottom of a cupcake paper cup. Fill with chocolate mixture ¾ full. Place a dollop of Cool-Whip on top, sprinkle with chopped nuts and a cherry. Freeze in muffin tins to keep shape. Store in a plastic bag after frozen. Makes 18.

Comments: Makes an excellent after-school snack for children.

Ramona Mouton

CHESS PIE

To make one pie:
1 stick butter
1¾ cups sugar
9 egg yolks
¾ cup milk
1 teaspoon vanilla
1 teaspoon nutmeg

To make two pies:
2 sticks butter
3½ cups sugar
13-14 egg yolks
1½ cups milk
1½ teaspoons vanilla
1½ teaspoons nutmeg

Preheat oven to 400°. Cream butter until fluffy. Gradually add sugar and cream thoroughly. Add egg yolks one at a time. Reduce speed to slow and add milk and seasonings. Cook 20 minutes at 400°. Reduce heat to 300° and cook 30 minutes more.

Mrs. Margaret S. Chambley

SEA RANCH CHOCOLATE CHESS PIE

4 heaping tablespoons cocoa
1½ cups sugar
2 eggs
½ cup pecan halves
¼ cup butter

½ cup unsweetened evaporated milk
½ cup coconut
1 (9-inch) unbaked pie shell
vanilla ice cream or whipped cream

Preheat oven to 400 degrees. Mix all ingredients and pour into an unbaked pie shell. Bake for 30 minutes. Cool. Serve with a scoop of vanilla ice cream or whipped cream.

Christie Adams

SWEET GERMAN CHOCOLATE PIE

1 (4-ounce) package German sweet
   chocolate
¼ cup butter
1⅔ cups evaporated milk
1½ cups sugar
3 tablespoons corn starch

⅛ teaspoon salt
2 eggs
1 teaspoon vanilla
1 unbaked 9-inch pie shell
1⅓ cups flaked coconut
½ cup chopped pecans

Melt chocolate and butter over low heat. Stir until blended. Remove from heat. Gradually blend in milk. In a separate bowl, mix sugar, corn starch and salt. Beat in eggs and vanilla. Gradually blend in chocolate mixture. Pour into pie shell. Mix coconut and pecans and sprinkle over pie filling. Bake at 375 degrees for 45 minutes or until top is puffed. Cool for 4 hours before serving.

Mrs. Sam Hance

EGG NOG PIE

2 cups light cream or milk
3 eggs, separated
½ cup sugar
dash salt
⅛ teaspoon nutmeg
1 envelope plain gelatin

2 tablespoons cold water
1 to 2 tablespoons rum
1 teaspoon vanilla extract
½ cup whipping cream, whipped
1 prepared 8-inch pie crust

Scald cream in a double boiler. Beat egg yolks with half the sugar until pale. Add salt and nutmeg. Add yolk mixture to cream. Cook, stirring constantly, over simmering water until it coats a spoon. Soften gelatin in the water and add to custard. Stir until dissolved. Strain. Add the rum and vanilla extract. Chill until it begins to set. Beat egg whites until foamy. Gradually add remaining sugar and beat until stiff. Fold into custard. Fold in whipped cream. Pour into crust; chill until firm. Garnish with more whipped cream and nutmeg.

Miss Linda R. Smith

CHOCOLATE EGG NOG PIE

1½ cups chocolate wafer crumbs
2 tablespoons sugar
¼ cup melted butter
1 envelope unflavored gelatin
¼ cup cold water
⅓ cup sugar

2 tablespoons corn starch
¼ teaspoon salt
2 cups dairy eggnog
1 teaspoon vanilla
½ teaspoon rum extract
1 cup whipping cream, whipped

Crust:
Mix sugar and wafer crumbs together. Stir in melted butter. Press mixture firmly and evenly against bottom and sides of 9-inch pie pan. Bake in 350° oven for 5 minutes. Cool.

Filling:
Sprinkle gelatin over water to soften. Mix together sugar, corn starch and salt in heavy saucepan. Gradually stir in egg nog. Cook over medium heat, stirring constantly until thickened. Cook two additional minutee. Remove from heat and add softened gelatin until dissolved. Add vanilla and rum extract. Chill until slightly thickened. Fold in whipped cream. Pour mixture into cooled crust. Chill until set.

Anne Roberts Sonnier

CRANBERRY SURPRISE PIE

2 cups cranberries
½ cup sugar
1 cup finely chopped nuts
2 eggs
1 cup sugar

1 cup sifted flour
½ cup melted margarine
¼ cup melted shortening
whipped cream or Cool Whip

Grease well a 10-inch pie plate. Spread cranberries in bottom. Sprinkle with the ½ cup sugar and chopped nuts. In bowl, beat 2 eggs, gradually adding 1 cup sugar. Beat until well mixed. Gradually add flour. Then add melted margarine and melted shortening. Beat thoroughly. Pour over cranberries. Bake at 300° for 45 minutes or until golden brown. Serve warm with whipped cream or Cool Whip. Serves 8.

Vera Hardcastle
Beaumont, Tx.

AMAZING COCONUT PIE

2 cups milk
¾ cup sugar
½ cup biscuit mix
4 eggs

¼ cup melted butter
1½ teaspoons vanilla
1 cup grated coconut

Combine all ingredients except the coconut. Mix and then using your electric blender, blend for 3 minutes on a slow speed. Pour into a 9-inch greased pie pan. Let stand 5 minutes. Sprinkle coconut on top. Bake at 350° for 40 minutes. Can be served hot or cold.

Wallice O'Quin Durbin
New Orleans, La.

CHOCOLATE NUT PIE

1 cup sugar
½ cup flour
½ cup real butter
2 whole eggs, well beaten
2 teaspoons vanilla or bourbon
   (bourbon preferred)

1 cup semi-sweet chocolate morsels
1 cup chopped walnuts or pecans
1 (9-inch) pie shell, unbaked

Mix sugar with flour. Cream butter, add sugar mixture to butter. Then add 2 beaten whole eggs and flavoring. Mix thoroughly and add chocolate morsels and nuts. Pour into pie shell and bake 50 minutes at 350°. (Created especially for Derby week in Louisville, Kentucky.)

Katherine Robbins Krampe

FRUIT PIE

1 can pie cherries
1 flat can crushed pineapple,
　　drained
1¼ cups sugar
¼ cup flour

1 (3 ounce) package orange jello
6 mashed bananas
2 graham cracker crusts
½ cup chopped pecans
whipping cream, whipped

Cook cherries, pineapple, flour, and sugar until thick. Remove from heat and add 1 package orange jello. Add mashed bananas and let cool. Pour ingredients into crusts and sprinkle with chopped pecans. Cover with whipped cream.

Priscilla Sheperd
Beaumont, Tx.

LEMON CHESS PIE

2 cups sugar
2 tablespoons flour
1 tablespoon cornmeal
¼ cup butter or margarine, melted

4 eggs, well beaten
2 lemons, grated and juice strained
1 unbaked 8-inch pie shell with high
　　fluted rim

Combine sugar, flour and cornmeal. Add with melted butter to eggs. Beat well. Stir in grated lemon peel and juice. Pour in pastry shell. Bake at 375° for 40 minutes or until knife inserted near rim comes out clean. Chill until center is firm enough to cut.

Patricia T. Olson

FRESH PEACH PIE

1 graham cracker crust
1½ cups powdered sugar
1 stick butter
1 beaten egg
1 teaspoon vanilla

4-5 peaches, sliced
½ cup granulated sugar
1 pint whipping cream, whipped or
　　Cool Whip
1 graham cracker pie crust

Cream together powdered sugar and butter. Add 1 beaten egg and vanilla. Slice peaches and cover with granulated sugar. Let stand for 45 minutes. Drain. Pour cream mixture into a graham cracker crust and top with peaches. Top with whipping cream or Cool Whip. Refrigerate. Slice in wedges when ready to serve. May be frozen. Serves 8.

Boopie McInnis
Ruth Allen
Minden, La.

MAMA'S PECAN PIE

3 eggs
⅔ cup sugar
dash salt
1 cup dark Karo syrup

⅓ cup melted margarine
1 cup pecans
1 unbaked pie shell

Beat eggs well by hand. Add remaining ingredients. Bake in pie shell at 350° for 50 minutes or until a knife remains clean when inserted ¼ way into the pie.

Hilda K. Walker
Lake Charles, LA

CHOCOLATE FUDGE PECAN PIE

4 whole eggs
2 cups sugar
3 squares unsweetened chocolate
¼ pound butter

1 teaspoon vanilla
pinch of salt
1 cup pecans
1 unbaked pie shell

Break eggs into bowl and stir in sugar. Melt chocolate and butter together and add to sugar and egg mixture. Add vanilla, salt and nuts. Mix well but do not beat. Pour into unbaked pie shell and bake 60 minutes at 350°. Serves 6-8.

Dorothy Buie Brown

PUMPKIN PIE

1 (9-inch) unbaked pie shell
1 cup granulated sugar
½ teaspoon salt
1½ teaspoons cinnamon
½ teaspoon nutmeg
½ teaspoon ginger

½ teaspoon allspice
½ teaspoon cloves
1½ cups fresh mashed pumpkin or solid
    packed canned pumpkin
2 eggs

Mix all ingredients together until smooth. Pour into an unbaked pie shell. Bake at 425° for 15 minutes. Lower temperature to 350° and continue baking about 35 minutes or until custard is firm.

This pie can be frozen. To thaw, let defrost for about 1 hour at room temperature. Reheat at 325° for about 20 minutes.

Jeanette Dugas

SHERRY PIE

Crust:
1 stick butter, melted
½ cup light brown sugar

1 cup flour
½ cup chopped pecans

Filling:
½ pound miniature marshmallows
½ cup sherry

½ pint whipping cream

Mix all crust ingredients in a 9-inch pie pan. Bake at 375° for 15-25 minutes or until golden brown. Stir occasionally. Reserve ½ cup of crust mixture for topping. Press pastry into pie plate with spoon while still hot. Set aside to cool.

For filling, melt marshmallows in sherry in a double boiler. Cool mixture. Fold mixture into ½ pint stiffly beaten whipping cream. Pour into a cold pastry shell and sprinkle with reserved crumbs. Refrigerate overnight. Serves 8.

Mrs. John A. Bolin

FRESH STRAWBERRY PIE

1 baked 9-inch pie shell

½ pint whipping cream, whipped

Filling:
1 (8-ounce) package Philadelphia
    Cream Cheese
2 tablespoons lemon juice

½ cup sugar
1 teaspoon grated lemon rind
2 tablespoons milk

Glaze:
¾ cup sugar
3 heaping tablespoons corn starch
pinch of salt
1 cup water

1 tablespoon lemon juice
½ teaspoon red coloring
2 pints of hulled strawberries,
    sliced if desired

For filling, mix the cream cheese, sugar, lemon juice, rind and milk. Spread on pie shell.

For glaze, mix sugar, corn starch and salt. Mix into a paste with 2 tablespoons water. Boil remaining water and stir into the sugar mixture. Cook until thick and clear. Remove from fire. Add lemon juice and coloring. When cool, fold in the berries, reserving some for garnish. Pour over cream cheese mixture. Top with whipped cream and garnish with whole berries. Refrigerate.

Nancy Crawford

PEACH CHANTILLY

4 cups pureed fresh peaches
2 tablespoons lemon juice
2 tablespoons unflavored gelatin
½ cup reserved juices
2 tablespoons orange liqueur

4 tablespoons sugar
2 cups whipping cream
1 baked 11 inch pastry shell
7-8 peeled fresh peach halves
raspberries and grapes, garnish

Mix peach puree with lemon juice. Place mixture in fine sieve and allow juices to drain into bowl for 20 minutes. Reserve juices. Stir gelatin and juices over low heat until gelatin has completely dissolved. Mix peach puree with liqueur, sugar and cooled gelatin mixture. Whip cream and fold into puree. Spoon mixture into flan shell and refrigerate 4-6 hours. Before serving, arrange peach halves on top of chantilly mixture. Garnish with grapes and raspberries. Serves 8.

Boopie Procter McInnis
Minden, LA

EASY PIE PASTRY

1 stick margarine, less 1 inch
1 cup flour

2 tablespoons powdered sugar

Melt margarine in pie plate. Sift in sugar and flour and pat out. Bake at 400° for 10 minutes or until golden brown.

Grace Cox Black
Quitman, Texas

FRENCH ALMOND PIE

3 cups slivered or sliced almonds
3 cups heavy cream
9 whole eggs

dash vanilla extract
2 cups sugar
1 uncooked pie crust

Combine all ingredients in mixing bowl and whip. Then put in uncooked pie crust and bake in 350° oven for 35 minutes.

Jacob's Restaurant

SOPAPILLAS

3 cups flour	1 egg
1 teaspoon salt	milk or water
3 teaspoons baking powder	deep fat about 375°
¼ cup fat, shortening	powdered sugar

Combine flour, salt and baking powder. Add fat then well beaten egg. Add just enough milk or water to allow you to roll out the dough to about ½ inch thickness. Cut dough in rectangles about 2-3 inches. Let rectangles rise for about 5-10 minutes. Drop in deep fat and cook until golden brown, which takes only a very short time. The dough puffs up like little pillows. Drain and sprinkle with sugar. These delicious Mexican donuts are good plain, or pour honey over them or roll in a cinnamon sugar mixture for something out of this world with coffee. Kids love them. Serves 6-8.

Jean Hurley

CRUNCHY APPLES CARAMEL

½ cup walnuts, coarsely broken	3 tablespoons water
¼ cup butter or margarine	¼ cup golden raisins
1½ pounds (3 large) apples, cored and sliced into rings	⅛ teaspoon nutmeg
⅓ cup firmly packed brown sugar	dash of salt

Sauté walnuts in butter in large skillet until lightly toasted; remove from pan. Fry apple rings on both sides until tender. Place apples and nuts in shallow serving dish, 13x9 inches. Keep warm. Combine sugar, water, raisins, nutmeg and salt in skillet and stir over heat until sugar dissolves and mixture bubbles. Pour over apples and nuts. Serve warm. Good with pork as a side dish or as a dessert over vanilla ice cream. Serves 6.

Mrs. Stan D. McEacharn

FROZEN CHOCOLATE JUBILEE

40 vanilla wafers	1 teaspoon vanilla
4 tablespoons margarine	3 egg yolks
2 cups powdered sugar	3 egg whites
½ cup margarine	1 quart vanilla ice cream
2 squares unsweetened chocolate	1 cup chopped nuts, optional

Line 13x9 inch pan with vanilla wafers, crushed and mixed with 4 tablespoons margarine. Press firm. Cream sugar and margarine; add melted chocolate, vanilla and beaten egg yolks. Fold in stiffly beaten egg whites and spread on wafer crust and chill until firm. Spread softened vanilla ice cream over top of chocolate mixture; sprinkle with nuts. Freeze. Slice and serve. Variation: Try different flavors of ice cream. Serves 12.

Nancy W. McDonald

CHOCOLATE MINT FREEZE

1¼ cups finely crushed vanilla
  wafers (28)
4 tablespoons melted butter or
  margarine
1 quart peppermint stick
  ice cream, melted
½ cup butter

2 (1 ounce) squares unsweetened
  chocolate
3 well beaten egg yolks
1½ cups sifted confectioners sugar
½ cup chopped pecans
1 teaspoon vanilla
3 egg whites

Toss together crumbs and 4 tablespoons melted butter or margarine. Reserve ¼ cup crumbs mixture. Press remaining crumb mixture into 9x9x2 inch baking pan. Spread with ice cream, freeze. Melt ½ cup butter and the chocolate over low heat; gradually stir into egg yolks with the sugar, nuts and vanilla. Cool thoroughly. Beat egg whites until stiff peaks form. Beat chocolate mixture until smooth. Add egg whites folding into chocolate mixture. Spread mixture over ice cream. Top with reserved crumb mixture. Freeze. Serves 9-12.

Sally Brockschmidt Herpin

CHOCOLATE SOUFFLE

Mold:
½ tablespoon butter

2-3 tablespoons confectioners sugar

Souffle:
3½ ounces semi-sweet chocolate
2 tablespoons strong coffee
3 tablespoons corn starch
1 cup milk
⅓ cup granulated sugar

2 tablespoons butter, softened
5 egg whites
1 tablespoon granulated sugar
3 egg yolks
2 tablespoons confectioners sugar, sifted
  fresh, unsweetened whipped cream

Preheat oven to 375°. Butter and dust with confectioners sugar a 6 cup mold or individual molds. Stir chocolate and coffee in a pan over simmering water until smooth. Remove from heat but keep over simmering water. In a separate pan beat corn starch and 3 tablespoons of milk until smooth. Beat in remaining milk and ⅓ cup sugar. Stir over moderate heat until it comes to a boil. Boil and stir 3 seconds. Take off heat and beat in hot melted chocolate. Divide butter over chocolate sauce. Allow to cool until tepid. Beat egg whites until soft peaks are formed. Add a pinch of salt while beating. Sprinkle 1 tablespoon sugar and continue beating until stiff peaks are formed. Scrape chocolate into a large mixing bowl. Beat in egg yolks. Beat in ¼ of the egg whites. Fold in remaining whites carefully. Pour into mold and bake at 375°, preheated, for 35 minutes. Rapidly sprinkle with 2 tablespoons sifted powdered sugar. Then bake 10 more minutes. Serve immediately with fresh unsweetened whipped cream. Serves 4-6.

Martha A. Hiatt

SWEET SOUFFLE WITH GRAND MARNIER

Preheat oven to 400°. Grease a 6 cup mold with ½ tablespoon softened butter and coat the sides and bottom with granulated sugar.

1 orange	⅓ cup granulated sugar
2 lumps sugar	4 egg yolks
3 tablespoons flour	2 tablespoons softened butter
¾ cup milk	

Rub the sugar lumps over the orange and mash. Grate the orange peel. Mix the flour with a little of the milk and then add the rest of the milk, sugar, orange peel. Using a wire whip, stir these ingredients over moderately high heat until mixture thickens and comes to a boil. Stir about 30 seconds more. Remove from the heat and beat to cool down slightly. Stir a little of the hot mixture into the egg yolks and then return to pan. Beat in the butter.

Meanwhile whip, slowly at first, 5 egg whites. When they are foaming add a pinch of salt. Beat until soft peaks form and sprinkle on 1 tablespoon sugar. Beat until stiff peaks are formed.

Stir into the sauce:

2 teaspoons vanilla	3-4 tablespoons Grand Marnier

Scoop ¼ of the egg whites into the sauce and stir until mixed. Delicately fold into each other the egg whites and sauce. Do this mixing of egg whites as gently and quickly as possible. Turn mixture into prepared mold. Run around the middle of the mixture with a spatula. Bake in middle of the preheated oven 30-35 minutes. (The oven should be preheated at 400° and reduced to 375° when souffle is put in.) (If souffle is rising unevenly, you may open the oven after 20 minutes and turn the souffle. You might also sprinkle with powdered sugar at this point, but it is very tricky and should be done with utmost speed and caution.)

It is done when nicely browned on top and a trussing needle or knife punched into the puff comes out clean. Sprinkle with powdered sugar and take to the table immediately. To serve: Take a large tablespoon and fork, back to back, and plunge into the center. You may wish to pour on a little more Grand Marnier and whipping cream.

Felicia Elsbury

CREPES GRAND MARNIER

¾ cup flour
¾ cup milk
3 eggs
dash salt

8 ounces sweet dark chocolate
⅓-½ cup orange juice
⅓-½ cup Grand Marnier

Put first column of ingredients into blender. Mix well. Let sit 30 minutes. Heat 7 inch crepe pan, spread with unsalted butter, using brush for each crepe. Turn with fork and stack on plate. If more than 12 are obtained from this recipe, the others can be frozen well.

Melt chocolate with orange juice in a chafing dish or shallow pan over a medium heat. Add Grand Marnier and blend well. Add crepes one at a time and turn each crepe over in the sauce. Fold into quarters and place on dessert saucers. Serve hot. Serves 6.

Mrs. Richard R. Kennedy

STRAWBERRY CREPES CREAM FILLING

2 pints fresh strawberries,
   hulled and sliced
⅓ cup sugar
1 (8 ounce) package cream cheese,
   softened

1 cup confectioners sugar
2-3 tablespoons rum
14-16 crepes

Sprinkle the ⅓ cup sugar over the strawberries, set them aside for at least 1 hour. Beat cream cheese and confectioners sugar together until light and fluffy. Stir in the rum and 2 cups of the strawberries. Fill each crepe with mixture then fold up or roll. Spoon reserved strawberries on top. Serves 14-16.

Mrs. John Tolson, III

STAINED GLASS FRUIT DESSERT

1 can cherry pie filling
1 can blueberry pie filling
1 large can chunk pineapple
1 can mandarin orange slices

2 sliced bananas
1 teaspoon vanilla
1 teaspoon almond extract
¼ teaspoon salt

Mix well in large bowl and chill. Serve in individual dessert dishes topped with sweetened sour cream. (Add vanilla extract, ½ teaspoon and 1 tablespoon of sugar to ½ pint sour cream.) Delicious. Will keep in refrigerator a week. Serves 15.

Variation: Serve over pound cake or plain. Kids love it.

Mrs. Eugene P. Cella

FUDGE SAUCE

½ cup cocoa
1 cup sugar
1 cup light corn syrup
½ cup light cream

3 tablespoons butter
¼ teaspoon salt
1 teaspoon vanilla

Put all ingredients except vanilla into a small saucepan and bring to a boil. Boil for 5 minutes. Remove and stir in vanilla. (Can be refrigerated indefinitely.) Yield 1½ pints.

Carolyn Flournoy
Shreveport, LA

FONDUE

2 cups semi-sweet chocolate, chopped
½ cup heavy sweet cream
2 tablespoons Cointreau, Triple Sec
2 tablespoons brandy
2 tablespoons coffee liqueur

marshmallows
dried fruit
cubes of fresh tropical fruit—bananas, pineapple, strawberries
Angel food cake, cubed

In chafing dish, combined chocolate and cream over low fire. Stir. Add whiskeys. Dip in the cake and fruits with fondue forks.

Truley Juneau

PEACH ICE CREAM

12 medium size (3 pounds) ripe peaches peeled and pitted
2¾ cups sugar
1 tablespoon lemon juice
1½ quarts heavy cream

¼ teaspoon salt
1 teaspoon vanilla extract
1 teaspoon almond extract
crushed ice
rock salt

Wash and scald cover, container and dasher of a 4 quart ice cream freezer. Chill thoroughly. Force peaches through a sieve or food mill. Stir the sugar and lemon juice into peaches and set them aside for 20 minutes. Blend the cream, salt and extracts. Mix with peaches until blended. Fill freezer container ⅔ full with mixture. Cover tightly. Set in freezer tub. (For electric freezer, follow manufacturer's directions.) Fill tub with alternate layers of 8 parts crushed ice and 1 part rock salt. Turn handle slowly 5 minutes. Then turn rapidly until handle becomes difficult to turn. About 15 minutes add crushed ice and rock salt as necessary. Wipe cover free of ice and salt. Remove dasher and pack down ice cream. Cover with aluminum foil or other moisture-vaporproof material. Replace and plug opening for dasher. Repack freezer with alternate layers of ice and salt, using 4 parts ice and 1 part rock salt. Cover with heavy paper or cloth. Allow to ripen 2-3 hours. Yield 3 quarts.

Lynn McCarthy Ferguson

ICE CREAM CAKE ROLL

Preheat oven to 325°. Prepare 15½x10½x1 inch jelly roll pan. Grease bottom of pan only; line with waxed paper cut to fit bottom, grease waxed paper.

Sift together and set aside:

¾ cup sifted cake flour　　　　　**¼ teaspoon salt**
5 tablespoons cocoa

Beat until very thick and lemon colored:

5 egg yolks　　　　　　　　**1 tablespoon lemon juice**
¾ cup sugar

Fold in dry ingredients on low speed in mixer. Set aside.

Beat until frothy:
5 egg whites

Add and beat slightly:
½ teaspoon cream of tartar

Add gradually, beating well after each addition:
½ cup sugar　　　　　　　　**confectioners sugar**

Beat until rounded peaks are formed and whites do not slide when bowl is partially inverted. Spread egg yolk mixture over egg whites and gently fold together well. Turn batter into pan and spread evenly to edges. Bake at 325° 20-25 minutes or until cake tests done. Loosen edges with a sharp knife. Turn immediately onto a soft dish towel sprinkled with sifted confectioners sugar. Remove waxed paper and cut off any crisp edges of cake.

To roll: begin rolling nearest edge of cake. Using towel as a guide, lightly grasp nearest edge of towel and quickly pull it over beyond opposite edge. Cake will roll itself as you pull. Wrap in towel and cool about ½ hour. When ready to fill, carefully unroll and spread with ½ gallon vanilla ice cream. Re-roll and sift top of roll with confectioners sugar. Serves 12.

Marianne Schneider

OLD FASHION CUSTARD ICE CREAM

½ gallon milk　　　　　　　　**½ teaspoon vanilla**
6 eggs　　　　　　　　　　**1 teaspoon butter flavor**
4 heaping tablespoons corn starch　**1 (14 ounce) can condensed milk**
1¾ cups sugar　　　　　　　　**2 (5½ ounce) cans Pet milk**

Put milk on medium heat in heavy pot. Do not stir. Let it heat until it makes a film. In medium bowl, mix eggs, corn starch and sugar. Beat until frothy. Add to milk, stir constantly until it reaches the thickness of a cream sauce. Remove from fire and add the ½ teaspoon of vanilla, 1 teaspoon of butter flavoring, condensed milk and the 2 cans pet milk. Put into 1 quart ice cream freezer. If refrigerated and allowed to cool before putting into ice cream freezer, less ice is needed for freezing. Yield 1 freezer.

Mrs. Edgar G. Mouton, Jr.

PECAN GLAZE SAUCE FOR ICE CREAM

¼ cup butter or margarine
½ cup firmly packed light brown
  sugar
2 tablespoons light corn syrup

¼ cup evaporated milk
½ teaspoon vanilla
½ cup chopped pecans

Melt butter in small saucepan over low heat. Add brown sugar, corn syrup and milk. Cook and stir over low heat until mixture comes to a full boil. Add vanilla and chopped pecans. Continue cooking and stirring for another 1½ minutes. Serve warm over individual servings of vanilla ice cream. Serves 4.

Ramona Mouton

LEMON MOUSSE

1 (3 ounce) package lemon Jello
1 cup hot water
2 lemons—juice and grated rind
6 eggs, separated

1 cup sugar
1 pint whipping cream, whipped
vanilla wafers crushed and mixed with 2
  tablespoons melted butter

Line 13x9x1½ inch pyrex dish with vanilla wafer crumbs. Dissolve Jello in hot water. Add juice and grated rind of lemons. Add beaten yolks to Jello mixture. Cook over low heat or double boiler until slightly thickened. Cool. Beat egg whites until stiff, gradually adding sugar. Mix with above. After completely cooled, add whipping cream. Pour over crumbled vanilla wafers. Sprinkle top with crumbs. Freeze. Serves 8-10.

Marianne Schneider

CORITA'S PARTY MOUSSE

18 fig newtons, crushed
1 cup evaporated milk
½ cup sugar
½ teaspoon instant coffee
1 cup water

½ teaspoon cinnamon
2 teaspoons vanilla
1 pint heavy cream
1 cup toasted walnuts or pecans
1 quart chocolate ice cream

In a saucepan add the following: fig newtons, milk, sugar, instant coffee and 1 cup of water. Mix well while heating for 3-5 minutes. Remove from heat and add ½ teaspoon cinnamon, 2 teaspoons vanilla. Empty into bowl and refrigerate. When cold, add 1 pint cream, 1 cup toasted nuts. Mix. Add 1 quart chocolate ice cream and mix quickly. Pour into parfait glasses or mold. Freeze. Serves 16.

Corita Crist Owen

MARDI GRAS MOCHA MOUSSE

1 spring pan
½ cup unsalted butter
½ cup white sugar
5 egg yolks
½ pound German sweet chocolate
1 tablespoon vanilla

¼ cup brewed strong black coffee
5 egg whites
½ cup sugar
whipped cream
lady fingers

Cream butter and sugar. Add egg yolks one at a time until blended. Add melted and cooled chocolate, vanilla and coffee. Blend well. Fold in stiffly beaten egg whites (with ½ cup sugar). Pour into a spring pan that is lined on the bottom and the sides with lady fingers. Chill in refrigerator 24 hours and serve topped with whipped cream. Serves 10-12.

Blair Bowden Cabes

BAKED SPICED PEARS

2 large cans pear halves
choice of, or combination of: currant
  jelly, orange marmalade

cinnamon, nutmeg, allspice, cloves,
  (whole), brown sugar and brandy

Preheat oven to 350°. Drain pear juice, set aside. Fill pear halves with jelly or combination of jellies. Sprinkle cinnamon, nutmeg and allspice over pears. Add brown sugar to taste to the pear juice as well as 3 whole cloves. Stir. Add ½ cup brandy. Pour over prepared pears, heat to 350° until hot or place in radarange for 1-2 minutes. This is an excellent substitute for a salad with many meals. It is versatile due to the choices of combinations of jellies as well as spices. Serves 10.

Eleanor Hall Lasseigne

CARAMEL CUSTARD

6 eggs
2 cups sugar
1 quart milk

2-3 teaspoons vanilla
¾ cup sugar, caramelized

Preheat oven to 300°. Mix eggs and sugar thoroughly. Set aside. Scald 1 quart of milk. Slowly add the scalded milk to the egg and sugar mixture stirring constantly. Add vanilla and set aside. To caramelize sugar place ¾ cup sugar in a heavy aluminum saucepan over a medium heat and stir constantly until the sugar turns a golden brown. Place 1 teaspoon of caramelized sugar into each custard cup. Fill cups with custard mixture. Place cups in a pan of hot water. Bake for 45 minutes to 1 hour. Watch closely. When custard shakes like jello remove that individual cup. Let custard cups set until cool enough to refrigerate. When thoroughly chilled and ready to serve, run a knife around the edges and turn upside down on individual dessert plates. Serves 13-14.

Marian Odom Knight

LEMON PUDDING

1 tablespoon butter, creamed well
1 cup sugar
3 egg yolks, beaten well
juice of 2 lemons, about 4 tablespoons
rind of 1 grated lemon
2 tablespoons flour, sifted

pinch of salt
1 cup milk
3 egg whites, beaten until stiff
whipped cream sweetened with 1
   tablespoon sugar and 1 teaspoon
   vanilla

Preheat oven to 250°. Cream butter, add sugar and cream thoroughly. Add egg yolks, stir. Add juice of lemons and rind. Sift in flour and salt. Add milk and mix well. Makes thin batter. Beat egg whites until stiff and fold into mixture. Put into well buttered pyrex cups and put into shallow pan of warm water. Bake at 250° for 1 hour. Garnish with whipped cream topping. Serves 4-6.

Mrs. Billie M. White

FROZEN CHRISTMAS PUDDING

2 (3 ounce) packages cream cheese
1 cup egg nog mix, commercial
1 medium can fruit cocktail, drained
½ cup maraschino cherries, finely
   chopped

1 cup whipped cream
2 cups miniature marshmallows
pinch salt
few drops red food coloring

Whip at high speed cream cheese and egg nog mix until fluffy and light. Add all other ingredients and pour into ring mold and place in freezer to freeze. Unmold about 15 minutes before serving. Serves 8.

Earlene McCallum

CHOCOLATE PARFAIT

1 (6 ounce) package semi-sweet
   chocolate pieces
pinch salt
1 egg

1 teaspoon vanilla
¾ cup hot milk
Creme de Menthe
whipped cream

Combine in blender chocolate, salt, egg, vanilla and milk. Blend at high speed 1 minute. Pour into parfait glasses and chill about 3 hours. Top with 1 tablespoon Creme de Menthe, whipped cream and a cherry. Serves 4.

Mrs. James Kuykendall

RAGIN' CAJUN

Rodney Fontenot, an architectural-antique dealer in Ville Platte, Louisiana, reflects the Cajun culture in a thundering manner that is strictly his own. He has had no difficulty in finding his identity in a town of 6,000, almost 4,000 with the name of Fontenot, none claiming to be related to the others.

Here I show Rodney holding his three most prized possessions, which he refuses to sell. In one hand is one of my early paintings which he probably got for nothing; in the other hand is one of the few remaining cans of Jax beer which shows his taste is not in his mouth; the third possession is an old Coca-Cola ice box which he has converted to a beer cooler.

LAGNIAPPE
(Something Extra)

WINING AND DINING

Generally speaking, a red wine may accompany beef, game, veal, lamb, pork and poultry, keeping in mind—the richer the food, the heavier the wine. These wines should be served at room temperature, 72°. Place them in the room the morning of the dinner and allow the wine to breathe for 30 mintues to one hour, the more full bodied wines requiring the longer time. A white wine may accompany veal, pork, poultry and seafood. These wines should be chilled for 2-3 hours before dinnertime and kept chilled during the meal.

Rosé is an individual wine, good in its place. It should not be referred to as a compromise between red and white wines. Chill 2-3 hours before serving. Rosé is a delightful choice with cold buffets, barbecues, picnics, luncheon sandwiches, highly seasoned foods, or with dinner on a hot summer night. It is also an excellent cocktail or appetizer wine. Champagne is the one all-purpose wine. Serve properly chilled, (35°-40°), any time, with or between meals. Experiment with the various kinds and find your favorite. The words "brut" or "natur" on a champagne label indicate the driest. Extra Dry is not as dry as Brut; and Demi Sec is fairly sweet and served only with desserts. Serving more than one wine throughout the evening—remember white before red; if both wines are the same color, serve the younger first; and dry before sweet.

What type of glass? A good all-purpose glass for any wine is the standard 8 ounce wine glass, however a 6 or 9 ounce glass is also suitable for most wines. Fill about halfway to allow the wine to continue breathing. For German wines, the traditional Rhine-wine rahmar about half-full is a good choice and a bubble glass, one-third full is nice for sparkling burgundy. Dessert wines in dessert wine glasses, no more than one-third full, and for sherry—a pipe-stem sherry glass. A balloon brandy snifter is the choice for brandy as it lends itself to warming the liquor and releasing the aroma. And to preserve the fizz of champagne, try an elegant tulip glass, two-thirds full.

BUYING YOUR WINE

Remember, depending on the vintage year, some French red wines, such as chateau bottled Bordeaux and Burgundy often require bottle aging. It is a good idea to buy these wines from a knowledgeable dealer who can give you an idea of when they'll be ready to drink.

Also, there is not necessarily any relationship between the quality of the wine and the age or between the current drinkability of the wine and the price. Unless you are interested in starting your own wine cellar, it would be best to buy wines that are ready to drink when they are bottled, such as the regional Bordeaux. Also some of the Rhone Valley wines are ready when they are young and most Beaujolais wines are best young. These wines live and die in the bottle and most become a risk after they are five years old.

WINE AND COOKING

Wine is as essential to the flavor of foods as your basic seasonings. Added to soups, salads, desserts, meats, fish, poultry, vegetables and sauces, it can turn the simplest of foods into quite an experience. Use a wine that is acceptable for drinking, not necessarily the one being served with the meal, but it should be in the same family.

Remember that wine will act as a tenderizer when added to meat marinades and will also intensify the flavor of salt.

How much to use? There's no need to be exact, but it is better to use too little than too much. If wine isn't an ingredient of the recipe, don't hesitate to substitute it for some of the liquid. If you'd like to concentrate the flavor of the wine without diluting the taste of the dish—reduce the wine. Boil it down until it resembles syrup. And don't worry about the alcohol effect on guests; it is burned off while cooking, leaving only the flavor.

In your kitchen it would be a good idea to keep within reach a white table wine, Chablis, for poultry and fish; a red table wine, Burgundy, for red meats and game; a dry sherry for sauces; and a sweet dessert wine, Port, for desserts.

WINE WITH DESSERT?

Certainly! The fortified wines, such as Sherry, Port, Madeira and Angelica, are specifically appetizer and dessert wines. There are also some sweetish table wines, Sauternes and late harvested Rieslings, as well as the sweet, sparkling wines, Asti Spumante and Muscats that compliment desserts. Try these desserts with these wines:

Cheeses
  Mild, runny type (Brie, Camembert) . . . . Dry red table wine, the same
                                                          as with dinner, Port, Cabernet,
                                                          Sauvignon
  Mild, solid type (Gruyère) . . . . Rosé, light bodied reds
  Sharp . . . . full bodied red wines
Chocolates . . . . Rich cream sherry, Tokay, Angelica
Choconut . . . . Sparkling wines
Fresh Fruit
  Apples . . . . fruity white, late Riesling
  Apricots . . . . Sweetish red, Port
  Grapes . . . . Any wine, continue dinner wine
  Nectarines . . . . Any wine, continue dinner wine
  Oranges . . . . Inexpensive, low-acid red
  Peaches . . . . Sparkling or still Muscat, Port
  Pears . . . . Any wine, continue dinner wine
    very ripe . . . . Sauternes, Barsacs

	American	American	Import	Family Favorites
EGGS				
Quiche	Chenin Blanc	Chablis	Vouvray	
GAME				
Dove	Cabernet Sauvignon	Pinot Noir	Bordeaux	
Duck	Petite Sirah	Cabernet Sauvignon	Chateauneuf du Pape	
Goose	Zinfandel	Pinot Noir	Hermitage	
Quail	Beaujolais	Zinfandel	Beaujolais	
Rabbit	Cabernet Sauvignon	Vin Rosé	Valpolicella	
Squirrel	Cabernet Sauvignon	Vin Rosé	Valpolicella	
Turkey, wild	Cabernet Sauvignon	Zinfandel	Burgundy	
Venison	Petite Sirah	Pinot Noir	Bordeaux	
GUMBOS				
Game	Burgundy	Zinfandel	Cote du Rhone	
Poultry	Pinot Chardonnay	Vin Rosé	Pouilly Fuisse	
Sausage	Beaujolais	Vin Rosé	Chianti	
Seafood	Pinot Chardonnay	Chablis	Muscadet	
LAMB	Cabernet Sauvignon	Zinfandel	Bordeaux	
LIVER	Petite Sirah	Zinfandel	Hermitage	
MEATS, RED				
Ground meat	Burgundy	Beaujolais	Burgundy	
Roast & Steaks	Cabernet Sauvignon	Pinot Noir	Bordeaux	
Stews	Zinfandel	Petite Sirah	Burgundy	
Barbecued	Petite Sirah	Barbera	Burgundy	
MEXICAN MEALS	Rosé	Chianti	Rosé	
ORIENTAL MEALS	Chenin Blanc	Pinot Chardonnay	Wan Fu Saki	

PORK

Chops	Chenin Blanc	Pinot Chardonnay	Riesling
Ham	Vin Rosé	Riesling	Spätlese
Ribs	Vin Rosé	Chenin Blanc	Chardonnay
Roast	Pinot Chardonnay	Riesling	Chablis
Sausage	Zinfandel	Rosé	Chianti

POULTRY

Chicken	Pinot Chardonnay	Chenin Blanc	Riesling
Cornish Hens	Pinot Chardonnay	Rosé	Chablis
Turkey	Riesling	Chenin Blanc	Vouvray

SALADS

Meal-in-one	Burgundy	Zinfandel	Barolo
Seafood	Chablis	Riesling	Liebfraumlich

SEAFOOD

Fish	Chablis	Pinot Chardonnay	Pouilgny / Montrachet

SHELLFISH

Crab	Chablis	Chenin Blanc	Riesling
Crawfish	Beaujolais	Vin Rosé	Riesling
Lobster	Chablis	Rielsing	Pinot Chardonnay
Oysters	Chablis	Pinot Chardonnay	Muscadet
Shrimp	Chenin Blanc	Vin Rosé	Vouvray

SOUPS

	Rosé	Chenin Blanc	Rosé

VEAL

	Pinot Chardonnay	Beaujolais	Mosel

—COMPLEMENTS FOR THE CHEF—

ALLSPICE—A sweet, mildly sharp spice with a combined flavor of cinnamon, cloves and nutmeg. Marketed in whole berries and ground variety. Use ground allspice in pastries, breads, canned foods, jellies, spiced fruits, eggs, beef, ham, lamb, carrots, tomatoes, eggplant and red cabbage. Add whole allspice to pea soup, steaming or boiling fish and shellfish. For four servings use ¼-1 teaspoon ground allspice or 3-6 whole allspice berries.

ANISE SEED—A licorice like flavored herb belonging to the parsley family. The seed is the dried fruit of the herb. Marketed as ground and whole seeds. Sprinkle the whole seeds on cheese and shellfish appetizers, coffeecakes and sweet breads, cakes and cookies, fruits, raw and cooked, compotes. Also use in stews, sweet pickles and beverages. For four servings use ¼-1 teaspoon ground anise or ¼-2 teaspoons whole anise seed.

SWEET BASIL OR BASIL—A peppery, tangy, clove-flavored herb belonging to the mint family. Available as dried leaves or fresh leaves as this herb is easily home grown. Essential to Italian meals and tomato dishes. Adds tang to mushrooms, scrambled eggs, duck, rabbit or venison casserole, beef, pork and veal roasts. Try in salads, soups and stews. Add to water when boiling lobster, shrimp and vegetables. For four servings use ⅛-¼ teaspoon dried basil, 2-3 teaspoons chopped fresh leaves or 1 small sprig fresh leaves.

BAY LEAVES (LAUREL)—Strong, woodsy herb with a light cinnamon flavor. Be careful because it becomes bitter when over used. Available in either whole leaf or ground. Add to sauces, stews, soups, pot roasts, tomato sauces with fish, stuffings and water when boiling vegetables. For four servings use 1-2 crushed leaves or 1-3 whole leaves.

BEAU MONDE SEASONING—A full tasting, balanced blend of basic seasonings which adds to most foods except sweets. Use in eggs, meats, seafood stews, tuna and cheese sandwich spreads, sauces and stuffings. For four servings use ¼ teaspoon.

CARDAMON—A spice with a lemon-ginger flavor. Available as whole seeds or crushed. Try in barbecue sauces, on ham, pork, fruit salads, cakes and cookies, breads, tea and coffee, honey and jellies. Use sparingly. For four servings use ¼-1 teaspoon ground seed or ½-2 teaspoons whole seed.

CHIVES—A delicate, onion flavored herb used fresh as much as possible as it is easily grown. A great all purpose herb. For four servings use 1 teaspoon to 2 tablespoons chopped stalks.

CINNAMON—A delicate, sweet, hot spice derived from the dried ground bark of the tree. Available ground or in sticks. Use in cookies, cakes, spicy beverages, fruit pies, compotes, mashed sweet potatoes. Try on lamb chops, pork chops, salt pork and ham. A treat when added to ice cream. For four servings use ¼-1 teaspoon ground cinnamon or 4 small sticks.

CLOVES—A strong, pungent, almost hot spice which are the unopened flower buds of the clove tree. Its name came from the French and Latin words meaning nail as it resembles a round-headed nail. Available ground or whole. Use ground clove powder in breads, pickles, preserves, mincemeats, soups, stews and sweet potatoes. Whole cloves added to vegetable water when cooking produces a warm taste as well as adding to beverages and studding baked hams. For four servings use ⅛-½ teaspoon ground cloves of 1-2 whole cloves for beverages.

CUMIN—A strong, nutty flavored herb which is the dried fruit of the plant and belongs to the parsley family. Available ground or whole. Use in cabbage, soups, sausages, cheeses, Oriental dishes as well as most Mexican dishes. Should be used sparingly until you become familiar with it. For four servings use ⅛-½ teaspoon ground or ½-2 teaspoons whole.

CURRY POWDER—One of the world's oldest seasonings which is a blend of many spices ranging from mild to hot depending on the manufacturer. American blends tend to be of the milder variety. Most will contain allspice, black and red pepper, ginger, cayenne, cinnamon, cardamon seed, coriande seed, mustard seed, nutmeg, saffron and turmeric. Use in eggs, fish, game, meats and vegetables, salad dressings, any Indian or Far Eastern dishes. For four servings use 1 teaspoon for a mild flavoring or 2 teaspoons to 1 tablespoon for a strong flavor.

DILL—A pungent, tart, lemon-flavored herb good for use in most foods. Available as ground dill or whole seeds and fresh stems and leaves of the herb as it is easy to grow. Try in seafood, eggs, cheese, vegetables, soups and stews and of course pickles. For four servings use 2 tablespoons to garnish and 1 sprig with the leaves for flavoring.

FINE HERBS—A mixture of 4-5 minced herbs always including chives and parsley or chervil. Some of these combinations are:

     chives, parsley, burnet, tarragon, chervil

     chives, chervil, basil, burnet, thyme

     chives, chervil, savory, burnet

The ones including the stronger herbs should be used sparingly and not allowed to cook but for a few minutes in soups, sauces and stews. To prepare a mixture of fine herbs use 1 tablespoon of fresh herbs or 1 teaspoon of the dried variety.

FILE POWDER—A woodsy, root-beer like seasoning made from dried sassafras leaves. An accent to gumbos and creole dishes added after cooking, just prior to serving. Sassafras can be easily home grown. Start with 1 scant teaspoon per serving.

HORSERADISH—A *peppery*, turnip flavored root herb. Available in fresh leaves during the summer or ground root or whole fresh root. Also available as a prepared condiment. The leaves, minced, add greatly to a mixed green salad while the root is used mostly to flavor sauces, dips and salad dressings. For four servings use 2-4 teaspoons freshly ground root as a condiment or 1-2 tablespoons freshly ground root in sauces.

GINGER—A biting, sweet spice derived from the root of the ginger herb which is available ground, crystallized ground root, root preserved in syrup and as a whole dried root. It is a must for baking, canning, Oriental sweet and sour dishes. Really something special when mixed with regular seasonings on meats, poultry, pork and lamb. Don't forget to add the whole root to beverages. For four servings use ¼-1 teaspoon ground ginger, 1-4 tablespoons preserved ginger in sauces.

MACE—A spice derived from grinding the middle layer of the nutmeg shell. It has a stronger flavor than nutmeg and can be used solo or in combination with other spices. It is an all-purpose spice available ground or whole dried. Try in biscuits, cakes, fish, preserves, fruit salads, cream sauces, shellfish, soups and creamed vegetables. For four servings use ⅛-½ teaspoon ground or 1 small whole, minced.

MARJORAM—A musky-mellow, nutty herb sometimes used as a lighter substitute for sage, because of its weaker flavor. Available in crushed, dried leaves, whole dried leaves, powdered leaves or fresh. The species, Pot Marjoram, is a great window sill herb and is easily started from a cutting. Use in veal, lamb, fowl, vegetables, seafoods, eggs, soups and brown sauces. For four servings use ¼-½ teaspoon crushed dried leaves, 3-4 small fresh leaves, ⅛-¼ teaspoon powdered leaves.

MINT—There are 30 varieties of this delicate, aromatic herb such as Apple Mint, Peppermint, Orange Mint and Spearmint. It is one of the most widely used herbs and the leafy tops of all varieties add flavor to many foods. Available as dried leaves, honey, fresh leaves as it is easily home grown and even wild in some damp climates. Use in cream cheese, teas, fruit and wine punches, marinades for seafood, jellies, lamb and veal and as a seasoning in the water of boiled vegetables. Also good in many desserts. For four servings, use ¼-1 teaspoon crushed, dried leaves, 1 teaspoon to 2 tablespoons chopped, fresh leaves, 4 sprigs fresh mint or 2-8 fresh leaves.

MUSTARD—A bitter and biting spice derived from crushed, ground and sifted mustard seeds. It comes in varying strengths—white is the mildest while the brown and Oriental types are extra strong. Available as dry mustard or prepared mustards of which the Dijon type is considered to be the best. This is one spice that lends itself to the taste of the individual user. The more used, the more pungent the flavor. Try in appetizers, cheeses, eggs, fish, salad dressings, steaks, poultry, shellfish and vegetables. Use as desired.

NUTMEG—A mellow, sweet, nutty, all-purpose spice which is a little more delicate in flavoring than mace. Available ground or whole and the whole nutmegs are rather bitter when grated. Use in beverages, cakes, cookies, eggs, fruits, meats, desserts, sauces, soups and vegetables. For four servings use ⅛-1 teaspoon ground nutmeg or a few grains grated nutmeg.

OREGANO—A bitter, marigold-like flavored herb, also known as Wild Marjoram. It has a much stronger flavor than Marjoram and should be used sparingly. Available as dried leaves or fresh as this herb is easily home grown. It is a must for Italian, Spanish and Mexican dishes. Also try in tomato juice, fish, poultry, potato salad, vegetables and shellfish. For four servings use ¼-2 teaspoons dried, 1-2 teaspoons chopped fresh leaves or 1 small sprig.

PAPRIKA—A nourishing, mild to slightly hot spice derived from the large sweet peppers of the plant. Available ground and is used mostly as a garnish for color and a browning agent. Add to any and all foods. For four servings use 2 teaspoons of the mild variety.

PARSLEY—A sweet, spicy all purpose herb which is a must to an herb garden. The plain leaf variety is a little more pungent than the curly leafed one. Used mostly as a garnish.

ROSEMARY—A heady, lemony flavored herb common to most moist climates. Available as dried leaves, fresh leaves or in honey. Good in summer drinks, appetizers, eggs, fish, beef, lamb, pork, veal, chicken and fricassée sauces. Also add to the cooking water of fresh vegetables. For four servings use ¼-1 teaspoon dried leaves, ½-1 teaspoon fresh leaves or 1 sprig.

SAFFRON—A somewhat bitter, medicinal flavored spice which is very expensive and a must in French, Italian and Spanish dishes. Available as a powder. Use for coloring confectionery, rice dishes and sauces. Use sparingly. For four servings ¼ teaspoon is ample.

SAGE—A musty, lime-scented herb with over 500 varieties available. The taste varies with the variety. The common garden sage is easily home grown. Available as dried leaves, powdered and fresh. Add sparingly to cheeses. Try in fish, stuffings, poultry, pork, Italian dishes, soups and vegetables. For four servings use 1 whole dried leaf, 1-4 fresh leaves or ¼-1 teaspoon powdered sage.

SAVORY—There are two varieties of this herb; Summer Savory is the delicate type and may be used in place of parsley in eggs, fish, salads, stuffings and vegetables. Winter Savory is pungent and more bitter than the summer. Also it is a good substitute for parsley. Both are available as dried leaves or fresh. It is easily grown in a sunny spot. For four servings use ½-1 teaspoon dried leaves, 1 teaspoon to 1 tablespoon fresh leaves, chopped or 4-8 sprigs for garnish.

TARRAGON—A sweet, licorice flavored herb which is easily grown in an herb garden. Also available as dried leaves. Use sparingly in seafood, veal, poultry, vegetables, soups and salad dressings. For four servings use ¼-½ teaspoon dried, ½-1 teaspoon fresh leaves or 1-4 whole fresh leaves.

THYME—A minty, tea-like flavored all-purpose herb which is also easily grown in an herb garden. Available also as dried leaves, ground and as a honey. Great in seafood cocktails, gumbos, meats, poultry, cottage and cream cheese, creole and tomato sauces. For four servings use ⅛-1 teaspoon dried, 1-2 teaspoons fresh or ⅛-½ teaspoon ground.

TURMERIC—A rich, warm, sweet, root spice which is the chief ingredient of curry powder. Available ground or in whole roots and should be used sparingly and carefully as it stains. Try in condiments, pickles, French dressing, eggs, beef and lamb. For four servings use ⅛-1 teaspoon ground.

SUBSTITUTIONS

1 teaspoon baking powder	¼ teaspoon soda plus ½ teaspoon cream of tartar
1 cup butter	1 cup margarine ⁴/₅-⅞ cup clarified bacon fat or drippings for sautéing ⅞ cup lard or solid shortening
chocolate	
1 ounce unsweetened	3 tablespoons cocoa plus 1 tablespoon fat
1 square	¼ cup cocoa
cream	
1 cup, half and half	1½ tablespoons butter plus ⅞ cup milk
1 cup, coffee	3 tablespoons butter plus ⅞ cup milk
1 cup, commercial sour	1 tablespoon lemon juice plus evaporated milk to equal 1 cup 3 tablespoons butter plus ⅞ cup sour milk
1 cup, whipping	⅓ cup butter plus ¾ cup milk
1 tablespoon corn starch	2 tablespoons flour (for thickening)
1 cup bread crumbs	¾ cup cracker crumbs
1 whole egg	2 egg yolks 2 egg yolks plus 1 tablespoon water (for cookies)
flour	
1 tablespoon, for thickening	½ tablespoon corn starch, potato starch, rice starch or arrowroot 1 tablespoon quick-cooking tapioca
1 cup all-purpose (for baking breads)	1 cup plus 2 tablespoons cake flour Up to ½ cup bran, whole wheat flour or cornmeal mixed with enough all-purpose flour to fill a cup
1 cup, cake flour (for baking)	1 cup less 2 tablespoons finely sifted all-purpose flour
1 cup, self-rising	1 cup all-purpose flour plus 1 teaspoon baking powder and ½ teaspoon salt

1 clove fresh garlic	1 teaspoon garlic salt ⅛ teaspoon garlic powder
1 tablespoon fresh herbs	1 teaspoon ground or crushed dry herbs
1 teaspoon lemon juice	½ teaspoon vinegar
milk	
1 cup fresh, whole	1 cup low fat milk plus 2 tablespoons butter
1 cup, sour	1 cup fresh milk plus 1 tablespoon vinegar or lemon juice
1 pound fresh mushrooms	6 ounces canned mushrooms
1 teaspoon onion powder	2 teaspoons baking powder
sugar	
1 tablespoon maple	1 teaspoon white granulated sugar
1 cup maple	1 cup brown sugar
1 tablespoon tapioca	1½ tablespoons all-purpose flour
tomatoes	
1 cup, packed	½ cup tomato sauce plus ½ cup water
1 cup, juice	½ cup tomato sauce plus ½ cup water
2 cups, sauce	¾ cup tomato paste plus 1 cup water
1 cup, sour	1 cup tomato sauce plus ½ cup water
1 cup yogurt	1 cup buttermilk or sour milk

EQUIVALENTS

	Amount	Approximate Measure
Apple, chopped	1 medium	1 cup
Bacon	8 slices, cooked	½ cup, crumbled
Breadcrumbs	2 slices, fresh bread	1 cup
Butter, shortening	1 pound	2 cups
Celery, chopped	¼ pound, 2 stalks	1 cup
Cheese		
Bleu	¼ pound	¾-1 cup
Cheddar, American	4 ounces	1 cup, shredded
Cottage	1 pound	2 cups
Cream	3 ounce package	6 tablespoons
	8 ounce package	1 cup
Chocolate		
chips	6 ounce package	1 cup
unsweetened	8 ounce package	1 cup
Coconut, shredded and		
flaked	4 ounce can	1⅓ cups
Coffee, ground	1 pound	80 tablespoons
Crackers		
Graham	12	1 cup fine crumbs
salted	20	1 cup fine crumbs
Vanilla wafers	22	1 cup fine crumbs
Zwieback toast	8-9	1 cup fine crumbs
Cream		
Sour	8 ounces	1 cup
Whipping	½ pint	1 cup—2 cups whipped
Eggs		
Whites	8-10	1 cup
Yolks	12-14	1 cup
Flour		
All-purpose	1 pound	3½ cups
Cake	1 pound	4 cups
Lemon		
Juice	1 medium	2-3 tablespoons
Peel, grated	1 medium	1½-3 teaspoons
Macaroni	1 cup uncooked	2¼ cups cooked
Marshmallows	1 large	10 miniature
	11 large = 110 miniature	1 cup

	Amount	Approximate Measure
Noodles	4 ounces, uncooked	2 cups, cooked
Nuts		
Almonds	1 pound in shell	1-1¾ cups meats
	1 pound shelled	3½ cups
Pecans	1 pound in shell	2¼ cups meats
	1 pound shelled	4 cups
Peanuts	1 pound in shell	2¼ cups meats
	1 pound shelled	3 cups
Walnuts	1 pound in shell	1⅔ cups meats
	1 pound shelled	4 cups
Onion, chopped	1 medium	½ cup
Orange		
Juice	1 medium	⅓-½ cup
Peel, grated	1 medium	1-2 tablespoons
Potatoes	1 pound	4 medium
Rice	1 pound	2 cups
Shrimp, in shell, raw	1½ pounds	2 cups (¾ lb) cleaned, cooked
Spaghetti	7 ounces, uncooked	4 cups cooked
Sugar		
Brown	1 pound	2¼ cups, firmly packed
Confectioners	1 pound	4 cups
Granulated	1 pound	2 cups
Tomatoes	3 medium	1 pound

A BREEZE TO FREEZE

AVOCADO—peel and purée ¾ cup, add 2 teaspoons lemon juice

BERNAISE OR HOLLANDAISE SAUCE—freeze leftovers, reheat in double boiler and use for basting, not as a sauce

BREADCRUMBS—dry out crusts and stale bread in oven, crumble

CAKES—wrap in foil, plastic wrap, freezer paper or plastic bags. When firm store in strong containers.

CHEESE—Swiss, Gruyère, Parmesan—buy whole, grate and freeze. Bleu Cheese, Roquefort—wrap in plastic, then foil, freeze, thaw at room temperature.

COFFEE—to preserve freshness use straight from freezer

CREAM—freeze leftovers in containers, use for cooking, not whipping or coffee

CROUTONS—cube stale bread, toast, freeze, thaw for 5 minutes at room temperature

EGG WHITES—pack separately in ice cube tray, thaw at room temperature, keeps 1-2 days

EGG YOLKS—hard boil, grate and freeze, great for garnishes.

FISH, SLICED LIVER & VEAL—wrap first in plastic then freezer foil

GAME BIRDS, TROUT & OTHER FRESH FISH—Freeze in water or stock

HERBS—basil, mint, tarragon, dill—wash, dry, discard stem, freeze in small bags, chop and use frozen

LASAGNA-CANNELLONI—freezes well, plain pasta doesn't

LEMON JUICE—freeze fresh juice in ice cube trays, 2 tablespoons/cube, freeze rind with juice and strain before using

MEAT—to seal in juices and prevent freezer burn on large cuts, coat the cut surface with a little vegetable oil and don't forget a double thickness of paper over bone ends

MILK—pasteurized and homogenized freeze at 0°F for 3 weeks

MUSHROOM CAPS—sprinkle with butter, broil 2 minutes, freeze, thaw 10 minutes and stuff or finish cooking

MUSHROOMS, RAW—don't wash, quick freeze, use frozen, keep up to 3 weeks

NUTS—frozen whole or chopped nuts last indefinitely, toast before using

ONIONS & SHALLOTS—chop coarsely, drain, quick freeze in single layer, use frozen

PARSLEY—chop and freeze

PIES—to keep the top crust intact place a paper plate over it before wrapping

    CRUSTS—don't prick, quick freeze, stack with plastic wrap between, thaw 15 minutes

    FILLINGS—1 quart fruit will fill a 9″ pie, line plate with foil, fill, cover with foil and freeze, remove from plate and store

RICE—freeze plain, reheat over steam in colander or in microwave

SOUPS—freeze bases for cream soups without cream

STOCK—freeze in milk cartons and ice cube trays

QUANTITIES TO SERVE FIFTY

Beef Roast	18-20 lbs.
Brunswick Stew	14 lbs. beef, 3 lbs. lean pork, 1 fowl, 7 cans tomatoes, 4 cans corn
Butter	1-1¼ lbs.
Cabbage Salad, Slaw	8 lbs. cabbage, 2 bunches carrots, 1 bunch celery, dressing
Cabbage-Apple Salad	6 apples, 6 lbs. cabbage, 2 boxes raisins, nuts
Chicken, dressed	
creamed	15-18 lbs.
baked	25-30 lbs.
for chicken salad	20-25 lbs.
Coffee, Regular	1-1¼ lbs.
Ham	
fresh	20-25 lbs.
Hamburgers	12½-15 lbs.
Juice for Cocktail	6½ quarts
Lemons for lemonade	6 dozen
Lettuce	12 medium heads
Peas	10-12 No. 2½ cans
Potatoes	
white	
creamed	16 lbs.
buttered, whole	20 lbs.
Au Gratin	15 lbs. with 4 cups medium sauce, 1 lb. cheese
Salad	12 lbs., 2 bunches celery, 2 dozen eggs, pickle, 4 green peppers, mayonnaise, seasoning to taste
sweet	
candied	18-20 lbs.
Rice	3 lbs.
grits	2½ lbs.
Rolls	15 dozen or 6 yeast cakes made into rolls
Sausage	16 lbs.
Tomatoes	
fresh	10 lbs.
Turkey, dressed &	
drawn	22-25 lbs.
Vegetables, canned	14 No. 303 or 11 No. 2 cans

BAKING PANS AND CASSEROLES

	Approximate Number of Servings
LOAF PANS	
Oven-proof glass	
8¾x5x2¼	6-8
Metal	
7⅜x3⅝x2¼ (Non-stick)	6-8
8½x4½x2½ (also Non-stick)	
9x5x3	8-10
10x5x3	
Disposable	
5-11/16x3¼x2	4-6
7⅞x3⅞x2½	6-8
PIE PLATES	
Oven-proof glass and Metal	
9″	6-8
10″	8-10
Disposable	
8¾″	6-8
ROUND	
Oven-proof glass	
7½″	4-6
8½″	6-8
Metal	
8x1½ layer cake (2 layers)	10-12
9x1½ layer cake (2 layers)	12-14
Disposable	
8½x1½ layer cake (2 layers)	10-12
SQUARE	
Oven-proof glass	
8x8x2	8-10
Metal	
8x8x2	8-10
9x9x2	10-12
Disposable	
8½x8½x15/16	8-10
OBLONG-RECTANGULAR	
Oven-proof glass	
10x6x1½	6-8
11¾x7½x1⅓	8-10
13½x8½x2	10-12
Metal	
11x7x1½ (also Non-stick)	8-10
13x9x2 (also Non-stick)	10-12
Disposable	
11⅝x8½x13/16	8-10

VOLUME OF MOLDS AND BAKING PANS

Volume	Size & Kind	Approximate Number of Servings
4½ cups	8½ x2¼ ring mold	8-10
6 cups	7½x3 Bundt tube pan	10-12
	7x5½x4 Melon mold	
7½ cups	6x4½ Charlotte mold	12-14
8 cups	9½x3¼ Brioche pan	14-16
	9¼x2¾ ring mold	
9 cups	9x3½ Fancy tube or Bundt	14-18

CAN SIZES

8 oz.	1 cup	250 ml.
Picnic, 10½-12 oz.	1¼ cups	312 ml.
12 ozs., vacuum	1½ cups	375 ml.
No. 300, 14-16 oz.	1¾ cups	438 ml.
No. 303, 16-17 oz.	2 cups	500 ml.
No. 2, 20 oz.	2½ cups	625 ml.
No. 2½, 29 oz.	3½ cups	875 ml.
No. 3, 46 fluid oz.	5¾ cups	1.4 l.
No. 10, 6½-7 lbs.	12-13 cups	3-3¼ l.
Condensed milk, 14 fluid oz.	1⅓ cups	333 ml.
Evaporated milk, 5⅓ & 13 fluid oz.	⅔-1⅔ cups	166-416 ml.

METRIC MEASURES

1 teaspoon	⅓ tablespoon	5 milliliters
3 teaspoons	1 tablespoon	15 milliliters
4 tablespoons	¼ cup	62 milliliters
16 tablespoons	1 cup	250 milliliters
2 cups	1 pint	500 milliliters
4 cups	1 quart	1000 milliliters
2 pints	1 quart	1000 milliliters
4 quarts (liquid)	1 gallon	4000 milliliters

INDEX

Talk About Good II

Complements the Junior League of Lafayette's first cookbook, *Talk About Good!*
First published in 1967, it boasts a record of over 350,000 international sales.
Although different in format and theme, it contains over 650 succulent recipes.
Talk About Good! is high on the list of best League cookbooks.

To complete the set,

order from

Junior League of Lafayette

504 Richland Avenue

Lafayette, Louisiana 70508

(337) 988-2739 • (800) 757-3651

Fax (337) 988-1079

www.juniorleagueoflafayette.com

Talk About Good II

The Junior League of Lafayette
504 Richland Avenue
Lafayette, Louisiana 70508
(337) 988-2739 • (800) 757-3651
Fax (337) 988-1079

Please send me information on ordering additional copies of *Talk About Good* II
or our first cookbook, *Talk About Good!*

Name _____

Address _____

City _____ State _____ Zip _____

Phone (_____)_____

- -

Talk About Good II

The Junior League of Lafayette
504 Richland Avenue
Lafayette, Louisiana 70508
(337) 988-2739 • (800) 757-3651
Fax (337) 988-1079

Please send me information on ordering additional copies of *Talk About Good* II
or our first cookbook, *Talk About Good!*

Name _____

Address _____

City _____ State _____ Zip _____

Phone (_____)_____

- -

Talk About Good II

The Junior League of Lafayette
504 Richland Avenue
Lafayette, Louisiana 70508
(337) 988-2739 • (800) 757-3651
Fax (337) 988-1079

Please send me information on ordering additional copies of *Talk About Good* II
or our first cookbook, *Talk About Good!*

Name _____

Address _____

City _____ State _____ Zip _____

Phone (_____)_____